The New School of Architecture

AMERICAN ARCHITECTURE AND URBANISM

AMERICAN ARCHITECTURE AND URBANISM

New Revised Edition

Vincent Scully

Henry Holt and Company

New York

For my wife and family

Copyright © 1969, 1988 by Vincent Scully
All rights reserved, including the right to reproduce this book
or portions thereof in any form.
Published by Henry Holt and Company, Inc.,
115 West 18th Street, New York, New York 10011.
Published in Canada by Fitzhenry & Whiteside Limited,
195 Allstate Parkway, Markham, Ontario L3R 4T8.

Library of Congress Cataloging-in-Publication Data
Scully, Vincent Joseph, 1920–
American architecture and urbanism / Vincent Scully.—New rev. ed.
p.   cm.
Bibliography: p.
Includes index.
ISBN 0-8050-0105-0.   ISBN 0-8050-0813-6 (pbk.)
1. Architecture—United States.   2. City planning—United States.
I. Title.
NA705.S36   1988
720'.973—dc19   87-37111
                                                        CIP

First published in the United States by Praeger Publishers, Inc., in 1969.
Printed in the United States of America
10 9 8 7 6 5 4 3 2 1

ISBN 0-8050-0105-0 HARDBOUND

ISBN 0-8050-0813-6 PAPERBACK

The founders' faith was in decay,
and yet their building seems to say:
"Every time I take a breath,
my god you are the air I breathe."
            Robert Lowell, *Fourth of July in Maine*

You are the buffalo-ghost, the bronco ghost
With dollar-silver in your saddle-horn,
The cowboys riding in from Painted Post,
The Indian arrow in the Indian corn . . .
            Stephen Vincent Benét, *John
            Brown's Body*

Some remove the landmarks. . . .
. . . .
They turn the needy out of the way: the poor
of the earth hide themselves together.
            Job xxiv: 2, 4

Contents

Preface

I am indebted for discussion and advice to many students, colleagues, and friends, such as George Hersey, Neil Levine, Helen Searing, and Robert A. M. Stern. As always, Helen Chillman's help at Yale has been indispensable. To the many people who kindly supplied photographs I am also deeply indebted; specific acknowledgment is made elsewhere.

It will be obvious to the reader that this book is intended not as a definitive chronicle but as a critical essay. Every effort is made in it to push the history of architecture toward a proper urbanistic scale and an active role in society, with what only partial success the author is entirely aware. It is the environment as a whole—how to see it, how it got that way, what to do about it—which we must learn to write about at the present time. No history of architecture can deal any longer with individual buildings only, or with buildings in a vacuum. There is no difference between architecture and city planning; all must now—or, rather, again—be treated as one.

This must especially be so because of the fact that every citizen must now share an active and critical responsibility for the future of the American city, as for that of the American community as a whole. His vote and his direct personal intervention in his own community can help determine the kind of world we will make, and we are in the bitter crisis of that making now. It is hoped that this book can bring some historical perspective to bear and so offer a minor contribution toward the peaceful resolution of that crisis and the shaping of a kinder and more civilized future for everyone. New Haven, Connecticut, receives rather more than its share of space in these pages because it is the field of battle which the author best knows. But this labor is one to which we are all drawn in agony and love for the whole of the American place and its people, as time runs out on us, while the curtains flap in the windows of the old brownstones, and the grasses bend in the water by the gray-shingled houses, and the neon begins to glow on the lifting plain under the darkening sky.

VINCENT SCULLY

New Haven–Nantucket
1966–67

8

Preface, 1988

The ideas expressed in the Preface of 1969 still seem valid enough today. It is also true, though, that the relative contemporaneity of any historical subject affects the permanence of our interpretations of it. The relative intensity of contemporary events also plays a part. This book was written in the late sixties during a period of intense social concern and civil strife. That climate of feeling led me toward a more socially activist treatment of architecture than I had ever practised before and tended to subordinate my own leaning toward a fundamentally aesthetic approach. Was that emphasis incorrect? Certainly it focused on some things at the expense of others, an imbalance which one would always be glad to rectify—as I hope I have done to some extent in the Notes and Postscript here—but it did direct attention toward the city as a whole, and from that, it now seems to me, the proper way to evaluate architectural form arises.

I now disagree with some of my original judgments and am indeed embarrassed by one or two of them. I was terribly wrong in my appreciation of Habitat, for example, and in my optimism about the urban possibilities of megastructures in general, and in my lack of understanding of the stripped "Modern Classic" of the twenties and thirties. The revival of traditional ideas about architecture has gone farther than could have been imagined at that time, and the myths of modernism have been deflated in ways unimaginable then. A lot has changed since 1969, I think for the better, and it is as well to let it all show plainly. Because of that I have tried to leave the original text much as it was, in its original present tenses and so on, only adding a few notes in places where the original discussion now seems to me to be especially inadequate or egregiously wrong. A few additional illustrations have also been added to supplement the old ones. Beyond that there is a long, new, illustrated chapter which tries to bring the topic up to date, again as a selective essay rather than in terms of comprehensive coverage. The bibliographical note has been considerably extended in the same way. It cannot cover everything, but it is much more comprehensive than the original note was intended to be.

Despite the sometimes somber tone of it all, I find that I do in fact feel relatively sanguine about the urbanistic future, though at present only in a professional rather than a political sense. There is so much more understanding of the city and of architecture as an urban art now than there was twenty years ago, and so many more professional and economic resources available to change it for the better, that it would take only a shift in political priorities (but what a shift) to bring some great things about and to improve the environment as a whole beyond measure. Architects and critics have been saying something like that for more than a hundred years, perhaps since time immemorial. But their ideas about the city, shaped by their own romanticism, have often been destructive ones—especially, and most spectacularly, in the recent past. We can only hope that someday soon the proper professional means and political will can come together. Certainly the public mood, perhaps counter to that of our present political leaders, runs toward preservation and healing rather than reckless aggression and destruction. We lean toward smaller, gentler things and set ourselves more modest objectives. We understand the city better than we did and have learned to respect the traditional development which made it what it is. We would like to save it, mend it, preserve it, and hold out till a better day.

I should note again the students I cited in the first edition: George Hersey, Neil Levine, Helen Searing, and Robert A. M. Stern. All of them have been distinguished scholars and teachers for many years, and to them should be added, among others: Allan Greenberg, Alex Gorlin, Leland Roth, Eve Blau, Robert Grant Irving, Ellen Shapiro, Esther da Costa Meyer, Blair Kamin, Paul Goldberger, Maya Lin, Isabelle Gournay, and my wife, Catherine Lynn, to whom I owe a considerable professional as well as personal debt. I continue to owe Helen Chillman more for her help than I can ever properly repay, and I am grateful to Rebecca Stone and Wanda Bubriski for their help with the new illustrations.

VINCENT SCULLY

New Haven
1988

AMERICAN
ARCHITECTURE
AND URBANISM

This book is concerned with the meaning of American architecture and with an assessment of the kind of human environment it has created in that geographical area which is now occupied by the United States. The splendid pre-Columbian, colonial, and modern achievements of South and Meso-America are not treated. In one sense, that restriction, though long if rather foolishly sanctioned by historical custom, seems especially artificial here, since all the architectures of this hemisphere can be shown to exhibit common hemispherical traits. Obvious cultural differences between them do not obscure those similarities which have grown out of the common experience of living on this side of the world. A vast landscape, a more or less scarifying contact with the Indian population, certain racial crimes, colonialism, a sense of distance from the centers of high civilization, a feeling at once of liberation and of loss: all these attitudes and phenomena have been shared in varying degree by every post-Columbian

culture in America, and they have marked its architecture in various essential ways. Together they build toward a kind of uneasiness, a distrust of the place, a restlessness shared to some extent even by the Indian civilizations which preceded them.

Yet, though present throughout the hemisphere, that restlessness and all it entails have been most intensely experienced in the area of the United States. Its people have always been the most adrift from precedent; their culture has consistently remained that of a frontier—at first a physical, later a social and technological one. The cataclysmic modern shift from the small, pre-industrial world to a new world of mass population and industrialism did not begin in America, but when it came to these shores it developed faster and more completely in the United States than anywhere else in the world. This must have taken place partly because there was less of the old in America to hold off the new and partly because of the character of the American

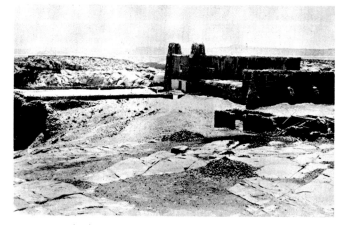

A. Acoma, New Mexico. San Esteban. *Ca.* 1630.

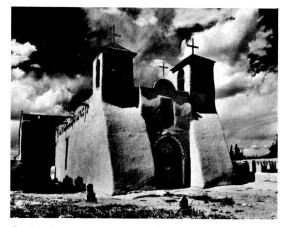

B. Ranchos de Taos, New Mexico. San Francisco. 1772. Entrance façade.

himself. The rush of immigration which began in the 1840's exacerbated an archetypal colonial sense of uprootedness and partial alienation, and it eventually swept away that anchor in classical learning and in the cult of intellectual attainment which had been the true distinction of, and, indeed, the spur to, reasoned revolutionary action in late colonial and early republican society. So the American became the first mass man, the first modern man, trampling over the earth and all old things. It is no wonder that the first characteristic forms of twentieth-century architecture began to take shape in his hands.

In all this rests whatever justification there may be for restricting this discussion to the architecture of the United States and to some of its predecessors in this continental area. Forms of a special flavor, deriving from various amalgams of colonialism, primitivism, technological experiment, and social and geographical expansion, indeed arise out of it, setting it off in kind, degree, and historical position from the other architectures of the Americas. So the mission churches at Acoma *(Fig. A)* and Ranchos de Taos *(Fig. B)* share critical characteristics of linearity, planarity, and simplification of mass with seventeenth- and eighteenth-century houses in New England *(Figs. C , D)*, and all exhibit a similar colonial relationship to the architecture of the mother cultures from which they derived. Each also shares special qualities with later architecture in the United States, with its industrial buildings, for example *(Fig. E)*, or, in other ways, with the work of Frank Lloyd Wright, or with the curtain-wall skyscrapers of this generation, or the buildings of Louis I. Kahn. Mid-twentieth-century-vernacular architecture, too, shows a clear impress of its American past, as well as some of the liveliest examples of peculiarly American adaptation and, perhaps, invention.

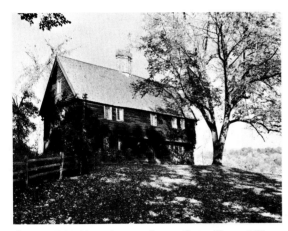

C. Topsfield, Massachusetts. Parson Capen House. 1683.

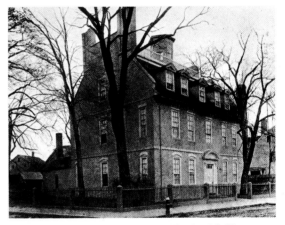

D. Portsmouth, New Hampshire. Macpheadris-Warner House. 1716–23.

E. Lima, Ohio. Ohio Steel Foundry Roll Shop. 1939. Albert Kahn.

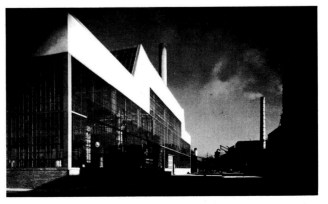

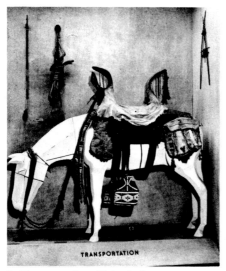

1. Horse trappings, Plains Indians.

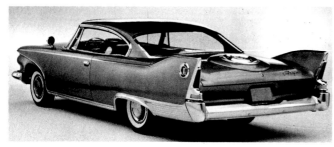

2. Plymouth automobile.

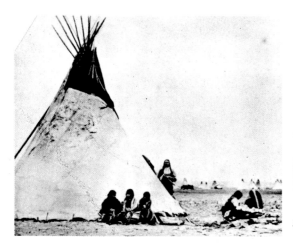

3. Fort Dodge, Kansas. Arapaho camp. Photograph taken *ca.* 1867–74.

It should be no surprise that such is the case. There is surely a *daimon* that dwells in places—not least, as D. H. Lawrence claimed long ago, on this grand and ruined continent, disquieting to inhabit, small enough to spoil, too large to own. It moves through its people like a vengeful ghost, giving them their dreams of space and journeys, of Europe on one side, war drums on the other, calling them on. It can be no accident that twice in its history a good percentage of its population has enthusiastically given up everything tending toward sedentary, civilized life in order to exploit a new means of transportation, a new vehicle of transcendence and escape: first the horse, then the automobile. The high-pommeled saddle trappings of the Plains Indians *(Fig. 1)* and the fins of the 1950's *(Fig. 2)* are not so far apart in effect and intention; nor are the wind-adjusted flapped tepee of the plains and Buckminster Fuller's Dymaxion House rotating on its mast: mobile both, unfixed to the ground *(Figs. 3, 4)*. And in 1967, one-fifth of the houses constructed were trailers themselves, mobile homes, huge in size, some of them expandable, opening out in all directions *(Fig. 5)*. Colonies of them, generally geriatric in program, sprawl in the desert *(Fig. 6)*.

4. Dymaxion House. 1927–28. R. Buckminster Fuller.

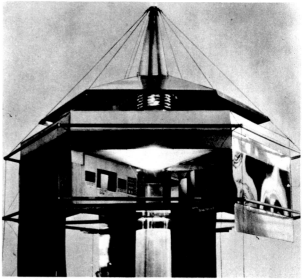

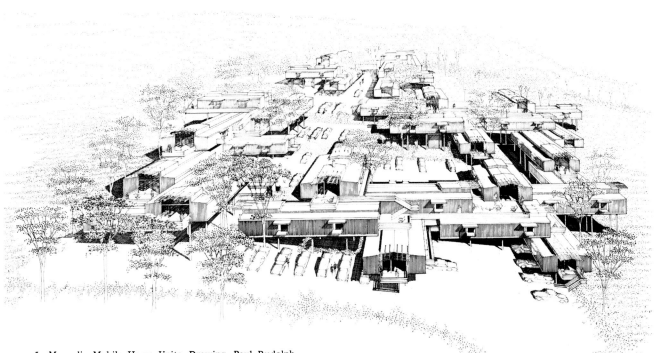

5. Magnolia Mobile Home Units. Drawing. Paul Rudolph.

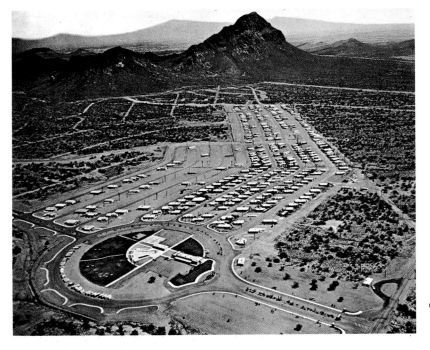

6. Tucson, Arizona. Tucson Estates.
Mobile home colony.

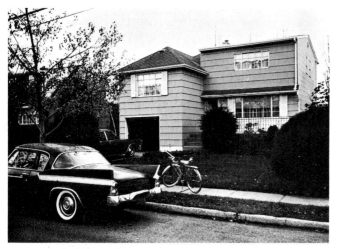

7. Merrick, Long Island. Suburban house. *Ca.* 1955.

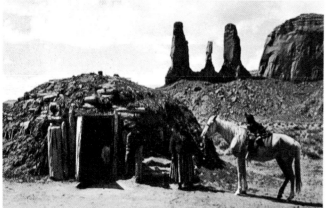

8. Monument Valley, Arizona. Navaho hogan.

The more general pattern as it has taken shape by the second half of the twentieth century is equally convincing: a tiny, highly efficient house, big automobile, and camper—hogan, horse, and travois; small difference between them *(Figs. 7–9)*. Similar, too, are the human qualities which brought the primitivistic and nomadic patterns forth, alike among post-conquest Plains Indians and contemporary Americans: a sense of open horizons, an impatience with communal restraints, an instinct for the continuation throughout life of childish joys, a taste for violence, hard use, quick turnover, lonely fantasies, eternal change. The feathered lance and the neons of the Strip are alike heraldries of American culture, of its Stone Age, chromium heart, windy gestures, and vacant lands *(Fig. 10)*.[1]

— ◈ —

Yet the general pattern of American architecture is perhaps best introduced by the strongest exception to it, within which, nevertheless, the pull of its influence can be perceived. Reference here is to the Pueblo Indians of the Southwest, who were the most communally minded builders of urban ar-

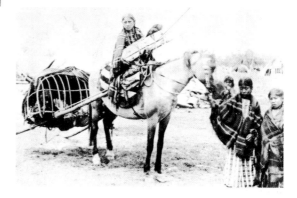

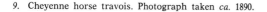

9. Cheyenne horse travois. Photograph taken *ca.* 1890.

chitecture that these continental limits have yet known. Monumental architecture, ultimately deriving from that of Meso-America, was built by Indians other than the Pueblos. One thinks of the Mound Builders of the Mississippi and the Ohio, and of their cosmic snakes, earth-molded, rising out of the river bottoms *(Fig. 11)*. There were towns, too, of many types: the plastered sod hemispheres of the Pawnee *(Fig. 12)*, the long houses of the Iroquois, the fortified villages of the Mandans. But the Pueblos and their architecture have special meaning. They formed a frontier at once agricultural and urban, eventually surrounded by nomad marauders; they were cities in the heart of the American wilderness, rocks in the flood. Civilized, the Pueblos never entirely succumbed to barbarian pressure or temptation. One might say that they are still resisting it today. The nomad made himself a horseman, and in the brilliant twilight of his history he fashioned for himself a gaudy role. But the Pueblo Indian, though he loves his horses, has never let them bear him away—nor his pickup truck either. He is still exercising his obsessive passion, which is for the earth and for the life that grows out of the earth. His history begins with that image.

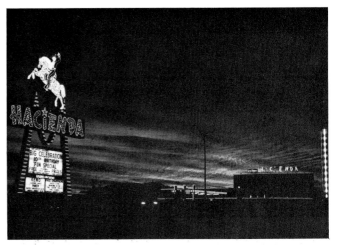

10. Las Vegas, Nevada. Evening.

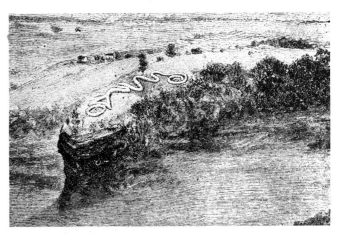

11. Bratten Township, Adams County, Ohio. Serpent mound and cliff.

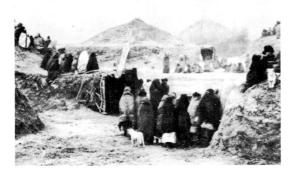

12. Pawnee earth-lodge village. Photograph taken 1871.

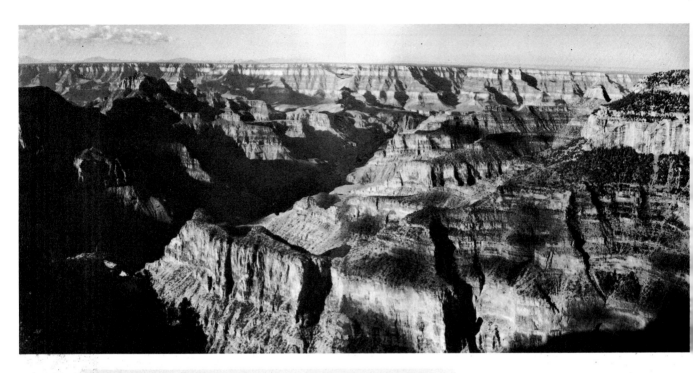

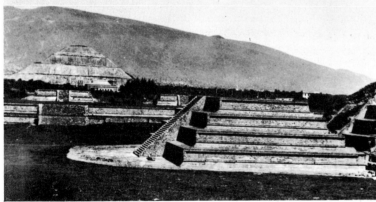

13. Grand Canyon, Arizona. View from north rim.

14. Teotihuacán, Valley of Mexico. Temple bases, pyramid, and mountain.

15. Mesa Verde, Colorado. Pit house. Modified Basketmaker. Section.

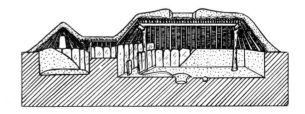

In the gorges of the Colorado the wind wakes with the touch of the sun *(Fig. 13)*. At dawn the buttes of the Grand Canyon lie sunk in darkness below the continental rim. Slowly the red light models their sides, revealing their bastions step by step, the vastest and most strictly constructed architectural forms on the continent and still, after all their aeons, wholly ignorant of man. No human dialogue can engage their archaic presences: a Greek temple would be riding chaos on their mesas, a Gothic cathedral lost among the spires. Far to the south, indeed, the temple bases of Mexico echo their forms and, in a more manageably sacred landscape, call the mountains to themselves *(Fig. 14)*; but there are no such temples here. It is the empty soul of the Great American Desert and the ultimate image of its power: a place of vast silence, the pilgrimage center of the continent, Delphi lost in it, Apollo Colorado-drowned. Out of those depths, so the Pueblos believe their primal ancestor emerged and climbed to the upper world.

Pueblo history, most clearly in the Mesa Verde area, repeats and then partly reverses that process. The first Anasazi people, the earliest Basketmakers *(ca. A.D. 1–450)* apparently lived in caves on the sides of their deep canyons and raised corn and squash on the flat mesa-tops far above. The Modified Basketmakers, of *ca.* 450–750, moved up out of the caves and dug themselves pit houses on the mesa near their fields *(Fig. 15)*. The first pits were more or less circular; development was toward oval and, finally, rectangular types. A timber frame, eventually carried on four posts, rose above the pit, supported slanted rafters, and was covered with brush and earth. Entrance came to be by ladder through the

smoke hole in the roof. The earlier side entrance shrank to the size of an air vent; between it and the fire pit an upright slab protected the flame and distributed the air. Beyond the fire, a shallow spirit hole, a *sipapu*, like a posthole, recalled the canyon depths whence the ancestor had sprung. Already there were kivas among the houses, even some so-called Great Kivas, and the appearance of these underground rooms for meeting and worship shows that architectural specialization had already begun *(Fig. 16)*. But the house itself was dwelling and temple at once, a clean, cool darkness, invoking the caverned earth and lit, like the Roman Pantheon, by a single shaft of sunlight from above.

Specialization increased in the Developmental Pueblo Period, of *ca.* 750–1100. Rectangular houses of masonry, with vertical walls and flat roofs, were grouped first in curved, then in E- and L-shaped rows, forming garden apartments for their clan groups *(Fig. 17)*. In the open courts which they defined, more elaborately stylized kivas were dug, perfectly circular and wholly below ground, with cribbed ceilings of cedar beams. In them the ceremonial functions of the older houses and kivas alike must have been elaborated, and the oldest circular house-shape was permanently memorialized. They were mainly, but not exclusively, reserved for the men as clubhouse, workshop, and retreat. Here they renewed contact with the earth and climbed skyward through the smoke. High rose the ladder poles. Above them, the cubes of the dwelling units proliferated until they lifted in massed tiers, set back story by story to provide living terraces on their roofs *(Fig. 28)*.

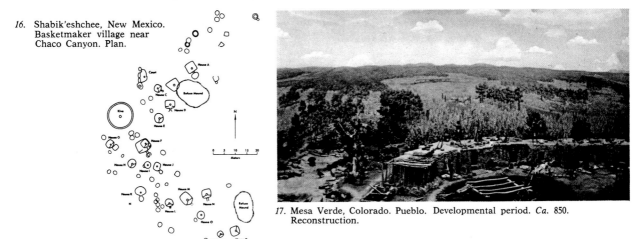

16. Shabik'eshchee, New Mexico. Basketmaker village near Chaco Canyon. Plan.

17. Mesa Verde, Colorado. Pueblo. Developmental period. *Ca.* 850. Reconstruction.

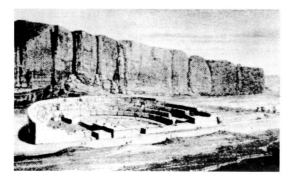

18. Chaco Canyon, New Mexico. Pueblo Bonito. Classic Pueblo period. *Ca.* 1100–1300. Reconstruction drawing.

19. Pueblo Bonito. Plan.

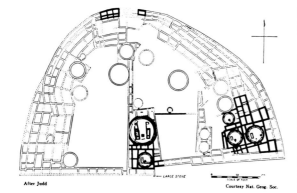

After Judd · — LARGE STONE · SCALE OF FEET · Courtesy Nat. Geog. Soc.

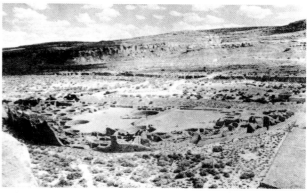

20. Pueblo Bonito. General view.

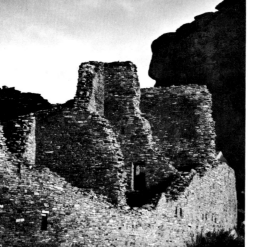

21. Pueblo Bonito. East wall and cliff, detail of construction.

During the Great, or Classic, Pueblo Period, of *ca.* 1100–1300, a much higher proportion of kivas was built and, for whatever reason—defense, proud monumentality, or both—the apartment-house villages, with their courts and kivas, began to be enclosed as a single shape within one thick wall. The finest known of such great buildings is the so-called Pueblo Bonito in Chaco Canyon, south of the Mesa Verde *(Figs. 18–21)*. Its rubble masonry is faced with various patterns of tiny slim stones, as elegant as wafers, laid flat and making a fluid wall-mosaic far more flexible than Roman *opus incertum.* Those sinuous walls housed a thousand people in a vast D-shape, rising to five sweeping stories in the curve and closed by a one-story section across the flat side. Large kivas were constructed and then packed about with earth in the court. They might be much expanded in size and surrounded with peripheral rooms, so forming monumental interior spaces, as in the Casa Rinconada and others in Chaco Canyon, or in the pueblo at Aztec *(Fig. 22)*. Many of these Great Kivas were also sited in topographically commanding positions, as if making enlarged contact not only with an increased congregation but also with the grander natural forms of the land *(Fig. 23)*. In consequence, much of the kiva's cylinder might now project above ground—as at Aztec itself or in some of the modern pueblos of the Rio Grande. There they still call to the sacred mountains around them and set up a beautifully direct relation between man-made and natural forms, which patterns of the dances in the plazas before them complete *(Fig. 24)*.

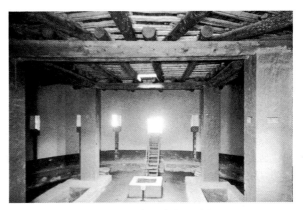

22. Aztec, New Mexico. Interior of Great Kiva. Reconstruction.

23. Chaco Canyon, New Mexico. Great Kiva "Kin Nahasbas," with butte.

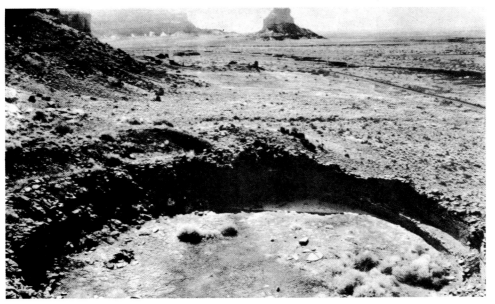

24. San Ildefonso, New Mexico. Kiva.

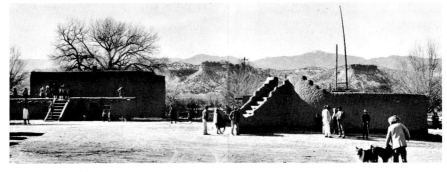

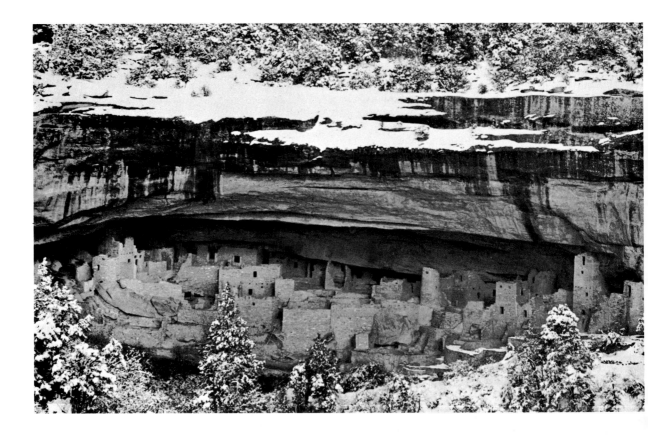

25. Mesa Verde, Colorado. Cliff Palace. *Ca.* 1200. Distant view.

26. Cliff Palace. Kivas and dwellings.

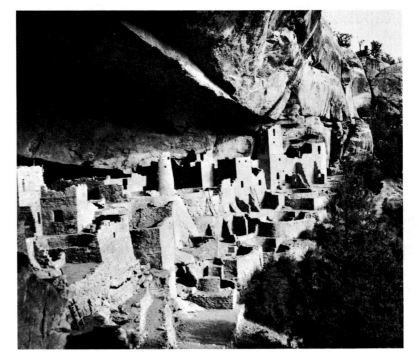

22

During prehistoric times, the whole complex of the Pueblo Bonito had been canyon and mountain in itself, a labyrinth of communicating cells, a galaxy of circular pits. Rectangle and circle moved symphonically together. But it was in the Mesa Verde that the most startling development took place. Late in the Great Pueblo Period, *ca.* 1200, most of the population moved its villages back off the mesa tops to long, shallow caverns in the canyon walls *(Figs. 25–27)*. Others left the area for good. The motive remains unknown, but there is good reason to believe that prolonged drought and progressive desiccation played a major role. Perhaps for this reason, new structures, tending toward symmetrical shapes and apparently of purely ritual use, such as the so-called Sun and Fire temples, made their appearance.

There were, it is true, many tiny groups of houses at the Mesa Verde in the clefts of the canyon, built of loaf-shaped, bread-colored stones. But the few large concentrations of dwellings, such as Cliff Palace and Spruce Tree House *(Figs. 25–27)*, show the structural and spatial rhythm developed to its fullest, a melody of square and circle, of rectangular and cylindrical towers, with kivas sown like raindrops among the cubical cells. Most of all, the kiva tops formed courtyards watched by several levels of doorway-eyes. The women held the houses, as the kivas the men. The space so formed is instinct with emotion still, a true urban theater, suspenseful, like a stage, as if, at a shout, the actors would appear: surely women in the doorways, but up the long ladders projecting from the kivas might climb— what? The men give themselves many parts, and they mount through the smoke in their disguises, embodiments of the gods or of the great nations of animals. The old towns still seem to await the mask and the rattle and the feet pounding the drum of the earth, and in the modern pueblos the dance goes on *(Fig. 24)*.

27. Mesa Verde, Colorado. Spruce Tree House. Court over kiva.

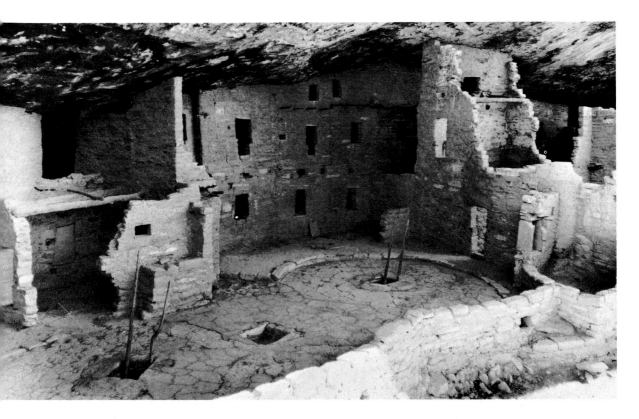

By the thirteenth century, the old Anasazi sites were almost all abandoned, and their people had moved south, probably dispersing among the so-called Regressive Pueblos of modern times, founding the high Hopi towns and moving down into the drainage of the Rio Grande, and since then repeatedly moving their pueblos tiny distances, as if working off some psychic restlessness within them. Splendid Taos *(Fig. 28)* has moved several times, but its two pyramidally stepped-back house-blocks still dance the sacred mountain before its face and receive its waters in the stream between them. The simple geometry of their trabeated, flat-roofed units, massing up their hollow cubes with unsophisticated profiles and plain surfaces, should be seen, like Anasazi architecture before it, in contrast to the elaborately sited, richly profiled, large-scaled and massively sculptural temples of Mexico *(Fig. 14)*. Where the two cultures can be seen side by side, as

at Casas Grandes in Chihuahua, each remains discrete, and the contrast between them is enormous. Despite its own changes of style, and indeed its spartan aridity and hardness when contrasted with Mayan shapes, Mexican architecture may be regarded as of an almost baroque complexity when compared to the simpler Pueblo forms.

That contrast between the architecture of the Valley of Mexico and of New Mexico is particularly clear and cogent in Spanish colonial times. Here it was in fact a question of modifying European Baroque forms in accordance with the primitive resources of the New Mexican frontier. The Pueblo of Taos, under its sacred mountain, and the mission church of San Francisco at Ranchos de Taos to the south *(Figs. 28–31)* both show how building with adobe tends naturally to produce simplified, strongly modeled shapes which, because of the necessary

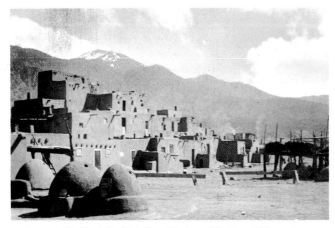

28. Taos Pueblo, New Mexico, with Sacred Mountain.

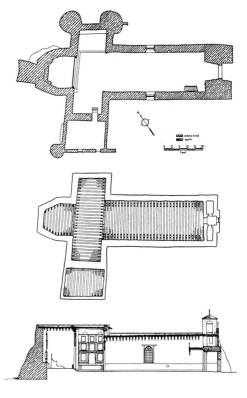

31. San Francisco. Plans and section.

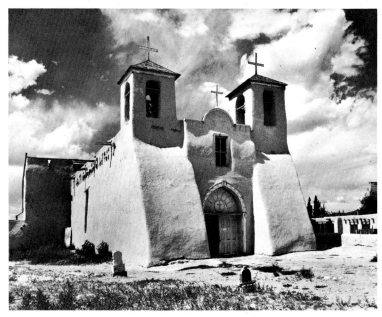

29. Ranchos de Taos, New Mexico. San Francisco. 1772. Entrance façade.

30. San Francisco. Rear view.

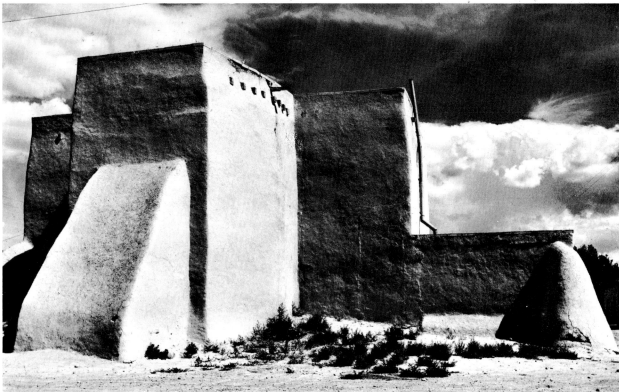

avoidance of detail, seem strangely scaled and abstract. The Cathedral of Mexico *(Fig. 32)* and San Francisco or, better, the much earlier church of San Esteban at Acoma *(Fig. 33)*, can demonstrate with exactitude the contrast between what we may now be permitted to call Mexican and American forms. One derives from the other, but the former defines the great plaza of a metropolitan capital, the seat of Montezuma's power and the center of systematic Spanish urbanism in the New World. The other stands high on the edge of a monstrous boulder whose summit supports an Indian pueblo. It faces as in a dream the so-called "enchanted" mesa across the valley, not the Renaissance splendors of a thronged urban square. What in the Mexican church is elaborate in profile, movemented in surface, and fluid in the modulation of part to part, has all disappeared. The massive walls are static in mass,

32. Mexico City. Cathedral. 1563–*ca.* 1667.

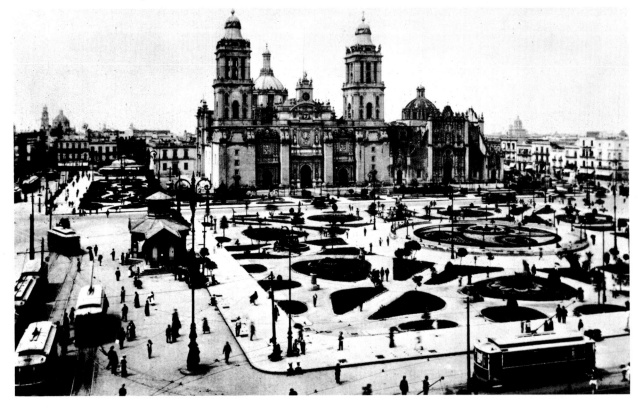

plain and flat of surface. The cathedral embodies a civilized conversation of many complicated scales; San Esteban is a simple heavy chant. Bearing walls, cedar beams, flat roofs, and buttressed corners make an architecture which, in relation to that of Mexico, is simplified, clarified, and primitivized. These qualities, at Acoma as at Ranchos de Taos, become positive ones, like the beginning of something which—though deriving or degenerating from a more developed style—has worked its way back to first principles, from which a new kind of growth may well be possible. The fact that no such development occurred in New Mexico indicates no more than the area's own general lack of development. The qualities its colonial architecture shares with that of the Eastern Seaboard were in fact to play an obvious part in the history of American architecture as a whole.

33. Acoma, New Mexico. San Esteban. *Ca.* 1630.

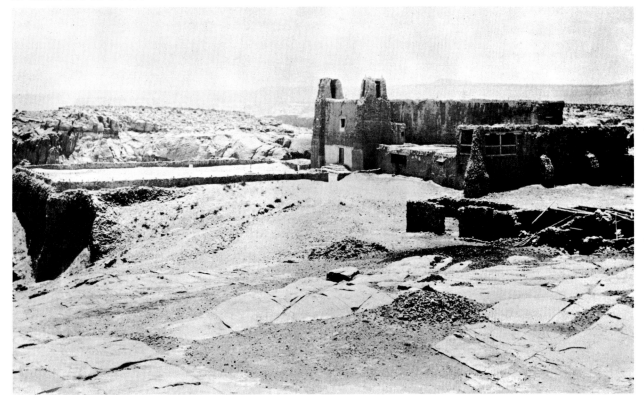

But Acoma is much more than a demonstration of frontier conditions. It creates a monumental interior space, which is one of the first and noblest to be built above ground on the northern part of the continent—a high, shadowed volume, vast and austere *(Fig. 34)*. So the bearing walls of flat stones and adobe brick are thick and battered inward in order to rise high, while the projecting cedar beams which span between them rest on carved and painted wooden corbels, which stretch and swell with an Etruscan exaggeration of profile. Before remodeling, a bloom of light enveloped the altar from a transverse clerestory over the choir. The device still exists at Ranchos de Taos *(Fig. 31)* and elsewhere in New Mexico, to which it is unique. It seems at once a primitivization of the European windowed dome and a recollection of the smoke hole in the kiva *(Figs. 15, 27)*, which, of course, still functions in the pueblos in more or less the traditional way. The light from above is another exact description of the American position between two worlds. So is the mass of Acoma as a whole, riding like a ship over the desert. It is built of Indian materials, but it rejects the hived, stepped massing of Indian forms *(Fig. 14)*. Its verticality is uncompromised, but its horizontal axis is intensified as well. Its assertions are fierce and heroic, ultimately Hellenic in origin, and it physically introduces the divine pretensions of the European individual into the savagely innocent American land.

The late-medieval colonial forms of the Eastern Seaboard, like their landscape, are less tragic and

34. San Esteban. Interior.

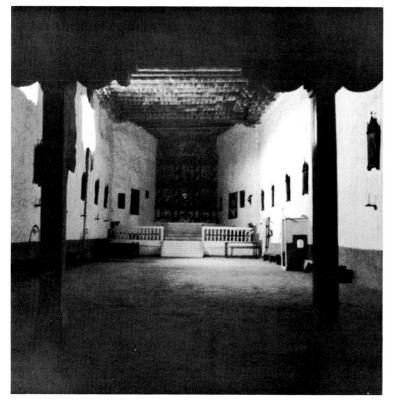

grand than those of New Mexico, but their relationship to their European antecedents is much the same. Their history has been more than adequately explored elsewhere, so that they need be treated only in these particular connections here. In the architecture of the English colonies there are three significant differences from that of the Southwest. There is no Indian influence; the house is more important in social terms and as the bearer of style; and most of all, the East Coast had what the Southwest lacked, a pattern of middle-class urbanism which was to form the dominant cultural strain of the United States as a whole. Here, therefore, as in Florence 300 or so years before, the middle class directed its energies toward the creation of a kind of classicism in its own image, seeking out reasonable, balanced, closed, and ordered forms. The existing English elements were more rigorously systematized than had generally been the case at home. It is true that some early towns, such as Boston, *(Fig. 35),* followed the old, loose pattern of communal growth: grouping its buildings around the harbor, filling out on the footpaths that climbed the contours of the site and ran along the crests, spreading along the roughly radial system of roads that linked the port with the rest of New England. An irregular tract of land at the edge of the town was reserved as a common. All of this was English enough, though reproducing in a few years, perhaps, some centuries of Saxon and Norman growth. But in the plan of New Haven, Connecticut, the regular grid system which was to become the dominant

35. Boston, Massachusetts. Plan of 1722.

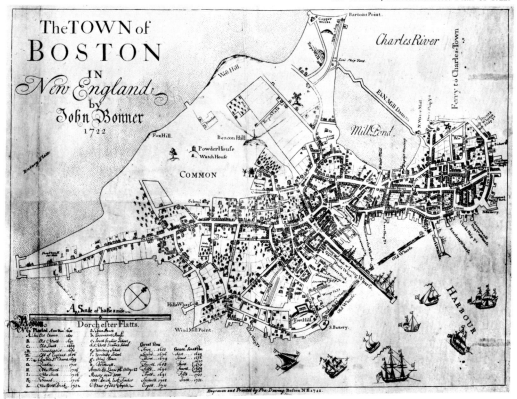

American scheme appeared very early *(Fig. 36)*. The grid was archetypally colonial as well, ideal for impatient settlers on a continental coast; it had been current long before Hippodamos and was used by the Greeks at Smyrna in the seventh century B.C., and at Metapontum and Akragas in the sixth. The English were employing it in ravaged Ireland during precisely the period when their colonization of America was taking place. But New Haven's grid is of a special and distinguished kind. It is a purely Vitruvian figure, a perfect square, canted a little off the north-south axis to adjust to the rivers that mark its site by the shore. It is divided by open streets into nine smaller squares, with the central one reserved as common land, in New Haven called the "Green." From the earliest days, a meeting-house, itself a perfect square, stood near the center of the Green. Later, when most of the squares were quartered by new streets, a single north-south avenue, named Temple Street, divided the Green; along it, early in the nineteenth century, three churches were strung, facing eastward like temples *(Fig. 37)*. They replaced the old meetinghouse, and their stee-

ples rose high into the Green's wide swell of open air. A State House in temple form stood behind them, until it was pulled down late in the century *(Fig. 38)*. Westward, the open space was defined by the Old Brick Row of Yale College, long gambreled barns turning their flanks to the street and punctuated by frontally faced buildings with churchlike towers *(Fig. 39)*. Elsewhere around the Green, each house stood free on its own plot of ground, defining the central open space as ships moored around it, not as a wall. The urban structure was widely spread but shaped by taut cubes, exact and self-contained, each a small grid in the large, in an order as integral as, if less fixed than, Peking's *(Fig. 40)*. The concept of the row house was resisted in such towns. New Haven gained only a few in the nineteenth century. The major definition of space was eventually to be accomplished by trees. With romanticism, elms were planted, and the whole, indeed almost all, of New Haven became Canterbury Cathedral, the streets long naves with sacred names: Church, Chapel, College, Temple, Court, Crown, and Elm.

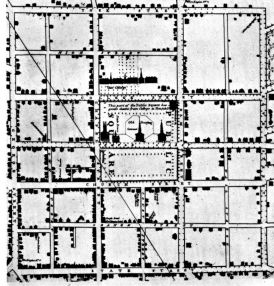

37. New Haven, Connecticut. Doolittle Map of 1824.

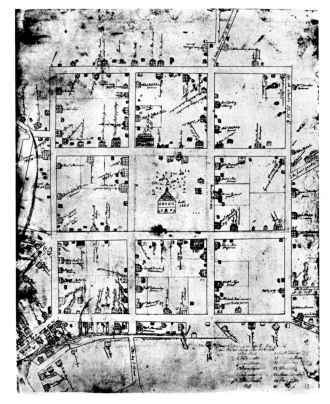

36. New Haven, Connecticut. Wadsworth Map of 1748, showing original plan of 1641.

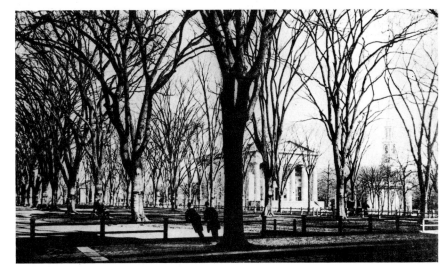

38. New Haven, Connecticut. The Green, with the State House (demolished) and Center Church.

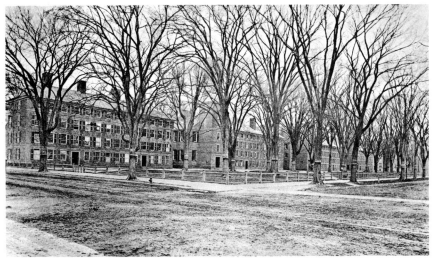

39. New Haven, Connecticut. Yale College. The Old Brick Row on the Green. 1750–1824.

40. Peking. Plan of 1765.

By the middle of the twentieth century, the elms were dying without remedy. Towns like Litchfield, Connecticut—though there the plan is the great cross-axis of a linear, ridge-top site—still hold the feeling: separate houses, broad lawns, the elm forest marching in dark pillars and arching and interlocking over all *(Fig. 41)*. The space is wide, but the order, made up of self-sufficient individual units, is fixed and complete. Hence, the New England town was the first and perhaps still the most beautiful of all those several syntheses of Europe and America, of the garden and the woodland, of

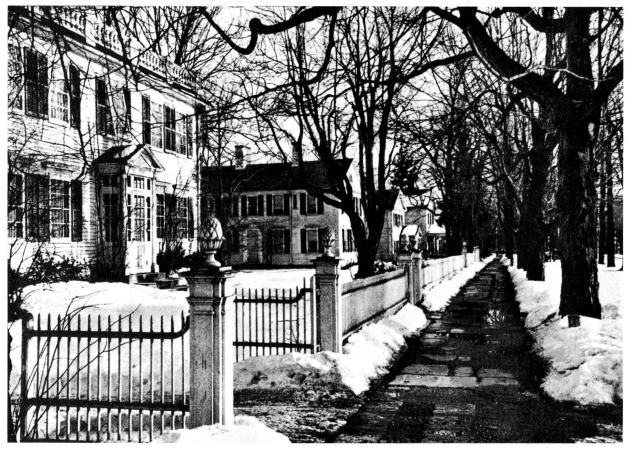

41. Litchfield, Connecticut. Main Street.

the street and the savannah, which American architecture was to bring into being.

William Penn clearly had London in mind when he
planned Philadelphia—not labyrinthine medieval
London, but plans like those of Evelyn, Holme, and
Craalinges for its rebuilding after the fire of 1666.
Philadelphia was again a grid, this time made up
of rectangles forming one long oblong of city
stretched between its rivers and divided by two
avenues crossing at a square in the center (Figs.
42, 43). Four additional squares enlarged the scale
of the rectangles and were reserved for parks.

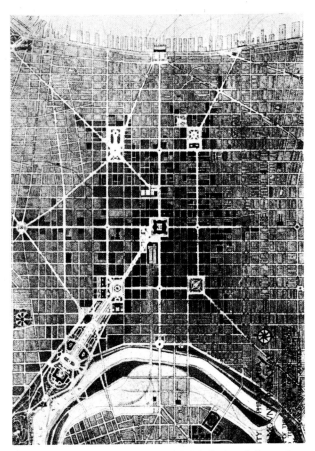

42. Philadelphia, Pennsylvania. William
Penn's plan of 1682.

43. Philadelphia, Pennsylvania. Plan of 1919. Projected diagonal
avenues.

The radial avenues of Sir Christopher Wren's plan for London *(Fig. 44)* had no takers in the colonies, unless the ceremonial axis at Williamsburg may be felt to derive from a similar baroque impulse toward movement and climax *(Fig. 45)*. Wren's scheme was a dynamic one, of unified order based beyond Versailles on the radiating avenues and obelisked intersections of Baroque Rome. The new republic was to seize upon its unifying gesture, but the colonies preferred the order of separate, repeated shapes. The plan of Savannah, for example, intensified the contrast between the closed and open units of the grid; the squares of park were separated by only a few blocks of built-up rectangles, so that a beautiful rhythm of street and square expanded and contracted through the city *(Fig. 46)*. The system was retained during Savannah's growth through the early nineteenth century right up to the Civil War, and it was given monumental stability by the splendidly abstract Greek Revival architecture which was built during that period. Hence, the urban solids and voids of the center of Savannah attain a sculptural balance worthy of the three-dimensional, modular-grid schemes of Francesco di Giorgio, though gentled by the American river of trees *(Fig. 47)*.

Behind the trees, all along the East Coast, stand the houses, though originally they stood stark and alone in pitiless, Iron Age clearings. In New Eng-

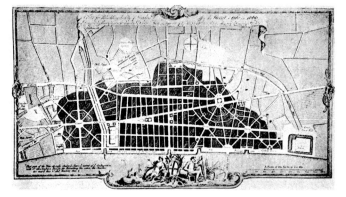

44. London. Sir Christopher Wren's plan of 1666.

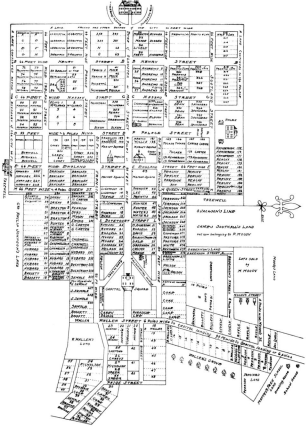

45. Williamsburg, Virginia. Plan of *ca.* 1800.

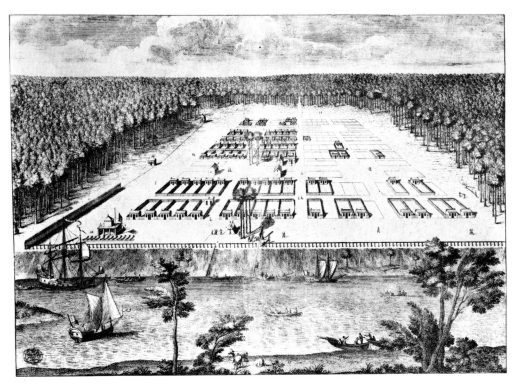

46. Savannah, Georgia. View in 1734.

47. Savannah, Georgia. View in 1855. After a painting by J. W. Hill.

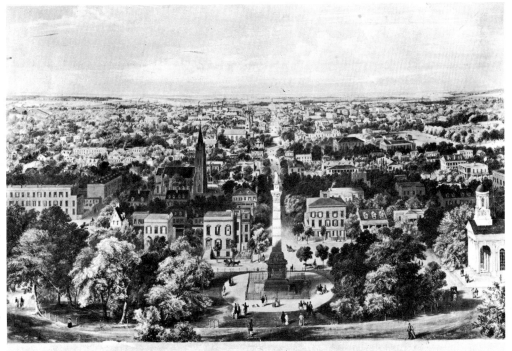

land, it was an English medieval wood-frame dwelling imported *in toto* *(Figs. 48, 49)*. Rapidly, however, modifications were made in it which led its forms in the direction taken by those of New Mexico. The thatched roof was changed to shingles, creating a tighter, harder profile. The skeleton frame, which in English examples might be weatherboarded, plastered, tiled, or left exposed as half-timber, was soon uniformly sheathed in thin, narrow American clapboards. Windows and doors were pushed tight up to the forward plane of the clapboards to keep a weather seal. The extremes of the American climate so played a part in closing the surface, making it more planar, more linear, and thinner than in the general run of English houses. A frontal gable was common in England. It occurred in the colonies, too *(Fig. 48)*, but soon was almost universally sheared off, so tightening the profile further *(Fig.*

48. Salem, Massachusetts. Lewis Hunt House, showing frontal gables. After 1698; destroyed 1863.

50. Parson Capen House. Plan.

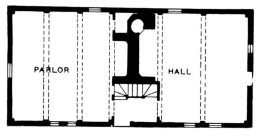

49. Topsfield, Massachusetts. Parson Capen House. 1683.

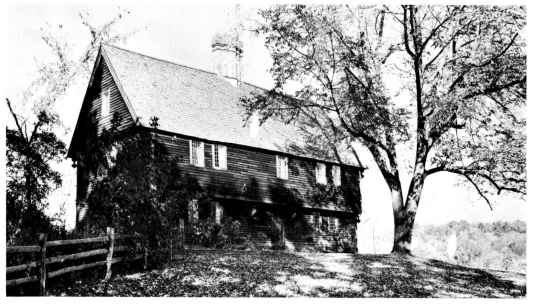

49). As in New Mexico, everything became simplified and clarified; the virtues sought were now the elemental ones of strong, obvious shapes and plain surfaces. Plan and structure, despite some variations, were also systematized *(Figs. 50, 51)*. The great fireplace mass, the only sculptural solid in the house, soon assumed a central position, stabilizing the heavy skeleton of the frame, which was sheathed to make a hollow box of space around it. The rooms, low and with the frame largely exposed *(Fig. 52)*, naturally assumed their positions in the system; their windows found a regular, more or less symmetrical placement. The English original was thus distilled into a more rigid order, less compromised by variety, less rich in modulation.

Those qualities became standard in America. The provincial baroque house of the mid-eighteenth century has them too: a regular plan, thin shell, taut,

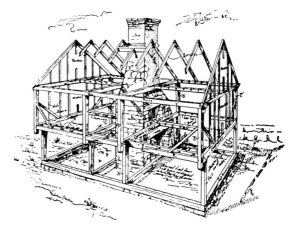

51. Farmington, Connecticut. Gleason House. *Ca.* 1660. Drawing of the frame structure.

52. Parson Capen House. Parlor.

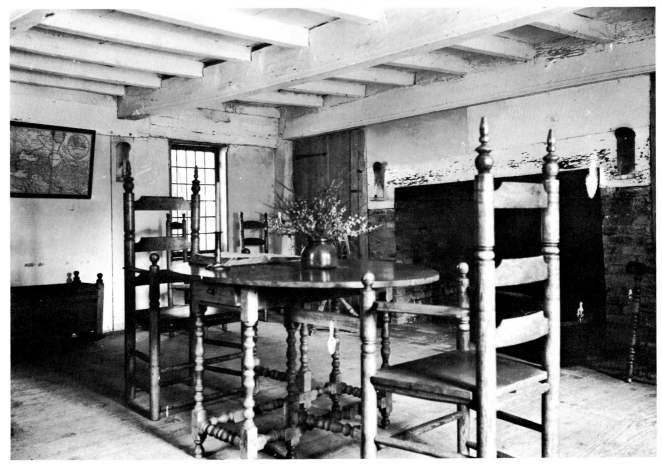

linear details, windows tight on the surface—in general, a flat pattern of sharply separated shapes like that of colonial painting *(Figs. 53, 54)*. While the linear and flattened architectural forms can be matched by some English examples, the paintings so far cannot quite be. It would thus seem to have been a matter of instinct and choice; Englishmen in America came actively to want perfect, precise, fleshless, puristic shapes—first dark, but soon incandescent with light blue or yellow paint against

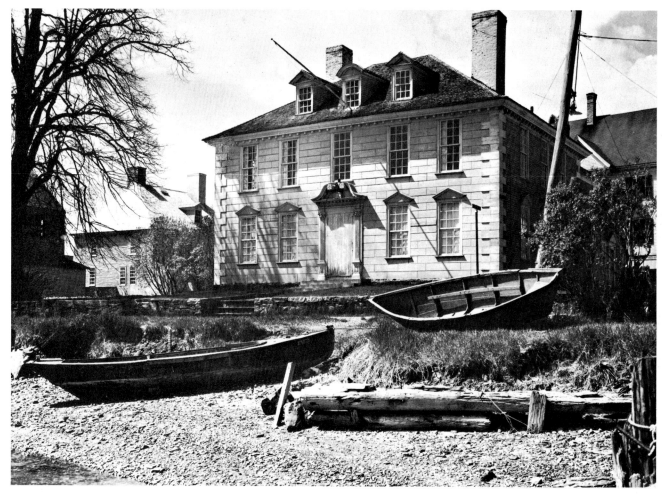

53. Portsmouth, New Hampshire. Wentworth-Gardner House. 1760.

New England's heavy greens. The Greek Revival was to bring most of them to the ultimate luminescence of glowing white, electric in violet air and autumn's haze. Hence, New England architecture's ultimate derivation from deep Puritan sensibilities, encouraged by a colonial situation, should not be denied in favor of simple technological explanations. It was indeed middle-class building, self-contained, even smug, not generous, but square and straight, like decency made visible, highly lit and clear. Its

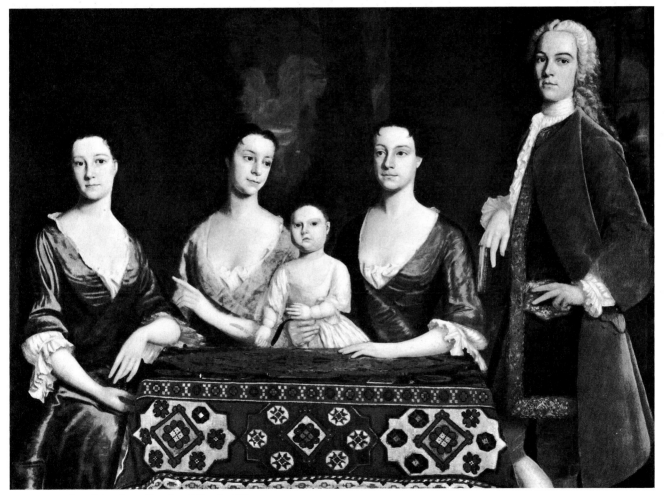

54. Robert Feke: *Isaac Royall and Family.* 1741.

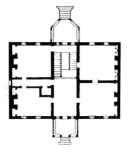

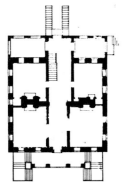

rooms are paneled or plastered cabinets, obsessive containers at generally very small scale. Slowly, they became more elaborate, with larger stair halls and walls papered with landscape scenes *(Figs. 55–57)*. Late in the eighteenth century, the painter of its occupants might throw up a double-hung window behind them to show a landscape with the house itself sitting bright on its steading *(Fig. 58)*, but it is in fact closed off against the place. It makes no overtures to the land, assumes no grand postures of any kind. And it was this way because its builders wanted it to be so, not simply because it was built of wood. In brick it was the same *(Fig. 59)*. The window frames are pressed forward so that no depth of wall is apparent, and the brick surface seems as tightly stretched and thin as wooden sheathing. Conversely, English window frames of

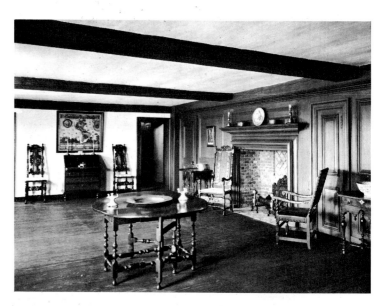

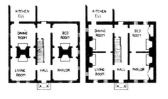

55. (*Far left*) Plans of eighteenth-century houses. *After Morrison, Early American Architecture.*

56. (*Above*) Portsmouth, New Hampshire. Room from Samuel Wentworth House, 1671. Paneled *ca.* 1710. Now in The Metropolitan Museum of Art, New York.

57. (*Left*) Portsmouth, New Hampshire. Moffatt-Ladd House. 1763. By Captain John Moffatt. Stair Hall.

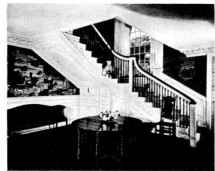

40

this period were pushed back by law, an urban regulation to protect them from fire. So the English surface became more plastic by legislation, and the American thinner by aesthetic choice, while the eighteenth-century gambrel roof tended to complete the effect of an interior volume of space tautly contained, even ballooning, as within a stretched fabric. The provincial-baroque details of pedimented doorways or coigned corners look as if they could be sliced off with a razor; the intrinsic qualities remain simplicity of mass and continuity of surface. How similar in all these ways were the fine factories built of metal and glass in the twentieth century by Albert Kahn *(Fig. 60)*.

In the Southern colonies, the pattern of domestic architecture was similar but somewhat more monumental in character. The general English vernacular

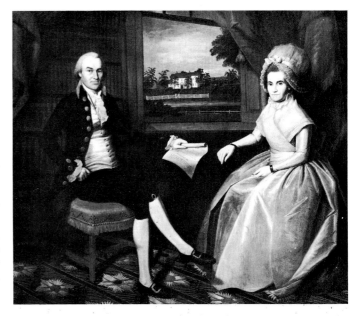

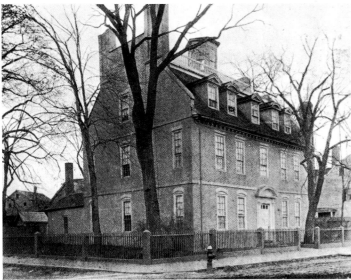

58. Ralph Earl: *Oliver Ellsworth and His Wife.* 1792.

59. Portsmouth, New Hampshire. Macpheadris-Warner House. 1716–23.

60. Lima, Ohio. Ohio Steel Foundry Roll Shop. 1939. Albert Kahn.

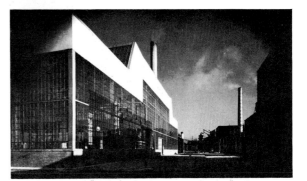

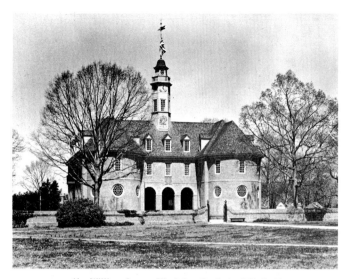

61. Williamsburg, Virginia. Capitol. 1701–5. Reconstructed 1928–34. View from the southwest.

was perhaps more in accord with American conditions here, and the vernacular line, high-roofed and exuberant, in red brick with white, semibaroque trim, runs with rather papery elegance to Westover *(Fig. 62)* and well beyond. But the H-plan of the colonial Capitol *(Fig. 61)* and the corner pavilions of Mulberry *(Fig. 63)* seem rather different, and they lead to Stratford, the Lee mansion, which is the most distinguished exception to the general rule *(Fig. 64)*. Here one may be allowed to cite Sir John Vanbrugh's Blenheim Palace for comparison and contrast *(Fig. 65)*. The change of scale is significant: Blenheim, tremendous; Stratford, its plan taken from a book of 1667 by Stephen Primatt, very small. Both houses group their chimneys in fours, with striking sculptural effect; but Blenheim, though more cubistic and waywardly fanciful than the European Baroque architecture by which it was inspired, still advances its masses in serried compa-

62. Charles City County, Virginia. Westover. 1726–30.

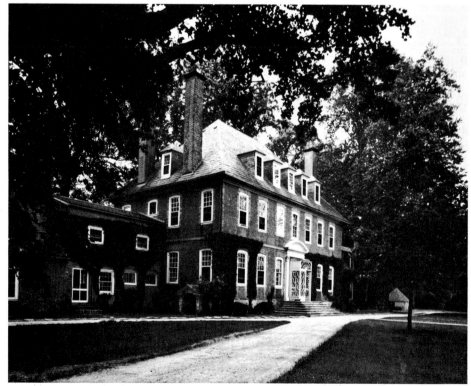

nies, rhythmically reaching out to its splendidly designed park, and building inward and upward toward the split pediment of its central block. Men and nature are thus juxtaposed and related to each other in the fine theater of a dance. Stratford avoids all such movements, climaxes, and relationships. Its side wings are clearly separate blocks, cubical and clear-cut. The dependencies, held on the Vitruvian quadrants, are far out in space. The scale is strange; there is a sense of disorientation. The stair to the hall is a ladder. The house is above the land, not of it, a stern image of humanity isolated in the world. Once more, the virtues are those of simplification and primitive directness. We are reminded of Acoma; indeed, the abstract cubism of Stratford, too, was to come into its own in the early tendency toward severe, geometric classicism which the American colonies as a whole were to exhibit during the second half of the eighteenth century.

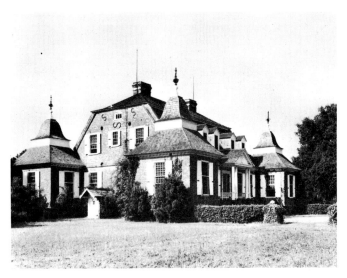

63. Berkeley County, South Carolina. Mulberry Castle. 1714.

64. Westmoreland County, Virginia. Stratford. *Ca.* 1725.

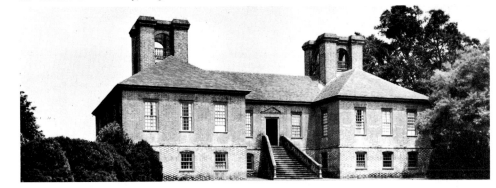

65. Oxfordshire, England. Blenheim Palace. 1705–24. Sir John Vanbrugh. North front.

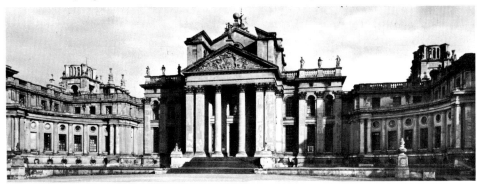

Colonial public buildings largely conformed to the predominantly domestic scale. Richard Munday's generous Colony House in Newport *(Fig. 66)* is no larger than a substantial English house. It retains a medieval frontal dormer, which recalls those in wood of Boston's First Town House but which has now been transformed in a Wren-like semibaroque frontispiece, lifting the façade into a vertical continuity that is the finest kind of climax to the hill slope above the harbor it crowns. A cupola leaps from the roof, as in the Governor's Palace at Williamsburg or in many English houses. But in Philadelphia's Independence Hall, all protuberances—cupolas, pediments, frontispieces—were sheared away until only a taut surface pattern of red and white remained. The building had to be monumentalized by the addition of a huge church steeple, wildly out of scale on the garden side and in any distant view but falling into perspective from the street *(Fig. 67)*.

This was appropriate enough, in a way, because the church—not city hall or its equivalent—was the center of community feeling and hence of monumental expression in the colonies. It was the major meeting place, and in New England the first churches were in fact nonconformist meetinghouses, even closer in function to the Moslem mosque than to the Jewish synagogue from which they so nearly derived. Like the mosque, they had been rigorously emptied of the physical presence of the divinity. Pieter Saenredam's paintings of the interiors of Dutch Catholic churches as reformed show the naked intensity of that iconoclastic desire. The altar is thrown out; the congregation is turned away from the old long axis down the nave and is instead faced across it toward the side of the church where a new pulpit rises. The disorientation from old foci is complete. The congregation is alone with itself, a meeting of conspirators against the old order. At Hingham, the Puritan meetinghouse as it evolved is seen in its purest form *(Figs. 68, 69)*. Light is concentrated behind the pulpit, but the whole is one volume of space more or less square and so nondirectional, its peaked roof surmounted by a single bell.

66. Newport, Rhode Island. Old Colony House. 1739. Richard Munday.

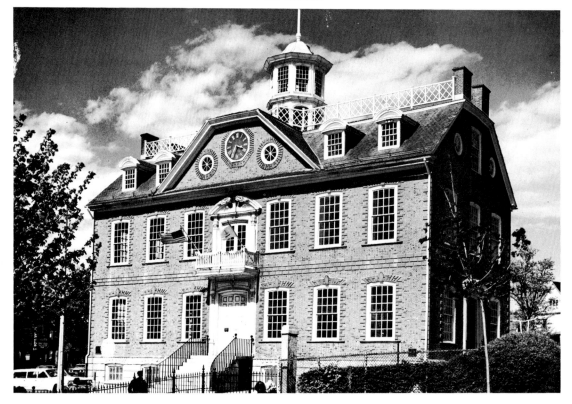

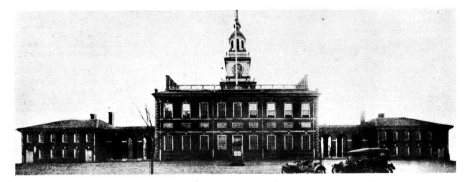

67. Philadelphia, Pennsylvania. Independence Hall. 1730–35.

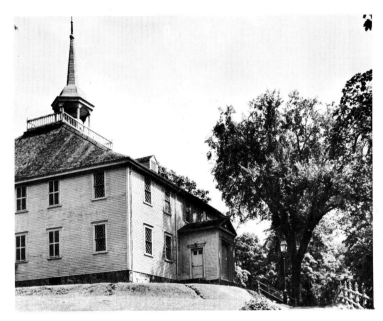

68. Hingham, Massachusetts. Old Ship Meeting House. 1681.

69. Old Ship Meeting House. Interior.

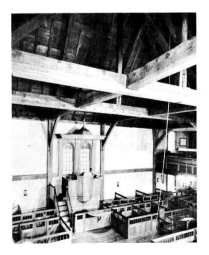

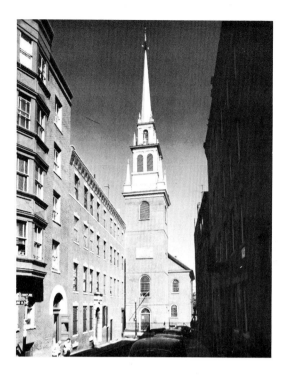

In Boston, the Old South Meeting House is just beginning to turn back into a church. Once more, the congregation sits closely together in a U-shape, the members stiff and straight, looking into each other's faces in the cold, clear light. It is the ultimate Protestant experience. A steeple, inspired by those of Wren and his followers, eventually marked the entrance on the crowded street, as Wren's had done in London, and it rises like Wren's into the sky as the single vertical marker of the Puritan town, the measure of its urban space and its only overt link with the heavens *(Fig. 70)*. But the forms of the colonial spire are Puritan too, sharpened from their English prototypes. Whether in wood at Trinity Church in Newport or in wood and brick at Old North Church in Boston—both Anglican churches with axial naves—the American spires assert their

70. Boston, Massachusetts. Old North Church. 1723. William Price.

71. "A View of Part of the Town of Boston in New England . . . 1768." Engraving by Paul Revere.

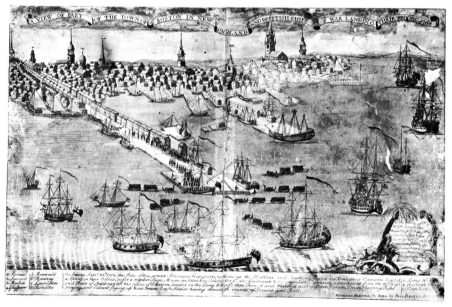

colonial compulsion toward shapes which are un-
wavering and pure *(Figs. 71, 72)*. The lanterns
burned for Paul Revere in a tower which, compared
with its English ancestors, is pointed as a sergeant's
pike, an icicle, a northern spear *(Fig. 70)*. Inside,
too, the contrast is striking. Linear and simplified
though the English churches are in contrast to their
own European contemporaries, the American interiors have in fact been swept clean *(Fig. 73)*. They
burn with that passion for reason, intellectual clarity, and legalistic justice *(Dike, in fact)* which made
the Revolution at last. Even most of the Gothic Revival churches of the next century in America retain
that character when contrasted with the English
work of A. W. N. Pugin, William Butterfield, the
Camdenians, and so on. They too, are sharply spired
outside, taut within *(Fig. 294)*.

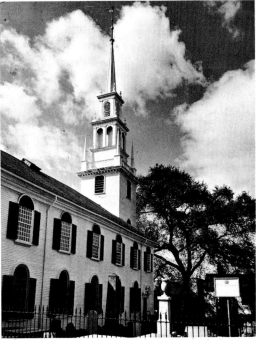

72. Newport, Rhode Island. Trinity Church. 1725.
Richard Munday.

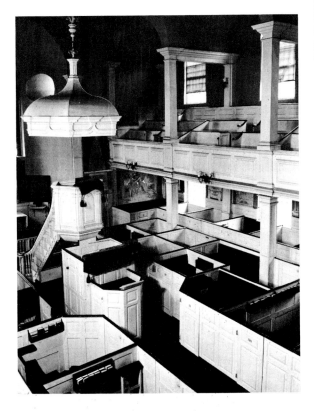

73. Trinity Church. Interior.

The classic reference is the correct one; the work of Peter Harrison in the middle of the eighteenth century already confirms it. Harrison should perhaps be called the first American architect. His dependence upon English example is only part of the story. He uses the books of the English Palladian architects and, like them, those of Vitruvius, Vignola, and Palladio. It is Palladio who is recalled in Harrison's Redwood Library of 1748–51; central pedimented portico, side wings, but strange scale —not mignonne like Lord Burlington's Chiswick, but lumbering, big in detail *(Fig. 74)*. Hence, though Harrison is clearly part of an English movement, and especially close here to James Gibbs, yet his intention is so heroic, in a building so small, that a new and primitive force is felt. His kind of freshness, even of welcome ineptitude, tends to remind us less of the obvious protoclassicism of his contemporary English sources than it does of the very beginnings of English Palladianism, as in Inigo Jones's Tuscan St. Paul's, Covent Garden, of 100 years before *(Fig. 75)*. And we must look forward to find the like again, to the beginnings of the tough romantic-classicism of the last quarter of the eighteenth century, as to Chalgrin's St. Philippe du Roule, of 1774–84 *(Fig. 76)*. From this it is only a step to the purposefully revolutionary projects of Ledoux, with their stark geometry, sharp contrasts, and discontinuous juxtapositions of opposites *(Fig. 77)*. All of this goes well with the Redwood Library and, in general, with the New England of the middle of the century.

Harrison's own King's Chapel is the other most striking example of English-colonial protoclassicism, with its ponderous mass, large-scaled masonry, and heavy colonnade *(Fig. 78)*. Beside it, the small, eared stones lean in the churchyard. Inside, slabs honor the dead; one of them is called "Friend of Virgil." Stern duty and classic learning directed, as here, Boston's try for excellence, the toughest and most sustained that the United States was to know. The United States was born out of it.

74. Newport, Rhode Island. Redwood Library. 1748–51. Peter Harrison.

75. London. St. Paul's, Covent Garden. 1631. Restored after fire 1795. Inigo Jones.

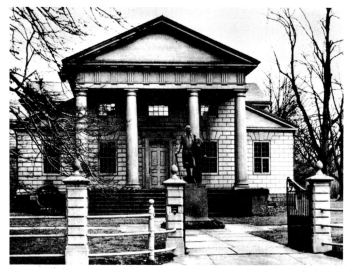

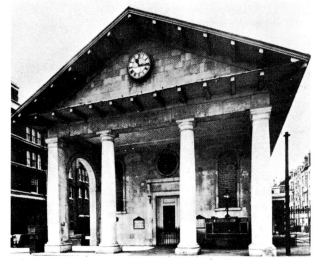

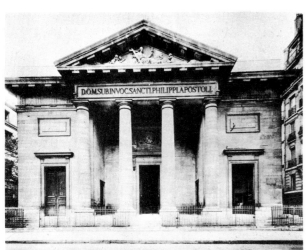

76. Paris. St. Philippe du Roule. 1774–84.
Jean François Chalgrin.

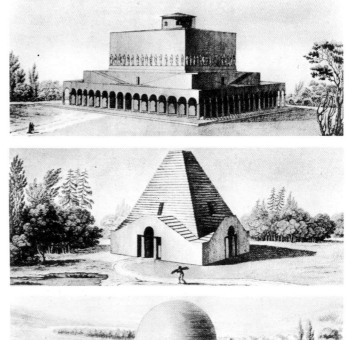

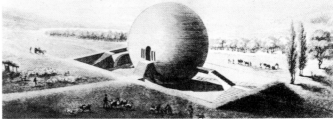

77. Designs for houses. After 1773. Claude-Nicolas Ledoux.

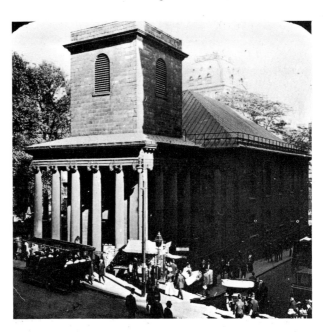

78. Boston, Massachusetts.
King's Chapel. 1753.
Peter Harrison.

49

But what was New England classicism directly after the Revolution? It is to be found in the work of Charles Bulfinch and Samuel McIntire, in a delicately attenuated decorative style derived from Robert Adam. Weight and mass have wholly disappeared; here middle-class energies were fixed for the moment upon the graceful proliferation of multishaped interior spaces and closed exterior surfaces elegantly inscribed. The heroic mood that made the Revolution had been dissipated. One must contrast Harrison's Brick Market of 1761 with Bulfinch's Boston State House, of 1798 *(Figs. 79, 80)*. Both are derived from Somerset House, an English government building. Harrison's details are big and strongly projected on a small mass; Bulfinch's are

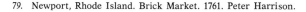

79. Newport, Rhode Island. Brick Market. 1761. Peter Harrison.

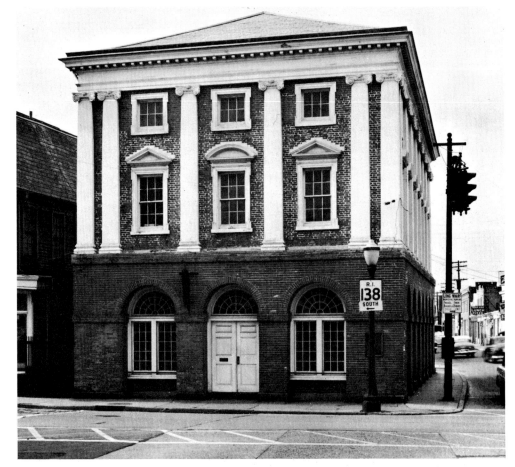

small and attenuated on a large one. Bulfinch's massing is romantic-classic enough; a block, a pedimented attic, and a dome; but his shapes are thin and stretched, like the skins of his houses. His dome especially is in marvelous tension between the cupped volume of its geometry and the glistening thinness of its golden surface: a balloon of air. So Bulfinch's architecture, though clear and luminous, is affluently inflated and institutional, perhaps an exact embodiment of Federalist New England. To match Harrison's sculptural force one must turn to Jefferson's work.

Monticello, as completed, seems to belong to the same world as Harrison's Redwood Library, derived from England but strongly awkward with new striv-

80. Boston, Massachusetts. State House. 1795–98. Charles Bulfinch.

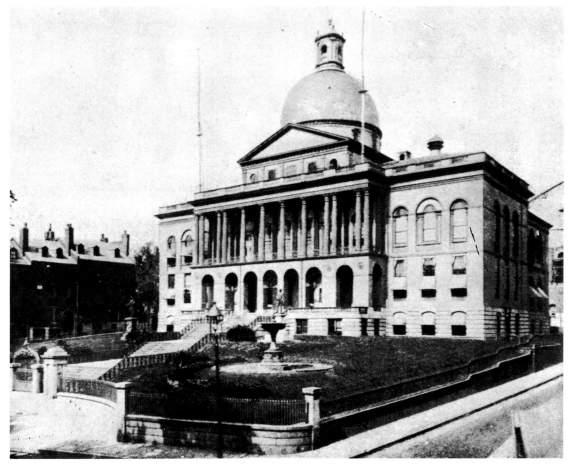

ings of its own *(Fig. 87)*. Yet Monticello shows that Jefferson's intentions were more complex than Harrison's had been, and some of them prefigure forms which were to be characteristic of American architecture during its most original phase in the late nineteenth and early twentieth centuries. Much of Jefferson's work should be seen, metaphorically speaking, as a struggle between the fixed European past and the mobile American future, between Palladio and Frank Lloyd Wright, between a desire for contained, classical geometry and an instinct to spread out horizontally along the surface of the land. The classical desire had always been obvious in America; horizontal continuity was largely to come later. But the first projects for Monticello are prophetic. A plan from a book by Robert Morris is the English source, showing a central block slightly projected beyond side wings *(Fig. 81)*. Quickly Jeff-

erson thickens the fireplace masses and thins out the containing walls, so recalling common colonial structure. At the same time, he changes the proportions of the side wings, so that both they and the central mass project widely from the block. In fact, Morris' cube disappears; instead, two axes begin to cross. Next, Jefferson clarifies these axes through a continuity in interior space and extends the major one outside by the addition of what would appear to have been, on the first floor, a piered and arcuated loggia *(Fig. 82)* like that which was later to grace Pavilion VII of the University of Virginia. Now Jefferson's plan itself closely resembles such an advanced, late nineteenth-century example as that of the Kent House, of 1885–86, by Bruce Price *(Fig. 220)*. But Jefferson does not stop there; he extends the two axes farther than Price was to do, pushing out columned porches on the entrance axis and

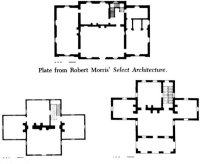

81. Charlottesville, Virginia. Monticello. Thomas Jefferson. Early plans, with plan by Robert Morris.

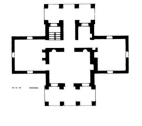

82. Monticello. Plan, fourth study. 1771–72.

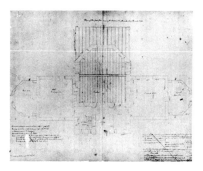

83. Monticello. Plan with porches and bays.

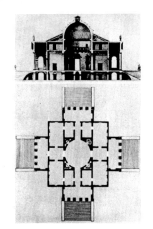

84. Vicenza, Italy. Villa Rotonda. *Ca.* 1560. Andrea Palladio. Plan and section.

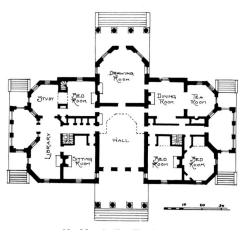

85. Monticello. Final plan.

popping out polygonal bays on the other *(Fig. 83)*. The fireplace masses remain grouped toward the center. Now Jefferson's plan prefigures that by Frank Lloyd Wright of the Ward Willitts House, of 1902 *(Fig. 224)*. Horizontal continuity has destroyed the English cube by crossing two extensible axes in space. But Jefferson cannot stop there either. He also desires a vertical axis, at least in massing, and a solidly monumental mass to fix the building sculpturally in place outside even more than in. This he finds in the dome and the drum, as well as in the pediment, of the Palladian-Burlingtonian tradition *(Figs. 84–87)*. Yet, unlike the Villa Rotunda, or even Chiswick, Jefferson's dome does not function inside; at Monticello there is only an attic room within it. No vertical volume of space contradicts the horizontal axes with a humanistic assertion of mankind's central position and vertical stance. Mon-

ticello's final plan, though heavily compromised, still retains its spatially horizontal organization; a strong axis leads into the body of the house from the hill slope and out again to the hill's flattened crest *(Figs. 85–87)*. The wings of the Palladian tradition are severed from that tradition's use of them as a humanistically embracing entrance element and are thrust underground to embrace, instead, the hill itself under its summit. We are reminded of Wright's first Taliesin, of 1911 *(Fig. 237)*. But where in the massing of Wright's houses everything was finally to give way before the horizontal extension of roof planes, in Monticello the mass is locked in a tense combat between vertical and horizontal: dome and wings fiercely striving, two stories made to look like one, huge classical details, like Harrison's, banding a tiny, struggling building and holding it together. Inside, too, the gadgetry which was to engage so much

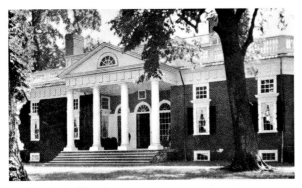

86. Monticello. East front.

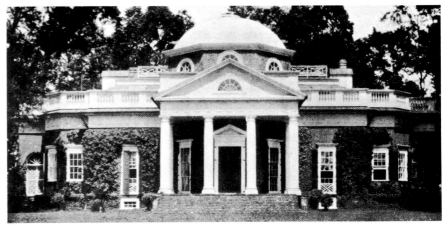

87. Monticello. West front.

American attention is obsessively in evidence, coupled with a dogged determination, prefiguring Louis Kahn's in the twentieth century, to shape and light each space separately in terms of its clearly articulated special function *(Figs. 88, 89)*. Probity and purism are still at work.

Monticello is not lacking in the fussiness of the cultivated amateur or in a kind of brittle American self-righteousness (inheritor of the ages, all the world to choose from, everywhere to go), but its abiding character is gentle and heroic. Its hill, *monticello*, is a perfect mound, like a king's tholos, swelling in profile and just small enough so that the compact house can cup its summit properly and the dome complete its shape *(Fig. 90)*. Higher hills swell like sea waves around it, and the Blue Ridge rises westward with the vast challenge of the frontier. In Monticello's hall, near the eight-day clock, hung an Indian painting on buffalo hide, and gifts from Lewis and Clark (as in Peter the Great's cabinet were trays of tribal objects in gold sent back from Siberian rivers). In the dining room, busts of Voltaire, Lafayette, and John Paul Jones were ranged. Hence, Monticello is in all ways a hero's place, where one human presence focuses the landscape's forms and is borne up by them. As such, Monticello is the exact complement to the Grand Canyon in terms of American pilgrimage, yet standing between it and urban, colonial Boston. It is the place where the decisive stance was taken on the continent, when all of European memory and civilization that a single brain could encompass were shaped to provide the foothold for the step to the western sea.

Jefferson had not meant to be revolutionary in Monticello, but its design shows how close the Palladianism of the middle of the century already was

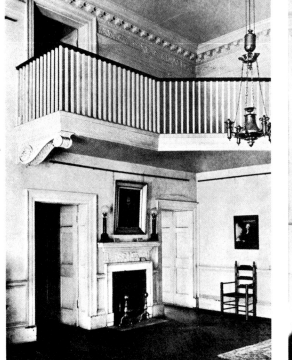

88. Monticello. Entrance hall.

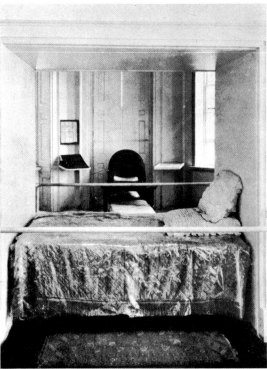

89. Monticello. Bedroom and study.

90. Monticello. Air view.

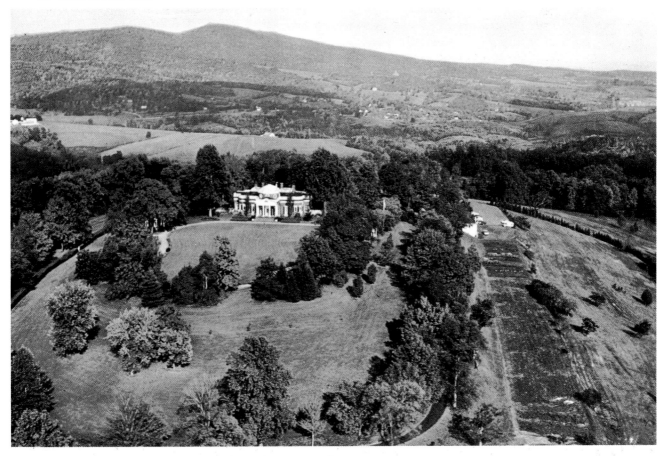

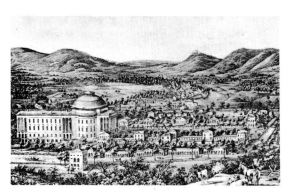

91. Charlottesville, Virginia. University of Virginia. 1817–26. Thomas Jefferson and Benjamin Latrobe. Engraving made in 1856.

to the revolutionary classicism of its close. Monticello shades over from one to the other. In the end, it is almost as abstractly romantic-classic as the work of Ledoux *(Fig. 77)*. But America was not France. Its revolution stopped short of a certain degree of violence, since the middle-class world that it wanted formed it already. Hence, baroque checks and balances shaped its constitution, so that when Jefferson was being consciously revolutionary and classicizing, as when he admired the revolutionary classicism of David or had an Augustan temple adapted for the first capitol of the state of Virginia *(Fig. 99)*, he was only developing further along the lines of intellectual rigor and visual order which had characterized the pre-Revolutionary colonies in general. So in that sense, the gray-granite or red-brick factories of New England's nineteenth century belong to the same righteous, hard-working family as the colonial house; they are taller and high-shouldered, but no less taut, with windows tight on the surface and a tense balance between their masonry piers and glass panes. Industrialized, they are New England still.

92. University of Virginia. Air view.

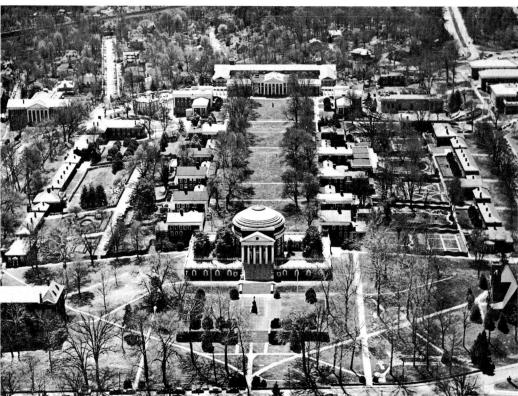

For these reasons, the University of Virginia, too, in which Jefferson was assisted by Benjamin Latrobe, grows easily out of his pre-Revolutionary work. Now, however, the project was wholly in accord with the widest scope of his talents, freed by revolution to shape a larger reality according to his ideals. These embraced the whole late-classical, almost Claudian landscape of nature and man, the one beneficent, the other articulate and wise. So the first component of the University of Virginia is the landscape, the hill among hills where the buildings are placed *(Figs. 91, 92)*. These human works frame the gentle hill slope, crown its summit, and balance, with their climactic Rotunda, the tapestry of hillside that rises southward across the narrow vale *(Fig. 93)*. The twentieth-century buildings which close off the south end of the complex are therefore wholly destructive of Jefferson's conception, which requires the Rotunda and the far hillside to be seen in relation to each other. From the Rotunda the lawn flows out like water over low mill dams, the last one steeper, a real rush which carries the eye across space to the hill beyond.

93. University of Virginia. View toward Rotunda, as rebuilt by McKim, Mead and White after the fire of 1898.

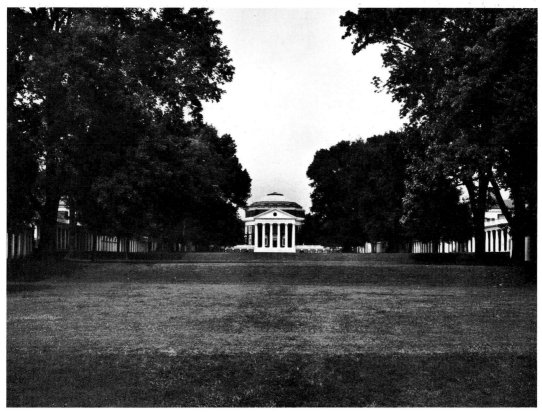

94. University of Virginia. View across Rotunda steps.

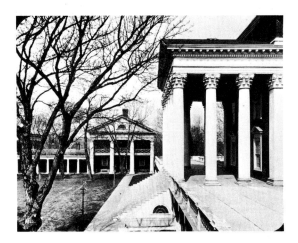

The hill and its view are framed by human individuals, organized into a disciplined company and stabilized by the subjects which bring them together. This union of men and ideas makes the human institution, the university, by definition a single embracing whole. The small columns, though a typical romantic-classic device, here especially evoke man-size, heightened; they are the students standing in the light; behind them, the small single doors lead to the restricted box of space which each inhabits. At intervals the pavilions stand; their columns are large, their capitals generous and varied *(Figs. 95– 97)*. They are the subjects of study, in truth the houses of the professors whose life they are. The students pass through them, line after line; coming into their shadow and out again. So the relationships between small columns and large, and the intersections at changes of level, are what they ought to be:

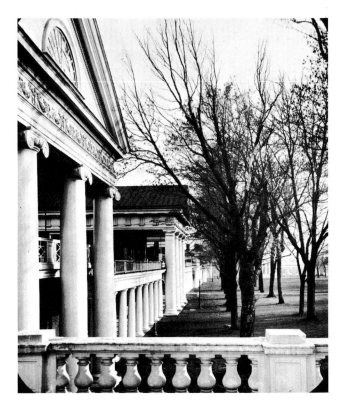

95. University of Virginia. View of pavilions.

intricate, complicated, anguished—highly studied, civil, and discrete. One is reminded again of Kahn's work of the early 1960's, as of all the dogged probity of American classical desires. But the University of Virginia is absolute in itself. Above its complex melody of columns, the Rotunda swells, expressive of interior volume, a container of books, the collective brain of the institution, keeper of the memory which sustains it. Men walk under it through its crypto-porticus, while the books are (were) lifted into the purely spherical geometry of its upper space. From this, the portico gives forth triumphantly, its stairs spilling down to the lawn (*Fig. 94*). Therefore, the form of the building as a whole, modeled upon that of the Pantheon, is consciously intended to bring memory into play and to confront nature across the way with what men bring to that tragic relationship anyway: the experience of the

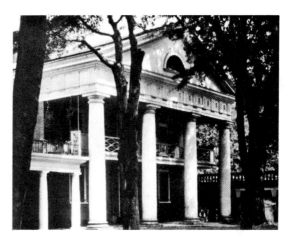

96. University of Virginia. Pavilion I.

97. University of Virginia. Pavilion IX.

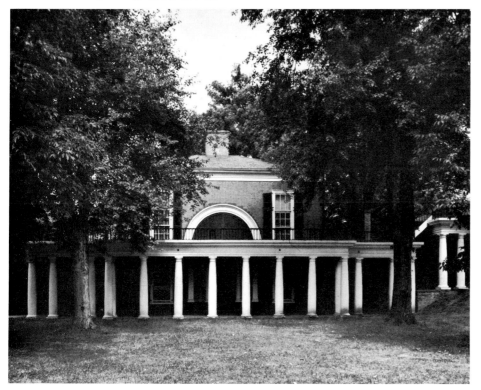

human ages, the quality of remembering through the arts which makes civilization, and which, at least at this complex level, is peculiar to the line of man.

Nowhere, at any scale, has a more intelligent image of classic wholeness been produced. The red brick and white columns of the colonial vocabulary are speaking good Greek and Latin here, while the hermetic romantic-classic geometry of Ledoux and Latrobe is calmed and broadened by this balance with the land. Pavilion IX, with its hemicycle behind a column screen *(Fig. 97)* especially recalls Ledoux. It became a favorite motif of romantic-classicism in Russia as well. There the instinct was, like Jefferson's, to stretch forms horizontally. (Already the image of a common Russo-American historical destiny, which was to create a new scale by spreading across continents, is physically apparent.) Jefferson slides the horizontal range of columns past the pavilion's restricted cube into the ranges as a whole. Thomas de Thomon, in his Stock Exchange for St. Petersburg, broadens out the entire body of his free-standing building *(Fig. 98)*.

Behind the lawns at Charlottesville, continuously

curving, single-brick walls flow out and downward to embrace the gardens and to make the transition from the columned hill to the service buildings and the farming countryside around *(Fig. 92)*. Never again was that structure of free nature, cultivated land, and human law and order to be so subtle and complete. The modern age was to destroy its proportion, scale, and frame of reference, and none of the other romantic-classic buildings of the early nineteenth century in America were really able to sustain it. Indeed, most of them are marked by classicism's limitations: by the struggle, for example, between a rigidly geometric exterior envelope and an interior space which came to demand more and more functional and visual variety. Jefferson's own State Capitol at Richmond, of 1785, closely adapted from the Maison Carrée at Nîmes, is the first of them all, either in Europe or in America, to use a pure temple form *(Fig. 99)*. Its rooms are arranged as reasonably as may be within its frontal, podiumed Roman shape. Windows burst forth gasping between its pilasters, but its skylit, domed central space is not expressed upon the exterior.

98. St. Petersburg (Leningrad), U.S.S.R. Stock Exchange. Design of 1803. Thomas de Thomon.

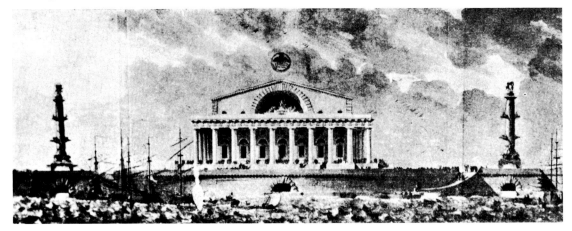

99. Richmond, Virginia. State Capitol. Model made in 1785 by
Thomas Jefferson and Charles Louis Clérisseau.

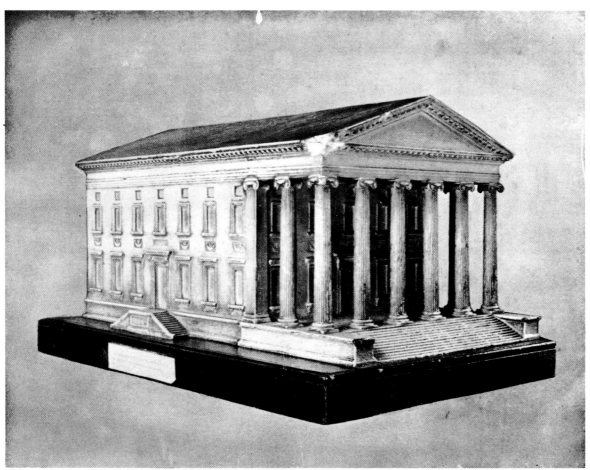

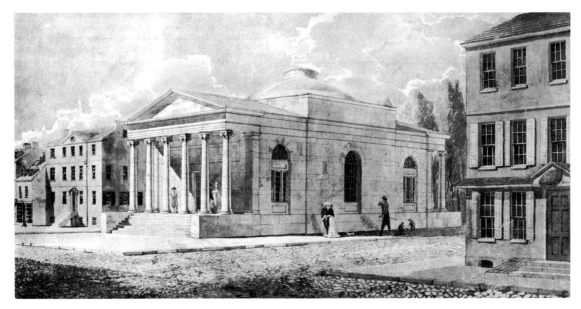

100. Philadelphia, Pennsylvania. Bank of Pennsylvania. 1799–1801. Benjamin Latrobe.

101. Baltimore, Maryland. Cathedral of the Assumption. 1804–18. Benjamin Latrobe.

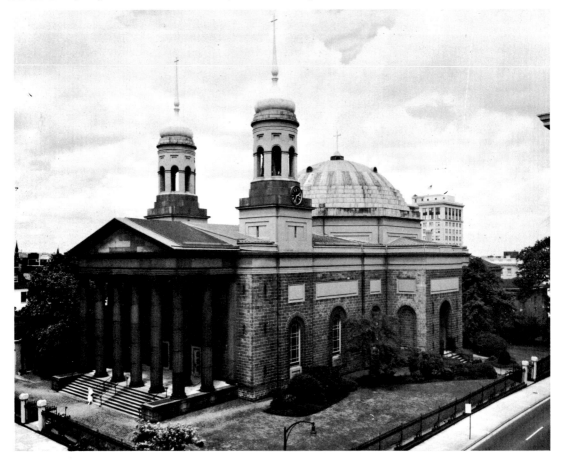

Latrobe was more rational and less obsessed. In his little Bank of Pennsylvania, of 1799–1801, with its good Greek order *(Fig. 100)*, and his grand cathedral in Baltimore, of 1804–18 *(Figs. 101, 102)*, he articulated entrance portico from rotunda volume and expressed both in the exterior massing. With its two towers, the cathedral recalls the Pantheon as it existed during the Baroque period, and its interior space, too, recalls not only the Pantheon itself but fine High Renaissance prototypes as well. Yet the clear separation of parts is very romantic-classic; here, as in his and Robert Mills's hallucinatory waterworks for Philadelphia *(Fig. 103)*, Latrobe manipulates a variety of geometric figures, as Ledoux had done. He does not squeeze all into a pure temple shape as Jefferson had already attempted and as the Americans, approaching their pervasive Greek phase, were soon everywhere to do.

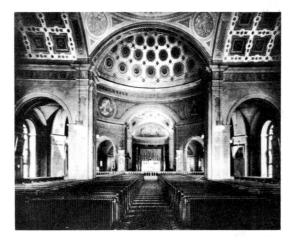

102. Cathedral of the Assumption. Interior.

103. Philadelphia, Pennsylvania. Schuylkill Waterworks, 1811–19. Benjamin Latrobe and Robert Mills. Engraving made in 1839.

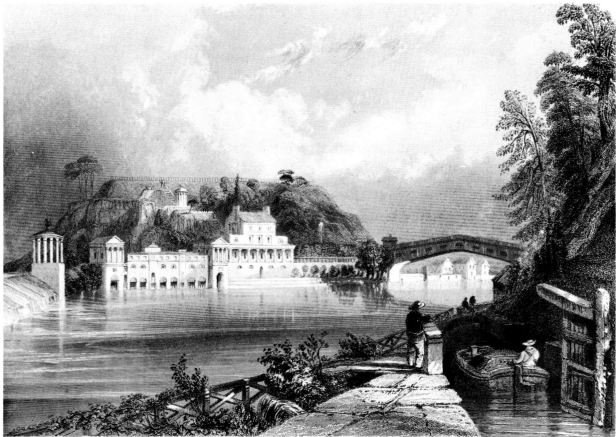

The main building at Girard College, by Thomas U. Walter, for example, was developed into a fully peripteral, if rather dry, Greek form *(Fig. 104)*. It somewhat resembles a Hellenistic Ionic temple but uses Corinthian capitals, as a Greek temple of its type would not have done, while Jefferson's building at Richmond, though based upon a Roman Corinthian prototype, had employed the Ionic mode. The interior spaces at Girard College are cut off more rigorously from the light than Jefferson had insisted upon. Encased in the walled and trabeated exterior, they hump wildly up into domes with oculi, like dolphins leaping to the air *(Fig. 105)*. It is Vignon and Huvé's system at the Madeleine. Its contrast between exterior and interior was clearly regarded as a positive virtue during this period, and it made some urban sense at the time. An old colonial street was instantly monumentalized and, one feels, "na-tionalized," by the columned exterior, while the domes supplied an ideal, top-lighted interior, a contrast and a surprise, wholly different from the space of everyday. The difficulty lay in the inability to develop in the temple form what Renaissance architecture had been so able to express: an articulate counterplay in the enclosing wall between the demands of interior and exterior space definition—the interior belonging to the building itself, the exterior defining the urban space of street, park, or square, and so belonging to the town as a whole. Thus the special American predilection for the purest possible temple form, so marked that romantic-classicism came commonly to be called "the Greek Revival" by American historians, may perhaps be regarded in the end as another demonstration of fundamental anti-urban tendencies on this continent *(Fig. 106)*. The Greek temple does not really want to get along

104. Philadelphia, Pennsylvania. Girard College. 1833–47. Thomas U. Walter.

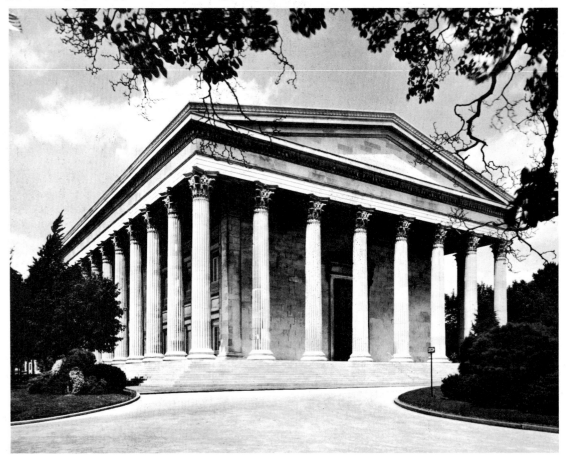

with other buildings in a street, but to stand free outside, preferably in a landscape, pure and unfettered. As revived, it demonstrates the puristic instinct to the utmost.

It was to have two more distinct revivals in America, that of the Beaux-Arts at the end of the nineteenth century and that of the late International Style of the 1950's. One striking difference lay in the fact that the romantic-classicism of the early nineteenth century, whatever forms from antiquity it employed, already tended to give them a machined quality, as in the Egyptian gates to the Grove Street Cemetery in New Haven *(Fig. 107)*, where the papyrus capitals are not soft and swelling, with rounded profiles, but hard, flat-planed, and edged like gears. They come to new life in this way. With some exceptions, the later Beaux-Arts forms tended to be softer or more archaeologically correct. The early period

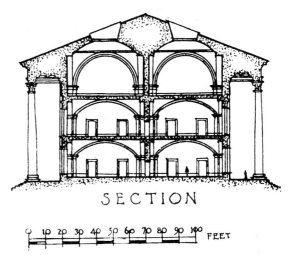

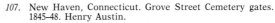

105. Girard College. Longitudinal section.

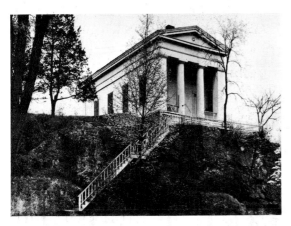

106. Woodbury, Connecticut. Masonic Temple. 1839.

107. New Haven, Connecticut. Grove Street Cemetery gates. 1845–48. Henry Austin.

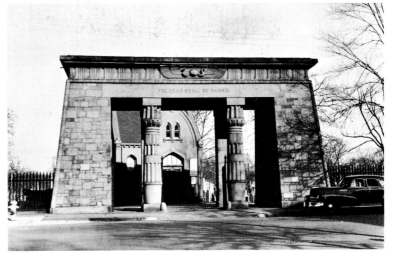

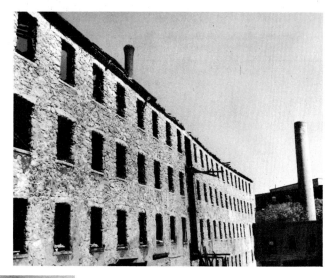

108. Fall River, Massachusetts. Falls Mill.

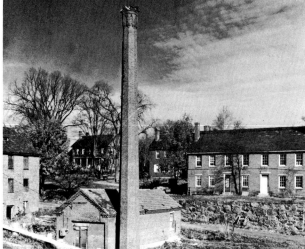

109. Harrisville, New Hampshire.
Mill town, 1818–50.

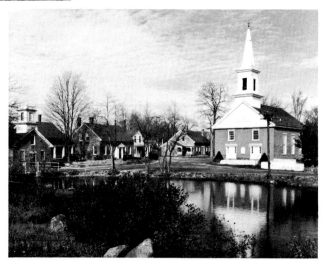

110. Harrisville, New Hampshire.

was also still part of a tradition which valued towns and was not yet caught up in the agonies of a mass world, so that its purism, inherited from its colonial past, could still function urbanistically, and could produce good housing, churches, and factories alike, and could group them in ways that made sense *(Figs. 108–10).* It also still understood or had faith in traditional hierarchies of function and of scale, in an urban landscape still idyllic *(Fig. 111),* and of good urban row houses to define streets with pre-cision *(Figs. 141–44).* The second period had lost its innocence but could still handle most of the urban elements, if somewhat less gently. The last period had lost the complex urban perceptions almost entirely, or had, at least, lost its respect for traditional urban methods and therefore, in large measure, its control over them.

The instinct toward cross-axial planning was still functioning during the early decades of the nineteenth century and sometimes found expression on

111. New Haven, Connecticut. Hillhouse House. 1835. Town and Davis. View from top of Hillhouse Avenue.

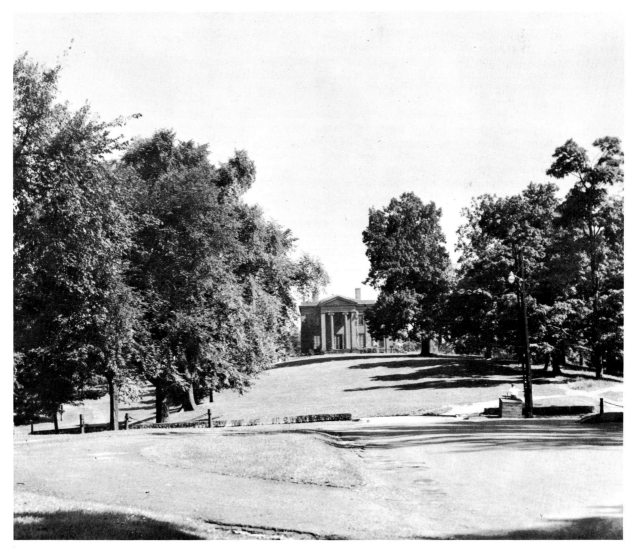

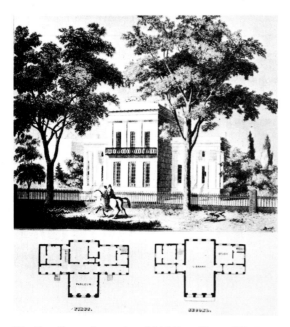

112. New Haven, Connecticut. Ithiel Town House. 1830. Town and Davis. Perspective drawing by A. J. Davis, and plan.

the exterior *(Fig. 112)*, so that the familial line from Jefferson to Wright remained alive; in combination with other factors, it eventually split the temple form. The Custom House in New York, of 1834–41, by Town and Davis, is an excellent example of the two modes, and of interior and exterior conflict as well *(Figs. 113, 114)*. In their competition design, Town and Davis had wanted to thrust their dome through the roof, so bursting the temple's envelope. Ammi B. Young immediately did so in Boston, and as that vertical axis broke loose it seemed to generate a horizontal cross-axis as well, so that a pedimented portico pushed out at the building's side—which then became its entrance front *(Figs. 115, 116)*. High above Nashville, Tennessee, William Strickland's capitol stretched on its hilltop, gullies cutting in

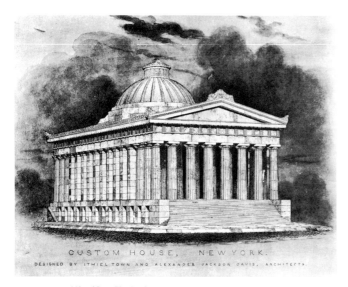

113. New York. Custom House (now Sub-Treasury). Original design. Town and Davis.

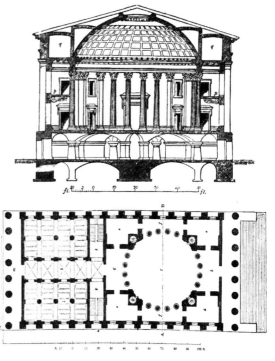

114. New York. Custom House. Plan and section, as built, 1834–41.

below it, roads running out to rolling horizons. The temple form became attenuated in its overextension; a tower, ostensibly the Choragic Monument of Lysicrates, but in effect a Gothic spire, leaped up from the long roof line to serve as a marker in the wide countryside *(Fig. 117)*. The scale of civilization and, indeed, of American frontier topography, was changing beyond the capacity of a temple form to control it. What happened to Young's Custom House in 1915 is a striking demonstration of that development, wherein the new industrialized, urban topography itself, no less than the demands of an exploding population, seemed to demand a similar explosion of scale if the old building were not to disappear entirely *(Fig. 116)*. Where those demands were least felt or most resisted, the old classic ideal

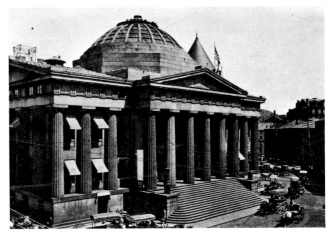

115. Boston, Massachusetts. Custom House. 1837–47. Ammi B. Young.

116. Boston, Massachusetts. Custom House, with addition of 1915.

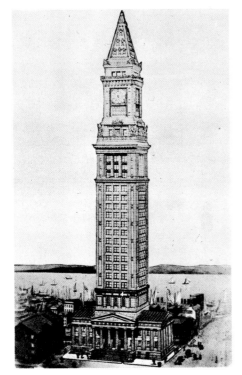

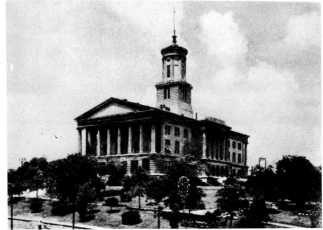

117. Nashville, Tennessee. State Capitol. 1845–54. William Strickland.

69

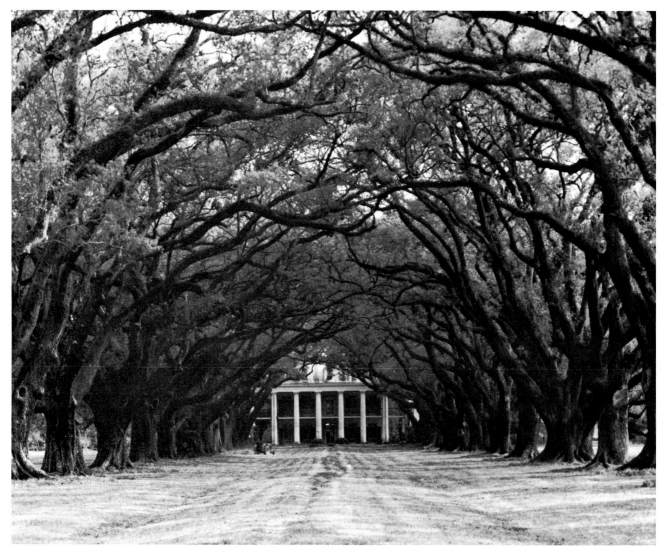

118. Vacherie, Louisiana. Oak Alley. *Ca.* 1830.

could be longest retained in its romanticized form. The late Greek Revival plantation houses of the deep South best embodied that condition and intention *(Fig. 118)*. Their softly gleaming column screens furnished the symbolic image around which Southern apologetics of the immediately pre-Civil War period and Southern mythology of the interminably postwar period were both to be fashioned. The more in ruin, the more Greek they seemed. Even so, before the war, they were already easing into the more complex articulations of international, mid-century design *(Figs. 119, 120)*.

120. Belmont. Stair hall.

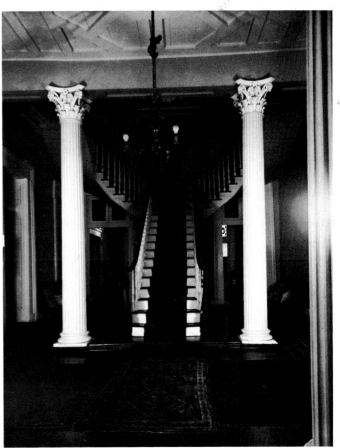

119. Nashville, Tennessee. Belmont. 1850. William Strickland.

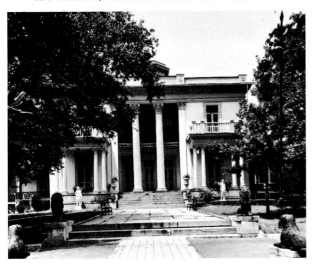

By way of contrast, the active sequence of nineteenth-century change and expansion can be seen in the development of the Capitol at Washington, from the winning design by William Thornton, of 1800, through the alterations and additions of Latrobe and Bulfinch, to the tall cast-iron dome of Thomas U. Walter, which was in building throughout the Civil War. The Capitol, too, had originally been partly modeled on Somerset House. Latrobe stiffened it into sharper, more cubistic romantic-classic forms *(Fig. 121)*. The vaulted series of interior spaces were also Latrobe's *(Figs. 122, 123)*; they ultimately derived from the fantasies of Piranesi and related well enough to the finest contemporary examples, such as those of Sir John Soane in the Bank of England. Bulfinch heightened the dome *(Fig. 124)*. The reason for this was inherent in Pierre Charles L'Enfant's plan for the city as a whole *(Fig. 125)*. It was a baroque plan, like Wren's for London and Le Nôtre's for Versailles. Long axial avenues led out

from the centers of power. The Capitol and the White House were the two major foci. The Capitol had the more commanding position on the height. The avenues were flung out from it like gestures of command. Hence, they needed a dominant vertical focus. It is appropriate that Walter's dome *(Figs. 126, 131)*, which finally supplied that element at proper scale, had most logically to be built in the new industrial material and was only a classicizing iron skin over a skeleton of openwork metal joists. Walter's beautiful section strikingly documents its technological and demographic revolution *(Fig. 126)*. At the same time, the Capitol was extended laterally by House and Senate office buildings. Two tenacious American instincts are thus juxtaposed in it: that toward central authority and union in the commanding dome, matched in iron only by the dome of St. Isaac's in St. Petersburg, and that toward horizontal expansion and dispersion in the proliferating wings. The Capitol is Monticello all over again, in mass

121. Washington, D.C. Capitol Building. Design of 1811. Benjamin Latrobe. After the original design by William Thornton.

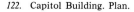

122. Capitol Building. Plan.

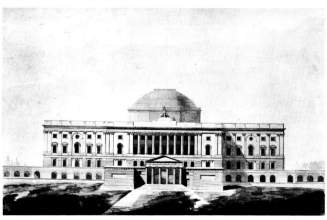

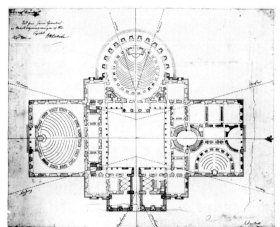

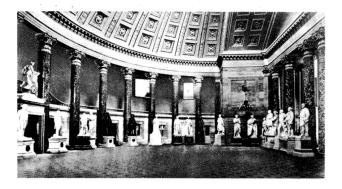

123. Capitol Building. Statuary Hall.

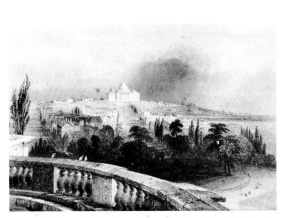

124. Capitol Building. Engraving showing dome by Charles Bulfinch, as seen from the White House in 1840.

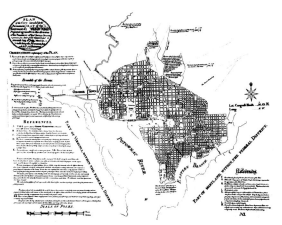

125. Washington, D.C. Pierre Charles L'Enfant's plan of 1791.

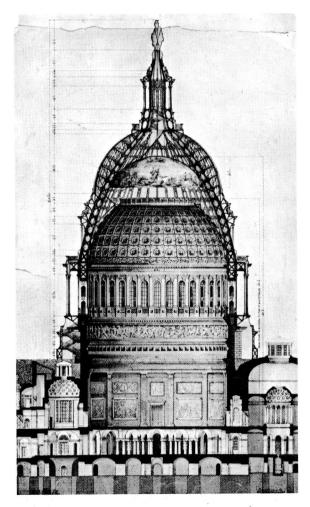

126. Capitol Building. Cast-iron dome. 1855–64. Thomas U. Walter.

73

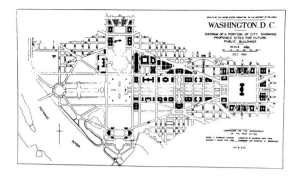

127. Washington, D.C. The Mall. Plan of 1901.

128. Washington, D.C. Perspective showing dome, with Washington Monument, Monument Gardens, and Mall, according to the plan of 1901.

129. Washington, D.C. Air view according to the plan of 1901. Left, Second Lincoln Memorial; 1914–20; Henry Bacon. Center, Washington Monument; 1848–84; Mills and Casey. Upper right, Capitol Building.

terms. It was severely mutilated in the 1950's and 1960's by the most spectacularly unqualified of a long line of incompetent Capitol architects.

The grandiose frame of L'Enfant's plan filled out over the century. The main axis of Mall from Capitol to Potomac was slowly cleared and furnished with two appropriate monuments *(Figs. 127–29)*. The 1880's miraculously produced the ideal puristic symbol in Washington's obelisk. A new wave of classicism came along in time to house Lincoln's gigantic presence in a simplified temple shape right out of Ledoux and much like the most popular Russian romantic-classic forms *(Fig. 130)*. It can be no accident that such a renewal of activity in the development of the Mall took place during America's period of imperial adventure in the late nineteenth and early twentieth centuries *(Fig. 131)*. Her next age of

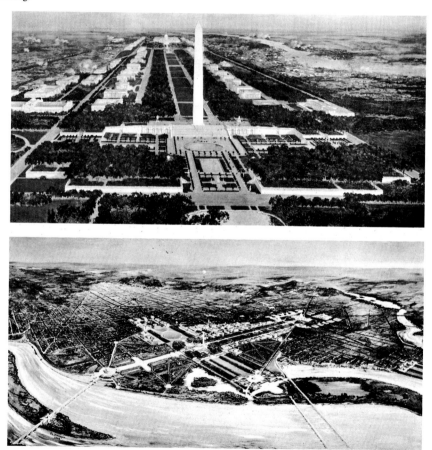

affluence, that of the early 1960's, itself not lacking in imperial assumptions, produced a scheme for the monumentalization of Pennsylvania Avenue and for the creation of new, paved squares which were based upon the garbled experiences of American architects as tourists abroad. L'Enfant's plan is strong enough to support such romanticisms *(Fig. 125)*. Its radial avenues overlay a grid, upon which Jefferson is supposed to have insisted and which recalls a plan much like Philadelphia's, proposed for Washington and supported by Jefferson himself. The grid held Washington steady under the whirl of the rotary intersections; only in the redevelopment of the northwest during the 1950's and 1960's has it been eliminated—along with most of the poor who once inhabited its streets—in favor of rather shapeless superblocks of luxury apartments and town houses.

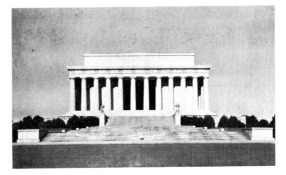

130. Washington, D.C. Lincoln Memorial.

131. Washington, D.C. Air view.

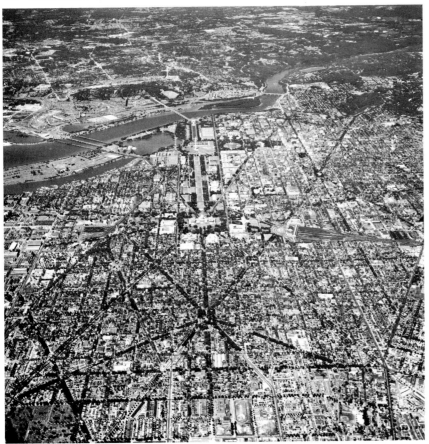

75

The ghastly effects of redevelopment programs carried out during the middle of the twentieth century according to principles which despised the street—the same in this whether they were those of Le Corbusier's Ville Radieuse or the Garden City—have necessarily brought about a re-evaluation of the old grid and the streets it shaped. Most American towns were made by it. Only a very few, such as Detroit *(Fig. 132)*, made use of the radial scheme or of a few radial avenues over the gridiron. New Orleans' fine old oblong of French Quarter, now hideously threatened by an expressway, was enlarged according to a scheme which extended blocks of grids on radial beams *(Fig. 133)*. Certainly the grid could be overdone and was normally employed as the grossest topographical device to facilitate speculation in land. New York's plan is a case in point. The old town spread loosely up Broadway from the Battery and east along Wall Street. By 1811, it still occupied only the tip of Manhattan. The Commissioners' plan of that date laid out the rest of the island in an implacable gridiron, leaving only a small area open as a park *(Fig. 134)*. The grid so applied might be slapped down anywhere, and usually all too little public space was left free in the process. The later American tendency toward private luxury and public squalor was already well in evidence here. The abstract shape, made up of units reproducible in

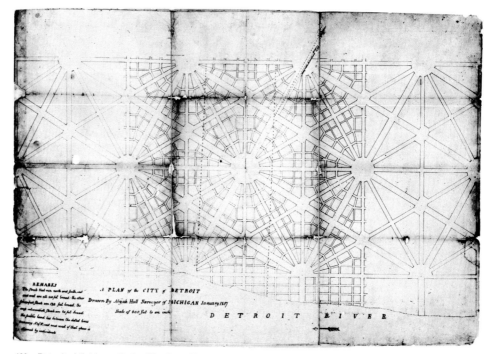

132. Detroit, Michigan. Judge Woodward's plan of 1807.

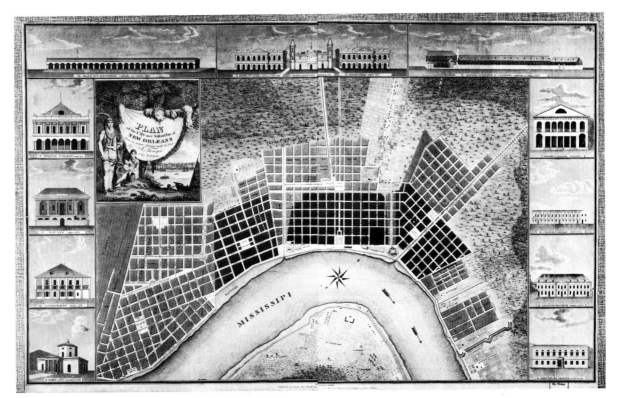

133. New Orleans, Louisiana. Plan of 1815.

134. New York. Commissioners' Map of 1811.

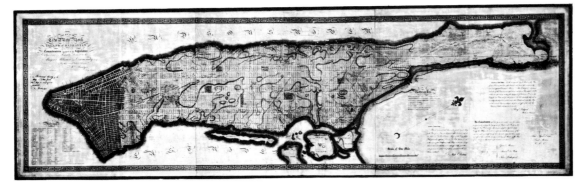

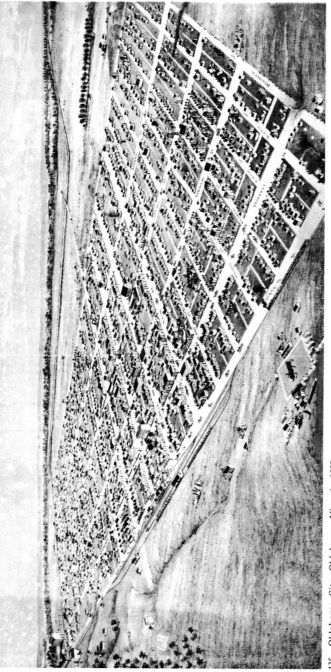

series, spread across the entire country, ideal on the prairie. A nineteenth-century view of Oklahoma City, Oklahoma, is famous in this regard *(Fig. 135)*. Even the map of the States turns into stricter rectangles *(Fig. 136)* as it crosses the Mississippi, and the one perfect right angle where four states meet falls right by the Mesa Verde. Yet it is a mistake often made to assume that the vastly extended grid was wholly without meaning or expressive architectural character. The interplay between natural shapes and human desires itself has force. The meeting of Colorado, New Mexico, Utah, and Arizona shows us high desert bounding away to crazily shaped moun-

135. Oklahoma City, Oklahoma. View in 1890.

78

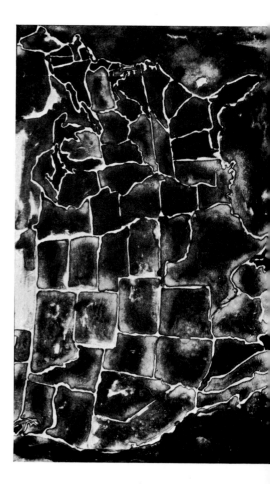

tains on all the quarters of the compass. The "Sleeping Ute" stretches out, and Ship Rock sails through the livid sand. It is a fine surrealist landscape, in which Renaissance energy, which discovered the continent, here lays claim, through the grid, to its archaic vastness. Or, seen in plan, Salt Lake City's rigid rectangles might seem only an unwarranted intrusion on the place. Nothing could be more false. The whole gridiron rides up the long slope to the capitol, which culminates the major axis in elevation as in plan; below it, a second great axis crosses to the immigrants' pass in the Rockies on one side and to the fertile valley on the other *(Fig. 137)*. So out in

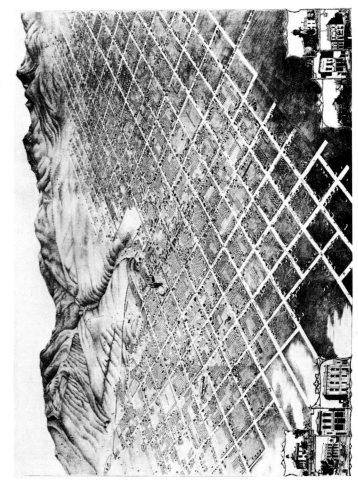

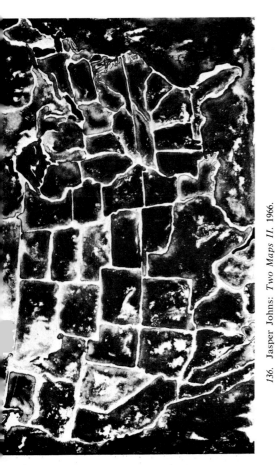

136. Jasper Johns: *Two Maps II.* 1966.

137. Salt Lake City, Utah. View in 1870.

little towns from the Dakotas to Oklahoma and the Panhandle of Texas, the crossing of two streets makes a place in the emptiness, the courthouse perhaps rising as the culmination of one of them, which may run endlessly into open desert on the reverse bearing. Along those Western streets the false fronts of the wooden buildings masked their gable ends to provide a true street façade, reaching for urban scale, for a shape in the vastness *(Figs. 138–40)*. The architectural instinct of their anonymous builders

was a good and right one, as it was when they provided their streets with resonant boardwalks shaded over by the porches of buildings, supported on wooden posts. It was the American stoa, where, in popular mythology, the boys shot it out, and which, in fact, functioned as the stoa had done in antiquity, as the place of urban meeting of man with man.

Yet the Western image of the street should be seen only as a reflection and adaptation of that of the more urbanized nineteenth-century East. There

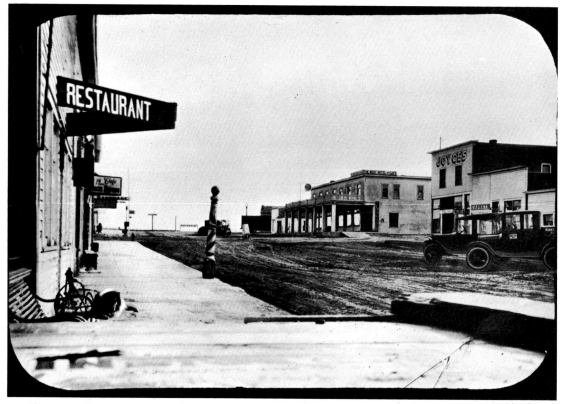

138. Faith, South Dakota. *Ca.* 1915.

80

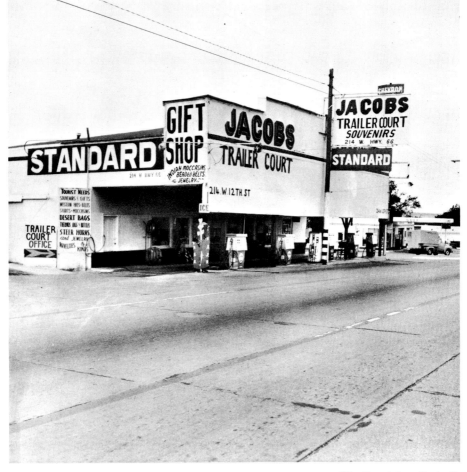

139. Gas station, Route 66.

140. Utopia, Texas. False fronts.

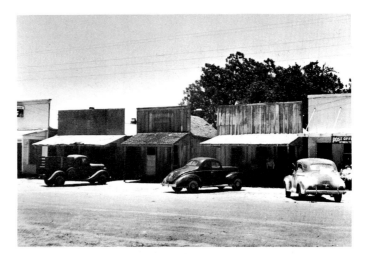

81

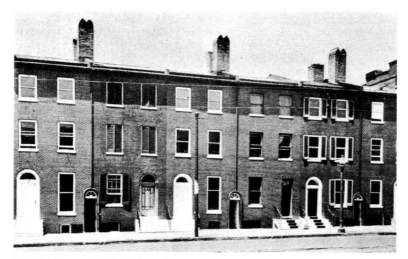

141. Baltimore, Maryland. Row houses. South Broadway. *Ca.* 1840.

142. Baltimore, Maryland. Row houses. Waverly Terrace. *Ca.* 1850.

143. Baltimore, Maryland. Row houses. Mt. Vernon Place. *Ca.* 1850.

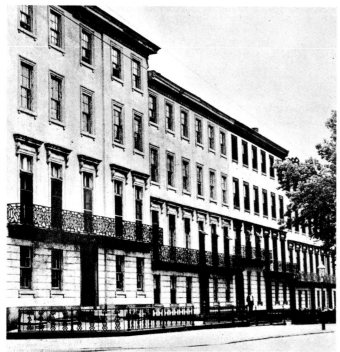

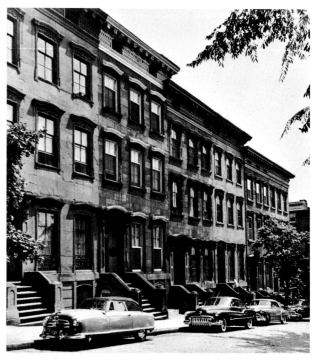

the row house was the main tool for the definition of the space of the street. Row houses had been very rare in eighteenth-century America. Philadelphia had a few, apparently to Jefferson's agrarian horror. By the early decades of the nineteenth century, they shaped many square miles of central Philadelphia, there with a peculiarly intimate and loving scale. The beautiful streets of Baltimore, with their stone steps and fine doorways, also show some of the best examples *(Figs. 141–43)*. The proportions are decisive; the buildings are high enough to give the street a shape, the doors and windows showing the scale of human use, the red brick of the defining walls varying in tone and therefore seeming to flow in and out down the street, the window cornices marking a beat, syncopating the rhythm, the major cornices giving the whole street-shape a volumetric definition. On Beacon Street in Boston, the cylindrical bays of the Sears House billow out into the hollow of the street with Regency buoyancy. Such variations in the row house might produce striking points of life.

So could the introduction of larger movements, along with small variations in the street's line. The area around St. Philip's in Charleston, of 1839 *(Fig. 144)*, showed all the elements: row houses, the projection of a columned portico into and over the public space, the vertical marker of the spire—in what beautiful scale with the width and length of the street. The importance of the sidewalk should be noted. It was one of the nineteenth century's triumphs, and it always manipulated the scale of the town in favor of the individual. It personalizes the street, gives release from traffic flow and a place for loitering, provides a hierarchy of spaces and a multiplicity of uses in what would otherwise be a passage. Indeed, once vehicles dominate, individuals on foot are banished from, literally have no place upon, those suburban streets where sidewalks are omitted. Police cars investigate them all.

Main Street in Nantucket did not use row houses, but the fine, flat-fronted or columned mansions of the Starbucks and other shipowners and whaling

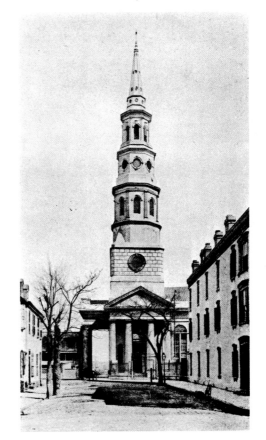

144. Charleston, South Carolina. St. Philip's. 1839.

captains stood close to each other and to the cobbled pavement *(Fig. 145)*. Dappled in sunlight, these blocks seem hardly to belong to the United States but to an island jewel, like Calypso's in the heart of the ocean. Here the captains slept uneasily, heads starting up with the grate of iron on cobbles, accustomed as they were, so Melville tells us, to pillow on the lucid rush of porpoises and whales. Down to the harbor, since suburbanized by Beinecke, their main street flowed. Its cobbled surface is now an excellent demonstration of a properly urban method for slowing up automobiles in essential areas *(Fig. 146)*.

Only a few row houses in America were organized into single monumental unities on the street, like some of those of London. Columned Lafayette Terrace in New York, by Town and Davis, was one *(Fig. 147)*, but New York's galloping avenues and taut side streets came to be defined by row houses which were livelier and more varied. Their scale, as in Baltimore, for example, can be observed growing throughout the Greek Revival period, the buildings becoming higher until they attained their fully canonical basement, three stories, and attic floor. The street became a stronger, if darker, shape by virtue of that development. Finally, as the true urban culmination of the century, the somber brownstones appeared, stately and marvelous, looming above the iron-speared sidewalks, bold and warm in their presences, varied in their forms *(Fig. 148)*. They were the strongest definers of domestic streets ever produced in America. Some of their like can be found in other towns *(Figs. 141–43)*, but they were the very blood and fiber of New York; wherever they appeared, they brought with them something of its special physical arrogance and its pride.

That quality came about in part from New York's density, arising from the confinement of the heart of the city to an island. Its vertical expansion was only a matter of time; even the streets soon seemed to require multilevel treatment *(Fig. 149)*. Such eventually produced not only the elevated railway and the subway but also vast dreams of soaring towers and bridges in the sky, which were to affect the European no less than the American image of Metropolis in the early twentieth century.

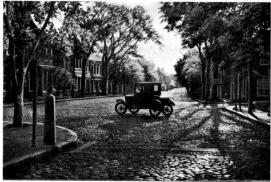

146. Nantucket, Massachusetts. Main street in the 1920's.

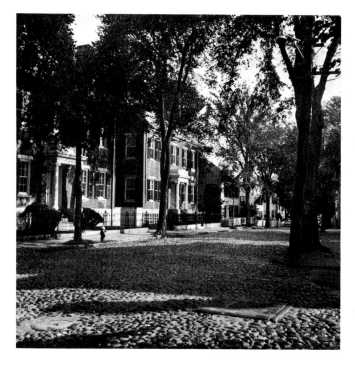

145. Nantucket, Massachusetts. Main street, with Starbuck houses. 1837.

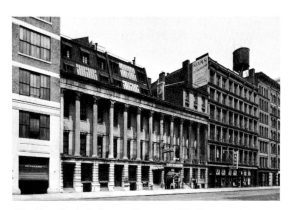

147. New York. Lafayette Terrace. 1836. Town and Davis.

148. New York. West 103rd Street. Brownstones. Photograph, 1964.

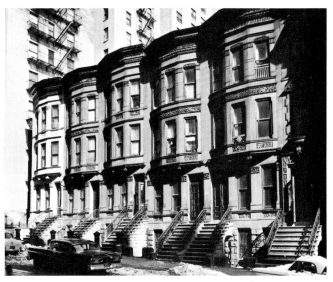

149. New York. "Proposed Arcade Railway Under Broadway." 1870.

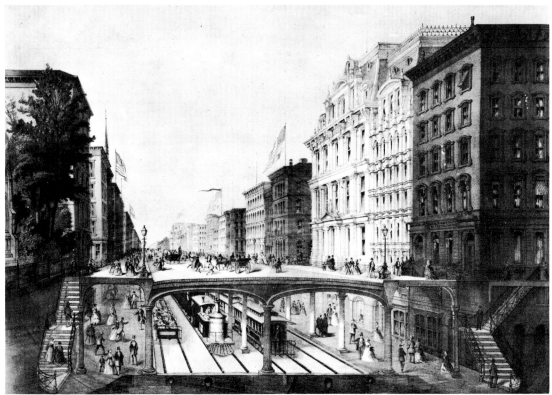

Yet there can be no doubt that the grid, uninflected and endlessly repeated, could be too much of a good thing. The Commissioners' New York would surely have been a dreary monster among cities. Central Park saved it. The park was one of the finest products of that picturesque mode of garden design which had been developed in eighteenth-century England *(Fig. 150)*. Its winding paths and tree-clumps shaped what the continent had come to know as the *jardin anglais*. Its picturesque variety and asymmetrical building types had their prototypes in the arcadian classicism of Claude, which was itself adapted to the American continent by the painters of the Hudson River School *(Fig. 151)*. Their shapes tended, not surprisingly, to resemble those of the picturesque garden itself. The studied asymmetries of its roads and buildings formed a kind of contemporary romantic-naturalist comple-

150. New York. Central Park. Frederick Law Olmsted and Calvert Vaux. View in 1863.

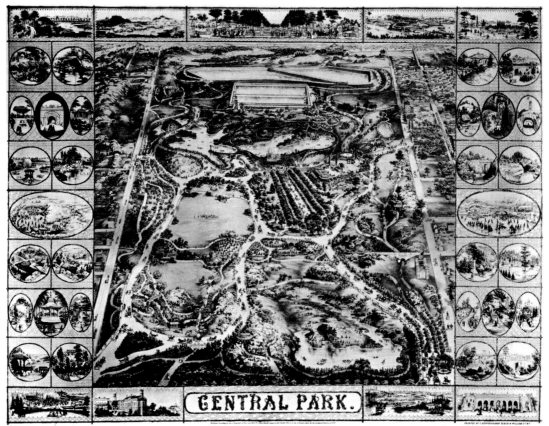

CENTRAL PARK.

ment to the strictly symmetrical and bare geometry of the late eighteenth-century's romantic-classic mode. It was the other side of the emotional coin, and the two represented the separation and intensification of shapes which during the Baroque period had formed a systematized whole. The picturesque garden and its architecture were popularized in America by Andrew Jackson Downing. They seemed to him to offer a necessary antidote to the inflexible urbanity of the Greek Revival. His books, *Treatise on the Theory and Practice of Landscape Gardening Adapted to North America*, of 1841, *Cottage Residences*, of 1842, and *The Architecture of Country Houses*, of 1850, were enormously successful; they initiated a general development in wooden domestic architecture, disseminated through pattern books, which I have elsewhere called the "Stick Style." Downing's principles of picturesque plot planning

151. Asher B. Durand: *Kindred Spirits.* 1849.

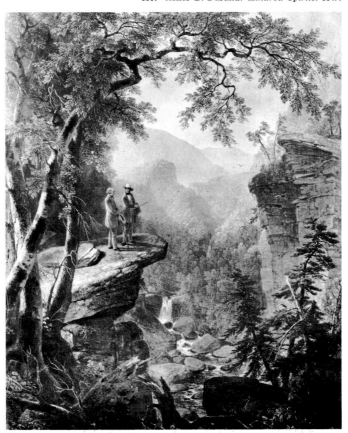

were adopted by Frederick Law Olmsted, who developed them to the generous scale of parks and suburbs, as in his plan for Riverside, Illinois *(Fig. 152)*. Central Park derives from Downing's and Olmsted's conceptions, with winding roads, underpasses, and a sustained illusion of natural variety in the heart of the city. Such principles were later to dominate the conceptions of Garden City planners and even of Le Corbusier, where they created the *jardin anglais* platform for his skyscraper towers. Combined with the colonial grid and the baroque radial avenues, the winding roads and irregular shapes of the picturesque mode completed the urban configurations which the modern formal imagination has so far been able to grasp. One supposes that the turning radius of the automobile has become the only other factor of form-making obsessive enough to override them. Usually in combination, they have between them shaped most nineteenth- and twentieth-century city plans.

Picturesque buildings were meant to unfold to the viewer over time, as he approached them along the contrived curves of their site plans or, inside, wandered from room to room according to an asymmetrical pattern which created the affect of freedom and discovery. Any kind of prototype might be employed in the making of such forms: Italian villas, Gothic cottages, and so on. Most of their shapes, too, can be found in the paintings of Claude. They might be "Tuscan" or "Italian Villa," as in Richard Upjohn's King House *(Figs. 153, 154)* or "Moorish" for Frederic Church in his grandly sited Olana above the Hudson *(Figs. 155, 156)*, but in essence they are all of the same style: that of free fancy dramatized, at once optical and allusive, hence doubly picturesque. The permissive choices of the middle-class suburban situation permitted and encouraged that "picturesque eclecticism." Indeed, it was the only kind of architecture that could have made sense in its period; the twentieth century,

152. Riverside, Illinois. Plan of 1869. Frederick Law Olmsted and Calvert Vaux.

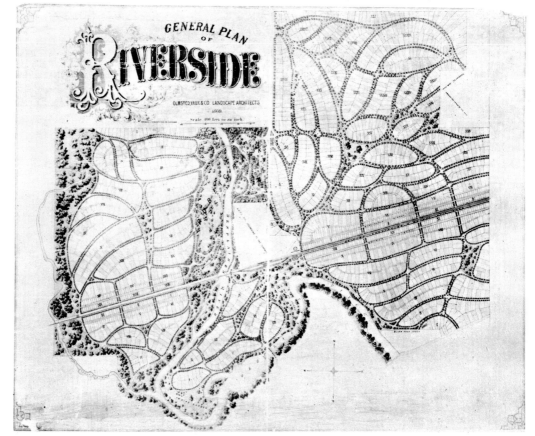

glass houses or no, is in no position to throw stones at it, and it is by no means dead. Yet its introduction into the city in both plan and buildings tended to break up the city's old intrinsic controls and to work toward the fragmentation of its fabric and the suburbanization of its forms. That, too, served deeply seated American attitudes, strong in Jefferson: a distrust of urban civilization, a tendency to equate physical dispersion with political freedom (which might be the most dangerous fallacy of all, as the political development of southern California can show). It is therefore no wonder that some of the liveliest adaptations of nineteenth-century American architecture took place in single-family suburban houses, and especially in those built of wood. That material was commonest throughout most of the United States. By the 1830's, it was undergoing a technological revolution: sawmills could most handily mass-produce thin, easily transported structural studs and joists rather than the massive tim-

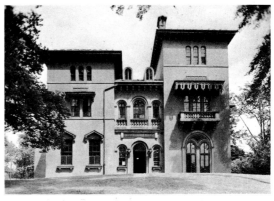

153. Newport, Rhode Island. Edward King House (now a home for the aged). 1845–47. Richard Upjohn.

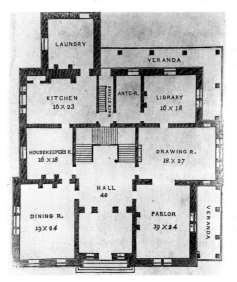

154. King House. Plan.

155. Hudson, New York. Olana (Frederic Church House). Calvert Vaux. 1870–72, 1888–89.

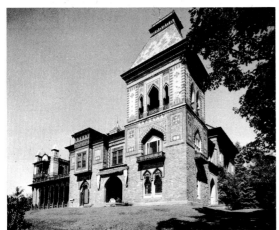

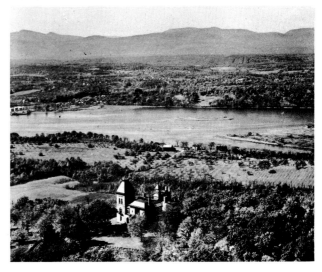

156. Olana in its landscape.

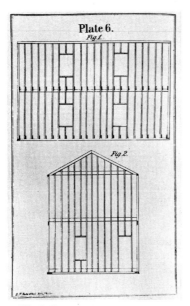

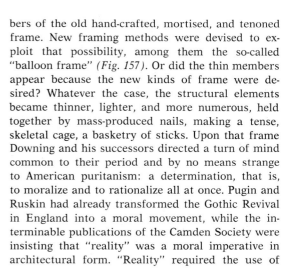

157. Balloon frame.

bers of the old hand-crafted, mortised, and tenoned frame. New framing methods were devised to exploit that possibility, among them the so-called "balloon frame" *(Fig. 157)*. Or did the thin members appear because the new kinds of frame were desired? Whatever the case, the structural elements became thinner, lighter, and more numerous, held together by mass-produced nails, making a tense, skeletal cage, a basketry of sticks. Upon that frame Downing and his successors directed a turn of mind common to their period and by no means strange to American puritanism: a determination, that is, to moralize and to rationalize all at once. Pugin and Ruskin had already transformed the Gothic Revival in England into a moral movement, while the interminable publications of the Camden Society were insisting that "reality" was a moral imperative in architectural form. "Reality" required the use of

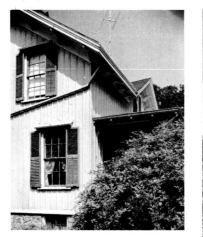

158. Newport, Rhode Island. Board-and-batten house. *Ca.* 1845.

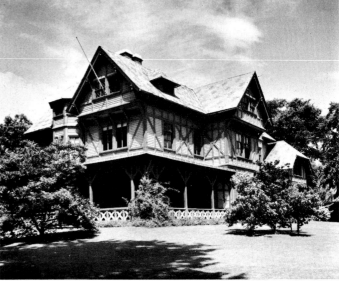

159. Newport, Rhode Island. J. N. A. Griswold House. 1862. Richard Morris Hunt.

common materials unadorned. That union of ethics and materialism remained the single most popular architectural slogan well into the second half of the twentieth century. Yet, for all its intellectual confusion and later bowdlerization, the demand for "reality," coupled with a lively visual imagination, was able to produce forms of considerable "masculinity," and that, too, became a favorite mid-century term of praise. For Downing and his followers it was the skeleton of the wooden frame whose expression "reality" demanded. Hence, the American house visually shed its sheathing skin and clad itself in vertical boards and battens to express its vertical studs, and pushed out the light frames of porches as picturesque viewing platforms and as pretexts for the visual exploitation of all the members of the frame *(Fig. 158)*. The Stick Style was to be found to some extent all over the world, from Istanbul to Buenos Aires, but its importance, again largely because of its comparatively large volume in contrast to pre-existing work, was apparently greater in the United States. Its forms developed during the period 1840–70 from simpler to more complex. They intersected French Gothic Revival rationalism, like that of Viollet-le-Duc, in the early work of such an architect as Richard Morris Hunt, who was the first American to study at the Ecole des Beaux-Arts in Paris. His Griswold House in Newport emphasized those diagonal bracing members, a kind of rationalized half-timbering, of which Viollet-le-Duc was so fond *(Fig. 159)*. A building like the Sturtevant House of 1872 represents the apogee of the movement: a highly articulated plan, deep porches, high, jagged, movemented silhouette, full of "masculine" activity, the surface exploded into a basketry of sticks *(Figs. 160, 161)*.

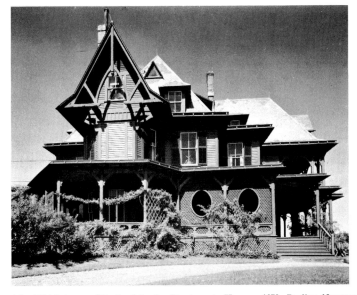

160. Middletown, Rhode Island. Sturtevant House. 1872. Dudley Newton.

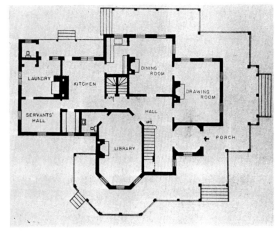

161. Sturtevant House. Plan.

91

Love of the frame was to be found in other materials as well, especially in those mass-produced by the new industrial processes. Cast iron could also form a skeleton, and as such it knew its greatest days in the middle of the century, before its lamentable tendency to melt in fires became too well known *(Fig. 162)*. The solution to its fireproofing was to create Chicago skyscraper construction in the 1880's. But, during the middle of the century, a feeling for skeletonized design permeated even buildings in more traditional and massive materials. The tendency was to break up and articulate all masses into active, compartmentalized components. The Smithsonian Institution is an early and good example *(Fig. 163)*, while the old Boston City Hall *(Fig. 164)* shows how a kind of classic reaction in the middle of the century, based upon French Second Empire prototypes, might squeeze the masses back into a symmetrical envelope but could even increase the skeletonized compartmentation of the

surface. In such larger buildings, of whatever eclectic mode, the general development of form was exactly the same as in the Stick Style; it reached a climax of active, even jagged, articulation by the early 1870's. Memorial Hall at Harvard *(Fig. 165)* should be contrasted with the Smithsonian, and Philadelphia's City Hall *(Fig. 166)* with Boston's, while both should be compared with the contemporary Sturtevant House and Olana *(Figs. 155, 160)*. Here, consequently, was clearly a mid-century style with early and late phases, overriding eclectic considerations or structural differences. It was highly varied in a complex of rather broken up interior spaces, and in massing it became sharp, energetic, and tough, a not unworthy expression and enhancement of the hard, pluralistic, and expanding urban environment of the period after the Civil War.

Of this phase, the finest architect was Frank Furness of Philadelphia. In his own way, Furness was the first great architect in America after Jefferson

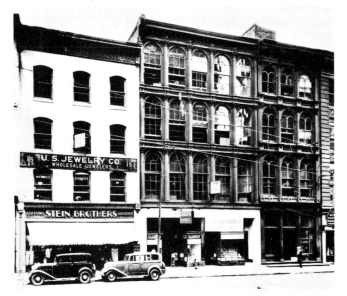

162. Baltimore, Maryland. Cast-iron building, 11 E. Liberty Street. *Ca.* 1855–60. James Bogardus.

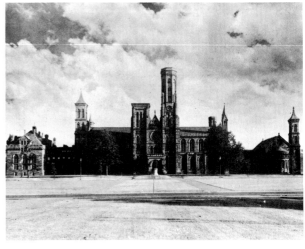

163. Washington, D.C. Smithsonian Institution. 1846. James Renwick.

164. Boston, Massachusetts. City Hall. 1862. Bryant and Gilman.

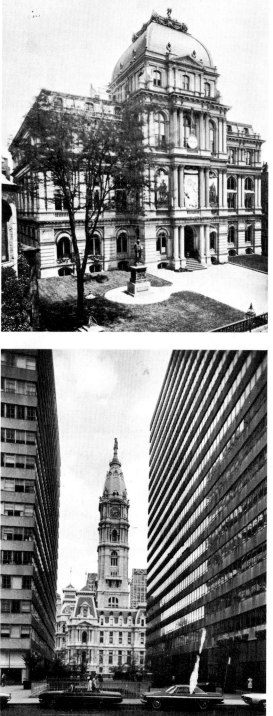

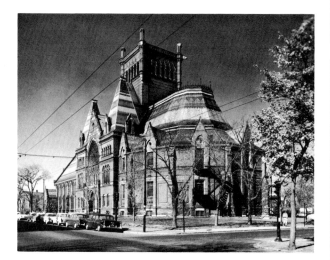

165. Cambridge, Massachusetts. Harvard University. Memorial Hall. 1871–78. Ware and Van Brunt.

166. Philadelphia, Pennsylvania. City Hall. 1874–80. John MacArthur. View through Penn Center.

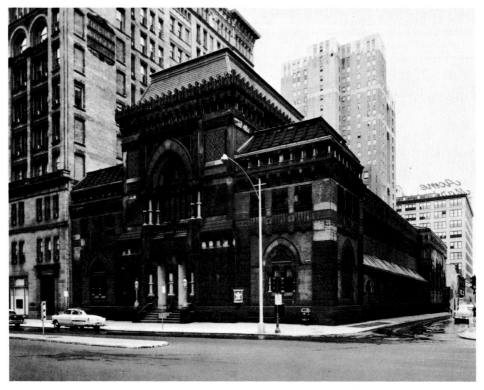

167. Philadelphia, Pennsylvania. Pennsylvania Academy of the Fine Arts. 1871–76. Frank Furness.

168. Pennsylvania Academy of the Fine Arts. Stair hall.

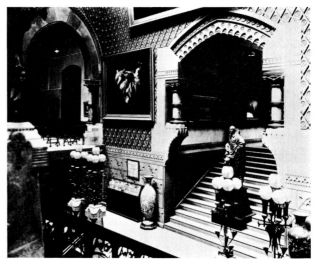

and certainly the most original American up to his time. Yet Furness, too, had his own kind of dependence upon European precedents, and in his case, as in that of his master, Hunt, the precedent was French. His Gothicism derived mainly from Viollet-le Duc, rather than from ecclesiological English Goths like William Butterfield, William Burges, or E. B. Lamb, as the strident polychrome of his Pennsylvania Academy of the Fine Arts might otherwise have led one to suppose *(Fig. 167)*. Its flat-arched portal, pushed up and divided by a taut, metallic column, is Viollet-le-Duc's, and Neil Levine has demonstrated how the symmetrical wall-paneling in flattened pilasters and screens was what the French called *neo-grec*, and was ultimately derived in their minds from the articulated column-and-wall system of the Temple of Zeus at Akragas. The intensity of the combinations is peculiar to Furness, as is the Academy's massing: a frontispiece of compacted Second Empire pavilions, behind which the galleries stretch out like a railroad-train shed. These two elements are strikingly joined in the interior space *(Fig. 168)*. Behind the divided front door, the stairs mount one sudden half-flight to the gallery entrance, where huge engaged columns and brutally machined entablatures like vises are screwed, unsupported, into a flat, diaper-patterned wall. Up the stairs the sad harsh trumpets of the iron lighting fixtures lift, prefiguring the shapes of Antonio Gaudí—who, after all, was also directly inspired by Viollet-le-Duc.

That great Frenchman's characteristic space and detailing underlay Furness' beautiful Guarantee Trust Company, of 1875, now, inconceivably, demolished *(Figs. 169–71)*. The interior space was high and squeezed, not voluminous but a well. Entrance to it was again divided in the middle, and it was threatened by the arched open-work metal trusses far above, visually unsupported high up on the smooth cliffs of the masonry walls. Outside, the masses rose like some exotic gate, its towers squeezed together, built of hard red brick with white impost blocks blown up but ruthlessly sliced off, flattened in the frontal plane. How similar, curiously, is Independence Hall, though the structural expressionism is absent there. Furness' gates are active and dangerous; the arched openings in them are visually fractured, interrupted, or compressed. The polychrome dances; everything is electric and snappingly alive.

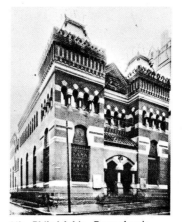

169. Philadelphia, Pennsylvania. Guarantee Trust Company. 1875. Frank Furness.

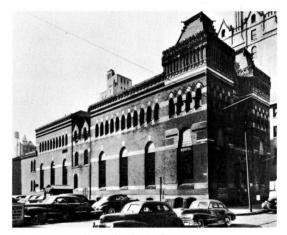

170. Guarantee Trust Company. Exterior.

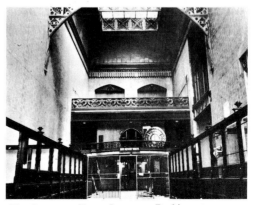

171. Guarantee Trust Company. Banking room.

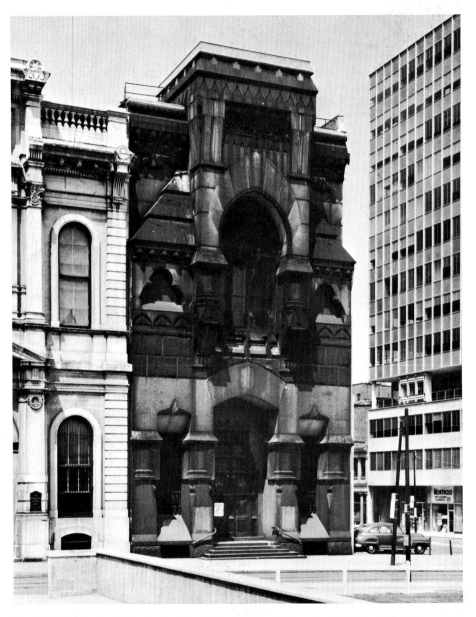

172. Philadelphia, Pennsylvania. Provident Life and Trust Company. 1879. Frank Furness.

Yet Furness' adaptation of Viollet-le-Duc's forms is also indicative of the optical rather than programmatic impetus behind most American work. Furness will take a motif, separate it from its function, blow up its scale, and make a whole building out of it. For the Provident Life and Trust Company, of 1879 (Fig. 172), surely his grandest success, he appropriated one of the entrance pavilions of Viollet-le-Duc's Château de Pierrefonds, lifted it off the ground, and dropped it, as from a great height, upon a tough little building whose walls all compacted under the impact, arches fracturing in compression, while the roofs of the wings fell into the main mass and, most of all, the polished columns were driven like brass pistons into rupturing cylinders, screeching with heat. Inside, the high, narrow space was threatened as by a falling drill press. The whole building is (was, alas) a great machine looming out of technology's archaic beginnings, a cast-iron marvel by Jules Verne, like those horrifically displayed at the Philadelphia Centennial of 1876. So its façade became massively active, embodying sculptural forces of compression and support which the viewer could empathetically experience through his own body's sense of such forces. The concept of "empathy" had already been proposed by Leopold Eidlitz (as Neil Levine has now shown), whose buildings, too, like those of Hunt, surely affected Furness. I used the word some years ago to describe the bodily effects of uprightness, compression, and tension which were to be developed by Louis Sullivan in his skyscrapers. The connection with Eidlitz lies in Furness, because it was the buildings of Furness which

the young Sullivan discovered for himself the day he walked through the streets of Philadelphia to find an architect whose work attracted him. Furness was the man, and he employed Sullivan for some months, until, so Sullivan tells us, the depression of 1873 forced him to cut down his staff. But this sense of bodily force he must somehow have passed on. It was to remain unique in his and Sullivan's mature work. With him, in 1879, it marked a kind of climax and ending. The Provident Trust was, after all, only a Philadelphia row house worked up into a paroxysm at once athletic and mechanical, of mass man hulking forward, a great golem of industrialism clanking away. One street could have taken only a few of those, so that, in a sense, Furness was releasing forces which could destroy the urbanism he exploited. How marvelous a monument the Provident Trust was, therefore, to the pressures taking place across the generations in modern cities as a whole; how absurd, in consequence, that it should have been destroyed in a modern redevelopment program—just as the Guarantee Trust was torn down to release Carpenter's Hall to a space it was never intended to control and which is too big for it—demolished with the united approval of Beaux-Arts backers, Bauhaus planners, and Garden City humanitarians. The buildings were too tough for everyone, apparently, too rough for the rather prissy gentility which has substituted for taste in most recent urban projects. "Masculine" indeed they were.

They marked Furness' highest moment. True enough, his library for the University of Pennsylvania, of 1880, is a splendid building, with several expressively different scales and, behind its hugely proportioned tower window *(Fig. 173)*, an inspired iron stair which gets smaller as it turns up the consistent volume of the stair well and finally, like a demented ladder, pierces the roof as a baroque saint the heavens. Yet the continuous hemicycle of the stacks, as well as the low, sweeping arches *(Fig. 174)* of the reading room (though not their power-press savagery) are echoes of the work of H. H. Richardson and mark the beginning of the submer-

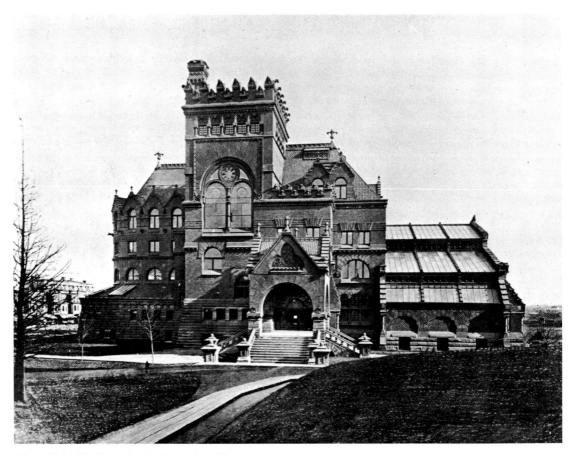

173. Philadelphia, Pennsylvania. University of Pennsylvania. Library. 1880–91. Frank Furness.

gence of Furness' own bodily active style in favor of
the swelling spatial volumes and continuous surfaces of Richardson's work. Furness continued to
practice for many years; he initiated the tradition
which has given modern Philadelphia far more than
its share of architects of first importance (Eyre,
Howe, Kahn, Venturi). But, despite flashes of his
old brimstone, he seemed to have passed his time.
He was a man of the 1870's, the strongest and
bravest.

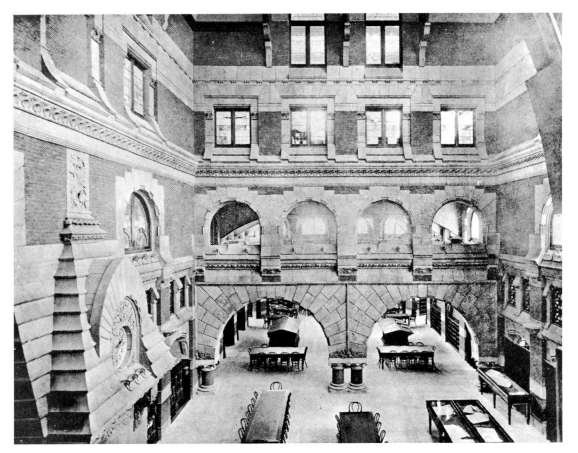

174. University of Pennsylvania. Library. View of main reading room in 1891.

With Richardson, American architecture entered its mythic phase: mythic itself, more or less consciously, in its content; mythic surely in the historical significance which what might be called the present American Studies generation has assigned to it. Brooklyn Bridge can mark its beginning *(Fig. 175)*. The towers are still mid-century Gothic, sharp and linear, but the roadway sweeps out into the new continuity of space which was to be the salient feature of the architecture of Richardson, Sullivan, and Wright, and hence America's major contribution to the first phases of international modern architecture in the early twentieth century. The bridge itself towered over the city; the curve of its road cut high above the old buildings. So it introduced all at once the scale of a new urban world and released into space its symbol of the roadway rushing continuously onward. It is no wonder that the bridge, with

its taut, singing cables, was to gain increasing force as an image of all America as the twentieth century wore on. Hart Crane gave it everything:

O sleepless as the river under thee,
Vaulting the sea, the prairies' dreaming sod. . . .

Hence, Montgomery Schuyler, who was one of the spokesmen of the new generation of the late 1870's, though in some ways a constantly disappointing one, admired the bridge's road and the curve of its cables, but disapproved of the towers. He was surely mistaken, since they are the finest kind of portals to New York, active in their shapes and hard as flint in their profiles. They energetically lift up the cables, and stand taut as the cables ride through them; how wrong they would have been in Richardsonian round-arched forms. They function as the

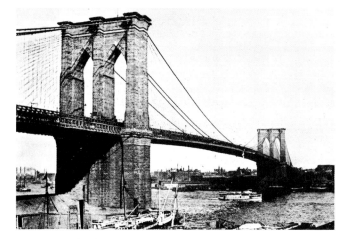

175. New York. Brooklyn Bridge. 1867–83. John A. and Washington A. Roebling.

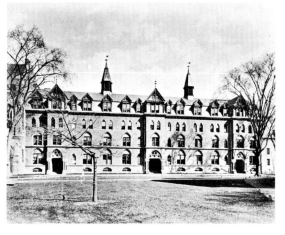

176. New Haven, Connecticut. Yale University. Farnam Hall. 1867–70. Russell Sturgis.

Roeblings obviously intended and give the road's area an actively vertical dimension for a measurable space, making it a cathedral of movement, ribbed with "choiring strings," an interval of psychic transformation in the passage over the water.

It is not too much to say that Richardson's design was dominated by the principle of spatial continuity. A comparison between his Sever Hall at Harvard and Russell Sturgis' Farnam Hall at Yale, an example of mid-century style, is instructive in this regard *(Figs. 176, 177)*. Farnam has walls which are flat and seem thin, with sharply-cut window openings, well separated on the wall plane and therefore strikingly discontinuous in effect. The roof is high and jaggedly articulated by dormers, while the perforated screens below the entrance arches wink with staccato points of light. Sever, on the other hand, connects its windows horizontally, suppresses

and stretches its dormers, bulges out in curving bays, and contains the whole volume in a continuous envelope of wall and roof plane. The entrance from the Yard *(Fig. 178)* is treated as a cavern in a wall of unimaginable thickness, modulated inward through plastically rounded profiles. A flat-planed, pedimented frontispiece pops forward overhead, as if pushed out by the interior air which is displaced by the act of entrance. On the other side of the building, that of exit from the Yard, the whole wall undulates outward, as if under interior pressure *(Fig. 179)*, while the semiclassical doorway is simply pinned to the surface, extruded, in contrast to the deep inhalation from the Yard. Hence, the shell of Sever is everywhere expressive of continuity and flow through the volume of space which it contains. It was this new continuity of space and shell which was to seduce Furness and to turn him from his

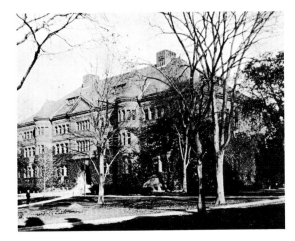

177. Cambridge, Massachusetts. Harvard University. Sever Hall. 1878–80. Henry Hobson Richardson.

178. Sever Hall. Entrance from the Yard.

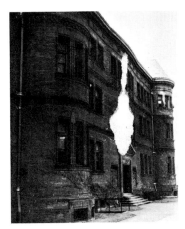

179. Sever Hall. Façade facing Quincy Street.

101

own active struggle between competing masses. Indeed, compared to Furness, Richardson seems a little soft and homogenized. Sullivan, influenced by both architects, was to make a humanistic synthesis of their objectives in industrial materials, for new programs at increased scale. But Richardson's work, no less than that of Furness, should not in any sense be primarily valued as transitional. It is unique in itself. Dark Trinity Church on Copley Square in Boston, with its single swelling volume of interior space and its firmly geometric massing, is one of his earliest and most conspicuous monuments but, in the long run, perhaps not one of his most characteristic or inventive. One thinks of the clear articulation of part from part in voids and solids in Austin Hall at Harvard: deep entrances swinging from the cylindrical stair-tower, vast panel of window for the stacks, other windows molding-stretched within the thick

stone walls, side wings holding classrooms with horizontal window bands *(Fig. 180)*. All is brought into one envelope; the neo-grec reminiscences are kept behind the earthy plane of the wall.

Richardson's libraries perhaps best show the two major elements of his design: the engulfing archways and the horizontally continuous windows of the reading rooms. Each library became more compact than the previous one; that at Quincy culminated the series *(Fig. 181)*. Its heavy-lidded roof engrosses even the frontal gable, which in turn contains its vertical stair-tower, pushed off center by the dark, staired entrance arch. Comparison should be made with the striking contrasts of functional areas in massing that Furness developed at the University of Pennsylvania. Still, Richardson's building is almost a creature. Other architects of the period apparently saw it as such—Bruce Price in a house or

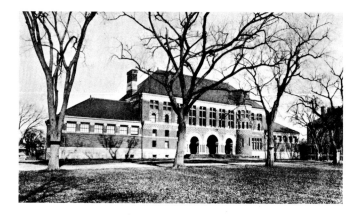

180. Harvard University. Austin Hall. 1881–83. Henry Hobson Richardson.

182. Chestnut Hill, Massachusetts. Boston and Albany Railroad Station. 1883–84. Henry Hobson Richardson.

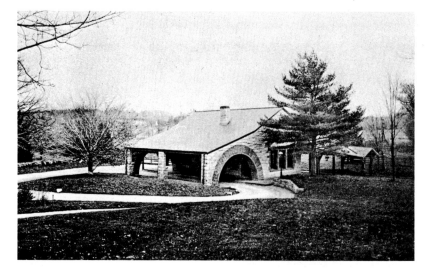

two, for example, or in his Osborne Hall at Yale, where the arches writhed back from short columns like teeth, sucking in and spewing out the stairs like Charybdis the sea. Yet no follower of Richardson's could match the image of engulfment which he could develop in even the smallest buildings. The tiny railroad station at Chestnut Hill, Massachusetts, is an insatiable monster, swallowing up vehicles *(Fig. 182)*.

Richardson's buildings were as geometrically ordered as any by Jefferson or Ledoux, but their latent and very American classicism was embodied in warm and earthy forms, not in the bright humanistic vocabulary of earlier classic design. So they combined two qualities previously considered to be natural opposites: "classicism" and "romanticism," if one wishes to call them that. They also combined the new continuity of space with weight and permanence of mass: archetypes of movement and stability synthesized. In all these ways they may be felt to have summed up the main conflicting aspects of modern, and peculiarly American, middle-class aspiration: to be free and protected all at once. In the same sense, they were both urban and suburban, place-fixing masses adjusted to expanding suburban patterns along the commuting railroad lines. They were thus a marvelously firm and satisfactory beginning for the modern phases of the city, and they laid a remarkable foundation for the further exploration of its themes. Aside from government buildings, such as the awesomely Cyclopean-Piranesian Allegheny County Court House and Jail *(Fig. 183)*, they did so in the two major and more revolutionary types of the new urbanism: in suburban domestic architecture, which we can best consider later, and in center-city commercial buildings. In the

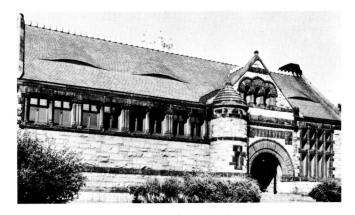

181. Quincy, Massachusetts. Crane Memorial Library. 1880–83. Henry Hobson Richardson.

183. Pittsburgh, Pennsylvania. Allegheny County Court House. 1884. Henry Hobson Richardson. Vestibule and main staircase.

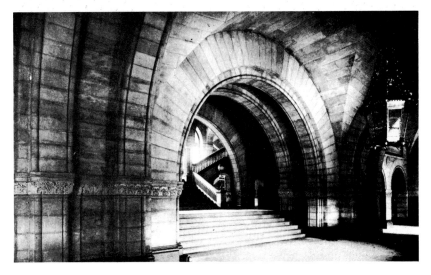

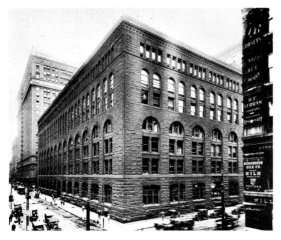

184. Chicago, Illinois. Marshall Field Warehouse. 1885–87.
Henry Hobson Richardson.

latter category, the Marshall Field Warehouse in
Chicago directly influenced Louis Sullivan in his
formulation of skyscraper shape *(Figs. 184, 185)*.
It is a single mass, but its surface swells vertically
and stretches laterally to contain its open interior.
Contrast should be drawn with its English prototypes, such as various warehouses in Bristol *(Fig.
186)*. There, too, several floors of windows are
grouped within high arches, but the reveals are deep,
the wall expressed as static and thick. Marshall Field
is stretched and taut, as ordered as a Renaissance
palazzo but expanding under the pressure of its continuous interior volume. If one moves from this to
Richardson's second Ames Building in Boston *(Fig.
187)*, where the arches rise the entire height of the
office floors (offering a fine contrast with the less
continuous forms of the first Ames Building, which
had influenced Furness in his library), it is only a
step to Sullivan's most advanced skyscraper, the
Guaranty, in Buffalo, of 1895 *(Fig. 197)*.

Sullivan did not come to that solution all at once.
His first buildings with Adler are secondhand Fur-

185. Marshall Field Warehouse. Plan.

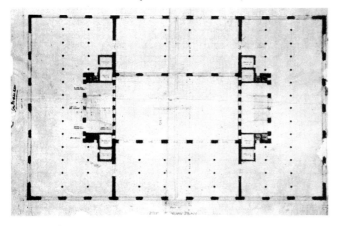

186. Bristol, England. Warehouse on Strait Street. *Ca.* 1870.

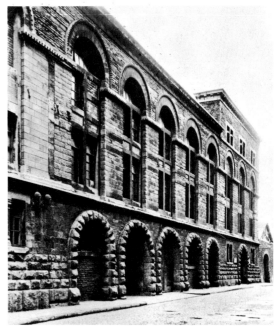

104

ness. By the time of the grandiose Auditorium he
was closely and perhaps not too successfully adapt-
ing the Marshall Field Warehouse to a program
overly complicated for it. In his Walker Warehouse
the relationship with the Marshall Field could be
closer in scale *(Fig. 188)*. The surface was simplified
and cut more sharply; already, and characteristi-
cally, it expressed less an interior volume than a
densely articulated fabric. The cubical order of the
massing was, if anything, intensified; as, in fact,
most of the architects of the late 1880's were in-
tensifying it. Indeed, Sullivan's tombs of the years
around 1890 closely recall the abstract geometric
solids of Ledoux; but across their surfaces a contrasting intention can be read, one which wishes
shapes to transform themselves into motion, to
shiver the light that falls upon them into continuously fluid patterns of form *(Fig. 189)*. This is the
way Sullivan uses his ornament, to enliven with
movement the stability of his masses. All these elements came together in the Wainwright Building, in
St. Louis, his first skyscraper *(Fig. 196)*.

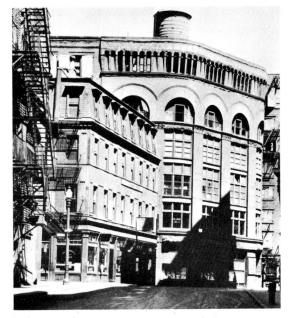

187. Boston, Massachusetts. Ames Building on Harrison Avenue. 1886–87. Henry Hobson Richardson.

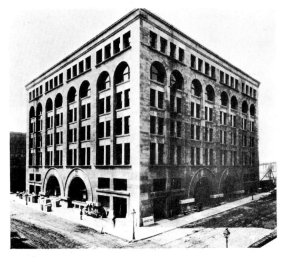

188. Chicago, Illinois. Walker Warehouse. 1888–89.
Adler and Sullivan.

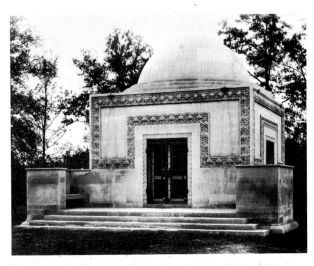

189. St. Louis, Missouri. Bellefontaine Cemetery. Wainwright
Tomb. 1892. Adler and Sullivan.

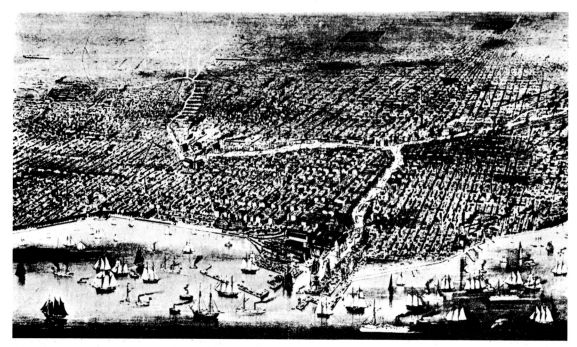

190. Chicago, Illinois. View in 1874.

191. Chicago, Illinois. Montauk Building. 1882. Burnham and Root.

192. Chicago, Illinois. Home Insurance Building. 1884–85. William Le Baron Jenney.

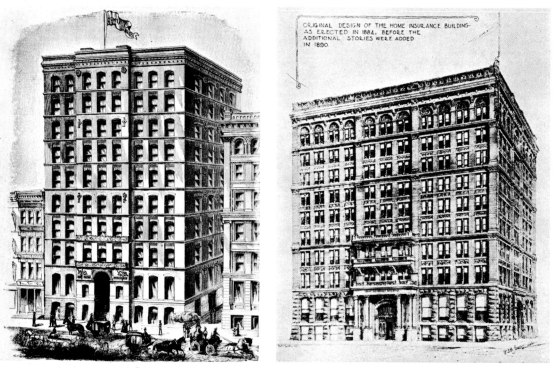

Yet to understand the Wainwright Building one must look to the larger development of its mode of construction in Chicago during the 1880's. The word "skyscraper" itself originally signified less a quality of height than a mode of building in which a steel frame supported its own fireproofing of masonry or terra cotta. But a desire for height had called it into being. The center of Chicago, though serving as transportation center of the continent, market for the West, and commissary of the East, was restricted in fact by its lake front, river, and loop of suburban railroad line *(Fig. 190)*. Land values in the Loop were high; buildings wanted to be tall and, if possible (in that swampy soil), light. The fire of 1871 had showed that iron frames were not the answer, since they wilted rapidly when the temperature rose.

The first tall office buildings, such as the Montauk, served by the first elevators, continuous vertical roads, were built of masonry *(Fig. 191)*. But how to scale the entrance? Masonry proved uneconomical because of the thickness of wall necessary in the lower floors, so that necessity fathered William Le Baron Jenney's Home Insurance Building, of 1884–85 *(Fig. 192)*, where a skeleton frame, partly of iron, mostly of Bessemer steel, supported its own fireproof cladding. But what to do with all those floors? Jenney's desperate horizontals seem based on those of the Montauk. The major accounts of the skyscraper so far written have emphasized the technological achievement and have tended to equate its eventual expression with aesthetic quality. It must be admitted that this approach has much to recommend it in practice so far as the metal-frame buildings in the Chicago Loop from that day to this are concerned. Yet technological determinism is always simplistic and, in the end, a dangerous evasion of the true complexity of all reality. The fact remains that the most splendid office building to rise in Chicago during the great early days was of pure, old-fashioned masonry construction: Burnham and Root's mighty Monadnock of 1889–91, lifting dark, smooth, and fast like one lovely pier, held thick at the corners, blossoming from within with shining window bays *(Fig. 193)*. In a sense, the Monadnock has outlasted the frame technique which was to outmode her, since contemporary wall-bearing concrete construction can call forth something of her profile,

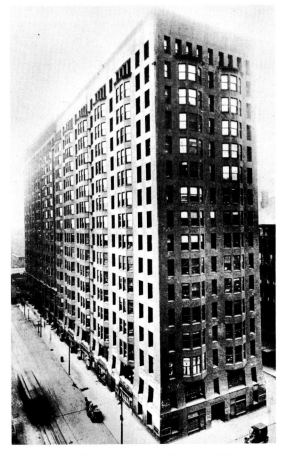

193. Chicago, Illinois. Monadnock Building. 1889–91. Burnham and Root.

although it is true that the buildings and projects which now evoke her curves in the Loop—the concrete Brunswick Building and the projected (steel framed) First National Bank—might better have tried something else.

The structural economics of the frame itself had two interconnected potentials: to rise high in bays of generally horizontal proportions. There was also a slight dominance of vertical over horizontal in the normal intersection of column and girder *(Fig. 194)*. It goes without saying that the interior spaces were low, horizontal volumes minimally obstructed by columns. The usual result in the hands of Chicago's best architects was clear in those particulars but not unduly elegant otherwise *(Fig. 199)*. The most famous success among them, the Reliance Building, of 1894, was also by Burnham and Root; its design was the last of Root's several fine achievements before his untimely death. Yet it is less the frame itself than the glass it makes possible—here set in projecting bays expressive of the interior volumes—which gives the building its special character *(Fig. 195)* and has caused it to be compared to Mies van der Rohe's glass-skyscraper projects of 1919–22. But there, indeed, the structure was intended to be of cantilevered slabs, not of a rectangular frame.

Therefore, the simple technological explanation of the skyscraper does not provide a complete or, in some cases, even the most relevant description of its qualities. Sullivan, who created its most influential shape, hardly thought of technology at all, but of the building as a functioning human institution with certain logical formal possibilities: a geometric cube containing an entrance floor as base, a honeycomb of identical office floors stressing the vertical dimension but repeating the scale of the individual window—which means of the individual human user, not of the framed bay of the construction—finally a service floor and cornice. The Wainwright Building in St. Louis has them all. *(Fig. 196)*. The office floors are a plait of vertical piers (structural columns within every other one only), threaded through by visually weightless spandrels expressive of the horizontal floors. The multiplied verticals force the eye to remain within the body of the building and to read it upward as a single sculptural shaft, not horizontally as layers of spatial volumes. The whole office grid of brick and terra cotta is set within the larger frame created by stone-sheathed base, stone-brick end-wall planes (some indecision there) and the richly shadowed service floor with its cornice; the piers have their own capitals and are placed on a projected slab. Upon the stone sheathing beneath the front of each pier a little ornament flares like a flower. The general effect is rich and discontinuous, of a grid in a frame. But it is both solid and elegant, dense enough to define the street as a plane, scaled enough with entrance floor and loving ornamental touches to articulate the street humanely.[2]

By 1895, in the Guaranty Building, all the contrasting elements had been drawn into one continuous plastic unity *(Fig. 197)*, into a vertical body standing on legs and stretching and swelling with muscular force. "A man on two legs," Sullivan called Richardson's Marshall Field Warehouse, but the progenitor of such body-image façadism, was, as we have seen, not Richardson but Furness *(Fig. 172)*. Now, however, the crochety individualism of the 1870's had passed by, and the overtly mechanical images abandoned. A new kind of giant stood high on his legs: mass man with steel muscles, tensile and springy. Richardson's continuities had now also been understood and extended; the doubled piers rose high and were connected by arches, so that they leaped up, over, and down. The screen now stretched the larger frame as well and merged with it. Compression and tension seemed to flicker across the whole skeleton, because the light terra-cotta sheathing was highly movemented in its ornament. Its decorative system strongly recalls that of the Irish manuscripts of the early Middle Ages; there, too, a derivation from metalwork sections was developed into calligraphic fluidity. Similar weight-destroying qualities had been developed in Moslem ornament, and Sullivan had clearly been influenced by its forms as well. The Irish and Islamic systems had once shared a common anticlassic intention at the edges of the European world; interesting that Sullivan, who so despised the classicizing design of the Beaux-Arts system, should have unerringly employed its ancient adversaries to set his own otherwise highly classical work in motion. Thus, the volume of the Guaranty as a whole has a classic integrity, but it is stretched into the scale of a new urbanism beyond classical boundaries. Ideally, though it does not deny the street, it could have served as a prototypal mid-space tower, and it prefigures those of Le Corbusier and Mies van der Rohe in the twentieth century. It is one of modern culture's most congenial developments, and in the long view hardly an accident, that Mies himself was eventually to bring Sullivan's demonstrations back to continuing use and was to do so in the Loop of Chicago.

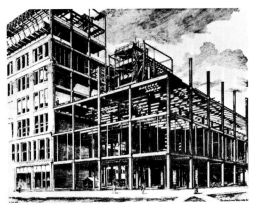

194. Chicago, Illinois. Fair Store. 1890–91. William Le Baron Jenney. Under construction.

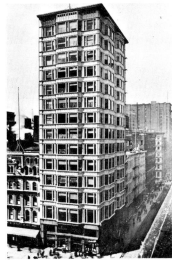

195. Chicago, Illinois. Reliance Building. 1894–95. Burnham and Root.

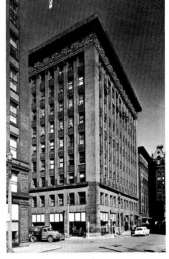

196. St. Louis, Missouri. Wainwright Building. 1890–91. Adler and Sullivan.

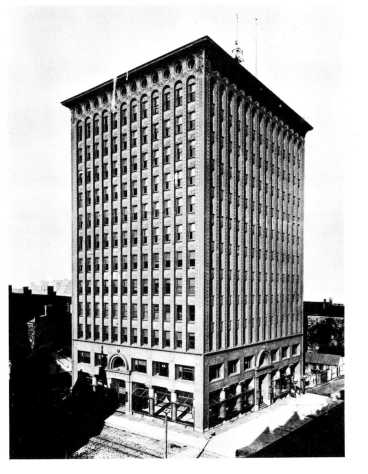

197. Buffalo, New York. Guaranty Building. 1894-95. Adler and Sullivan.

109

It is clear that Sullivan himself was thinking of his buildings as related to traditional street groupings, so that part of his urbanistic responsibility was to design appropriately planar façades. Such is clear in the Bayard and Gage Buildings; both are like taut screens dropped to define a public space. In the Bayard *(Fig. 198)*, Sullivan distinguished between bearing and nonbearing piers, as he had not done in either the Wainwright or the Guaranty buildings. Above the compressed capitals of the ground floor, the structural piers are thick in section, obviously heavy; the others are drawn tight, like cables in tension, stretched downward by the heavy spandrels dropped like sash weights above the first office floor. The Gage Building *(Fig. 199)*, on the other hand, is visually all hung from the top, its columns pinned there by vast ornamental brooches, the window frames clattering down between them like Venetian blinds.

Finally, in the Carson-Pirie-Scott Department Store, which we should regard as the last of his epoch-making metropolitan images (touchingly, those of small-town Main Street were to come last of all), Sullivan suppressed the vertical columns in order to stress and even to exaggerate the horizontality of the structural bays *(Figs. 200, 201)*. At the same time, he masked any sense of support by elaborating the interwoven ironwork ornament of the ground floor. The upper floors were thus liberated to take on a kind of horizontal velocity, like that of the busy street they so splendidly define. Yet their flat shell splits at the corner to let the interior space swell forward behind, as it were, stretched metal and taut glass, while the vertical columns measure off the curve and the modeled profiles of the intersection help change its pace and direction. It is regrettable that the original projecting cornice no longer enhances that movement, but the building

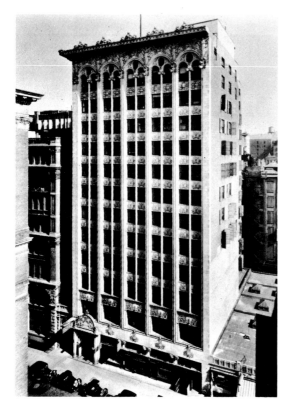

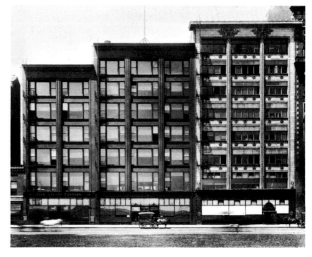

199. Chicago, Illinois. Gage Building. 1898–99. Louis Sullivan. View showing the Gage Building, far right, and two buildings by Holabird and Roche, on the left.

198. *(Left)* New York. Bayard Building. 1897–98. Louis Sullivan.

still rides to its intersection as the most effective embodiment so far created of the lush and exhilarating life of the downtown, big-city shopping street.

Carson-Pirie-Scott's coiling thickets of iron ribbons remind us of the European Art Nouveau which was contemporary with it. There, as in the work of Victor Horta and, even more, in some of the buildings of Gaudí, the principle of continuity tended to bring the whole building into liquid motion. That never occurred in America, except, curiously, in a more geometric way in the very late work of Wright. American continuity in architecture, like Sullivan's, was more strictly an affair of flat planes and directed avenues of space. In that sense, the only true Art Nouveau in America was probably to be found elsewhere, as in Tiffany's decoration. In urbanistic terms, the Carson-Pirie-Scott Store was the horizontal, space-defining complement to the potentially freestanding tower of the Guaranty. The two types,

though somewhat desiccated in the process, were to shape the major new urban groupings of the middle of the coming century. By that time, they were more than balanced by the millions of single-family suburban houses which blanketed the landscape, and whose inhabitants, in search of individuality and safety together, in fact led highly dangerous lives of continual, strictly directed movement on the proliferating net of automobile roads. The house and the road always go together in America, in symbolical no less than directly physical terms. The house is at the end of the road, or on it, or is abandoned for it *(Fig. 513)*; the colonial house hugged it; the twentieth-century house was to draw it into its huge garage and to enshrine its bug-eyed creatures there. The suburban houses of the nineteenth century multiplied along lines of growth defined by their access roads, railroads, and carriageways. By the 1870's, the Stick Style began to give way to a shin-

200. Chicago, Illinois. Carson-Pirie-Scott Department Store. 1899–1904. Louis Sullivan.

201. Carson-Pirie-Scott Store. Façade detail.

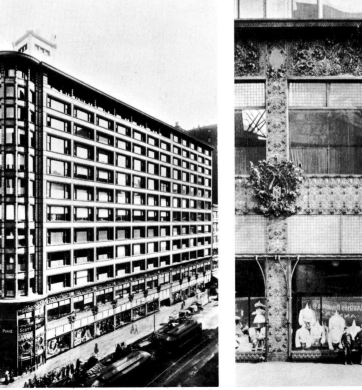

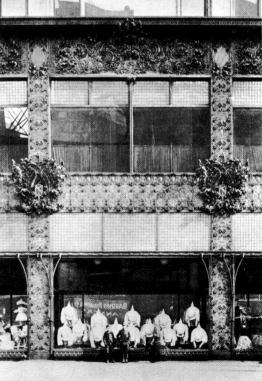

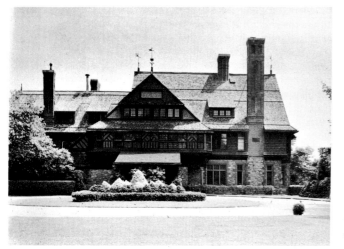

gled mode in which the space of the house itself opened up and stretched out horizontally like the space of the road.

Again, it was Richardson who initiated the new phase of style. His Watts Sherman House, of 1874 *(Fig. 202)*, should be contrasted with the Sturtevant House, of two years before *(Fig. 160)*. What is vertical in the earlier house is now turning horizontal. The windows are grouping in long horizontal bands; the gable is stretched for lateral rather than vertical massing. The shingled surface is continuous rather than paneled. Horizontal rather than vertical shadow-lines are everywhere emphasized. The house is becoming an affair of horizontal planes, rather than of an articulated skeleton. Most of all, the interior space is opening up through wide doorways off a large central living hall, making use of a monu-

202. Newport, Rhode Island. Watts Sherman House. 1874–76. Henry Hobson Richardson.

203. Watts Sherman House. Living hall. Drawing probably by Stanford White.

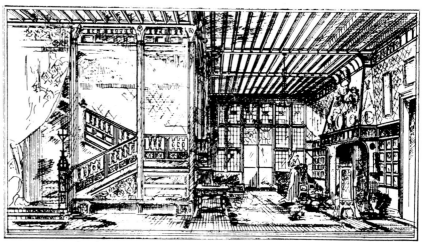

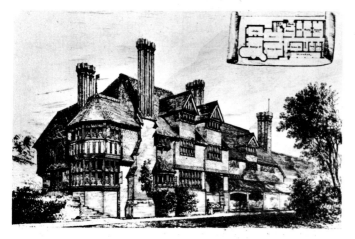

204. Surrey, England. Hopedene. Richard Norman Shaw. As published in 1874.

mental stairway, a massive fireplace, and a window wall *(Fig. 203)*. Everything is beginning to flow together in terms of continuous space and of surfaces defining it.

Richardson derived every one of these elements from English houses of the late 1860's and early 1870's, especially those such as Leyswood, of 1868, and Hopedene, of 1873, by Richard Norman Shaw *(Fig. 204)*. But Richardson exaggerated their qualities and amplified them. The horizontality is more continuous, the interior space more open. Again one senses the American instinct to clarify, systematize, and simplify. In fact, with the waning of the Gothic Revival, that stylistic phenomenon I have noted elsewhere, which was the tendency of the nineteenth century to revive earlier architectural styles in chronological order, became most marked. So

Gothic gave way to Jacobean and to the moment when American architecture itself began. Such is strikingly evident in Richardson's Stoughton House of 1882–83 *(Figs. 205, 206)*. Where both the English and American buildings noted above had employed the forms of English half-timber' construction, the Stoughton House was sheathed in a continuous skin, exactly as seventeenth-century American houses had been clothed *(Fig. 213)*. Now, however, the cladding was not clapboard but shingles, so that the whole surface—high, voluminous roof, thin walls and all— was even more multidirectionally continuous than in the earlier century.

The reference to early colonial architecture was intentional on Richardson's part. Nor was he by any means alone in his use of it. By the time of the Philadelphia Centennial of 1876, the country was de-

205. Cambridge, Massachusetts. Stoughton House. 1882–83. Henry Hobson Richardson.

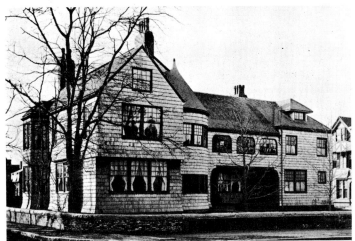

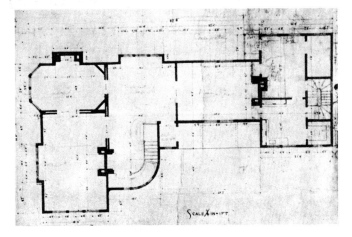

206. Stoughton House. Plan.

cisively embarked on a colonial revival which has, in one sense, never entirely subsided. The mood was not bumptiously confident, as during the mid-century, but nostalgic, a little discouraged and sad. The modern world was "too large," and, during the Grant Administration no less than that of the second Johnson, the United States as a dream of human goodness seemed to have lost its way. How to reevaluate the ideals of the founding fathers? How even to find them again? In the 1870's and 1880's, that question was answered largely in escapist terms. Civilized withdrawal from a brutalized society encouraged interminable summer vacations (the real decadence of New England here?) to Nan-

tucket, Martha's Vineyard, and the coasts of Massachusetts and Maine, where the old houses weathered silver, floating like dreams of forever in the cool fogs off the sea. So the Stoughton House in Cambridge, like the other suburban or resort houses of its type, recalls colonial practice in mass and detail and sheathes its open but cavernous interior space in naturally weathering shingles. Travel in Europe, too, was recalled in such houses; the swelling candle-snuffer towers of the châteaux of the Loire played a special part in their design (Fig. 205). Japanese influence, also felt strongly at the Philadelphia Centennial, was not absent either. The interior spaces were opened to each other and interwoven,

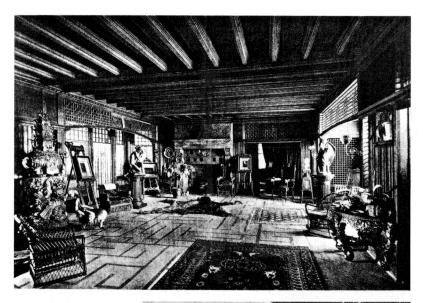

207. (*Above*) Elberon, New Jersey. Victor Newcomb House. 1880–81. McKim, Mead and White. Living hall.

208. (*Right*) Newport, Rhode Island. Casino. 1879–81. McKim, Mead and White. Fountain and piazza.

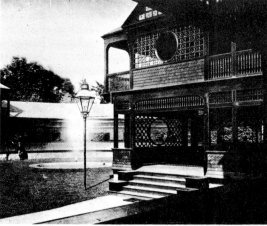

114

one with the other, through a system of Japanese moldings and screens derived from a close study of Japanese architecture but, typically, here developed toward more impatient continuities of space than the Japanese, with their firm sense of hieratic figures in framed volumes, had cared to employ *(Fig. 207)*. In fact, Japanese influence created a kind of countercurrent in the Shingle Style, tending as it did toward skeletal rather than cavernous effects. Its finest monument is surely the lovingly framed and screened piazza of the Newport Casino, by McKim, Mead and White *(Figs. 208, 209)*.

Yet the major image of the Shingle Style is of something dark in color and primitivistic in form, a warm, hollow body, earthy and rooted in a place: permanence, maternal peace. Richardson's Ames Gate Lodge is the archetypal example in masonry, not hard but soft, whose plum-pudding boulders are not unlike shingles, picturesque surface elements rather than lithic masses, while the whole building stretches out in lateral continuity and engulfment *(Fig. 210)*.

Architects like William Ralph Emerson of Boston used all these elements in free and varied pictorial combinations to create the special summertime world (the Impressionist world, one might say) of Manchester-by-the-Sea and other resorts. A house like that for G. N. Black, by Peabody and Stearns,

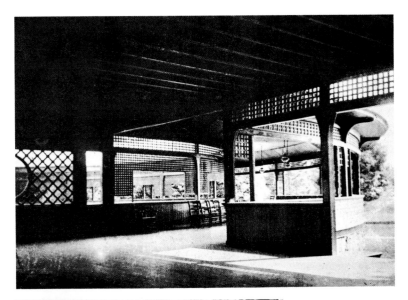

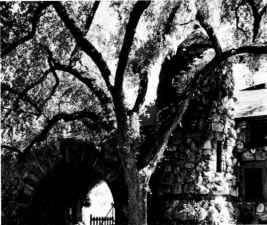

209. (*Above*) Newport Casino. Piazza.

210. (*Left*) North Easton, Massachusetts. Ames Gate Lodge. 1880–81. Henry Hobson Richardson.

115

shows how a single design might combine everything *(Figs. 211, 212)*: rough stone, weather: g shingles, Richardson's arch, and intersecting gabl:d and gambreled masses like those of colonial houses such as the Fairbanks House at Dedham *(Fig. 213)*. The massing has now become complex and voluminous; the interior, around its great fireplaces, is no longer a colonial box but a varied landscape of its own. It opens up at several levels and pushes out to porches, green-shadowed pavilions of permissive relaxation, of summer-stock assignations among the cane chairs and the gliders, middle-class heaven, somnolent with novels.[4]

Everything in such houses "accommodates" difference and variety. Yet the instinct of most American architects was to discipline that ideal world and to stretch it out horizontally, as Richardson had begun to do from the very beginning of his shingle phase.

211. Manchester-by-the-Sea, Massachusetts. G. N. Black House. 1882–84. Peabody and Stearns.

212. G. N. Black House. Plans and sketches by E. Eldon Deane.

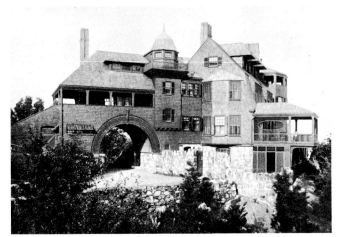

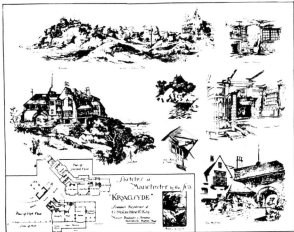

213. Dedham, Massachusetts. Fairbanks House. 1636, with eighteenth-century additions.

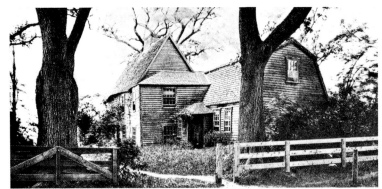

116

So architects like John Calvin Stevens of Maine interwove gambrels and porches in a direct expression of continuity between interior and exterior spaces, while the Ashurst House by Wilson Eyre, of Philadelphia *(Figs. 214, 215)*, shows a long axis of horizontal extension in plan; it is further developed in three dimensions by lowering the masses and stretching the window bands around the corners. McKim, Mead and White used the gable as a uniting device. In the William Low House (demolished by a later owner who built an indescribable ranch house on the site), it was mightily stretched, indeed as far as a gable could go *(Fig. 216)*. In this, the Low House recalls the distended cube of Richardson's Marshall Field Warehouse, of exactly the same time *(Fig. 184)*. In both buildings, a closed geometric shape is expanded to the utmost and made as continuous as possible through the pressure of interior volume.

214. Overbrook, Pennsylvania. Richard L. Ashurst House. *Ca.* 1885. Wilson Eyre.

215. Richard L. Ashurst House. Plan.

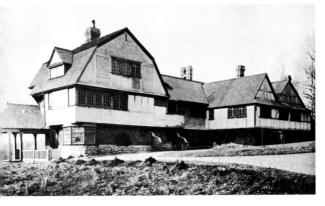

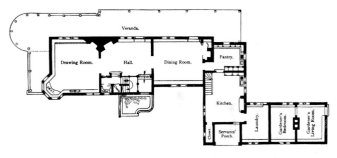

216. Bristol, Rhode Island. William Low House. 1887. McKim, Mead and White.

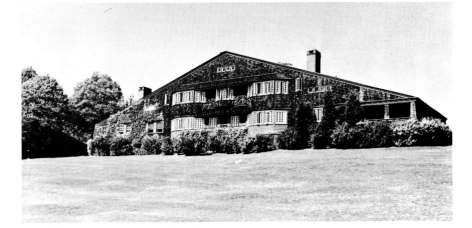

117

The next step in suburban domestic architecture had to be to burst the envelope or to relieve the pressure. I think we may say that larger cultural inferences are not absent from that statement of the problem. The Beaux-Arts architects of the late nineteenth and early twentieth centuries chose, among other things, the latter alternative. The elegantly colonially-planned, flat-planed, white-columned, Adam-detailed H. A. C. Taylor House, by McKim, Mead and White, was one of the best and finest examples of the second choice *(Figs. 217, 218)*. Frank Lloyd Wright found a way to accomplish the other alternative and to go forward in inventive terms.

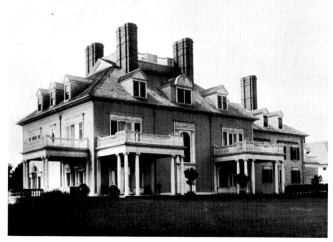

217. Newport, Rhode Island. H. A. C. Taylor House. 1885–86. McKim, Mead and White.

218. H. A. C. Taylor House. Plan.

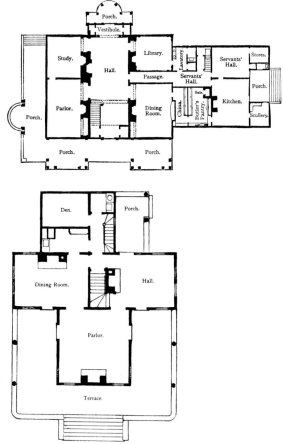

220. Kent House. Plan.

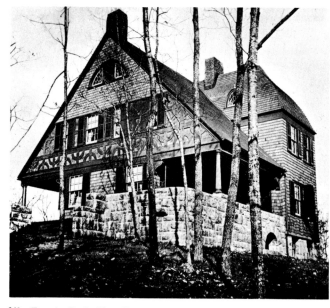

219. Tuxedo Park, New York. Kent House. 1885–86. Bruce Price.

Wright's work grew directly out of the Shingle Style. We have already noted, in connection with Monticello, the cross-axial plan of the Kent House at Tuxedo Park, New York, by Bruce Price *(Figs. 219, 220)*. Here, too, is the stretched gable with the horizontal window bands. Wright, as a young designer in Sullivan's office, building his own house, employed Price's forms almost exactly, those of the Kent House and of another, the Chandler House, together *(Fig. 221)*. Wright's plan was still the more loosely accommodating type of the earlier Shingle Style rather than the more rigidly disciplined cross-axis of the Kent House. But in less than ten years,

Wright had synthesized all the elements which the second half of the nineteenth century had developed. He did not neglect the H. A. C. Taylor House or the Beaux-Arts buildings at the Chicago World's Fair of 1893; he used both in designs of that year. The Turkish Pavilion at the Fair was also adapted, as was the Japanese "Ho-O-Den" there. By the time of the River Forest Golf Club, of 1898–1901, Wright had adopted the cross-axial plan and exploited it architecturally more fully than any architect before him had done *(Fig. 222)*. He eliminated both gable and gambrel, so flattening his hipped roofs into long planes and making his window bands completely continuous below

221. Oak Park, Illinois. Frank Lloyd Wright House. 1889. Frank Lloyd Wright.

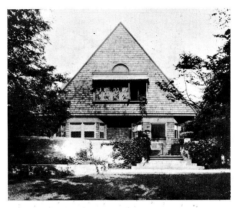

222. River Forest, Illinois. Golf Club. 1898–1901. Frank Lloyd Wright. Perspective drawing.

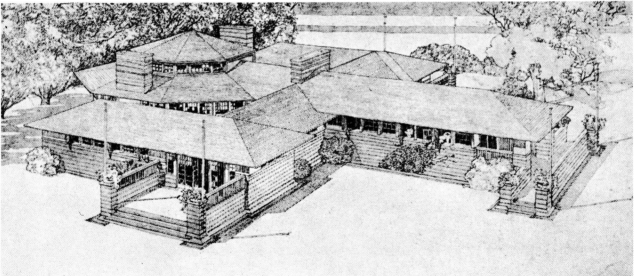

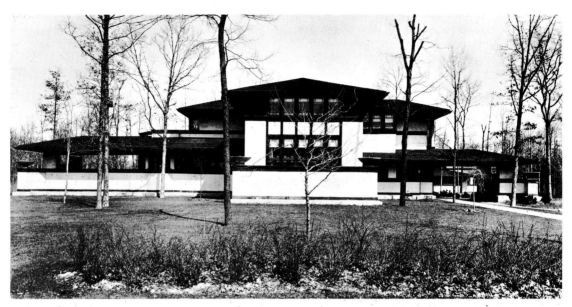

223. Highland Park, Illinois. Ward Willitts
House. 1902. Frank Lloyd Wright.

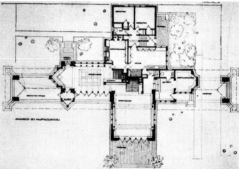

224. Ward Willitts House. Plan.

225. Project for "A Home in a Prairie
Town." 1901. Frank Lloyd Wright.
Section.

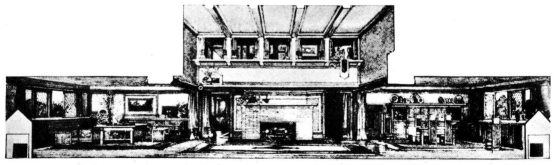

them. The shingles were abandoned in favor of horizontally-battened wooden siding — the exact opposite of the vertically-battened Stick Style. By 1900–1902, in the Ward Willitts House, Wright articulated the whole structure through the cross-axis, as by interwoven framing members, and the interior space was created by that total interweaving *(Figs. 223–25, 228)*. Such articulation grew out of the Japanese practice of the 1880's *(Fig. 207)*, but Wright intensified the integration of the elements and, drastically lowering the ceiling, correspondingly increased the scale of the details. Here again, despite the vast differences in formal vocabulary, the methods of Harrison and Jefferson are recalled *(Figs. 74, 87)*. Once more, the intention is to enforce the physical effect, here of horizontal continuity and expansion, by large details in small buildings. So the spaces are made to intersect and to stretch continuously outward from the dark fireplace in the center toward the dimmed light of the outside world. It is the solution of the seventeenth-century American house *(Figs. 49–52)*, where, however, the containing box has been split apart as if two roads had burst

through it, crossing in front of the flat frontal chimney mass, in whose depths the fire burns. It seems obvious that two deep-seated compulsions, both always very apparent in America, one seeking rootedness and protection, the other demanding freedom and mobility, are here woven together in a calm and expansive unity *(Fig. 228)*.

It was a new architecture. How it grew out of Richardson, but intensified his scale and reorganized his closed volumes into separate intersecting planes, can be seen by a simple comparison between Richardson's fine Glessner House in Chicago and Wright's Heurtley House of 1902 *(Figs. 226, 227)*. The ancestry is obvious, but a revolution has taken place; Wright's building, even darker and warmer in tone than the other, is already a piece of Constructivist sculpture. It has broken through the persistent American boxed form and prepared the way for numerous free experiments in Europe. It is no longer "colonial" in any sense. In Wright's work, American culture thus transcended itself, and tides of influence and release therefore flowed backward for a while from it to the mother continent.

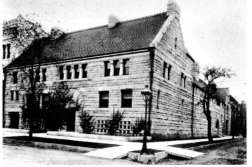

226. Chicago, Illinois. Glessner House. 1885–87. Henry Hobson Richardson.

227. Oak Park, Illinois. Heurtley House. 1902. Frank Lloyd Wright.

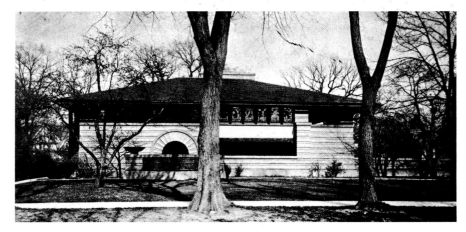

So Wright summed up his century and went on. The positivism of the Gothic Revival of its middle decades was of great importance to him. He imbibed it directly from the writings of Viollet-le-Duc; hence, he wanted to make spatial areas through regular structure if he could, and to justify his design in rationalistic terms if possible. At times, there was some conflict between that materialistic rationalism and his major objective of making continuously expansive spaces. All his cantilevered roofs conceal steel in them, for example, to make them look as if they were floating effortlessly in the void. The Martin House at Buffalo shows the two desires. Here Wright articulated a continuously horizontal cross-axis with vertical brick piers, whose groupings in bays of four at the intersections contain service spaces for heating and lighting between them. It is all very rationalistic and complete; yet the horizontal floor and ceiling planes push through to dominate all *(Fig. 228)*. But in the Larkin Building of 1904 there is no conflict whatever between structure and space. The Larkin is one of the very few buildings larger than houses that Wright was able to construct during these years

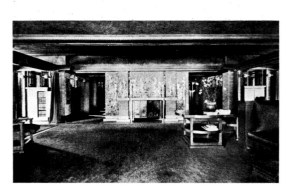

228. Buffalo, New York. Martin House. 1904. Frank Lloyd Wright. Living room.

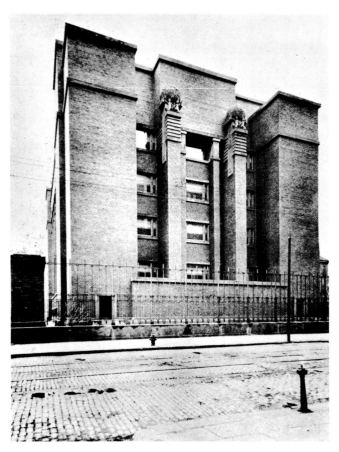

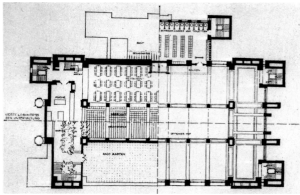

229. Buffalo, New York. Larkin Building. 1904. Frank Lloyd Wright.

230. Larkin Building. Plan.

(Figs. 229–31). Here structure and space, function and mechanical means, the demands of the inside and those of the outside were integrated perhaps more completely than in any other building ever built in America. Indeed, Wright's compulsion toward total unity was his most American trait. At the same time, the Larkin Building was one of the most important demonstrations of a significant architectural movement at the turn of the century in America and Europe alike, the final development of classicizing form into what can only be called mechanical or industrializing form, and the merger of one with the other. In Europe, one thinks of Olbrich, Wagner, and Behrens. We might remember Wright's Charnley House of 1891. There was pure romantic-classicism, sharp-cut and cubical, the equivalent, at domestic scale, of Sullivan's contemporary tombs on the one hand and his Wainwright Building on the other. We are reminded of Stratford *(Fig. 64)*; one senses the chunky blocks of Wright's Froebel kindergarten training as well. Their geometric solids also affect the Larkin Building *(Fig. 229)*, but now stairs are housed in the hollow corner-blocks, and the heavy structural frame of vertical piers and interwoven horizontal beams supports balconies of offices, high-windowed, with filing cabinets in the thickness of the piers. Top light pours down the central well. The exterior promises what the interior will be, but that space is entered from the side, through a low, dark doorway and under the office balconies, so that the central volume surprises with its burst of height and light at last. Furness, grain elevators *(Fig. 232)*, American factories by the hundred, Sullivan, are all recalled, no less than the medieval cathedrals—naved, bayed, and harmonically massed—whose pictures Wright's mother had hung in his room and which Viollet-le-Duc had so persuasively made a part of the nineteenth century through his technologically deterministic description of them. In that mechanistic sense, most of all, the Larkin Building was surely a monument of the machine age, a rationalistic engine to delight Henry Adams and to terrify him. The major European architects of its period, Behrens and Berlage, recognized it as such. It was not a humanistic image, like Sullivan's Guaranty *(Fig. 197)*, but an environ-

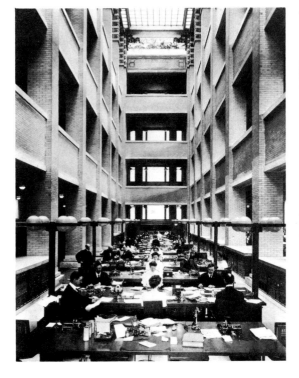

231. Larkin Building. Interior.

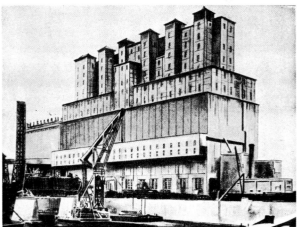

232. Buffalo, New York. Grain elevator. Reproduced by Le Corbusier in *Vers une Architecture*, 1923.

123

mental hollow, clifflike and cavernous, yet distributing people at work as within a great machine.

Only after the middle of the century would its lessons be absorbed or rediscovered by architects such as Kahn (*Fig. 451*). Wright complemented it immediately with Unity Temple, where he made the spaces with planes of poured concrete and lit them from above through darkly glowing squares of Froebel-decorated amber skylights set between crossed concrete beams. Again one saw the interior from the exterior but had to enter from the side to discover the top-lighted space at last (*Figs. 233, 234*).

That journey of Wright's, persistently recurring, seems the climax of Romanticism. It differs from the

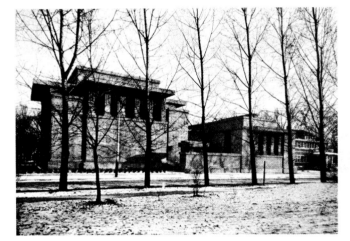

233. Oak Park, Illinois. Unity Temple. 1906. Frank Lloyd Wright.

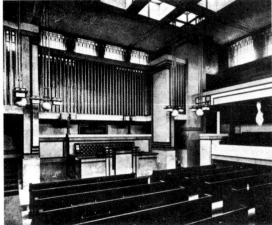

234. Unity Temple. Meeting room.

old Baroque progression of losing and finding in that its plan is asymmetrical, hence not that of a theater but of a quest. The Robie House, image of a century's research and desire, has it all *(Figs. 235, 236)*. The dark wings lift on concealed steel along the Chicago street—prairie symbolically only—and the entrance must be circuitously sought, with the low overhangs riding just barely overhead, until at last one mounts through the caverns, around the fire, to the lifting flight of the upper floor as it rises from the ground. Heavy as earth, but opening out into hovering planes and rising: the analogies with Cézanne and with Cubism have been made many times before. Wright's work was indeed America's contribution to that image of the world in flux which was the nineteenth century's major artistic legacy to the twentieth.

Wright himself fled his suburban milieu at exactly that moment. He was never to find it again. From that time forward, he was in fact a voyager in time and space: first in Europe, where his work had its most important publications in 1910 and 1911; then on his farm in Wisconsin *(Fig. 237)*, where he dug for his ancestral roots (matrilocal, like an Indian's); and finally when, in 1914, that dream blew up for him in blood and fire, in Japan, and, most of all, in pre-Columbian America.

The date of 1914 marks a decisive break in Wright's career; his work after 1914 properly belongs to a

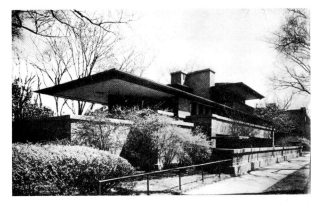

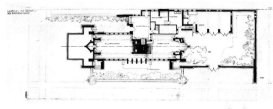

235. Chicago, Illinois. Robie House. 1909. Frank Lloyd Wright.

236. Robie House. Plan.

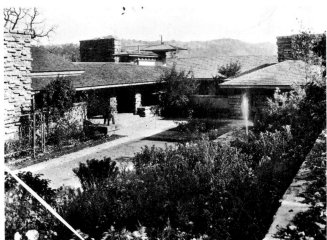

237. Spring Green, Wisconsin. Taliesin I. 1911–14. Frank Lloyd Wright. Burned in 1914, since twice rebuilt. Roofs and court.

125

different age, which he himself had done something to form but into which he was to grow only with the utmost agony of soul. After 1917, it was a new age for all America. Wright's many followers and associates in Chicago could not function in it, and they withered more or less rapidly on the vine. Indeed, now that a good deal of research has been done on the other members of the Prairie School—such as Marion Mahoney, Walter Burley Griffin, Purcell and Elmslie, Hermann von Holst, George Maher, and so on—it is important to note that while Wright may have been indebted to some of them for help in drafting and in other ways, so far as we can tell all the significant ideas were his, the innovations were his own, the development of their common style was wholly dependent upon him. The others tended to be eclectic upon his work; they were not driven, as he was, to invent and, most of all, to integrate. Instead,

they chose and combined. The Bradley House, at Woods Hole, by Purcell and Elmslie, is one of the most beautifully sited houses in America, skimming out toward Martha's Vineyard like a low-flying plane *(Fig. 238)*. It is a combination of several earlier buildings by Wright—Winslow House, River Forest Golf Club, Robie House—but it is shingled, and the box is closed at the corners despite the deep overhangs. Or take a bank by Purcell, Feick and Elmslie, the Merchants' National Bank at Winona, Minnesota *(Fig. 239)*. Here the large and small piers and the deep attic are picturesque adjustments after Wright's rigorously descriptive system in the Larkin Building *(Fig. 229)*. Indeed, the bank as a block enlivened by piers with stained glass between them is a *parti* which also goes back to Wright, to his project for a village bank, in concrete, of 1901 *(Fig. 240)*. Here there may even be evidence of influence from Frank

238. Woods Hole, Massachusetts. Bradley House. 1912. Purcell and Elmslie.

239. Winona, Minnesota. Merchants' National Bank. 1910. Purcell, Feick and Elmslie.

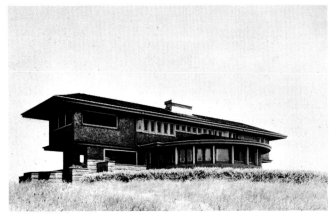

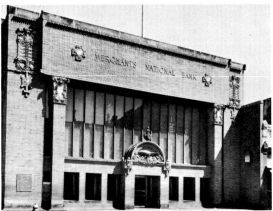

240. Project for a village bank. 1901. Frank Lloyd Wright.

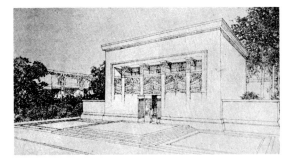

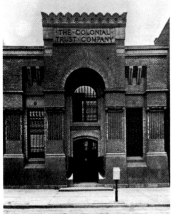

241. Philadelphia, Pennsylvania. The Colonial Trust Company. *Ca.* 1892. Frank Furness (?).

Furness, if the Colonial Trust Company in Philadelphia, of *ca.* 1892, can be attributed to that architect *(Fig. 241).* The high, sloping lintels between the engaged piers, common to both buildings, were often to be found in Furness' design, but otherwise almost never in Wright's.

But in approaching the small-town, Middle Western bank, we come to a critical area, where the last works of Louis Sullivan are involved. The most famous of such banks are his, and Purcell and Elmslie regarded themselves much more as his followers than as Wright's. Elmslie was still with Sullivan when, in the decadence of his fortune, but not of his talent, he designed the National Farmers' Bank, at Owatonna, Minnesota, in 1907–8 *(Figs. 242, 243).* A recent study has even assigned Elmslie the major credit for its design. If so, Elmslie himself was never so skillful again, and needed Sullivan with him. Contrast should be made with Elmslie's own bank at Winona mentioned above *(Fig. 239).* Whereas the bank at Owatonna has an unbroken ground-story base that defines street scale and controls the vehicles parked before it, the other has none, so that its integrity as a shape is constantly being compromised. Similarly, the bank at Owatonna has two clearly defined scales. That of the first level and of the office wing generally repeats the scale of the other buildings on the street. That of the banking room *(Fig. 244),* made generous in the single sweeping shape of its vast arch, is set firmly on the lower level and lifts to monumental proportions inside and out. The building both respects Main Street and ennobles it. Its urban lessons therein were to be pointed out by Robert Venturi in the 1960's and were significantly to affect Venturi's design. Again, in the cornice at Owatonna we are reminded of

242. Owatonna, Minnesota. National Farmers' Bank. 1907–8. Louis Sullivan.

243. National Farmers' Bank. View showing office wing.

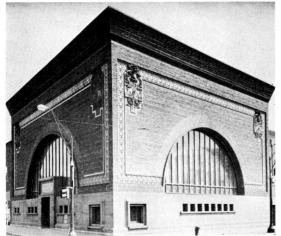

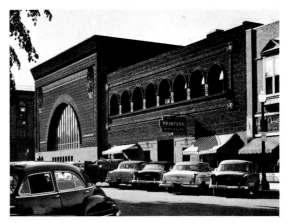

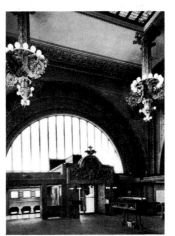

244. National Farmers' Bank. Interior.

127

Wright's bank, but Sullivan's large conception is obviously his own. He understands and manipulates the street, as in these instances neither Wright nor Purcell and Elmslie seem to do. So at Mason City, whose hotel was to exert a direct influence on Walter Gropius in 1914, Wright's bank is uncertainly scaled and feebly sited *(Fig. 245)*. But Sullivan is strong in both these ways in all the small-town banks he built during his final decade. Grinnell again uses two scales: the base with small windows, the big burst of form higher up *(Fig. 246)*. And these, along with the great piered side window (again, Wright), are exact descriptions of the interior functions as well: the offices at low window height, the precious vault, the vast room. Down the street at Grinnell there is a good, more or less contemporary Beaux-Arts bank in temple form with columns in antis. We may sub-

stitute for it here a far finer bank in New Haven, a nice building but faulty in its place *(Fig. 247)*, even more than Purcell and Elmslie's was faulty at Winona: no solid base; mass cut off and compromised by traffic; no small, everyday scale whatever to make the big assertion palpable; no connection between outside and interior functions. It is awkward on the street, says nothing about its inside; Sullivan's bank swells with a good small-town banker's pride, dominating the traffic. So do those at Cedar Rapids, Iowa, Columbus, Wisconsin, and elsewhere. That at Columbus exploits a beautiful site. It is a clanked-down jewel casket on its shopping street and a rich, deep wall along the gentle, parklike avenue at the side *(Fig. 248)*. But behind it—as at Cedar Rapids but not, thankfully, at Grinnell—the owners have torn the fabric of the town apart in order to

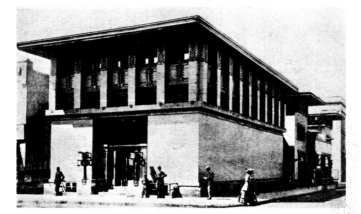

245. Mason City, Iowa. City National Bank. 1909. Frank Lloyd Wright.

246. Grinnell, Iowa. Merchants' National Bank. 1914. Louis Sullivan.

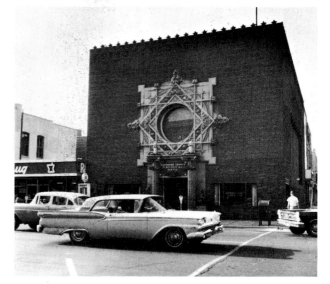

128

accommodate an outdoor teller's cage and a huge parking lot. Except where rigorously controlled by local opinion, banks were doing exactly that to towns and cities everywhere during the second half of the twentieth century. Not content with their suburban branches, they have been suburbanizing the center of town to trap the automobile trade where it should not be unduly encouraged to be.

Sullivan's banks were uniquely solid and permanent. The best of Main Street, perhaps what it would have liked to be, was interpreted and monumentalized by them. In contrast to most of the design of the Beaux-Arts, with which we will be concerned in a moment, they were local architecture, suggested by local conditions and adapted to them. The Beaux-Arts, on the other hand, like the so-called International Style of the next generation, was in

truth internationally based, and its forms employed ideal models of total order, which, like the Ionic bank in New Haven, often (though not always) resisted adaptation to local realities. Insistence upon another ideal model, that of the International Style, was to sack and denature scores of city centers later in the century. Sullivan's urbanism exploited the particular and respected, even loved, existing conditions. That lesson, too, was to be absorbed and used later by Venturi and others in the urban counterattack of the 1960's.

Sullivan, though nourished in a place and producing some of the last monuments which embodied its own Middle Western flavor, was still in no sense a "provincial" architect, especially as the word has been used earlier here. It can be better applied, perhaps, to his distinguished contemporaries in south-

247. New Haven, Connecticut. Connecticut Savings Bank. 1904–6. Egerton Swartwout.

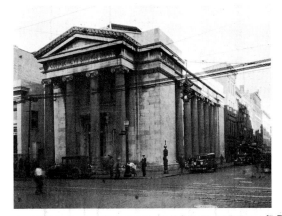

248. Columbus, Wisconsin. Farmers' and Merchants' Union Bank. 1919. Louis Sullivan.

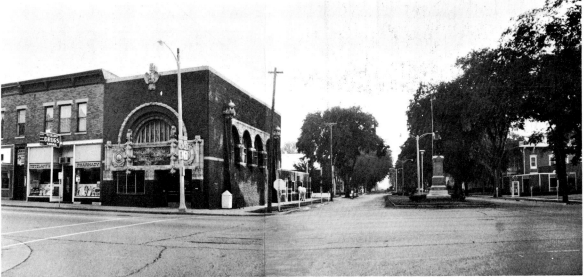

ern California, the brothers Greene. They, too, built in response to local traditions just before Beaux-Arts internationalism submerged them. But they were bound to a certain technique, as Sullivan was not, and produced forms deriving almost exclusively from their materials rather than from more complex humanistic or urban considerations. Their work was pure neo-Stick Style in suburban houses, exploiting and developing local timber techniques and more than touched by those of the Orient. Their plans were loose, sensitive, and unemphatic; everything went into the beautifully detailed skeleton structure, pegged and burnished *(Figs. 249, 250).* In large houses, such as the Blacker or Gamble, it was a luxurious super-Stick Style, but it also furnished the major inspiration for the California bungalows

which proliferated throughout the country during the first two decades of the century. These were popularized by Gustav Stickley as "Craftsman Homes." Rustic and self-conscious, they represented the final phase of the nineteenth-century American development of suburban houses and wood construction. But they, like the work of the Greenes which inspired them, were to act as a link between the early days of that development in the 1840's and its revival in California during the middle decades of the twentieth century by such architects as Harwell Harris (whose wife studied the work of Greene and Greene), William Wurster, Joseph Esherick, and, finally, though sharpened from additional sources, Charles Moore and others *(Figs. 379, 488).*

One is less satisfied to label Irving Gill a provincial

249. Pasadena, California. David B. Gamble House. 1908. Charles and Henry Greene.

250. Gamble House. Living room.

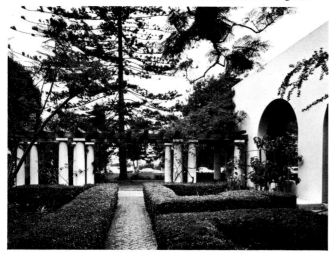

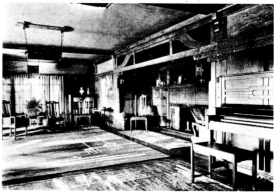

251. La Jolla, California. Women's Club. 1913. Irving Gill.

252. Women's Club. Plan.

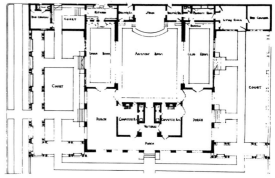

architect in the same way. Like Greene and Greene, Gill was limited to one technique; but his method did not involve a baroque elaboration of earlier techniques, rather a kind of primitively direct investigation of new ones. His material was cast concrete; he adapted tilt-slab methods from army engineers. His buildings were a direct expression of concrete cast in planes for walls, in cylinders for columns. His windows were metal frames, simply detailed. His spaces, as in the Women's Club for La Jolla *(Figs. 251, 252)*, or the Dodge House *(Fig. 253)*, were such as most directly derived from those structural elements. Gill was not spatially inventive otherwise. Yet he conceived of exterior spaces as well as of interiors, and he formed terraces with planar setbacks and ranges of columns marching across his lawns

(Figs. 251–53). Most touching of all Gill's projects, and one that has, like the others, been movingly described by Esther McCoy, is the low-cost housing development at Sierra Madre *(Figs. 254, 255)*. Here the general urbanistic relevance of Gill's simple architecture and humane site-planning is clearest. It reflected a burning social conscience on his part—in which he was fairly unique among American architects at that or any other period. McCoy describes his helpless fury when the entrepreneur took advantage of the success of the group at Sierra Madre to raise its rent out of the low-income category.

As Gill's buildings are appropriate to their place, they strongly recall the Spanish colonial architecture of the region, and consciously did so, but their industrialized technique made the old forms tauter,

253. Los Angeles, California. Dodge House. 1916. Irving Gill.

254. Sierra Madre, California. Lewis Courts. 1910. Irving Gill.

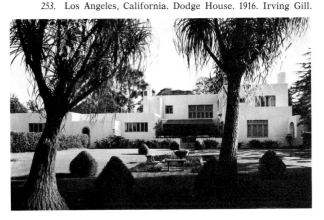

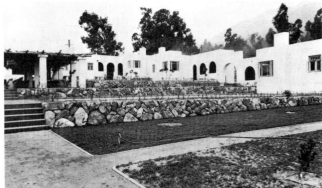

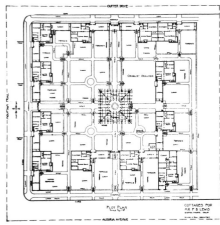

255. Lewis Courts. Plan.

131

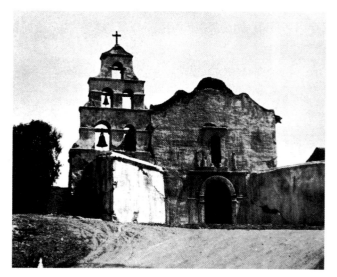

256. San Diego, California. San Diego de Alcalá Mission. 1769. Restored by J. Marshall Miller.

thinner, and more abstract. We should note here San Diego de Alcalá *(Fig. 256)* and Gill's Christian Science Church at San Diego *(Fig. 257)*. It is the American pattern mentioned before: even the change of religion further denies the flesh. Appropriate, then, that Gill's Wilson Acton Hotel at La Jolla *(Fig. 258)* should so closely resemble the garden façade of the Steiner House in Vienna, of 1910 *(Fig. 259)*, by Adolf Loos, whose hysterical polemic against ornament, imputing sexual perversion to those who employed it, had appeared in 1908. The visual relation of Gill's buildings to early puristic modern architecture, the forerunner of the International Style, seems very close indeed. It is more than a fortuitous relationship, because Gill apparently knew and passionately admired Loos's writings and his earlier works. Yet one cannot help feeling that Gill's deepest attitude was really technologically direct, not psychologically or philosophically purist. He was a straight builder, however much he might have wanted to be a poet or a polemicist; his flat, rendered wall planes are in fact concrete, not rubble stuccoed over, as in the European examples. Obvious comparison between his forms and those of Loos, or, later, Le Corbusier,

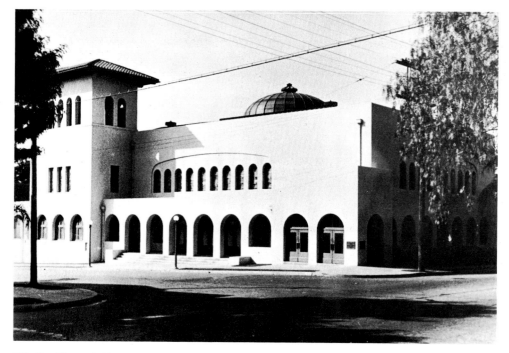

132

257. San Diego, California. Christian Science Church. 1909. Irving Gill.

should not be carried too far in iconological terms. Gill was, in architecture, a plain man, with the limitations as well as the strength of that condition. There was no emotional depth to his buildings, nor any irony. But in their own way they were profoundly integrated, like Wright's and generally unlike those of the Europeans, and they show us the American pattern of formal simplification and probity in one of its most sympathetic guises. So their relation to the Spanish colonial past was infinitely more integral than that of the work of Bertram Goodhue, whose eclectically picturesque Spanish colonial style, introduced by him at the San Diego Exposition of 1915, was to overwhelm Gill's work and, in the general triumph of the Beaux-Arts, to finish Gill as an architect, as it also finished Greene and Greene. Yet Goodhue's town of Tyrone, New Mexico, now ruthlessly bulldozed out, was a fine achievement *(Figs. 328, 329)*. It showed that, in the traditional sense at any rate, the Beaux-Arts architects knew what to do with urbanistic groupings.

The production of Bernard Maybeck, in San Francisco, also began to dwindle away by the 1920's, but Maybeck should by no means be bracketed with the

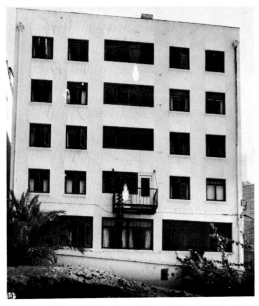

258. La Jolla, California.   Wilson Acton Hotel.   1908. Irving Gill.

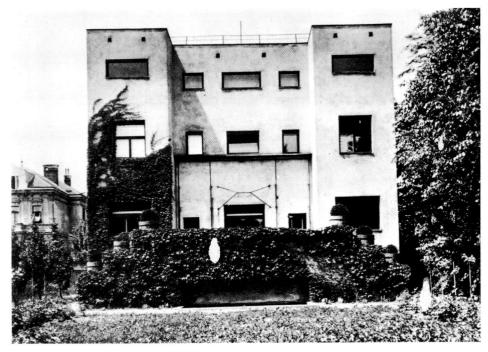

259. Vienna. Steiner House. 1910. Adolf Loos.

133

southern Californians. He was, first of all, himself a supremely Beaux-Arts designer and was trained in Paris. Beyond all else, he was an expressionist architect, of which there have been few in America, where folly and fantasy have rarely been encouraged. Perhaps Furness was one—he, too, Beaux-Arts trained, even if at secondhand. Earlier I compared Furness to Gaudí and noted their common debt to Viollet-le-Duc. That relationship to each other and to the same French Gothic Revival source also operates in the case of Gaudí and Maybeck, who were contemporaries. Maybeck's Hearst Hall for Berkeley (Fig. 260) is structurally expressionistic, calling to mind both the obliquely continuous structures of Gaudí and the German Expressionist forms of the late

teens. So Maybeck's Christian Science Church in Berkeley (Fig. 261) is fluid with energies running through it, the Gothic tracery squirming snakelike in continuous curves which, like Sullivan's ironwork, suggest in detail those of the contemporary European Art Nouveau, or the lava-like flow of Gaudí's neo-Gothic forms.

Thus Maybeck, unlike Gill or Greene and Greene, is formalistically flexible, eclectic, and emotionally varied in his design. He was surely consciously so. His pool for the Memorial Gymnasium at Berkeley, of 1925, for example, seems directly derived from Ryder's "The Temple of the Mind," and intended, from curved cornice to figured sarcophagus, to evoke the same melancholy mood (Figs. 262, 263).

260. Berkeley, California. University of California. Hearst Hall. 1899. Bernard Maybeck. Interior.

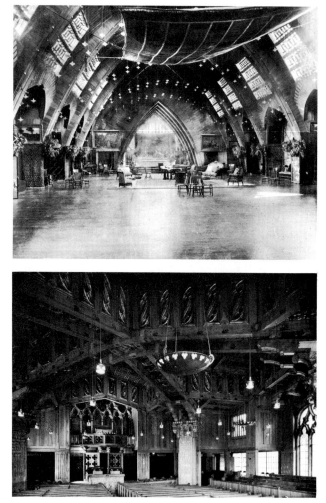

261. Berkeley, California. Christian Science Church. 1910. Bernard Maybeck. Interior.

134

In much the same vein, but at grandiose scale, Maybeck's Palace of the Fine Arts at San Francisco, built for the Fair of 1915, evokes lost baroque grandeurs as in a dream. Vanbrughian or Piranesian in scale, the paired columns lift their great blocks on luxuriant capitals, while a continuous entablature, with dentils like gigantic ratchets, slides through between them *(Fig. 264)*. The colonnade unrolls terrifically around its sculpturally swelling, empty rotunda. It all floats on the water, Jefferson's images adrift on the Pacific at last.

None of the other Beaux-Arts architects of the early twentieth century could equal Maybeck as expressive artists. Yet they were highly competent architects, better trained in many ways than those

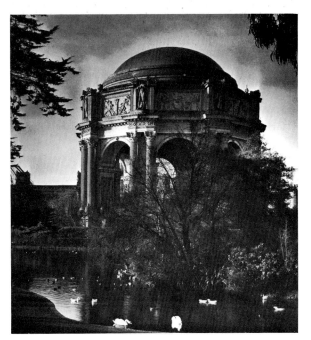

264. San Francisco, California. Panama Pacific Exhibition. Palace of the Fine Arts. 1915. Bernard Maybeck.

262. Berkeley, California. University of California. Hearst Memorial Gymnasium for Women. 1927. Bernard Maybeck.

263. Albert P. Ryder: *The Temple of the Mind.* Before 1888.

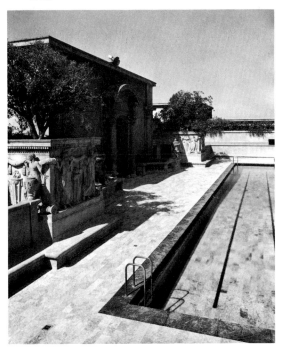

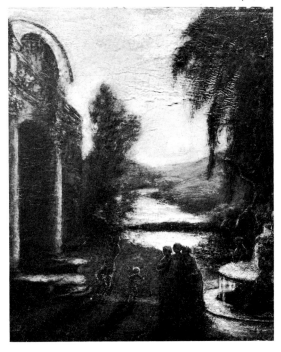

135

of any earlier generation and, in some ways, than those of this. They were the product of a French educational system in the arts which was fundamentally baroque in character and through which the solid virtues of the French academic tradition survived into the modern period. Hence, the Beaux-Arts did not believe in complete originality for individuals—since that idea was born of romanticism —but in the individual manipulation of forms within a common formal vocabulary, which had been the Renaissance way and which, in one sense or another, must usually be the way with architecture and always the way with schools. The French school had served America well. Hunt had trained there, and through him Furness; Richardson had learned his trade solidly in Paris, and Sullivan, hating everything but his mathematics during a year there, had come away nevertheless with a firm vision of formal order. It was that order—order and tradition—which the school offered to American architects just as the country entered its international, even imperial, phase. They began to attend it in increasing numbers toward the close of the century, and schools in its image, and often affiliated with it, multiplied in America. Once again, the Americans pictorialized and eclecticized the European forms, loosened their rationale, and mixed up their programs. So the American Beaux-Arts became much less systematic

265. Boston, Massachusetts. Public Library. 1888–92. McKim, Mead and White.

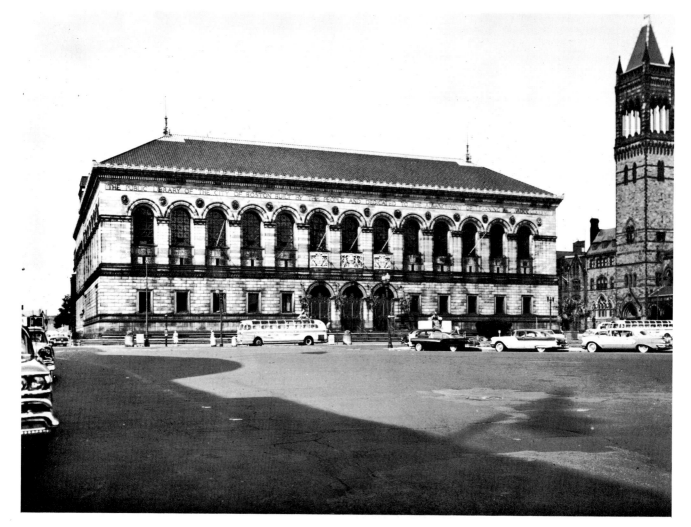

than the French, less intellectually rigorous, and more superficially tasteful. We have also noted a general movement toward order in American architecture as a whole around 1885, and have already mentioned the H. A. C. Taylor House of 1885–86 *(Figs. 217, 218)*, where McKim, Mead and White had found a sanction for order in semi-Palladian, late colonial, Adamesque forms. These remained the commonest vernacular in domestic architecture at various levels of elaboration or impoverishment right through the middle of the twentieth century. In that sense, the developed colonial house has been in almost continuous existence in the United States, with an interruption of hardly more than two generations, in some places none at all. In the Villard House, of 1883, McKim, Mead and White had already chosen more severe High Renaissance details for a midtown palazzo, excellent urban architecture, a dark and solid block. The same is true of the Boston Public Library, constructed of the light-colored stone which most Beaux-Arts design in classicizing forms was henceforward to favor *(Fig. 265)*. Roman though it seems, its Beaux-Arts rationale of wall, base, pier, and screen was the same old *neo-grec* which Furness had employed in his Academy; and it was fairly closely based upon a distinguished mid-century French prototype, the Bibliothèque Ste. Geneviève by Henri Labrouste *(Fig. 266)*.

266. Paris. Bibliothèque Ste. Geneviève. 1843–50. Henri Labrouste.

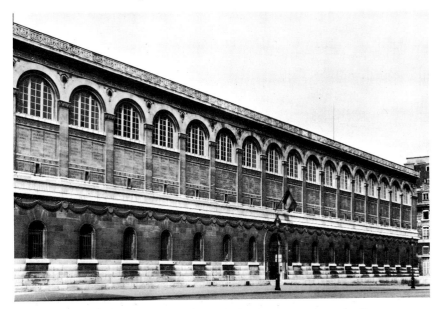

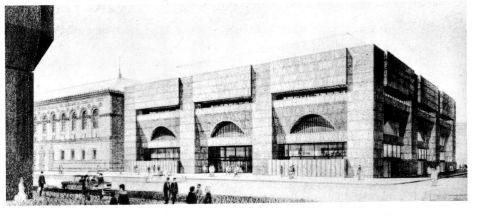

267. Proposed addition to Boston Public Library. 1967. Philip Johnson. Perspective drawing of revised project.

Order thus turned academic at the end of the century. But this again is not to be wondered at. The only model for complete, or almost complete, urbanistic form which existed was the baroque one. It must be remembered that neither the architects of the Shingle Style nor Sullivan nor, later, Wright really had any new vision of general urbanism to challenge it with. When Walter Burley Griffin of the Prairie School architects won the competition for Canberra, the capital city of Australia, he did so with a fundamentally Beaux-Arts plan. Or when Ebenezer Howard proposed his Garden City in 1898, his explanatory diagram looked much like a Beaux-Arts plan itself *(Fig. 326)*. It is therefore no wonder that the Chicago World's Fair, of 1893, was unified according to Beaux-Arts principles as a cross-axial, neo-baroque spatial composition in pictorially classicizing forms *(Fig. 268)*. It was an attempt to create once again an environment entire, like a Baroque environment, with sculpture set in it as an embodi-

ment of action in a theatrical play with the architectural setting. It was the American picturesque stageset to the life. Small wonder, since the Baroque theater may be said to have long since burned down, that the action of much of the sculpture was weak to the point of absurdity. Nor, since the nineteenth century lacked belief in the iconic physicality of sculpture, was it really there at all, except as a pictorial part of its setting. The act, already theater in the Baroque, now melted entirely into its environment—a very nineteenth-century phenomenon, and one found equally well in the work of Wright where the interwoven environment dominates all. Sculpture itself had therefore become wholly pictorialized and could find its special way again only by beginning all over as the ruthlessly physical embodiment of isolated beings, existing apart from environmental sanctions. That did not occur in America, where physicality was not valued in any event, but in Europe, with Maillol and Brancusi. (A few American Beaux-

268. Chicago, Illinois. World's Columbian Exposition. 1893. Grand Basin and Court of Honor.

269. Boston, Massachusetts. Boston Common. Augustus Saint-Gaudens: *Memorial to Robert Gould Shaw.* 1884–97.

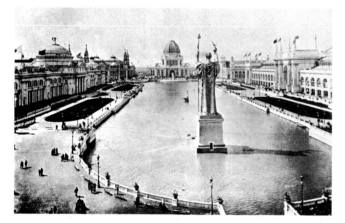

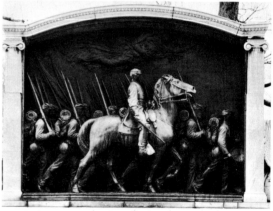

272. Washington, D.C. Folger Shakespeare Library. 1929–32. Paul Cret.

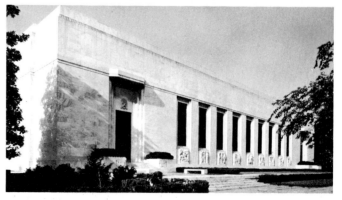

138

Arts embodiments of moral energy come to mind: Augustus Saint-Gaudens' Colonel Shaw and his Negro infantry in Boston *(Fig. 269)*, and his electric Sherman in New York: American heroes, migrained men.) Consequently, the insistence of the Beaux-Arts upon integrating academic sculpture with architecture, while admirable if rather simple-minded as an intention, and productive of some welcome, delicately conceived, and pictorial groups, nevertheless failed to revive sculpture itself in any significant sense and tended to cast a rather trivial pose across some otherwise highly effective buildings. And, as so artificially conceived, architecture and sculpture together were fighting a losing battle with aridity. A quick series can show the progression. The peristylar arch at Chicago is fairly sculptural itself, and its associated sculpture, while unbearably imperialistic in theme (the Indians take the places of conquered barbarians on Roman arches), works in fairly good scale with it *(Fig. 270)*. The corresponding arch at

San Francisco was already dried up, mass feeble, details out of scale, sculpture dwindling. We should note that Maybeck at that period could still carry all this off *(Fig. 264)*, but tended, wisely at the moment, to keep the figural sculpture in relief so that, as in his evocation of Ryder, he could convincingly achieve a fundamentally pictorial effect *(Fig. 262)*.

The entrances at Bertram Goodhue's Nebraska State Capitol, of 1916–28, a sort of modernistic Beaux-Arts, show the sculpture hideously growing out of the architecture or disappearing into it *(Fig. 271)*, brutal images of impotence and pretension which culminate in, at the worst, a deathly purity and the total lack of sculptural force, as in Nazi architecture, or, more generally, in the flattened, sterilized, and abstracted forms which marked, appropriately enough, the last phase of the Beaux-Arts in America, and which made a kind of bridge to the totalitarian forms of the 1930's in Europe *(Fig. 272)*.[5]

270. Chicago, Illinois. World's Columbian Exposition. 1893. Triumphal Arch. McKim, Mead and White.

271. Lincoln, Nebraska. State Capitol. 1916–28. Bertram G. Goodhue.

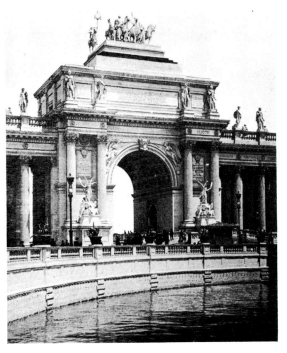

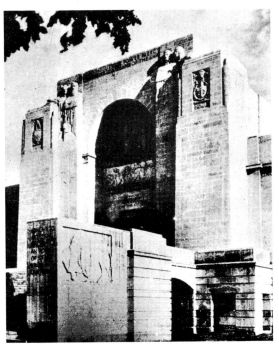

The Beaux-Arts environment and the kinds of acts it encouraged were already somewhat devitalized in the late nineteenth century. Old forms had to be stretched in it, like the proposed Civic Center in Daniel H. Burnham's projected plan for Chicago of 1909, where a dome on a drum had to be attenuated to skyscraper proportions in order to control a vast desert of central square *(Figs. 273, 274)*. Off it, the long radial avenues of the baroque system were to run. They were not in fact constructed in Chicago, but one of them, Benjamin Franklin Parkway, was cut diagonally through Philadelphia's grid at this period, running out to Fairmount Park *(Fig. 42)*. Venturi was later to propose a grand and ominously sculptural fountain here *(Fig. 483)*.

Burnham's plan for San Francisco was as ambitious as that for Chicago. Twin peaks were to have been exploited at the end of the main axis there, with a mighty image of a civic Athena, scaled like the Athens Promachos, standing below them and facing out to sea *(Figs. 275–77)*. It seems clear that

Burnham and his planners knew Athens itself, whose axis through the Acropolis from Salamis to the horns of Hymettos he all but reproduced here. But the Lincoln Memorial in Washington was the closest the Beaux-Arts came to producing a Parthenon, and, as we have already seen, that wholly austere building was closely related to the forms of Ledoux, and to their Russian derivatives as well *(Figs. 96, 98, 128–30)*. The extended Mall in Washington was, on the whole, the finest achievement of Beaux-Arts urbanism. The grandiose axis was everything; slums proliferated behind its façade. The method was a partial and self-satisfied one, seeking monumental grandeur and kicking the poor out of the way. It differed only in its lack of hypocrisy from most later redevelopment practice in the middle of the century.[6]

The Beaux-Arts also tended to build better monuments and urban spaces than the later period, at least in America, has yet been able to do. One should contrast, say, the New York Public Library and its

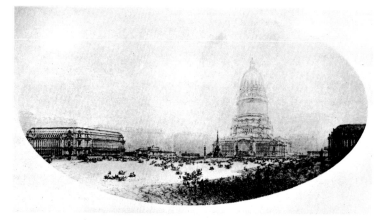

273. Plan for Chicago, Illinois. 1909. Daniel H. Burnham. Perspective view of proposed Civic Center, with central dome.

274. Plan for Chicago. View toward west, showing proposed Civic Center, the grand axis, and the Harbor.

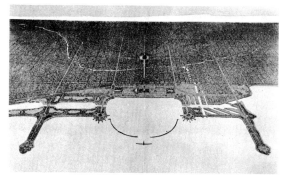

140

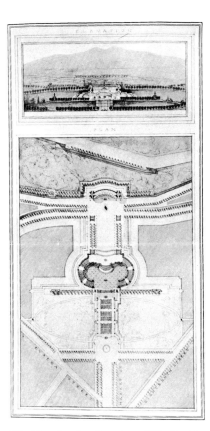

276. Plan for San Francisco. 1905. Daniel
H. Burnham. Plan and elevation of
main axis.

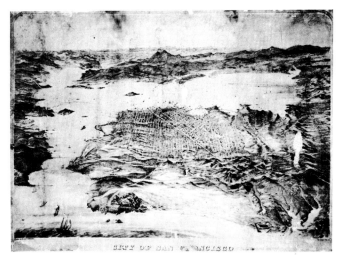

275. San Francisco, California. View in 1896.

277. Plan for San Francisco. Perspective view toward the sea.

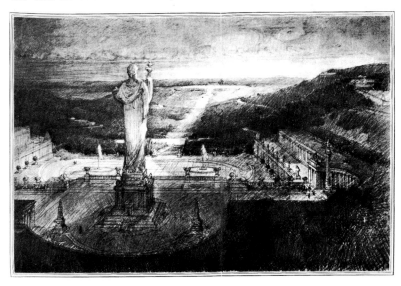

141

gentle park with the shambles around the new City Hall in Boston; or the Plaza Hotel in New York (where Wright always stayed) and the square and fountain before it with the scene as it will be when it is dwarfed by the huge if feeble new office building now rising across the way; or, since it is not merely a question of enlarged scale, old Pennsylvania Station in New York with the shoddy confection for which it was demolished *(Figs. 278–80).* The former was all public grandeur, embodying a quality too rare in America, as we have noted before. A later

generation was to deride its formal dependence upon the Baths of Caracalla. One is less sure than one used to be that such was a very relevant criticism at all. Much more memorable now that it is gone is the rhythmic clarity of the generous big spaces of the station and the majestic firmness with which the great piers and columns and the coffered vault defined them *(Fig. 279).* It was academic building at its best, rational and ordered according to a pattern of use and a blessed sense of civic excess. It seems odd that we could ever have been persuaded that it was

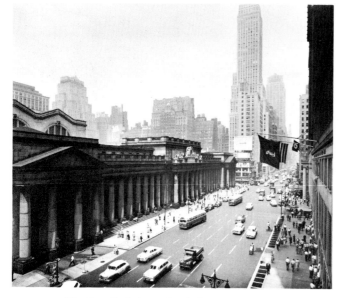

278.   New York. Pennsylvania Station. 1906–10. McKim, Mead and White.

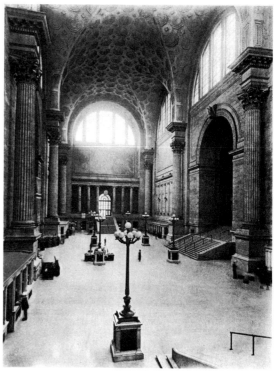

279.   Pennsylvania Station. Main waiting room.

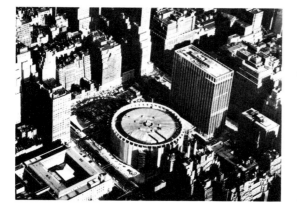

280.   New York. Madison Square Garden Center. 1966–68.

no good and, finally, permitted its destruction. Through it one entered the city like a god. Perhaps it was really too much. One scuttles in now like a rat.

Grand Central Station was an equally grand achievement and, urbanistically, an even more intricate and subtle one. Many levels interweave in it, below ground and above. Traffic is led in fine ramps around it up and down Park Avenue, while the great barrel-vaulted volume of the Grand Concourse glows within *(Figs. 281, 282)*. The slender tower of the

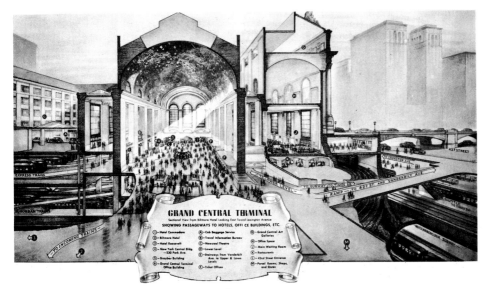

281. New York. Grand Central Station. 1903–13. Reed and Stem; Warren and Wetmore. Sectional view.

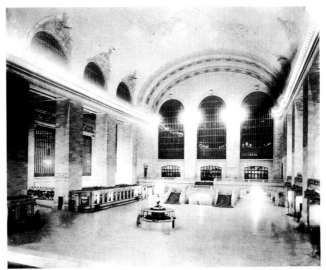

282. Grand Central Station. Grand Concourse.

Grand Central Office Building rose on the axis of the avenue, high enough to draw the space to it, narrow enough to let the eye slide around it on both sides *(Fig. 283)*. The Pan American Building later smothered that movement *(Fig. 284)*. The original buildings along the avenue, like McKim, Mead and White's Racquet Club, for example, defined its flow. The solid planes formed the street with façades designed for that purpose and so in scale with the width of the avenue. The whole was one shape flowing southward, an urbanistic achievement of a kind of design which still valued the street, as, later, the urban theory and practice of the 1950's were not to do.

Even the unique massing of skyscrapers which became the glory of New York, and, indeed, the major symbol of America as a whole, occurred because the street pattern was followed. At the tip of Manhattan that pattern was irregular, so that the towers jostled each other like the competitive crowd they were *(Figs. 285, 287)*. Each stretched for the limelight, and so the whole group tended to build toward one pyramidal mass at the point of the island. Precisely that passionate density made the group splendid, so that later, obsessed schemes to thin it out according to the principles of Le Corbusier could only have destroyed it. Or again, the last thing the narrow streets between the towers needed was to be widened or opened; they were canyons, not salubrious but sublime. By the same token, each building needed its upward-lifting shape, bursting upward in spires like that of Trinity Church below them *(294)*: vertical roads and attenuated mountains together. These qualities gave them their active force, so that later intrusions of inert slabs or boxes, like that of the Chase Manhattan Bank, for example, immeasurably injured the group as a whole *(Fig. 287)*. Now the huge, bland towers of the World Trade Center will wholly destroy the old

283. New York. Park Avenue in the 1930's, with Grand Central Terminal Office Building by Whitney Warren.

284. New York. Park Avenue in the 1960's, with Pan American Building.

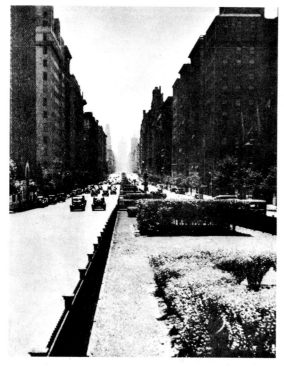

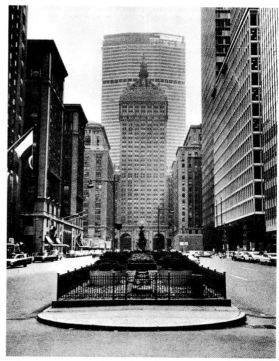

144

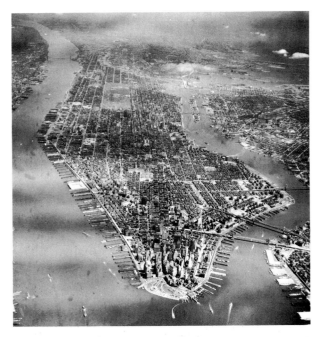

285. New York. Air view in 1953.

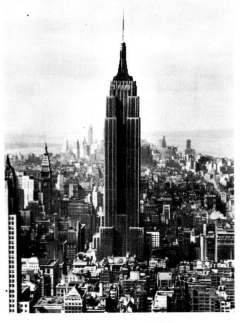

286. New York. Empire State Building. 1931.
Shreve, Lamb and Harmon.

287. Downtown New York. Skyscrapers from the bay.

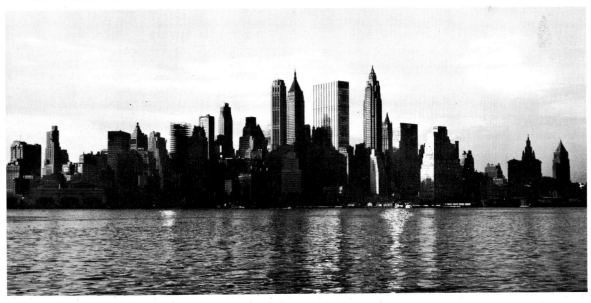

scale, as, for example, Paul Rudolph's proposed megastructure of trailers in towers, building up pyramidally, highly articulated and full of action itself, would not do *(Figs. 298, 299)*.[7]

Indeed, the Beaux-Arts skyscrapers of New York owed little to the square-cut shapes or the principles of Sullivan or, later, to those of the International Style; it is surely in large part for those reasons that they have been so undervalued during the past generation. They were the Beaux-Arts at its best, its most urbane and freest. They began appropriately enough with Hunt, whose Tribune Building of 1873–75 created the type: a tower set on a mass and tending to lift the lower volume with it *(Fig. 288)*. The whole was already rather higher, and looked higher, than most of the skyscrapers of Chicago. Then a Chicago architect appeared, with a semi-Sullivanian interlude. Daniel Burnham's steel-framed Flatiron Building, of 1902 *(Fig. 289)*, is a single volume of base, shaft, and capital; but it is more heavily clad than Sullivan's developed type

and is compressed to a fine edge at its acutely angled corner. Ernest Flagg's Singer Building, of 1908 *(Fig. 290)*, picked up Hunt's type but rose higher and capped its tower with a lush, *fin de siècle*, semimansard semidome. It is just now (1968) being torn down by Inland Steel. Cass Gilbert's Woolworth Building, of 1913 *(Fig. 291)*, continued the type, but now a splendid continuity between mass and tower, sanctified by medieval quotation, was eloquently encouraged. The semi-Gothic piers are as if bound together, and they lift in bundles of force from sidewalk to spire.

But the New York architects never followed a single solution. The skyscrapers that began to hedge in the Woolworth, for example, were all different beings. The group began to take on a fantastic quality; its members stood about and conversed. Others joined them, lifting châteaux, temples, and mausolea into the sky, their tripods smoking among the clouds; a city of genial giants was rising *(Figs. 292, 293)*. It was a world of fantasy at many levels, of the

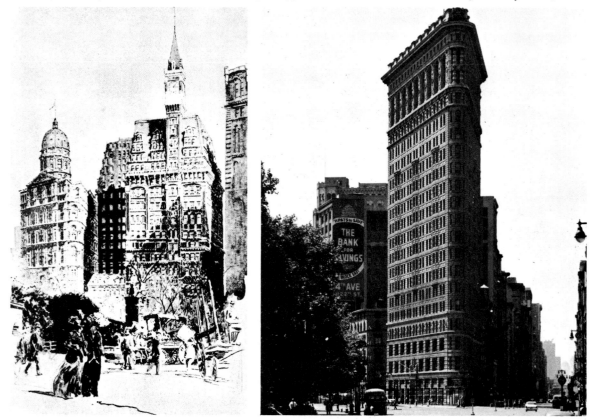

288. New York. Tribune Building. 1873–75. Richard Morris Hunt.

289. New York. Flatiron Building. 1902. Daniel H. Burnham.

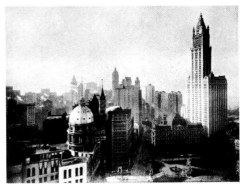

290. New York. Singer Building.
1906–8. Ernest Flagg.

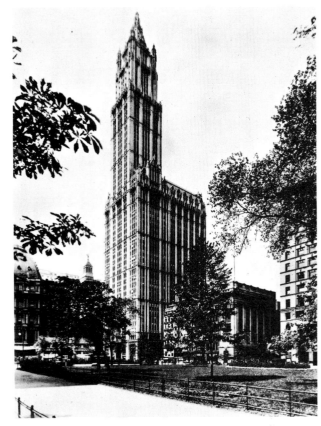

291. New York. Woolworth Building. 1913. Cass Gilbert.

293. Downtown New York in 1914, looking south from the Woolworth Building.

292. Downtown New York in 1914, looking south from the Municipal Building.

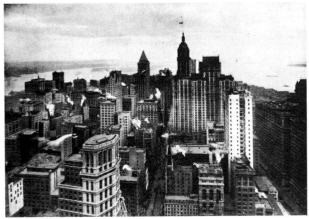

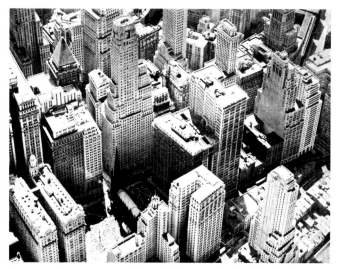

294. New York. Trinity Church. 1839–46. Richard Upjohn.

old world and its spires *(Fig. 294)*, or of the new multilevel city, the proto-Futurist image which was so directly to inspire not only the Italians and Le Corbusier but the Russians after the Revolution as well. So "King's Dream of New York" *(Fig. 295)* is Kharkov in the 1920's *(Fig. 296)*, while the Woolworth and McKim, Mead and White's Municipal Building were apparently to meet Stalin's dream of grandeur and to ring Moscow, echoing the Kremlin's towers with their forms *(Fig. 297)*.

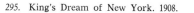

295. King's Dream of New York. 1908.

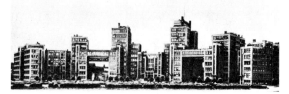

296. Kharkov. Dzerzhinsky Square and House of Industry. 1925–33. S. Serafimov.

297. Moscow. Red Square. Savior Gate of the Kremlin, St. Basil's, and skyscraper.

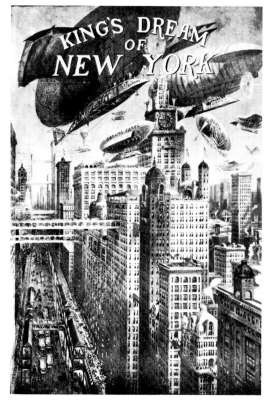

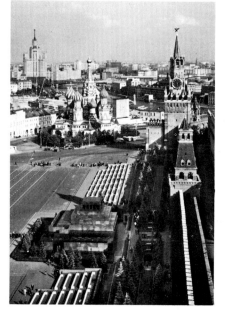

148

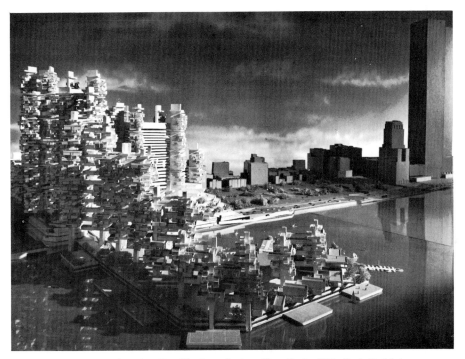

298. Megastructure project for Graphic Arts Center. New York. 1967. Paul Rudolph. View of model from the north, showing skyscrapers, and World Trade Center, by Minoru Yamasaki and Associates.

299. Megastructure project from the north.

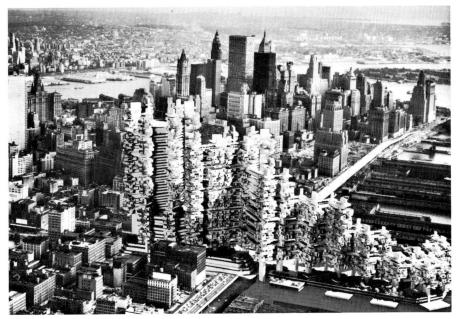

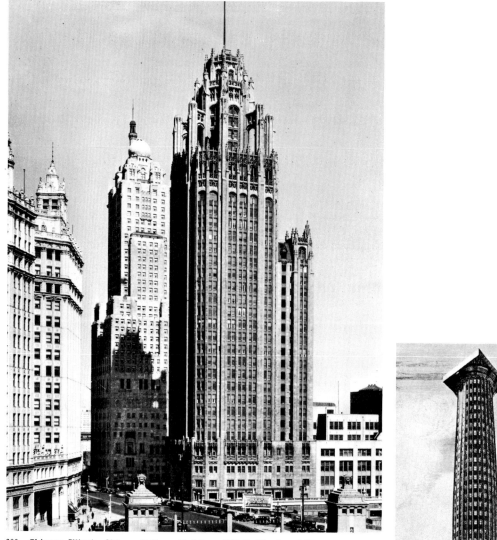

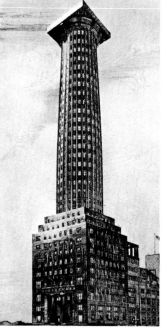

300. Chicago, Illinois. Chicago Tribune Building. 1922–24. Hood and Howells. View looking north on Michigan Avenue.

301. Chicago Tribune Building competition entry. 1922. Adolf Loos.

(*Opposite, left to right*)

302. Chicago Tribune Building competition entry. 1922. Heinrich Mossdor, Hans Hahn, and Bruno Busch.

303. Chicago Tribune Building competition entry. 1922. Walter Gropius and Adolf Meyer.

304. Chicago Tribune Building competition entry. 1922. Knut Lönberg-Holm.

The next major steps in skyscraper design were marked by an event not in New York but in Chicago, the *Tribune* Competition of 1922. The winning design by Hood and Howells was of the New York type, a vertically continuous tower lifting a subsidiary mass with it, but in this case a rather grotesquely buttressed Gothic chapter house overpowered the summit *(Fig. 300)*. Today, many other entries in the competition seem more interesting in one way or another. Adolf Loos demonstrated his contempt for sexual perversion with a Doric column, skyscraper size *(Fig. 301)*. The owner had specified that the building should have symbolic as well as utilitarian value. It is therefore surprising that he did not choose the Indian, with his tomahawk rather paralytically raised *(Fig. 302)*. Walter Gropius and Adolf Meyer gave evidence of direct knowledge of Chicago's good old skyscraper construction with a fine frame structure using Chicago windows *(Fig. 303)*. Their tower's more abstract play of balcony planes, perhaps intended to suggest its movement down Michigan Boulevard, seems related not only to the formal experiments of the Dutch De Stijl group of the teens (itself derived in part from Wright), but also to Russian Constructivism of the immediately post-Revolutionary period. In fact, the design of the building for *Izvestia*, of 1925, by Barkhin, was based directly upon Gropius' project in Chicago. A rather toned-down version was built. Sad that Gropius' entry did not win the prize. Who can say how much trouble might have been averted if *Izvestia* and the *Chicago Tribune* had shared the same design.

The other most advanced project was by Knut Lönberg-Holm *(Fig. 304)*. It too showed a debt to De Stijl. Its major innovation was an attempt to express the difference between the horizontal floor levels and the vertical articulation. As in De Stijl architectural projects generally, concern was primarily for flat wall planes of different colors, not for the structural skeleton—here, therefore, more or less for areas of different uses, not for the structure.

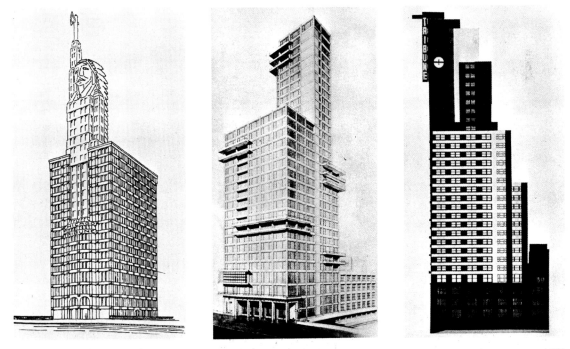

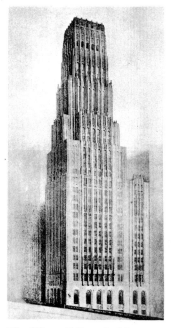

305. Chicago Tribune Building competition entry. 1922. Eliel Saarinen.

The entry of Eliel Saarinen, from Finland, won second prize and was the favorite of most architects and critics *(Fig. 305)*. Sullivan wrote a tribute to it. It was a stepped mountain plastically modeled, but with vertically continuous elements running up through it and receding gently in soaring ranges. It was the tower made mountain, a northern cathedral-image, and it instantly took hold in New York. Hugh Ferriss used it as his model in studying the massing possibilities of the new zoning laws. His stupefying drawings show buildings emerging from mountains, really more Mayan than Gothic in the visual weight of their profiled step-backs *(Figs. 14, 306, 307)*. Ferriss' drawings were a kind of recrudescence of romanticism's "sublime," here in its terminal stages: man small, the environment overwhelming; it was the Grand Canyon, in fact *(Fig. 13)*, now shaping the myths of New York and of the Metropolis of the future no less than those of the Anasazi. Nor can there be any doubt that there was a highly conscious awareness of Mayan architecture at this time. Much had been made of it as early as the Chicago World's Fair, of 1893, and Bruce Price had been directly in-

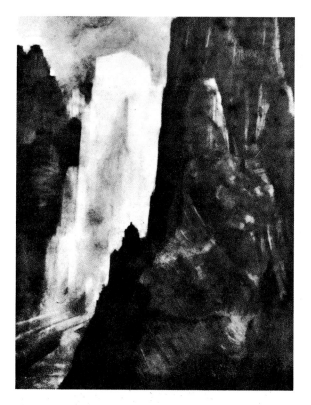

306. Hugh Ferriss: *Buildings like mountains.* 1929.

152

fluenced by it even earlier *(Figs. 316, 317)*. Such knowledge was essential to Wright's work throughout the 1920's; he shared a sympathy for the monumental permanence of Mayan temples with his rivals of the Beaux-Arts. The Barclay-Vesey Building of the later 1920's sums it up: Saarinen, Ferriss, mountain mass, and, edging the surfaces, a kind of flattened jazz-modern decoration which was the latest thing in its period and which had swept the board at the Exposition des Arts Décoratifs in Paris, of 1925 *(Fig. 308)*.

Influence from that source surely played some part in flattening out Raymond Hood's Daily News Building, of 1930 *(Figs. 309, 310)*. Here tower and mountain fused under pressure in a vertically uncompromised but flatly stepped-back slab. Unlike Sullivan's towers, it provides no sense of volume or cage, nor any terminating cornice. All those differences are reasonable enough, since the New York buildings were much larger and higher and would in one sense have dominated all too grossly were they not to dissipate their mass in an uninterrupted, open-ended dispersion of energy upward.

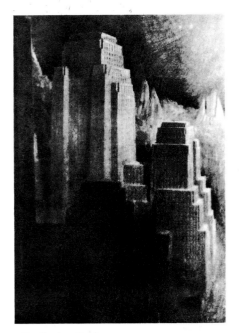

307. Hugh Ferriss: *The four stages.*

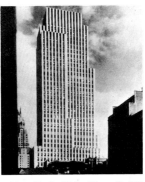

309. New York. Daily News Building. 1930. Raymond Hood.

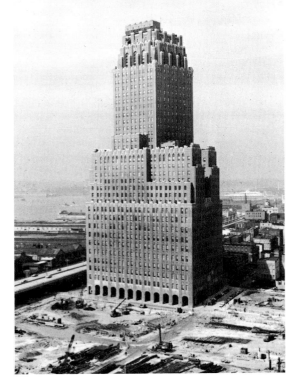

308. New York. Barclay-Vesey Building. 1927. Voorhees and Walker.

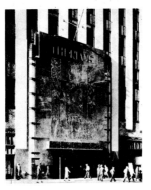

310. Daily News Building. Entrance.

Compressed to slab form, they also became essentially space-definers rather than mid-space elements, and it was as such that they formed what can still properly be called the finest spatial grouping of skyscrapers the world has seen: Rockefeller Center in New York *(Figs. 311, 312)*. In the deserved praise which Rockefeller Center has received, it has all too seldom been pointed out that the arrangement is pure Beaux-Arts, a little stolid perhaps, but axial, focused, and firm, shaping a shopping street with places to sit and a small square in which it is possible to do something or to watch people doing things. The huge vertical slabs dramatize that space and those actions, and the single basic alteration which the architects made in the first design succeeded in bringing them all to life: one slab was turned at right angles to the major axis, and so set the whole group in pinwheeling motion but left the central space axially defined. Rockefeller Center is wholly successful urbanism in its most restricted and easily grasped social and formal terms, those of the group design of mid-city commercial buildings, offices, and shops, with their associated amenities. None of the groups put together in the 1950's and 1960's came close to it. Indeed, the much advertised Penn Center in Philadelphia or, at smaller scale, projects like those for New Haven, or finally, the incoherent spatter of skyscrapers just west of Rockefeller Center itself, all seem to indicate in their various ways that Americans can no longer put the centers of cities together at all but can only destroy them. The new spaces tend to be disintegrated rather than shaped. Perhaps it was in part the Depression which began the process, because Rockefeller Center has integral opulence and solidity, while the new projects, whatever they cost, tend either toward weak aridity or cheaply meretricious gaudiness of form. Mary McCarthy once said that Americans were the world's poor; not true, at the moment, in financial terms, but psychically exact, so that perhaps the liveliest and most intrinsic aspect of the newest centers is their resemblance to penny arcades. But Rockefeller Center is one of the few surviving public spaces in America that look as if they were designed and used by people who knew what stable wealth was and were not ashamed to enjoy it. Flags snap, high heels tap: a little sex and aggression, the city's delights. Jefferson would have hated it all.

The Depression killed off the old skyscrapers and gave the American Beaux-Arts its death blow. The Empire State, a lonely dinosaur, rose sadly at midtown, highest tower, tallest mountain, longest road, King Kong's eyrie, meant to moor airships, alas *(Fig. 286)*. Westward, also alone, squatted the McGraw-Hill Building *(Fig. 313)*, another jazz-modern edifice, proto-jukebox in detail but obviously based upon Lönberg-Holm's differentiation between vertical circulation and horizontal office floors *(Fig. 304)*. Finally, the true last of the old and first of the new, but not a New Yorker, appeared. It was the Philadelphia Savings Fund Society Building *(Fig. 314)*, by the American George Howe, a Beaux-Arts architect consciously turned modern, and William Lescaze, a European semi-International Style designer. PSFS was built during the Depression to take advantage of lowered construction costs. Again, the symbolic articulation of circulation from office levels by cladding and color closely recalled Lönberg-Holm. Howe's first project for the building had been even closer, but the final one, in Lescaze's International Style mode of attenuated planes, still shows the relationship well. The exposure of the structural columns of the office floors was the result of client demand; the architects had hoped to be stylish by covering the columns and floating the floor levels. There can be little doubt that the building has worn better than would have been the case if they had gotten their way. As it stands, it closely prefigures some outstanding buildings of the 1950's and 1960's, like Skidmore, Owings and Merrill's for Inland Steel, or, even more important, the Richards Medical Research Laboratories *(Fig. 451)*, by Louis Kahn, who was Howe's lifelong friend and associate. But to understand the background of post-World War II architecture in America, one must turn back to the development of the International Style during the 1920's and 1930's, and before that to the work of Wright after 1914.[8]

154

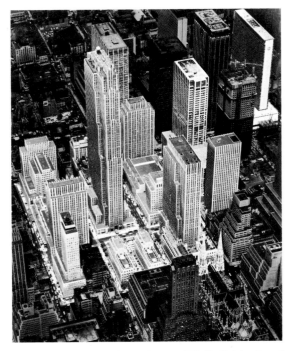

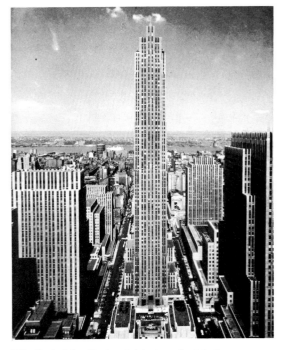

311. New York. Rockefeller Center. 1931–39. Reinhard and Hofmeister; Corbett, Harrison, and MacMurray; Hood and Fouilhoux. View beyond Center, showing skyscrapers built later along Sixth Avenue.

312. Rockefeller Center. Axial view of original group.

313. New York. McGraw-Hill Building. 1931. Raymond Hood.

314. Philadelphia, Pennsylvania. Philadelphia Savings Fund Society. 1932. Howe and Lescaze.

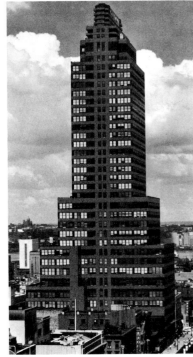

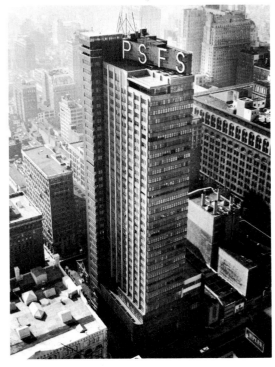

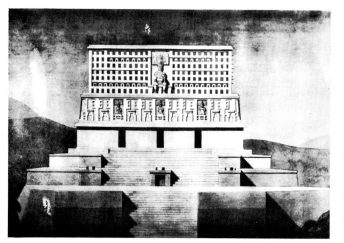

The second half of Wright's career—almost his second life—was remarkable in the depth of its break with the first. True enough, elements in it had been prefigured earlier, and a little of the old hung about for a while, like unfinished business. But on the whole, Wright began afresh, almost as if he possessed or wanted to possess nothing but his vision of perfect space to bring to the new life from the old. His use of Mayan and Mexican forms, for example, while scattered, hard to isolate, and even questionable earlier, instantly became obsessive, as if he were trying to start over with the most monumental and permanent shapes that the continent had produced. His warehouse in Richland Center, of 1915, is the Temple of the Two Lintels at Chichén Itzá with, in effect, only the proportions changed. Even the Imperial Hotel in Tokyo is more Mayan

316. Yaxchilan. Structure 33. Restoration after Bolles.

315. Hollywood, California. Barnsdall House. 1920. Frank Lloyd Wright.

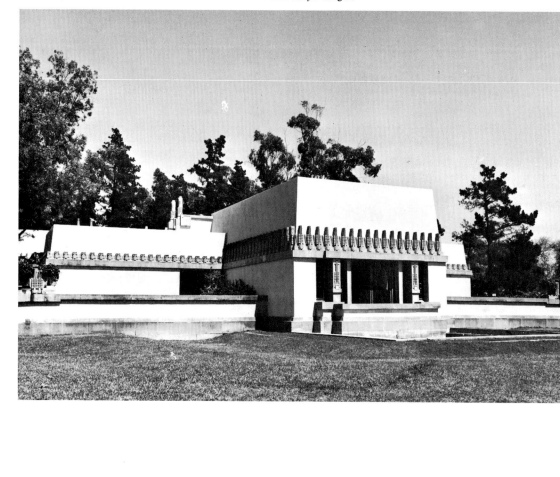

than Japanese in scale, and the Barnsdall House, of 1920, is the plaster model of a Usumacinta temple, squashed down *(Figs. 315, 316)*. One is reminded of Bruce Price, inspired through Pierre Lorillard by the same sources and inspiring Wright at his beginning *(Figs. 219, 221, 317)*. Now, however, it is as if nothing whatever remained of the lively American development in suburban architecture which Wright had culminated, especially nothing of its lift and flight. In a larger sense, we are indeed forced to acknowledge that the more inventive American movement as a whole had spent its energy by 1920. Curiously little was passed on from it which could be of use for the generation immediately following. It seemed an experience terminated once and for all, and one which, in a very American way, left no tradition. It sank without

trace, like the *Pequod* under Ishmael, leaving the American afloat once again on the measureless waters. One has almost the feeling that Wright had quit his suburban milieu in 1909 with the instinct of the experienced sailor who senses the first shudder under his feet. Yet the terror out of nowhere struck him, too, at last, fate completing, as always, choice's work, so that he did not escape without pain and became in truth the only survivor.

So he built temples to the continent based on Indian forms, as if it were the only program of work and source of power left to him. In exactly these years, D. H. Lawrence, on the slopes of the Sangre de Cristo, just above Taos, was calling for something not unrelated to this from American art. The Barnsdall House, and the Nakoma Country Club *(Fig. 318)* and Lake Tahoe projects of the early 1920's show us

317. Tuxedo Park, New York. Lorillard House. 1885–86. Bruce Price.

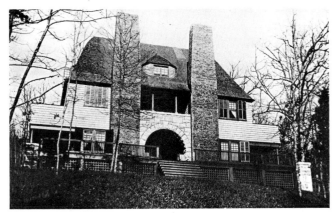

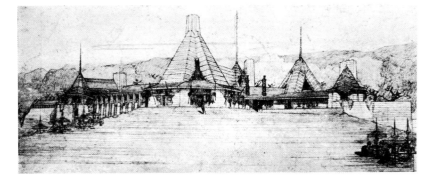

318. Project for Nakoma Country Club. 1924. Frank Lloyd Wright.

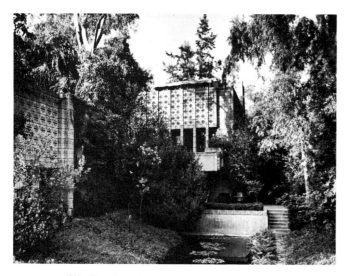

pictorial adaptations of mountain, tepee, and pine. But the Millard, Freeman, Storer, and Ennis houses show us Mayan cut-stone mosaic made structurally integral in precast concrete blocks, threaded on steel rods and packed with poured concrete. Here another source of inspiration may have showed itself, because the first *parti* of the Millard House closely recalls that of Le Corbusier's Citrohan house project published in the same year *(Figs. 319, 320)*. It seems likely that Wright knew of it, especially since he was closely associated at this time with Rudolph Schindler, who had emigrated from Vienna and was directly connected with advanced movements in Europe. One might indeed show a progression of forms leading directly from Schindler to Wright's masterpieces of the 1930's. Schindler's Lovell House, at Newport Beach, California, of 1925–26, is a rein-

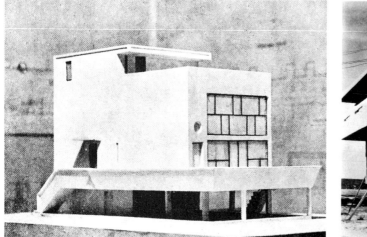

320. Citrohan House. Model with pilotis. Salon d'Automne, Paris, 1922. Le Corbusier.

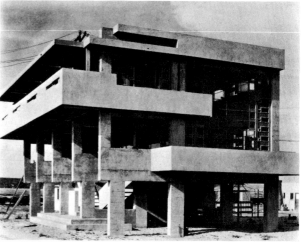

321. Newport Beach, California. Lovell Beach House. 1925–26. Rudolph Schindler.

158

forced concrete structure that lifts its cantilevered second floor for a view of the sea *(Fig. 321)*. Schindler then facilitated the immigration of Richard Neutra, who built a second Lovell House, in 1929, which cantilevered its steel structure and flat planes above a ravine in Los Angeles *(Fig. 322)*. The two together, transformed and integrated by the hand of an absolute master of design, grow splendidly into Wright's concrete and cantilevered Kaufmann House, of 1936 *(Figs. 323, 324)*. Evidence of influence from Mies van der Rohe, in the plan, and from Le Corbusier, in the terrace-envelope, may also be felt there; but the densely pyramidal composition is Mayan, now transformed from solids to sliding voids, from masses to spaces, and made structurally integral to the material as, for example, had not been done in the Barnsdall House *(Figs. 315, 316)*.

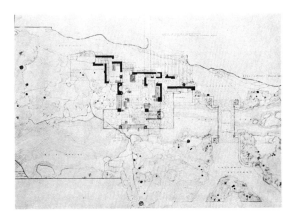

324. Falling Water. Plan.

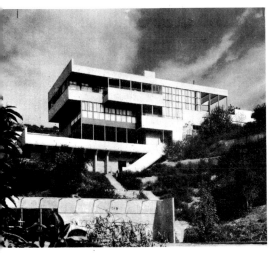

322. Los Angeles, California. Lovell House. 1929. Richard Neutra.

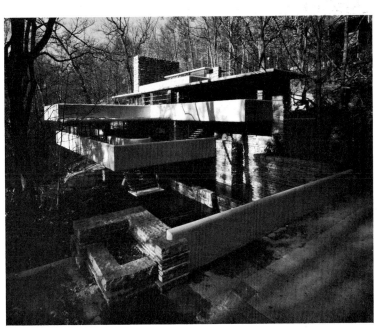

323. Bear Run, Pennsylvania. Falling Water (Kaufmann House). 1936. Frank Lloyd Wright.

159

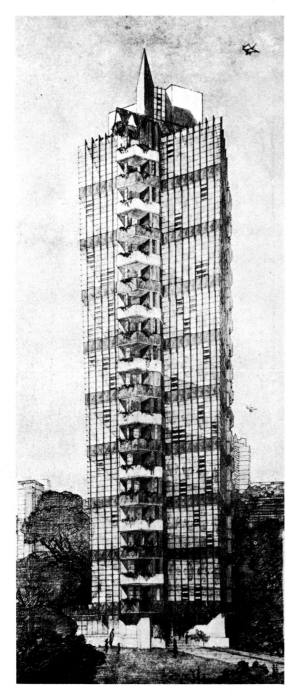

Hence, Indian foundations received European superstructures in Wright's new career. Yet Wright had made, as it were, his own European sources, because the early work of Mies, for example, owed much to him. It was a truly international phenomenon, in which Wright's own influence, reinterpreted by the Europeans, came back fresh to him when he needed it, helping him on to his second great decade, the 1930's just at the moment when totalitarianism was snuffing out creativity in Europe.

That counterplay with Europe in Wright's work is more complicated yet. His insurance company skyscraper project of 1924 recalls Antonio Sant'Elia and Italian Futurism, as some of Le Corbusier's projects of the same years also do, but it is richly Mayan in surface. So is the fine St. Mark's Tower project of 1929 *(Fig. 325)*. There, too, the prismatic surface is supported on horizontal floor slabs cantilevered off vertical fins of bearing wall—all strongly recalling a project by Mies of 1919. The depression of 1929 prevented the building of St. Mark's Tower. It left

325. Project for St. Mark's-in-the-Bouwerie apartment tower, New York. 1929. Frank Lloyd Wright.

Wright wholly without work, and he turned his thoughts, really for the first time, toward the problems of city planning as a whole. The proposal he arrived at, which he called, rather like a real-estate man, Broadacre City, had three important qualities. It was (a) Garden City in theory, but (b) rather Corbusian in practice, and (c) entirely in accord with the way things were going in America anyway.

The Garden City had been proposed in England by Ebenezer Howard, in 1898 *(Fig. 326).* Its satellite towns outside the metropolis were to combine the "Best of Town and Country." They were in reality the suburb rationalized with somewhat denser planning, a town center, and some local industry. The circular town with radiating avenues which Howard published was intended by him only as a diagram, but forms act like forms even if called by other names, and Howard's diagram, so like an ideal Renaissance or Beaux-Arts scheme itself, surely gave Letchworth, of 1903, its underlying formal framework. That diagram has not ceased to function. The

326. Diagram for a Garden City. 1898. Ebenezer Howard.

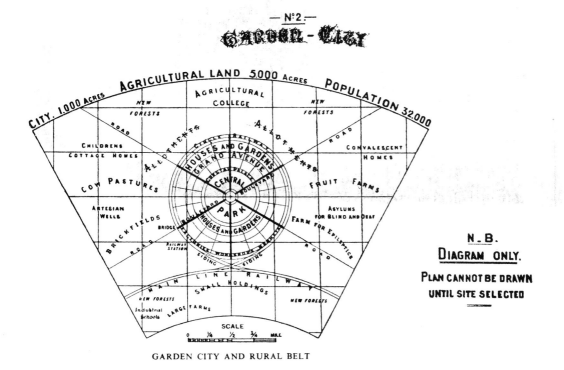

GARDEN CITY AND RURAL BELT

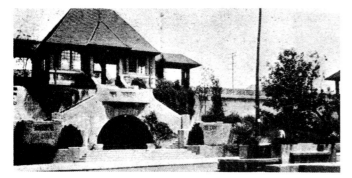

327. Long Island, New York. Forest Hills Gardens. 1910.
Grosvenor Atterbury. Railroad station and underpass.

first publications of Columbia, a Garden City town projected after much sociological research by James Rouse for a site near Washington D.C., shows its impress clearly, from the over-all scheme to the radial center and the curved, glazed shopping street. It and the somewhat more romantically conceived Reston, now in building *(Fig. 520)*, are only the most recent of a long line. At most stages (though not at Reston), the radiating avenues dominated, and Garden City planners, regarding the typical street largely as a source of danger to women with baby carriages (who perennially figured, hard to object

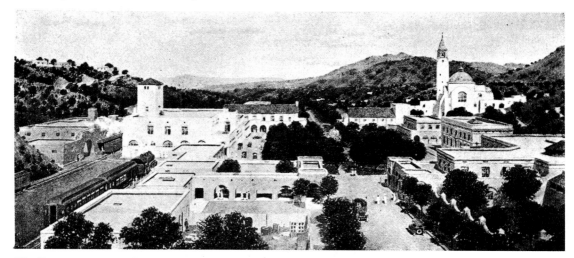

328. Tyrone, New Mexico. Civic Center. 1917. Bertram Goodhue.

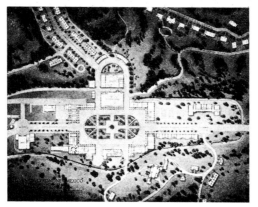

329. Tyrone, New Mexico. Plan.

162

to, in their visual propaganda), eventually used those avenues to mark off the living groups from each other, the housing clusters to be served internally by dead-end lanes if possible. True enough, Grosvenor Atterbury's breath-takingly good Forest Hills Gardens, of 1910 and after *(Fig. 327)*, and Goodhue's Tyrone, of the teens *(Figs. 328, 329)*, had a traditional solidity and a command of relationship and vista worthy of Camillo Sitte. The beautiful Sunnyside Gardens, of 1924–28 *(Figs. 330, 331)*, by Clarence Stein and Henry Wright, developed the superblock with considerable feeling for the street and with

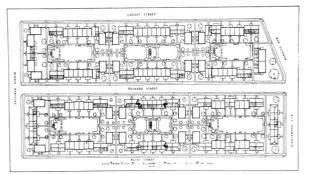

330. Long Island, New York. Sunnyside Gardens. 1924–28. Clarence Stein and Henry Wright. Plan of blocks built in 1926.

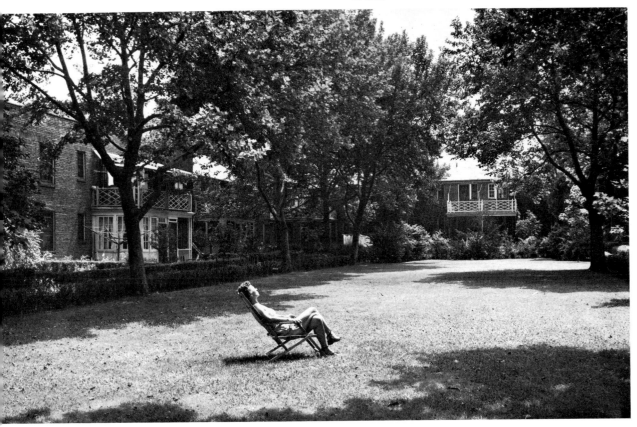

331. Sunnyside Gardens. View of Court built in 1926, photographed in 1949.

firm urban scale. But their famous Radburn, New Jersey, of 1928, was an amoeba-shaped fragment of a radial Garden City scheme *(Fig. 332)*. Working in a tradition as much Jeffersonian as picturesque, and following the professional lines developed by Olmsted, these two most dedicated of American housing experts and planners of the 1920's and 1930's had obviously come to loathe the density of the city and to hate its streets: they clearly used their radial roads to separate the buildings on both sides, not to connect them, as the city street had done, with a common, multiple-use public space. Greenbelt, Maryland, of 1936, as well as other "Greenbelts" throughout the country, were designed according to these principles *(Fig. 333)*. Some of the housing groups of this period, such as Chatham Village, of the early 1930's, and Baldwin Hills Village, of 1941 *(Figs. 334, 335)*, have great suburban, perhaps even village, charm, proper order, and a welcome sense of human relevance in terms of group design. They are still among some of the best housing built in America, and they exude today, as their planting has grown,

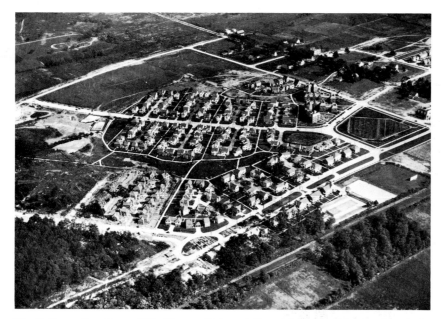

332. Radburn, New Jersey. 1928. Clarence Stein and Henry Wright. Air view in 1929.

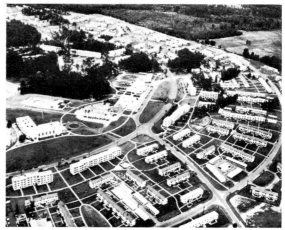

333. Greenbelt, Maryland. 1936. Hale, Walker; Douglas D. Ellington and Reginald J. Wadsworth. Air view.

164

a feeling of bliss that is almost arcadian. After World War II, the single-family-house Levittowns were their commercialized successors; declustered, considerably degraded in conception and impoverished in form, but serving the lower-middle-class dream-house market at close to the lowest prices the industry seemed able to attain (Fig. 336).

The concept of the superblock, with the multiple-use street as archetypal villain, was eventually to be employed with catastrophic visual and social results in the redevelopment projects of the 1950's and

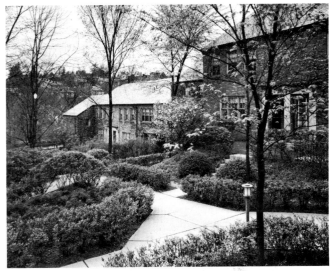

334. Pittsburgh, Pennsylvania. Chatham Village. 1931–35. Ingham and Boyd, architects; Stein and Wright, site planners.

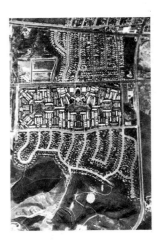

335. Los Angeles, California. Baldwin Hills Village. 1941. Reginald D. Johnson; Wilson, Merrill, and Alexander, associate architects; Clarence Stein, consulting architect. Air view showing contrasting speculative developments on both sides.

336. Levittown, Pennsylvania. 1952–58. Air view.

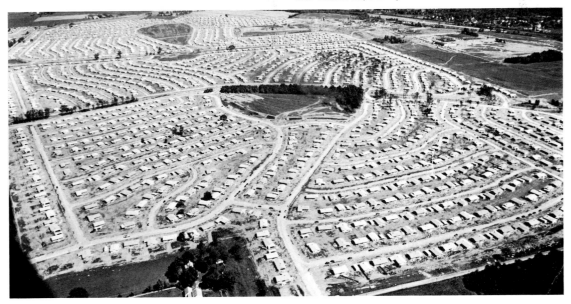

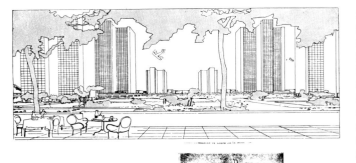

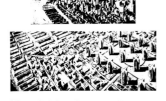

337. Ideal City for Three Million People. 1922. Le Corbusier. Center of the city and a general view, compared with New York to the same scale.

338. Ideal City for Three Million People. Plan.

1960's. It has also played its own technical part in that destruction of old neighborhoods which the sociological viewpoint of redevelopment (or its lack) has tended to encourage. Jane Jacobs pointed out this particular emperor's lack of clothes in her admirable *The Death and Life of Great American Cities*, of 1961. So a projected plan for the continued redevelopment of New Haven, Connecticut, for example, would show the city chopped into squirming segments by vast throughways and connectors *(Fig. 515)*. It is a pure Garden City frame, now applied to a city as a whole. But at large urban scale it had another ancestor also—Le Corbusier himself. His Ideal City, of 1922 *(Fig. 337)*, a clear descendant of the French academic tradition of L'Enfant's Washington *(Fig. 125)*, was based upon a system of crossing avenues at once Beaux-Arts and Garden City. The rectangular module was canted to produce diagonals which, at their intersections, were radial in effect *(Fig. 338)*. Skyscraper towers stood free in superblocks. Some streets were traditionally defined by blocks of courtyard housing, which closely re-

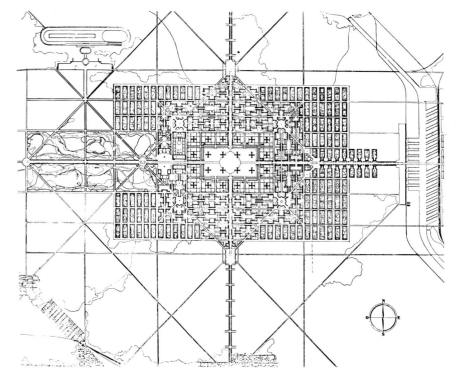

called the fine achievements of the Amsterdam School of architects of the immediately preceding years. Elsewhere, long horizontal slabs *à redents*, looking like Versailles, snaked through leafy parks. There the street was weakened as a defining force. Finally, a mall-like *jardin anglais* penetrated the town. Eventually the skyscrapers themselves were to stand free in that English garden, as in the magnificent housing group at Roehampton in London, built after World War II at the edge of Richmond Park *(Fig. 339)*. The street is gone and with it, even more strikingly than in Garden City examples, the old density of towns. These results were actively desired by Le Corbusier. In 1925, he wrote a diatribe against the street; he hated its complex multiplicity and what seemed to him its mess and confinement. By 1925, he showed his complete intention in his Voisin Plan for Paris. The old streets and blocks of Paris were to be destroyed in favor of towers standing in superblocks with tremendous throughways flashing between them *(Figs. 340, 341)*. The old city was gone; a vast proletariat advanced upon the Seine

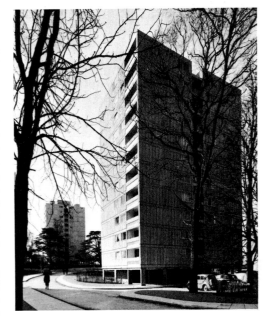

339. London. Alton Estate (West), Roehampton. 1959. Greater London Council, Department of Architecture and Civic Design. Hubert Bennett, architect.

340. Voisin Plan for Paris. 1925. Le Corbusier. Plan drawing.

341. Voisin Plan for Paris. 1925. View of model.

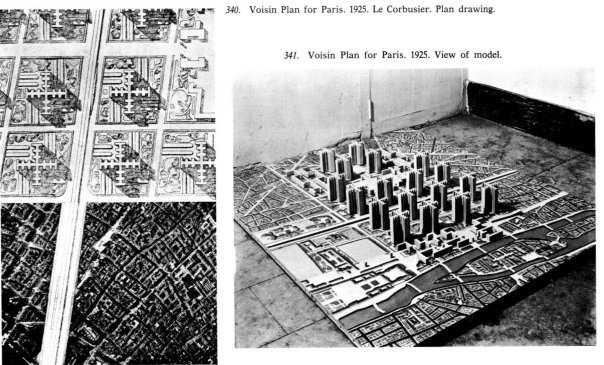

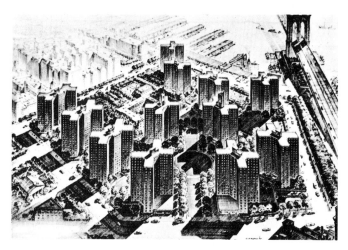

342. New York. Alfred E. Smith Houses. 1948. Eggers and Higgins. Low-cost public housing. Perspective drawing.

in massed towers *(Fig. 346)*. It was a striking image, and a revolutionary one. It quite naturally dominated most large-scale, low-cost public housing, what there was of it, in the next generation. In 1938, New York's Williamsburg houses were still low rise, but by 1948, the Alfred E. Smith Houses were *ville radieuse* towers, as were Metropolitan Life's contemporary, middle-class Stuyvesant Town and the Bernard Baruch Houses of the 1950's *(Figs. 342–44)*. During the 1960's, the Polo Grounds Houses arose, looming above their river, lumbering and cruciform, the Voisin scheme to the life *(Figs. 345, 346)*, except that the forms are somber, not glittering in the light as Le Corbusier's glass planes would have done. The same kind of thing happened in Chicago, culminat-

343. Alfred E. Smith Houses. View toward downtown New York.

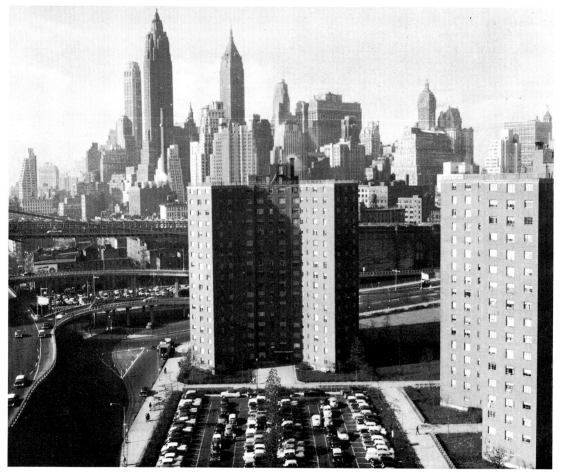

ing, visually at least, in Skidmore, Owings and Merrill's fine slabs at Lake Meadows. Yet few people have thought through the sociology of the housing towers, and indeed, by the 1960's, it was the striking visual effect of the *ville radieuse*, not its social intent, which came to dominate the conceptions of urban redevelopers. It constituted their preconceived formal image, which they discovered could be as appropriate for luxury apartments or for office buildings as for the proletarian army that Le Corbusier had paraded. Despite their protestations of functional objectivity, they tended simply to reproduce it for all functions, except that now the gardens between the towers were normally filled with parked automobiles *(Fig. 514)*.

344. New York. Stuyvesant Town. 1947. Middle-income housing.

345. New York. Polo Grounds Houses. 1964–67. Ballard Todd, Associates. Middle-income housing.

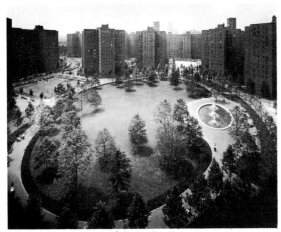

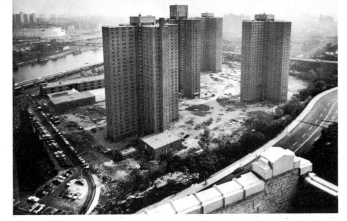

346. Voisin Plan for Paris. 1925. Perspective view.

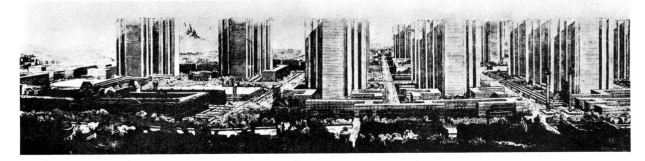

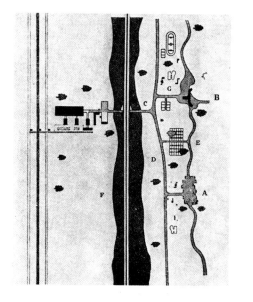

By the early 1940's, Le Corbusier had come to regard such *cités d'affaires* as the connecting points of long *cités linéaires*, the whole to form a marvelous triangulation of the world. These linear cities were to grow up along the "four routes" of canal (pure Simenon for Americans), railroad, highway, and air travel. They were to be decentralized cities, with *usines vertes* in industrial parks and various kinds of housing dispersed loosely on both sides of the throughways *(Fig. 347)*. As such, they exactly prefigured the development of suburban factories and garden-apartment housing which is now so obviously taking place along America's new highway and connector networks. Route 128 *(Fig. 348)* around Boston is an early and outstanding example; New Haven's excellent Long Wharf is one; there are many others. As automobile planning, the whole concept makes considerable sense; and as an affair of roads

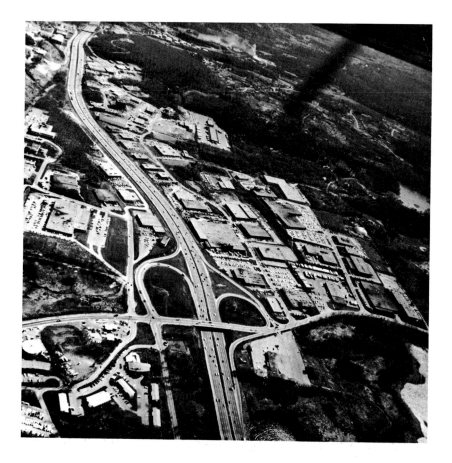

347. *(Above)* The Four Routes of the Linear City. 1942. Le Corbusier.

348. Boston, Massachusetts. Route 128.

and dispersion, it touches the mass American dream of *Lebensraum* as the concentrated city does not seem able to do.

It seems likely, in any event, that Wright's proposal for Broadacre City owed something to Le Corbusier's Ville Radieuse and prefigured his decentralized Ville Linéaire. Wright's own drawings *(Fig. 349)*, published in 1934, show striking similarities to some of those for the Ville Radieuse *(Fig. 350)*, even to the way the driveway connection of the individual buildings to the roads is made—though in Le Corbusier, such connections normally served apartment towers, in Wright, individual houses. Therefore, two conclusions seem inescapable: first, that—despite the opinion of many distinguished American planners and critics, such as Lewis Mumford—the Garden City and the Ville Radieuse have many points

of similarity between them and, in fact, came to ream out the traditional density of the town and to destroy its streets in much the same way; second, that Le Corbusier and Wright are not true polarities either, and that the two probably learned from one another, while the latter surely developed out of the European source what the American spirit most desired—the uninhibited automobile road, the decentralized city, the endless horizontal extension across the land *(Fig. 513)*. But in Wright, there was a romantically Jeffersonian agrarianism that Le Corbusier lacked (his image of the farmer heroic but more existentially French, like Zola's); so Wright threw out the *cités d'affaires*, at least theoretically. Yet when he spoke of what he would save from the old cities—a fine building here and there—he sounded like Corbusier himself, with his Louvre and Notre Dame, though with less to choose from.

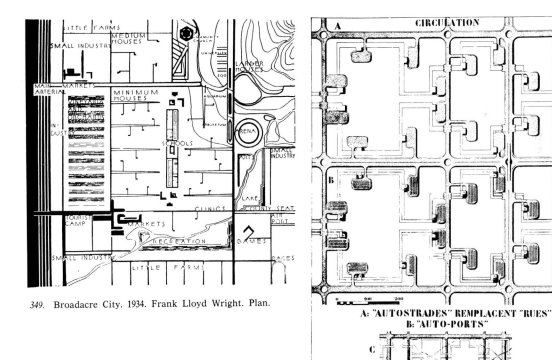

349. Broadacre City. 1934. Frank Lloyd Wright. Plan.

350. Ville Radieuse. 1922–35. Le Corbusier. *Circulation.*

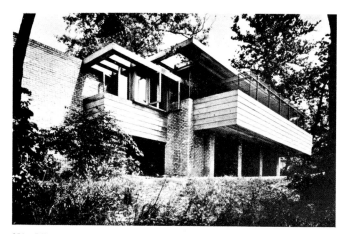

351. Libertyville, Illinois. Lloyd Lewis House. 1940. Frank Lloyd Wright.

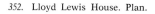

352. Lloyd Lewis House. Plan.

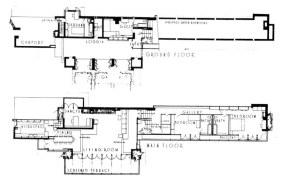

353. Lloyd Lewis House. Living room.

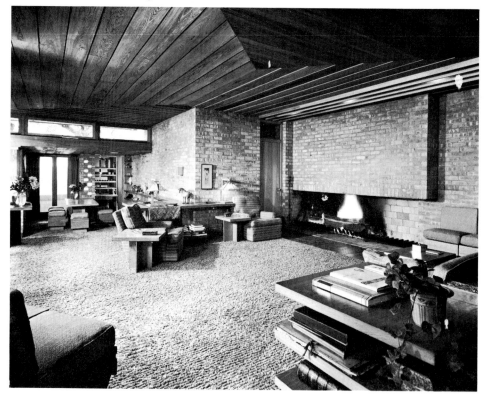

Hence, American purism used European purism to serve its own ends, which were of a perfect, cityless, endlessly suburban world, to which anyone could belong who possessed the following qualifications: (a) enough money to build his own house and to operate a car or two, and (b) the right color (once the right religion, too, but that requirement largely passed by) to be allowed to build in the suburbs at all. If one was poor (of whom there were comparatively few in America) or black (there were about the same number), there was no room in the dreamworld for him. Since a majority has been able to meet middle-class standards in the United States, it has usually been simply tough luck for those who couldn't; they have never controlled enough power, upon which architecture is ultimately based, to build a reasonable environment for themselves. They resentfully make use of the leftovers or are put up in barracks, their wishes unconsulted; and they are otherwise never included in the ideal environmental schemes—to make room for which, in fact, they are normally removed.

All of this was clear enough to everyone by the late 1960's, but in the general economic paralysis of the 1930's it was much less so. The pattern was not yet wholly formed. Yet Wright's lovely houses of that decade and later should be seen as archetypal dream images of the middle-class ideal, and prototypes for its ultimate, more or less mass-produced phase of the 1950's and 1960's. All on one floor, or interweaving two, expansive in space, radiant-heated, finished like a kind of lush hunting lodge in natural wood and warm red brick, combining Europe and autochthonous America in their forms, Wright's Usonian houses were indeed a dream of timeless suburban peace, an Indian-summer architecture, a last harvest of the land.

The Lloyd Lewis House is an excellent example among many *(Figs. 351–53)*, and it is "split-level" too, like so many builders' houses later. It stretches and lifts on its riverside, the gentle, mosquitoed, Middle Western prairie river, and celebrates its place, as all Wright's houses do. Some of them ease out in reflex diagonals *(Figs. 354, 355)*, flowing into

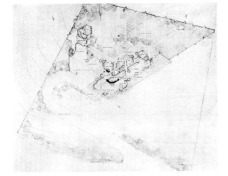

354. Palo Alto, California. Hanna House. 1939. Frank Lloyd Wright. Plan.

355. Hanna House. Living Room.

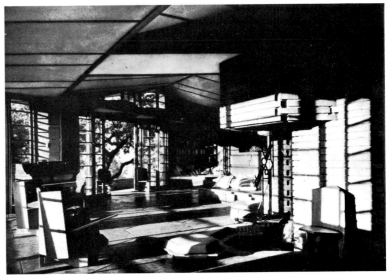

hexagons or circles *(Figs. 356, 357)*, mellow pumpkins of form. In the Pauson House in Arizona, the sculptural pre-Columbian masses took on a fiercely shadowed Mexican density and hardness, in keeping with the arid landscape and the bare mountain forms. Wright's own Taliesin West quite naturally shows the most complete set of the composite images and memories that are involved in it all *(Figs. 358–61)*. Beyond the desert, the pioneer succeeds in leaving all other men behind him and finds his own sacred mountain and his fountain of youth at last; so his canvas-covered Conestoga wagon becomes a patriarch's booth and an Indian temple, solid and compacted as the bases and pyramids at Teotihuacán *(Fig. 14)*, gripping and echoing the

landscape, its major cross-axis focused, as at Teotihuacán itself or in a Minoan palace, upon the mountain presence behind it. Along that axis through the house to the mountain, Wright, in the last days of his life, was building what he called a "menhir avenue" of standing stones, ending with a great rock he called "the Madonna," set up in the desert *(Fig. 361)*. Here the whole Mediterranean tradition of sacred mountains and goddesses of the earth must come to mind, as it does in so much of the work of Wright's last twenty years. But the modern world does not permit noble stances to go unqualified very long, and Taliesin West now receives its inevitable complement in Suburbia West not far away *(Fig. 362)*.

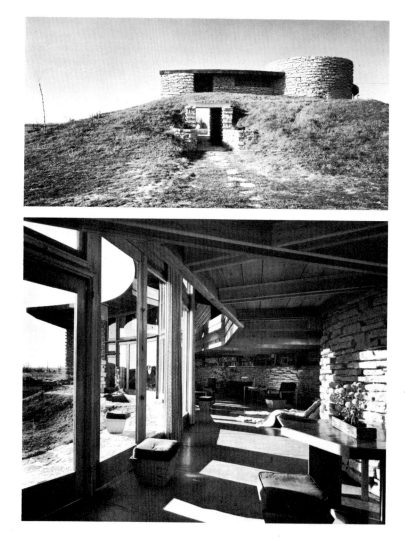

356. Madison, Wisconsin. Second Jacobs House. 1948. Frank Lloyd Wright. North, entrance side.

357. Second Jacobs House. Interior.

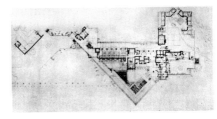

358. Maricopa Mesa, near Phoenix, Arizona. Taliesin West, 1938–59. Frank Lloyd Wright. Plan.

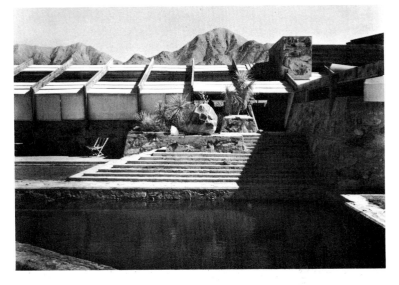

359. Taliesin West. Pool, boulder, house, and mountain.

360. Taliesin West. Interior.

361. Taliesin West. Axis from desert to mountain.

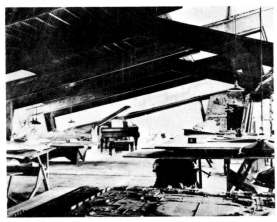

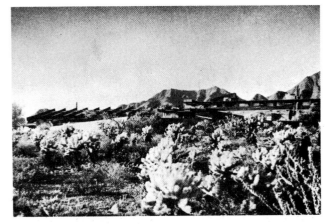

362. Phoenix, Arizona. Suburbia West. 1967.

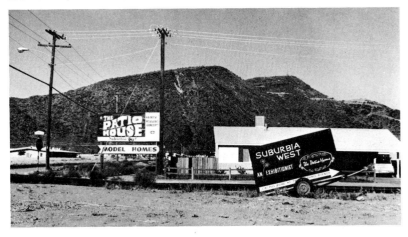

Wright's Johnson Wax Building of 1936 had moved toward the circular forms characteristic of the chthonian tradition; its Minoan columns rise in a pool of space, lighted from above as in a Roman building and enclosed within Roman shells of wall *(Figs. 363, 364)*. The Johnson Wax should, I think, be regarded as the equivalent in Wright's second career to the Larkin Building of his first. It, too, is a splendid achievement, noble and Pop, Roman and streamlined, at once. It creates most of all the culminating spatial progression of Wright's career: the pull of the masses from the street; the engulfment of the low entrance; the unexpected release of the great central space, and the escape from everyday reality which it implies. Yet how tough and young, by comparison, the lost Larkin Building seems *(Figs. 229–31)*, how harsh and lean; how soft and wily the other, manipulating sensation with such practiced ease and settling with the wisdom of age for relaxed standards and easy transcendence. So Wright's last phase is surely a space-dominated one, less hero-

ically integrated in structure and volume than that of his early days. He remembers Richardson's arches; beyond them, the circle and the helix conquer, culminating in the Guggenheim Museum, affronting the street's façade, calling hoydenishly to the park across the way, and offering, in tension with its supporting vertical piers and flat-ribbed dome, an illusion of continuous coiling movement, like that of the spirals carved in Neolithic caves *(Figs. 365, 366)*. It also markedly resembles the staircase in the Vatican Museum, by Giuseppe Momo, of 1932. Yet it is at once more spacious and more insubstantial, its road sweeping out in generous continuities like those of Jackson Pollock's paintings of the 1940's and 1950's. It is a dream of open space and endless movement, drawn out in spite of everything. In this, it shows us much of America at any time. But in its peculiarly arbitrary and theatrical quality it seems especially characteristic of American architecture as it tended generally to become in the 1950's and 1960's.

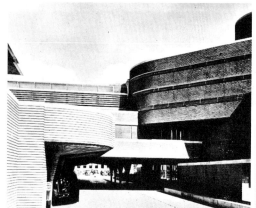

363. Racine, Wisconsin. Johnson Wax Administration Building. 1936–39, 1950. Frank Lloyd Wright.

364. Johnson Wax Administration Building. Main room.

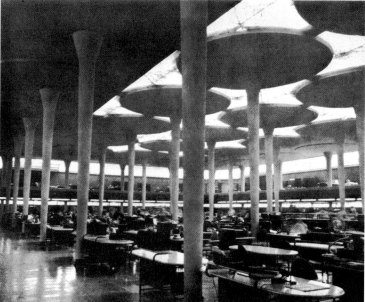

176

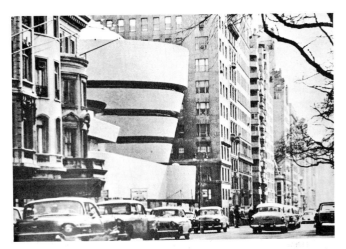

365. New York. The Solomon R. Guggenheim Museum. 1946–59. Frank Lloyd Wright.

366. The Solomon R. Guggenheim Museum. Interior.

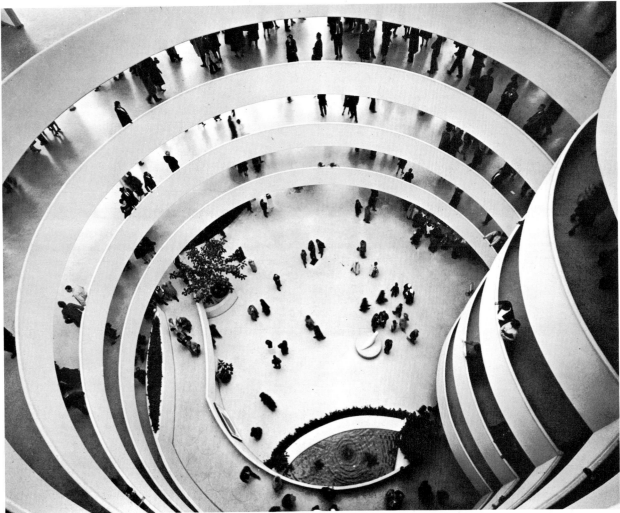

During the period after 1945, the Beaux-Arts fell apart in the United States, and what for lack of a more exact name has been called Modern Architecture became the standard of the profession. Like the Beaux-Arts, it was at that time an international style clearly enough, a compound of American and European work of the period circa 1890–1930, and in the America of the late 1940's it entered, as one might have expected, its at once most bowdlerized, classicized, and academic phase. Indeed, it was largely introduced to most Americans by Henry-Russell Hitchcock and Philip Johnson in their book, *The International Style*, of 1932, in a highly selective and rather tame form: no Futurism, no Russian Constructivism, no Amsterdam School, no German Expressionism—most of all, perhaps, no real urbanism, no social purpose to speak of, and none of the rationalistic passion which, whether always apparent in the forms or not, was the driving emotional force behind the European development as a whole. Once again, the American literally denatured his European sources, separating them from their programs and meanings and using them for whatever picturesquely conceived purposes they might be directed toward. Hitchcock's earlier book, *Modern Architecture*, of 1929, was more inclusive and less neat and closed in its conclusions, but *The International Style* had on it the true impress of the Museum of Modern Art and of most American scholars of modern art at that period. That is to say, it, too, sought a land of dream: hermetic, free of the world and the body, transcendent and pure. The book's virtue, not a small one, was that it was really examining the actual architectural forms as they existed and was generalizing therefrom. True enough, it saw those forms only picturesquely and rather superficially, but unlike some of the Europeans, it was not saying one thing and doing the opposite.

The major exception to this American picturesque approach to modern architecture in the 1930's was George Howe, who had consciously left the Beaux-Arts for reasons of intellectual probity and social conscience, and who with William Lescaze had built the PSFS in 1932 *(Fig. 314)*. Like Franklin Roosevelt, whose classmate he was, Howe was called a "traitor to his class" during the 1930's. What he himself referred to as his "Wall Street Pastoral Period" of the Beaux-Arts 1920's can be seen in the picturesque Newbold House, of 1925 *(Fig. 367)*. It reminds one of some of the most elaborate and visually successful Beaux-Arts Gothic, like that of James Gamble Rogers in the Harkness Quadrangle at Yale *(Fig. 368)*, which is surely better than the stiff but inflated Gothic forms of so much of Beaux-Arts ecclesiastical architecture. Howe abandoned this genial manner for the harsher International Style geometry of his Square Shadows, of 1935 *(Fig. 369)*. But here was no stucco, which Hitchcock had demanded, but instead an exposed surface showing the articulated structure of the wall, its concrete lintels and brick panels, carried outrageously on lally columns. Here one sees revived, and purposely exaggerated, the older structural theories of the authentic Beaux-Arts itself—and especially of the ubiquitous Viollet-le-Duc, who was always anxious to carry vast masonry weights on metal tubes—rather than the pictorialism of the late American Beaux-Arts and the American International Style alike. The work of Louis Kahn in the 1950's, which was to transcend the picturesque phase of modern architecture in America, derived from these principles and from forms such as these. The same kind of prophecy seems embodied in Howe's Clara Fargo Thomas House, at Mt. Desert, Maine *(Fig. 370)*, where the flat roof and rendered stucco of the International Style were both abandoned in favor of forms no less sharply, even ironically, defined, but more natural than those of the International Style to local techniques and conditions. It was a tautened Shingle Style. Here, rather than in Wright's wooden houses of the period, much of the domestic work in wood of the 1960's was prefigured *(Fig. 488)*.

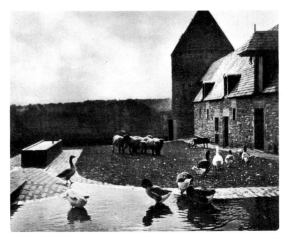

367. Laverock, Pennsylvania. Arthur Newbold House. 1925. Mellor, Meigs and Howe.

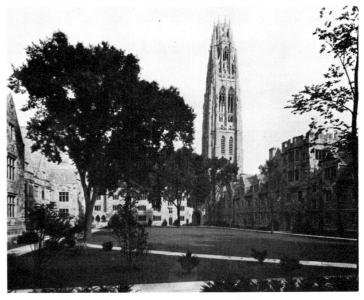

368. New Haven, Connecticut. Yale University. Harkness Quadrangle. 1921. James Gamble Rogers.

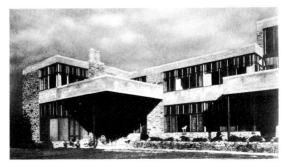

369. Whitemarsh, Pennsylvania. Square Shadows. 1935. George Howe.

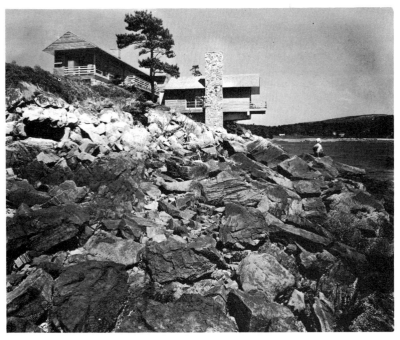

370. Mt. Desert Island, Maine. Fortune Rock (Mrs. C. F. Thomas House). 1939. George Howe.

But Howe's production was uneven and limited in quantity and influence. The major event of the late 1930's was Dean Hudnut's importation of Walter Gropius to Harvard. Gropius brought with him most of the few weaknesses and few of the many virtues that his Bauhaus of the 1920's and early 1930's had possessed. His antihistorical bias was stronger than ever, and since architecture at its true urban scale is largely history, he helped lay part of the groundwork for the general destruction of American cities which some of his pupils were to undertake in the following generation. Such was further prepared for by the selective rewriting of architectural events which was brilliantly accomplished at Harvard by Sigfried Giedion in his *Space, Time and Architecture*, of 1941. Most of us who began our work at that time can testify to the extent in which this book dominated our thinking during the late 1940's. In terms of effective force it was surely a great book. In it, only the International Style was given a history. Most of the nineteenth century was ridiculed, especially everything Beaux-Arts, while the traditional city was wholly condemned and the day when Le Corbusier's throughways would run uninterruptedly through it was ecstatically hailed. Giedion's book, like this one, lamented the passing of many fine buildings, but it sounded the death knell of many others equally fine by the persuasive contempt it lavished upon their kind of architecture. The destruction of Pennsylvania Station *(Figs. 278–80)*, Gropius' own *coup de grâce* to Park Avenue in the Pan American Building *(Fig. 284)*, the abortive attempt *(Figs. 521, 522)* on the New Haven Post Office (to move once again to the provinces), were a few among many grotesque results of that iconoclastic fury, and to them hecatombs of unnecessary victims of the Corbusier-Giedion throughways must also be joined.

Most of all, perhaps, though Gropius insisted in his teaching upon a functional, structural, and sociological basis for his forms, such had, in fact, been directly derived by him from those created by the Dutch painters, sculptors, and architects of the De Stijl movement of the teens and early 1920's— the obvious influence of which upon the early Bauhaus Gropius consistently deprecated. Hence, decrying what his students came to call "formalism" and, indeed, the whole concept of style as well, Gropius and his student collaborators of the American neo-Bauhaus were still dependent for their actual shapes upon a "style" created by painters and sculptors. The resultant "split between thought and feeling" was such as to indicate that when Giedion ascribed such a psychic condition to the nineteenth century, he can only have been indulging in the joys of projection.

The influence of the American dream of the rose-covered cottage (*le rêve à deux millions,* Le Corbusier called it) also acted toward the disintegration of earlier Bauhaus toughness and the further pictorialization of its forms. Gropius' own house in Lincoln, Massachusetts, of 1937, contrasted not only with the Bauhaus at Dessau itself, but also with his own house there, is an instructive example *(Figs. 371, 372)*. It is like a "space-time" construction by Moholy-Nagy, an asymmetrical affair of shifting planes, weightless interpenetrations, and ambiguous scale *(Fig. 373)*. Marcel Breuer's house at Lincoln also shows the designer's and graphic artist's scale at work *(Fig. 374)*, and the same taut, tensile, insectile quality, recalling a painting by Klee, is to be found in Breuer's own house at New Canaan, of 1947 *(Fig. 375)*, and, indeed, in almost all his later work. Despite its greater size, its scale tends to remain that of his own industrially designed chairs and tables, or of a Bauhaus graphic design, rather

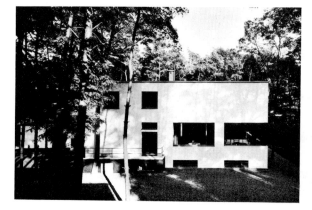

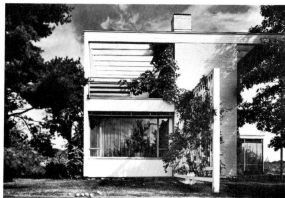

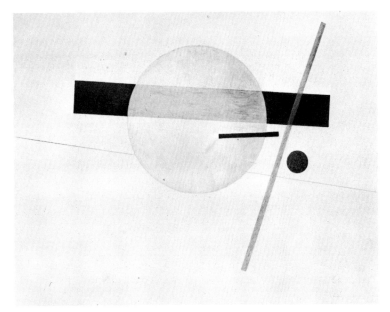

373. Laszlo Moholy-Nagy: *G 5.* 1923–26.

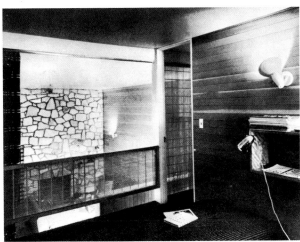

374. Lincoln, Massachusetts. Breuer House. 1939. Marcel Breuer and Walter Gropius. Interior.

375. New Canaan, Connecticut. Breuer House. 1947. Marcel Breuer.

(*Opposite Left to Right*)

371. Dessau, Germany. Gropius House. 1925. Walter Gropius.

372. Lincoln, Massachusetts. Gropius House. 1937. Walter Gropius and Marcel Breuer.

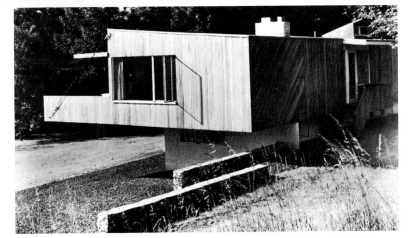

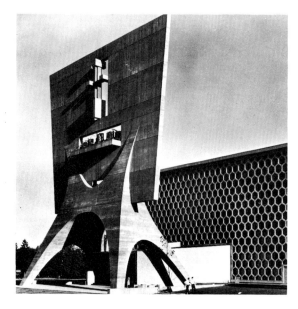

376. Collegeville, Minnesota. St. John's Abbey Church. 1961. Marcel Breuer. Campanile and screened façade.

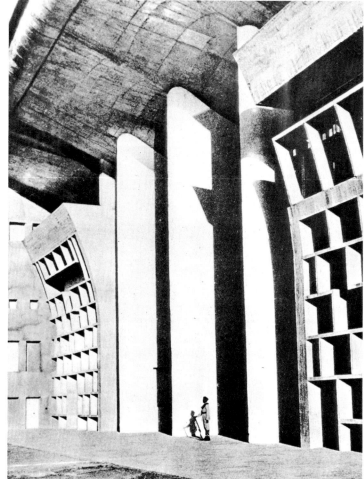

377. Chandigarh, India. High Court Building. 1951–56. Le Corbusier.

182

than of a monumental structure *(Fig. 376)*. His buildings are radio cabinets or table ornaments. Here, at every point, the humanistic unity and force of Le Corbusier's late buildings must be contrasted *(Fig. 377)*.

In the late 1940's, smallness of scale and compulsive asymmetry of design, coupled with a preoccupation with domestic architecture, were not confined to the Bauhaus or to the schools of the East Coast but were to be found as well among the architects of the Bay Region Style, in California *(Figs. 378, 379)*. The forms of the neo-Bauhaus and the Bay Region are more alike than different, and the two schools cannot be regarded as classic and romantic, or mechanical and natural, polarities, as some critics attempted to do at the time. They were both simply small-scale architecture, prevented by depression and war from the chance to tackle large social programs and monumental buildings, and perhaps already deprived by their own hermeticism from the capacity to do so. My own writing during this period on the Stick and Shingle styles was obviously not unsymptomatic of these conditions in general.

The Harvard Graduate Center offered an interesting demonstration of the difficulty the architects of the time had with groups of buildings of any size.

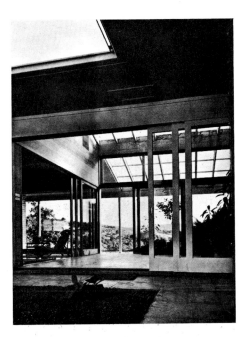

378. Lafayette, California. House by Clarence Mayhew. *Ca.* 1945.

379. Los Angeles, California. Johnson House. 1949. Harwell Hamilton Harris.

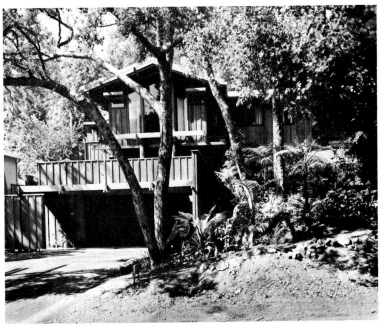

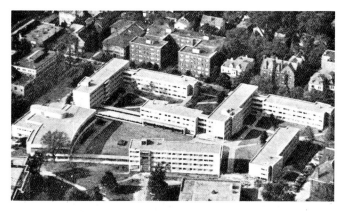

380. Cambridge, Massachusetts. Harvard University. Graduate Center. 1950. Walter Gropius and The Architects' Collaborative.

Everything was stretched into the sliding, interpenetrating planes which derived from principles fundamentally graphic rather than full-scale *(Figs. 373, 380, 381)*. It is, therefore, no wonder that the major new question which the most thoughtful architects were asking around 1950 was how they could learn to build properly firm, permanent urban structures once again. Most of all, they wanted the monumentality which Gropius had deprecated and that Giedion, though he was eventually to call for it, had derided in nineteenth-century work. The major polemical figure, unashamedly formalistic, was Philip Johnson, carrying the banner of his avowed master, Mies van der Rohe. During the early 1950's, the work of Mies did seem to many architects to be the answer to their problem. And it was exactly the kind of answer that Americans instinctively liked, whether they admitted so or not. It was simplified, pure, clean, generalized, reasonable, abstract: the colonial house all over again. Like that house, it also involved

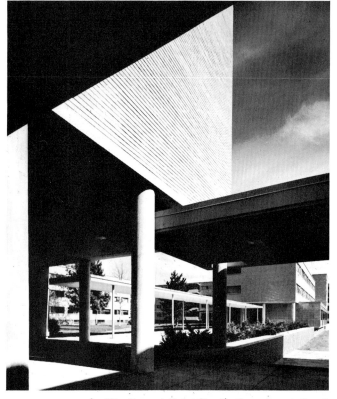

381. Harvard University. Graduate Center. Detail.

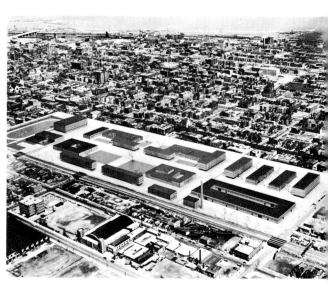

382. Chicago, Illinois. Illinois Institute of Technology. Mies van der Rohe. View of model in photo-montage, 1940.

a framed structure, now the ideal fleshless skeleton of ringing steel. It could hardly be resisted; and with what absolute quality and, in its own way, sweetness, Mies imbued it *(Figs. 382, 383)*. The site plan of the Illinois Institute of Technology expands gently from its symmetrical central space, as if in relaxed answer to the tortured flow patterns of the Harvard Graduate Center (which was in fact designed ten years later). The balance between small building block and symmetrical open space at IIT, along with the plastic precision of Mies's detailing, suggested Renaissance architecture to many architects and critics in America and England. This served the excellent purpose of helping to rescue that period from the fascist limbo to which Gropius, like Wright a Gothic-Revival phenomenon after all, had tended to consign it. But Mies's architecture and urbanism are not at all Renaissance in scale. His spaces at IIT, for example, are defined by really very low masses, gently articulated by their own thin skeletons and

rather far apart *(Figs. 380–84)*. Trees, not much higher than they, are meant to be planted in the grassed areas between them. There is nothing of Renaissance cubical density; little hard pavement. One is instead reminded of Corbusier's *jardin anglais (Fig. 339)*, and indeed the proportions are not urban in the old European sense but very spread out, approaching those, say, of a town in Chihuahua or Fort Garland in southern Colorado. Such is surely not ideal center-city building but is perhaps well suited to those vast gray urban areas of fairly low density anyway, like the South Side of Chicago, in which IIT is set *(Fig. 382)*. In housing, Lafayette Park in Detroit, though it is unfortunately a typical example of redevelopment for the middle class at the expense of the original inhabitants of the area, also offers a demonstration of that barely urban Miesian scale, here carried out wholly, as IIT was not, and heavily planted as Mies intended *(Fig. 385)*. It is his own kind of balance between the man-made

384. Illinois Institute of Technology. Crown Hall. 1956. Interior.

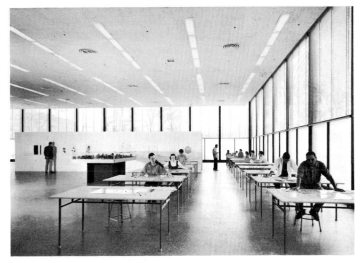

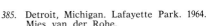

383. Illinois Institute of Technology. Alumni Memorial Hall. 1945–46.

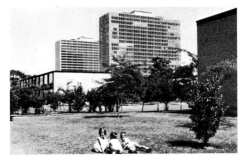

385. Detroit, Michigan. Lafayette Park. 1964. Mies van der Rohe.

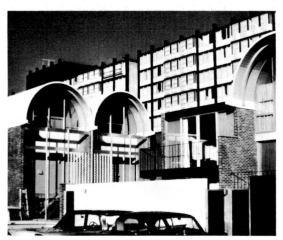

386. Washington, D.C. Southwest Redevelopment Area. River Park Cooperative Homes. 1963. Charles Goodman.

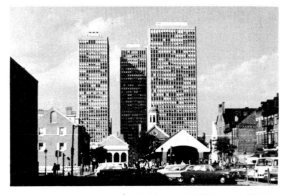

387. Philadelphia, Pennsylvania. Society Hill Towers. 1964–65. I. M. Pei.

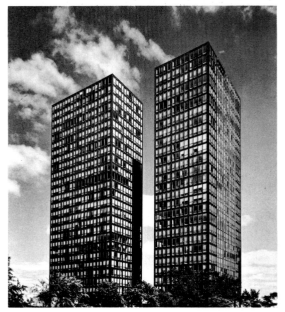

and the natural, and it is backed, perhaps not too successfully, by the flatly designed slab of an apartment tower. Stiffened, those Miesian slabs were sensitively translated into concrete by I. M. Pei in his University Village, finished in 1966. Somewhat lushed up, and combined with overly detailed town houses by Charles Goodman, they also backed up Washington's Southwest renewal project *(Fig. 386)*. Sited and scaled a little like Mies's Commonwealth Apartments, they were also used by Pei with rather quaint row houses in his Society Hill in Philadelphia *(Fig. 387)*.

As monuments to function in the denser groupings of Center City, Mies had designed such slabs with multiplied verticals to make them act as mid-space towers. The sequence runs from the Lake Shore Apartments in Chicago *(Fig. 388)*, where the horizontal bays are also read, to the Commonwealth Apartments, where the vertical piers are kept back, to the Seagram Building in New York, where the same thing occurs *(Fig. 389)*. The solution is basically Sullivan's in thinner metal sections, and the Seagram Building stands on Park Avenue as a body on its legs much like Sullivan's Guaranty *(Fig. 197)*. Contrast should be made with Lever House across the avenue. That first of the modern skyscrapers on the thoroughfare elegantly set the type for the famous American screen, or curtain wall, of the 1950's *(Fig. 390)*. Or perhaps the somewhat less elegant Secretariat of the United Nations was more typical; the whole group was a weakly achieved linearization of a sketch by Le Corbusier *(Fig. 391)*. The screen itself had a typically American ancestry and growth: a European original in Le Corbusier's *pans de verre* of the 1920's, made slicker, thinner, and more obsessively linear in the traditional American manner *(Fig. 53)*. Lever House was also a typical Bauhaus object: free-standing, shiny, weightless, asymmetrical, and fundamentally nonurban *(Fig. 390)*. It both cut the first serious hole in Park Avenue as a street and created an unusable plaza of its own. The Seagram Building, on the other hand, although it, too, clearly wanted to be free-standing in the *ville radieuse* rather than on a street *(Fig. 389)*, was not unwilling both to assume a firm cross-axis with the avenue, so creating a fine entrance plaza, and to stretch its own slab laterally with the movement of the avenue rather than against it, as Lever had done.

388. Chicago, Illinois. Lake Shore Apartments. 1949–51. Mies van der Rohe.

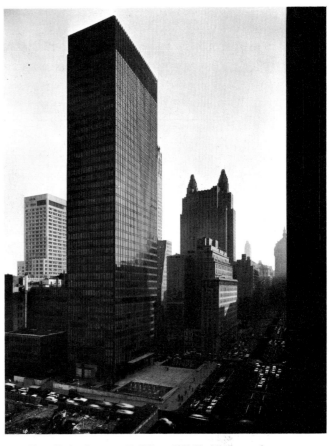

390. New York. Lever House. 1950–52. Skidmore, Owings and Merrill.

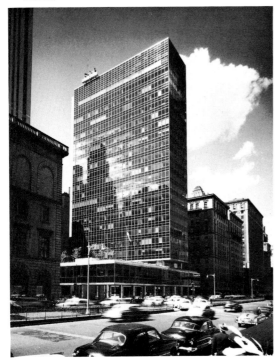

389. New York. Seagram Building. 1956–58. Mies van der Rohe and Philip Johnson.

391. New York. United Nations. 1951–52. Wallace K. Harrison and Associates.

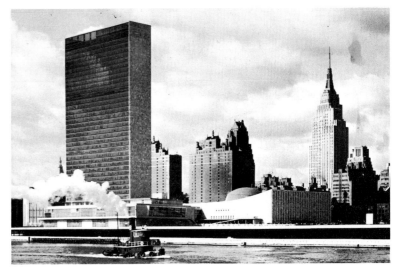

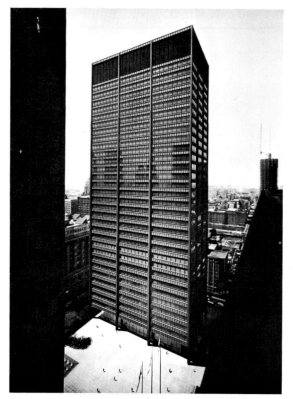

Mies might sometimes so stretch his slab and detail his vertical mullions that the whole mass lost its vertical dominance and gave up its quality as a body to become primarily a planar definer of space: such is the Federal Center in Chicago, sliding through its block. But in the Civic Center at the heart of Chicago's great Loop, Jacques Brownson, a pupil of Mies, reversed that movement toward refinement and small scale, abandoned the obsessive verticals, built up the columns, and reduced their number *(Figs. 392, 393)*. Hence, the floors were carried on great steel girders spanning like bridges. The Miesian system so broke free to a new lease on life at grander scale, and it might well do so again in ways not apparent at the moment. Brownson's solution was ideal for the Civic Center; the tensile stretch of his horizontal spans complemented the visually compressive vertical shafts of the columns of the old City Hall next door, and his horizontal voids their vertical solids, so that the two buildings of very different types get along splendidly together. It is

392. Chicago, Illinois. Civic Center. 1963–65. Jacques Brownson for C. F. Murphy Associates, supervising architects.

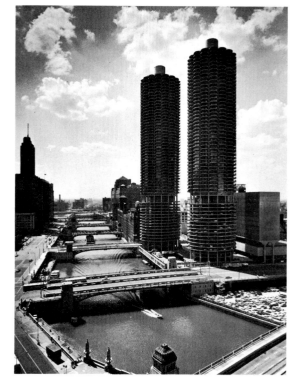

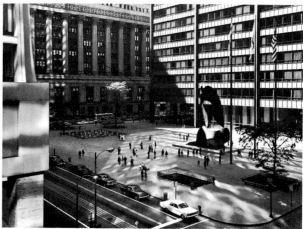

393. Civic Center. Court, with sculpture by Picasso.

394. Chicago, Illinois. Marina City. 1964. Bertrand Goldberg.

fine conversation between the generations and so a truly urbanistic relationship. Surely the weakest of the three buildings on the square is the reinforced concrete Brunswick, which feebly invokes the grand old Monadnock down the street. Marina City, across the river, is one of the few moderately successful exceptions to the Chicago School–Miesian frame, perhaps because its circular concrete shapes derived so directly from its slip-form method of construction *(Fig. 394)*. Or again, the towering John Hancock Center, by Skidmore, Owings and Merrill *(Fig. 395)*, introduces visual diagonal bracing and batters slightly inward, so recalling not only space-frame skyscraper experiments by Kahn but also Mies's beautifully expressed diagonals in his space-framed project for a convention hall in Chicago *(Figs. 396, 397)*. Indeed, one of the obvious phenomena of the 1950's and 1960's was the superior work done by bureaucratic firms when they followed Mies closely and, with some exceptions, the weakness of their pretensions to originality. Sometimes, though, their

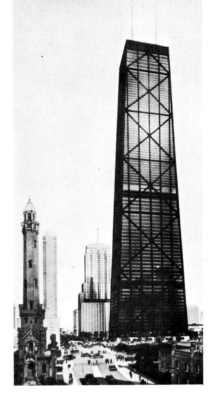

395. Chicago, Illinois. John Hancock Center. Under construction. Skidmore, Owings and Merrill. Perspective drawing.

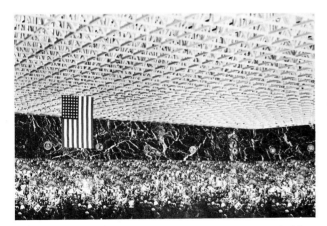

396. Project for a Convention Hall for Chicago, Illinois. 1953. Mies van der Rohe. Photo-montage.

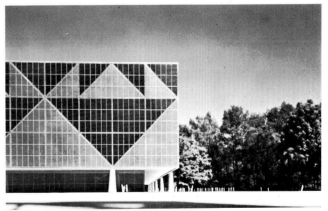

397. Project for a Convention Hall. Detail of model.

189

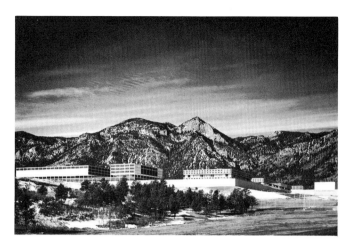

apparent lack of understanding of Mies's basic principles was hard to credit, like the nightmarish Crerar Memorial Library at IIT, which travesties Mies's Crown Hall next door. The Air Force Academy *(Fig. 398)* under Pike's Peak is a perhaps more characteristic example: hard to beat in the Americanized (sharpened, smoothed) Mies of the dormitories, and so on, but abortive in the wigwammy chapel, which seeks to invoke, a little like late Wright at Elkins Park or at Taliesin itself, the Rocky Mountains' serrated forms *(Fig. 399)*.

Architects clearly felt driven to such attempts because of the obvious limitations in Mies's intentions: *beinahe nichts,* indeed, as he said so often. His architecture cried on nobody's lapel; it made perfect, technologically appropriate cages, and pure, limpid

398. Colorado Springs, Colorado. U.S. Air Force Academy. 1956–62. Skidmore, Owings and Merrill.

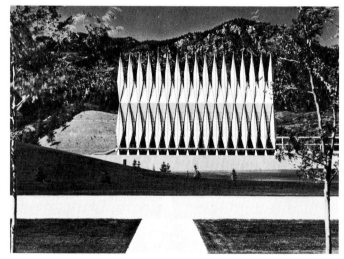

399. U.S. Air Force Academy. Chapel.

400. Houston, Texas. Museum of Fine Arts. Cullinan Hall. 1958–59. Mies van der Rohe.

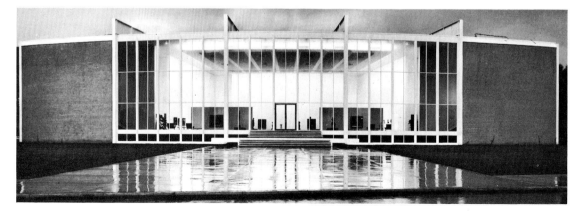

volumes of air, and that was all. Crown Hall itself, or the unbuilt convention hall, or Cullinan Hall, the fine addition to the Museum of Fine Arts in Houston *(Figs. 384, 397, 400)*, are excellent examples of that second mode, wherein the actions of men and the solid, active bodies of figural sculpture (Mies himself never used environmental constructivist sculpture, for the obvious reason that his own buildings were such) could occur in noble volumes of unthreatened space. We should contrast here the unsuccessful Beaux-Arts attempt toward the integration of architecture and sculpture. Mies was content to have one contain the other. His buildings were frames for action and, in a way, perfect ones; they served the American classicizing instinct well.[9]

But what to do if one wanted to vary the mixture?

The easiest and most common answer during the 1950's and 1960's was simply to decorate the container in obvious ways. Such is what Yamasaki did in his Reynolds Metals Building and in his designs for Wayne State University and just about everywhere else. It is superficial classicism; and it is, literally, superficial design, where the volume, into which the functions are more or less fitted, is fundamentally Miesian, symmetrical, and not overly studied, but the surface is as crumpled and laced up as the trade can afford *(Fig. 401)*. This is what Edward Durell Stone did with his gold columns and perforated screens at New Delhi *(Fig. 402)* and interminably thereafter, most repellently, perhaps, in Huntington Hartford's museum on Columbus Circle and, apparently, in the National Cultural Center for

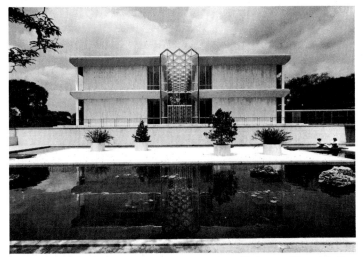

401. Detroit, Michigan. Wayne State University. McGregor Memorial Conference Center. 1957. Yamasaki, Leinweber and Associates.

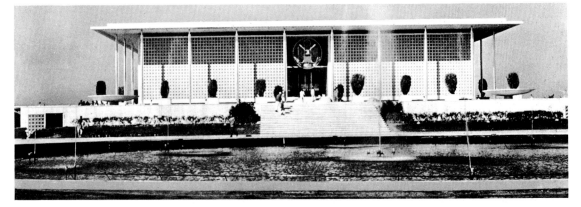

402. New Delhi, India. United States Embassy. 1957–59. Edward Durell Stone.

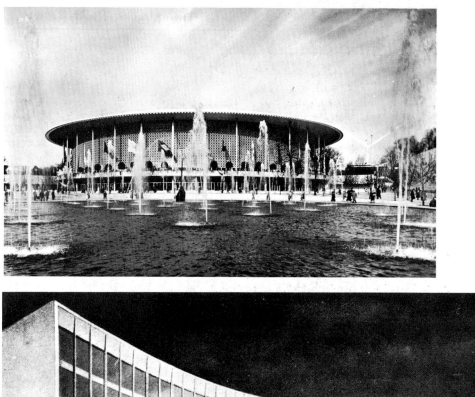

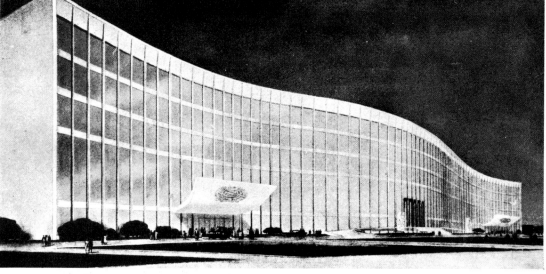

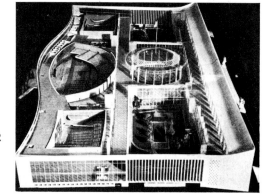

403. Brussels World's Fair, 1958. United States Pavilion. Edward Durell Stone.

404. Competition entry for the Palace of the Congresses, Moscow. 1959. I. Levinson and I. Fomin. Exterior.

405. Competition entry for the Palace of the Congresses, Moscow. Interior layout.

Washington *(Fig. 406)*. That center marks the rococo end of the International Style in its hermetically decorative American guise, but the Russians seem to like it very much as well. Indeed, the Cultural Center closely recalls Fomin's project for the Palace of the Congresses in Moscow, of a year or so before *(Figs. 404, 405)*; but this is no wonder, since Fomin's design and others in that competition had clearly been influenced by Stone's confection (gold columns, pierced screen) for the American pavilion at Brussels, of 1958 *(Fig. 403)*. The Russians finally built a Palace of the Congresses inside the Kremlin. It is

much of this type, but more austere, now recalling the Skidmore office and Pei more directly than Stone *(Fig. 407)*.

Such buildings are packages, whether built in Moscow or Washington, and the package is, after all, one of technology's most ubiquitous products, wherein the illusion of variety, unaffecting fundamental realities, can be most cheaply achieved. It is no wonder, in consequence, that most American architecture of the 1950's and 1960's became an affair of brightly colored bundles, gaudily bowed to catch the blearing eye.

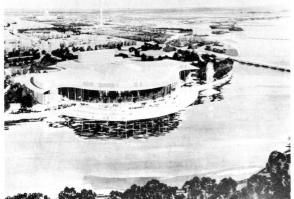

406. Project for the National Cultural Center, Washington, D.C. Early version. 1960. Edward Durell Stone.

407. Moscow. Palace of the Congresses in the Kremlin. 1961.

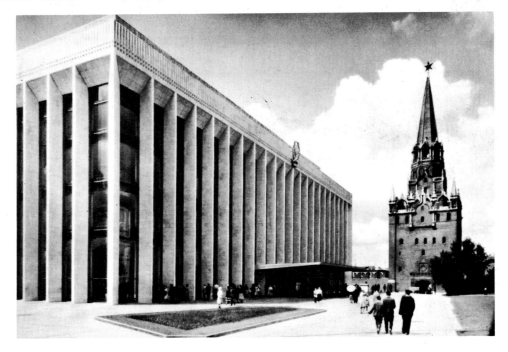

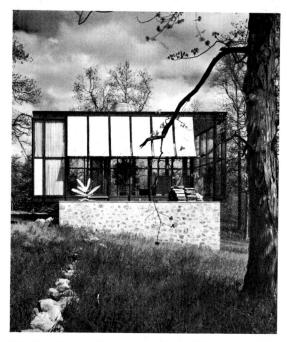

408. New Canaan, Connecticut. Robert Wiley House. 1953. Philip Johnson.

409. New York. Asia House. 1959. Philip Johnson.

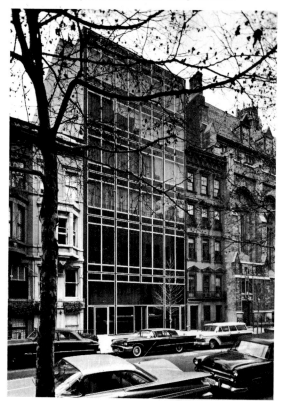

Philip Johnson, Mies's most intelligent follower, understood this phenomenon perfectly and, with uncommon discretion and taste, designed a whole series of buildings from the late 1940's onward that consciously manipulated the quality of container for dramatic effect. His own glass house contrasted with the solid brick house behind it and has served as a luminous setting in the landscape for that generous, informal, and continuous seminar on architecture through which every architectural student in America has come into Johnson's debt. The glass volume of the Wiley House stood on a masonry base containing bedrooms *(Fig. 408);* Asia House was an exquisite façade, indeed only a façade, but in this it fulfilled very well its primary urban responsibility to the street *(Fig. 409).* The Port Chester synagogue was a Ledoux-like, romantic-classic affair of ovoid and cubical containers *(Figs. 77, 410).* Here Johnson had also been inspired, like Piranesi, Soane, Le Corbusier, and Wright, by Hadrian's Villa near Tivoli. Like that villa, the synagogue was hung with ballooning handkerchiefs of vault within *(Fig. 411).* The interiors of the Kline Science Center at Yale were more or less designed by the scientists; the exterior is a rather portentously urbane skin by Johnson, pretending to be chunky cylindrical towers. The Kline Tower is the same, stretched *(Figs. 412, 413).* Perfectly sited, replacing a grand old house

410. Port Chester, New York. Kneses Tifereth Israel Synagogue. 1956. Philip Johnson.

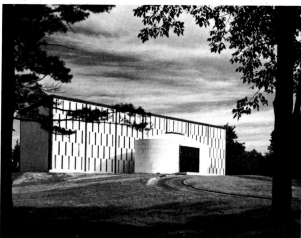

(Fig. 111), but respecting the hillcrest, it is a Seagram Building in concrete swathed in brick cylinders, a stiffened Sullivanian image standing as the pivotal tower in a whole landscape ·of hills, town, throughways, and arm of the sea. It is a considerable success. The difficulty, however, is clear and becoming harder to swallow: it is that so much sheer mass and expense goes into what is, after all, only surface embellishment, though one which, in Johnson's hands, intelligently seeks to fulfill its important architectural role in relating to other buildings and defining urban spaces. Yet, if the package is too obviously only a shell—as may be the case in Johnson's proposed addition to McKim, Mead and White's Boston Public Library *(Figs. 265–67)*, when compared to the more tautly articulated original—it runs the risk of appearing to be something empty, less than a building. Johnson's project for Boston also completes a kind of American Beaux-Arts descent from its rigorous French original, the admirably logical Bibliothèque Ste. Geneviève, by Labrouste, in comparison to which McKim, Mead and White's library is more eclectically picturesque, and Johnson's design is even more stagey (though much improved over his muffin-like first project, one should add). Still the progression reverses the usual American development toward harder forms and produces· softer ones. One looks in general, and perhaps un-

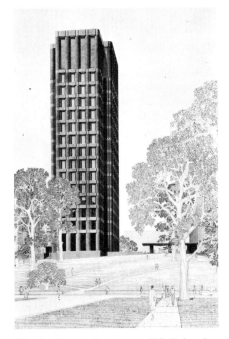

412. New Haven, Connecticut. Yale University. Kline Science Center. 1966. Philip Johnson and Richard Foster, Architects. Perspective from Hillhouse Avenue.

411. Kneses Tifereth Israel Synagogue. Interior.

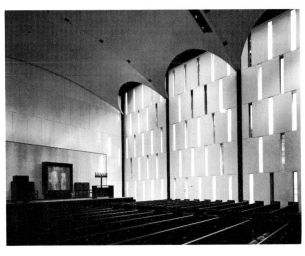

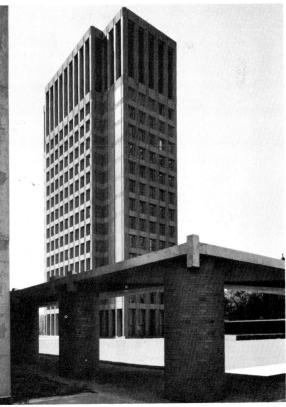

413. Kline Tower. Tower from inner court.

gratefully, for a less impatient analysis of the architectural problem, toward which Johnson's admirably unsentimental wit may one day lead him.

Eero Saarinen, the son of Eliel Saarinen, also designed packages, but with a rather different intention. He sought not urbanity, like Johnson, but a uniquely, even feverishly, expressive container for each and every particular program. It is a method which seems the opposite of that of Mies, and yet it, too, got its start from Mies. True enough, with his father, Saarinen had already designed a number of buildings in a rather undistinguished but sound and obviously thoughtful half-modern, semiclassic style. Their Crow Island Elementary School, of 1940 *(Fig. 414)*, did much to create the type of spread-out, suburbanized school building which replaced the stern old images of civic virtue and is to be found everywhere today. Their collaborators, Perkins, Wheeler and Will, did much to develop the type further in later years. But Saarinen's first important work on his own was the General Motors Technical Center: a perfect program in this connection and ideally exploited by him *(Fig. 415)*. In it, the Miesian forms became at once thinner, slicker, and more geometrically classicizing than they were ever to become anywhere else. In this supremely American combination, Saarinen was already showing his remarkable instinct for appealing to American taste; few architects have been so faithfully backed by their clients. General Motors stretches out across the landscape and glitters and snaps like something designed for the moon. The American had gotten right away at last.

The same combination is even more apparent in the Kresge Auditorium at MIT *(Fig. 416)*. Neoclassicizing willfulness, where everything is jammed into one scaleless shape, is sanctified by structural exhibitionism, where the whole carapace is a single, vast, bent slab, which nudges sullenly against its three connections with the ground, but which, from the exterior, is visually as thin and weightless as the glass skin. There, conversely, the mullions have become so large that they look as if they supported the slab, and do so in part. The conception is not structural but abstract. Is it a building? Can other buildings be related to it? This quality of uniqueness and intractability can make startling sculpture of gigantic size: Saarinen's arch in St. Louis shows that *(Fig. 417)*. Somehow, perhaps because of its very vastness, scalelessness, and uselessness, it does in truth function as a potent sculptural intrusion capable of menacing everything else and dominating space from afar. The great grain elevators of the wheat-bearing plains out beyond St. Louis are like that, without referential scale, gleaming, far-seen American cathedrals, devoid of images and congregation *(Fig. 418)*. Claes Oldenburg's inspired icons of inanimate threat, which, along with Venturi's somewhat similar fountain, are the most intelligent projects for modern urban sculpture we have yet seen, exploit that same scalelessness and disorientation *(Fig. 419)*. Saarinen has less hallucinatory force but still seems ahead of his time and much in the American spirit. But, of a building at normal size, such as that at M.I.T., the eye and mind ask: How does one get into it *(Fig. 416)?* There is a door but hardly an entrance.

414. Winnetka, Illinois. Crow Island Elementary School. 1940. Eliel and Eero Saarinen; Perkins, Wheeler and Will.

415. Detroit, Michigan. General Motors Technical Center. 1948–56. Eero Saarinen and Associates. View showing Styling Administration Building at left and Styling Auditorium at right.

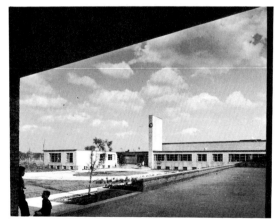

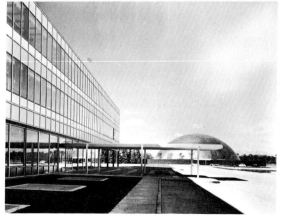

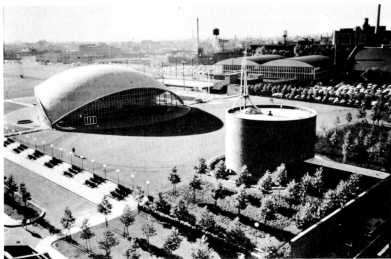

416. Cambridge, Massachusetts. Massachusetts Institute of Technology. Kresge Auditorium and Chapel. 1955. Eero Saarinen and Associates.

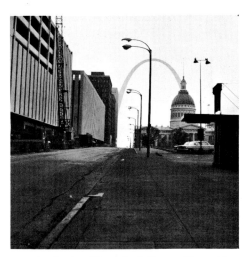

417. St. Louis, Missouri. Jefferson Memorial Arch. 1948–67. Eero Saarinen and Associates.

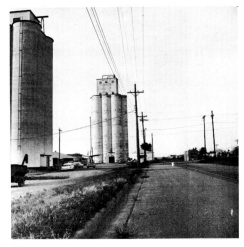

418. Grain elevators off U.S. 66.

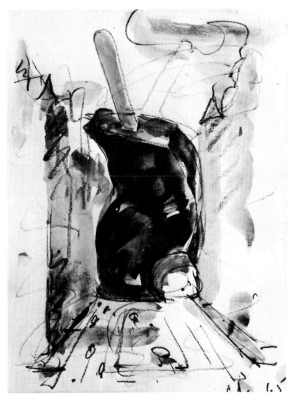

419. Claes Oldenburg: *Proposed Colossal Monument: Good Humor for Park Avenue.* 1965. Collection Carroll Janis, New York.

At Yale's Hockey Rink, Saarinen tackled the problem of entrance by making the space directional along one huge, high-arched concrete member, off which the roof was slung and from whose profile (or vice versa) the banks of seats took their shape (*Fig. 420*). It is a marvelous space in many ways, swooping like hockey, but the conception was again abstract and diagrammatic; the knock-your-eye-out concrete beam was fundamentally wobbly and two-dimensional; it required guying for lateral stability. The urbanistic effect of the whole was disastrous, the street destroyed. The only site such a building could have occupied was the top of a gentle hill in the open; instead, it was set at the foot of a hill among other buildings. In all these ways it embodied a good deal that was wrong with American architecture in the mid-1950's: exhibitionism, structural pretension, self-defeating urbanistic arrogance. It should in all these ways be contrasted with Kenzo Tange's otherwise rather similar Olympic stadia in Japan, where the conception was developed three-dimensionally, with integral structure, and with an understanding of the larger urbanistic responsibilities in-

volved. Again, the difference must be regarded as between a building thought through all the way and a PR package with a few calculated "features" for everyone. Such can be seen in Saarinen's offerings at Kennedy and Dulles airports (*Figs. 421, 422*). The ingredients are always obvious, and they have remained the clients' delight: (a) one whammo shape, justified by (b) one whammo functional innovation, here tubes for the one and Afrika Korps troop carriers for the other, and by (c) one whammo structural exhibition which is always threatening, visually at least, to come apart at the seams: pseudo-concrete choked with steel at Kennedy, finger-tip insecurity over marshmallow slab at Dulles, with a motel drain stuck down the middle.

Saarinen's buildings are the most popular packages of their time and a revealing image of it. Through them runs the insistent American instinct for simplistic and, in this case, spectacular solutions —though I do think that the beautifully sited and eloquently detailed John Deere Building for Moline is a fine exception here (*Figs. 423, 424*). But most of the other buildings give the impression of having

420. New Haven, Connecticut. Yale University. Ingalls Hockey Rink. 1956–58. Eero Saarinen and Associates.

421. Long Island, New York. Kennedy International Airport. TWA Terminal. 1956–62. Eero Saarinen and Associates.

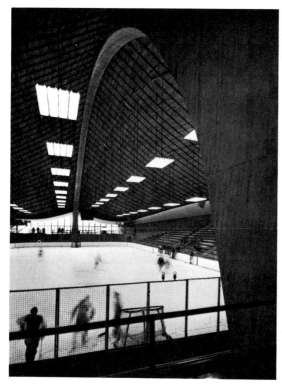

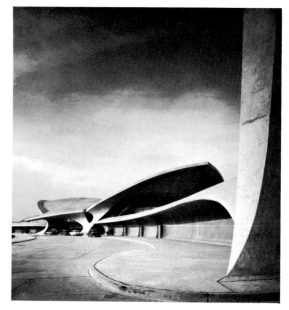

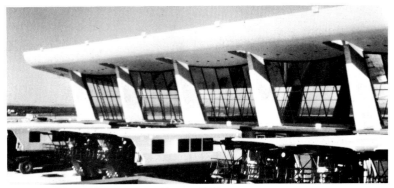

422. Chantilly, Virginia (near Washington, D.C.). Dulles International Airport. 1962. Eero Saarinen and Associates.

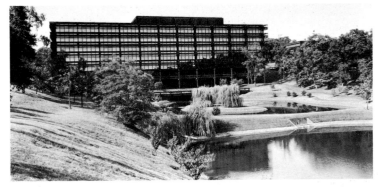

423. Moline, Illinois. John Deere & Company Building. 1961–64. Eero Saarinen and Associates.

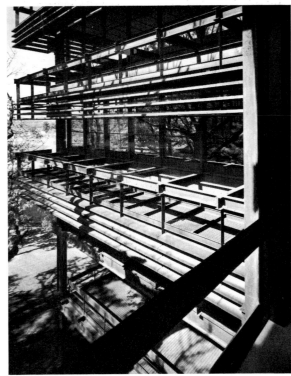

424. John Deere & Company Building. Detail.

been designed in the form of models for dramatic unveiling at board meetings and of having never been detailed beyond that point, so that, whatever their actual size, their scale reveals no connection with human use and remains that of small objects grown frightfully large. The effect is of arbitrary mass order and individual disorientation, and it is most obvious in the late projects and in those produced by Saarinen's organization after his death. They develop a quality at once cruelly inhuman and trivial, as if they had been designed by the Joint Chiefs of Staff. The diagrammatic impatience grows, as does the willful forcing of the structure, the total abstraction of the scale, and the science-fiction character of the image. A sequence to show it: CBS, in New York *(Fig. 425); Knights of Columbus Building*

(Figs. 426, 427), Coliseum project, and Mayor Richard C. Lee High School, a pillbox at the edge of the "Hill" *(Figs. 428, 429),* in New Haven. The last three all share a kind of paramilitary dandyism which seems especially disturbing at the present moment in American history. The Ford Foundation in New York is more complex but no less ominous: military scale on the street, sultanic inner garden *(Fig. 430).* So the firm continues to sense and to embody the most deeply seated, perhaps unconscious, aspirations of its political and corporate clients. That is a significant achievement of a kind, and it justifies so extended a consideration of the work.

During the late 1950's and the 1960's, the architect Paul Rudolph, somewhat younger than Saarinen, designed a number of buildings which are perhaps no

425. New York. CBS Building. 1965.
Eero Saarinen and Associates.

426. Project for Knights of Columbus Hall, New Haven, Connecticut. 1967. Kevin Roche, John Dinkeloo, and Associates.

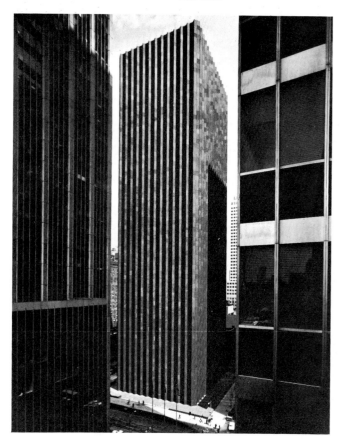

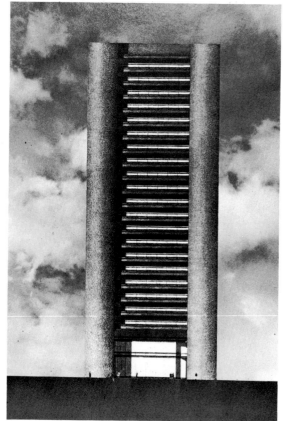

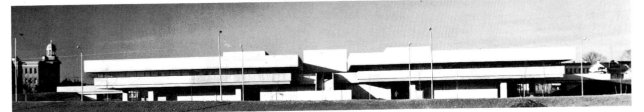

428. New Haven, Connecticut. Richard C. Lee High School. 1966. Kevin Roche, John Dinkeloo, and Associates.

429. New Haven, Connecticut. Project for Coliseum. 1967. Kevin Roche, John Dinkeloo, and Associates. View of model.

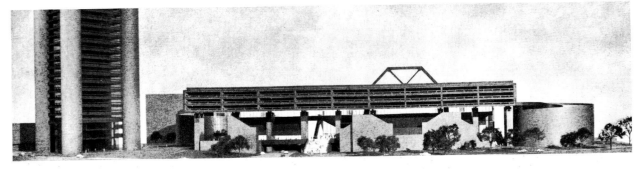

427. New Haven, Connecticut. Knights of Columbus Hall. Under construction.

430. New York. Ford Foundation Building. 1967. Kevin Roche, John Dinkeloo, and Associates.

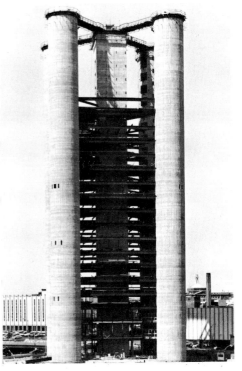

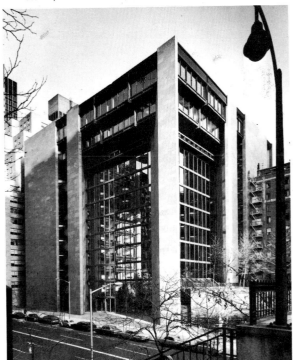

less exhibitionistic but so earnestly and intricately worked out that they can hardly be characterized as packages. Rudolph probably best represents that side of the American consciousness which is always trying to find and to identify the self. Hence he tends to emulate and to compete; architecture becomes a kind of heroic contest, an *agōn*. The self tries to encompass the whole of things; hence the megastructure toward which Rudolph's design, as he himself points out, now so determinedly moves. Strong echoes of Wright and Kahn run through his work, but his major inspiration is clearly from the late buildings of Le Corbusier. So he wants not the snappy technological package but the heroic humanistic image, that sculptural embodiment of human force and action which the late work of Le Corbusier, directly fed from Hellenic sources as it was, so richly accomplished.

The Art and Architecture Building at Yale *(Fig. 431)* recalls Wright's Larkin Building and Kahn's Richards Medical Research Laboratories *(Figs. 229, 451)*, but its primary act is the spectacular lift of its upper floors on continuous piers of vertically striated concrete. This is Le Corbusier dramatized, as is the design of the top floors to look like solid beams, without which the lift of the piers would seem absurd. But at La Tourette, which is the proto-

432. Eveux, France. Monastery of La Tourette. 1956–60. Le Corbusier.

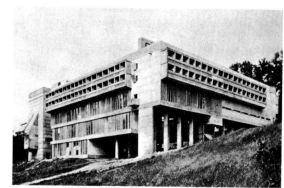

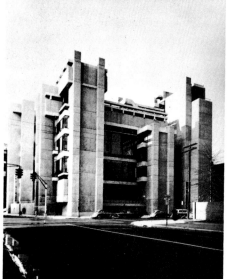

431. New Haven, Connecticut. Yale University. Art and Architecture Building. 1962–63. Paul Rudolph.

433. Yale University. Art and Architecture Building. Section, first project.

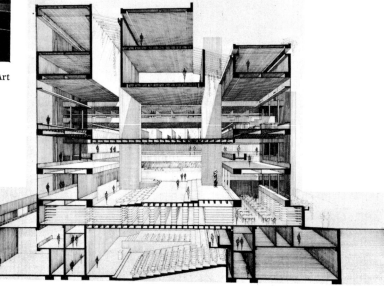

type here *(Fig. 432)*, Le Corbusier, with his usual ability to make sculptural forms out of functional spaces which are, nevertheless, decently respected and revealed themselves, was able to construct a convincing beam out of the horizontal floors of monks' cells. But Rudolph was housing painters' studios at that level, quite a different matter in terms of the height, flexibility, and light required, and one in which the function, confined in the beam shape, was badly squeezed *(Fig. 433)*. Again, the pattern is of a European original adapted by an American architect largely for visual effect. On the other hand, the Art and Architecture Building is splendidly designed for its corner site and in relation to the pre-existing university buildings along Chapel Street *(Figs. 434, 435)*. Its lifting gesture on the axis of the sidewalk complements and completes the chopped-off box of Kahn's new Art Gallery of 1951–53, which had in turn intensified the definition of the street and its direction set up by the older Beaux-Arts gallery, by Swartwout, of 1927, while that building in turn had taken off from the compact Gothic Revival prism of Street Hall, of 1869. It is an instructive sequence urbanistically, in that it shows a large part of what urban architecture really is: a creation of interior and exterior spaces and, most of all, a continuing dialogue between the generations which creates an environment developing across time.

435. Art and Architecture Building. View from west along Chapel Street.

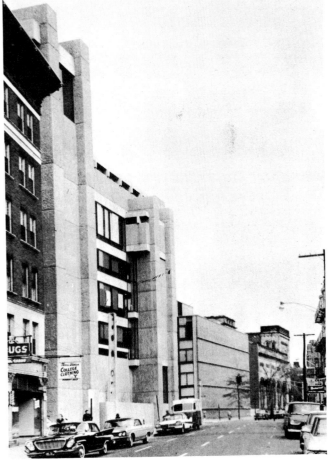

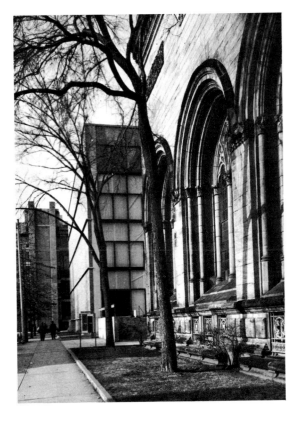

434. Art and Architecture Building. View from east along axis of Chapel Street, with Art Gallery of 1927–28 by Egerton Swartwout, and new Art Gallery of 1951–53 by Louis I. Kahn.

Rudolph's buildings, with the fairly catastrophic exception of his parking garage for New Haven, which should have spanned the Connector but was pushed grossly up a street *(Fig. 436)*, have always been well sited. His early Blue Cross Building in Boston, with its chamfered corners and its position on a raised plaza in an excellent relationship to the pre-existing street, surely prefigures the perhaps even finer Economist group in London by Alison and Peter Smithson, where the same features occur *(Figs. 437, 438)*. In broader architectural terms, one of Rudolph's most useful contributions was his consistent attempt to encourage contact between the young English architects and American students and colleagues; the Smithsons, James Stirling, Colin Wilson, come first to mind.

Rudolph himself has continued to pursue his lonely compulsions, a solitary performer, whose buildings always tend to look better than most of those around them, the work of a man with remarkable optical gifts and an unerring instinct not so much for creating space as for positioning objects in it. His tower of apartments for the aged, on the redeveloped Oak Street Connector in New Haven, spins up into the void and stands as the only building which so far gives any effective architectural definition to that area of urban cataclysm *(Fig. 512)*. It also seems to be very popular with its inhabitants, but whether old people should be piled up in towers as point markers over throughways is a more doubtful matter. It represents a solution which is popular with the New Haven Redevelopment Agency, which would like to mark off the Garden City segments of its scheme, Wren-like, with such towers *(Fig. 519)*. Kahn, who categorically refused to build one for the redevelopment of New Haven's "Hill" section, calls them "vertical cemeteries." But one notes that Rudolph seems to be driven toward stronger and stronger plastic sensation for its own sake and without foreseeable end or rest. So his Government Services Building for Boston will join the new City Hall by Kallmann, McKinnell and Knowles as one of the few elements of that redevelopment area which give the impression of even minimal competence in urbanistic design *(Figs. 439–41)*. There, as in so many group projects today, one feels that civilization must already have ended. Yet the exaggeration in Rudolph's building can be sensed; a little as in late Wright, everything is flowing faster and faster for Rudolph, lifting higher and higher. On the one hand, his problem seems to be that of most of the generation which matured in the 1950's; how to

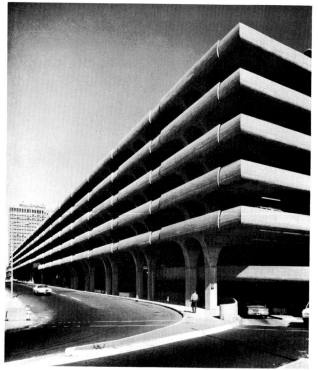

436. New Haven, Connecticut. Temple Street Parking Garage. 1962. Paul Rudolph.

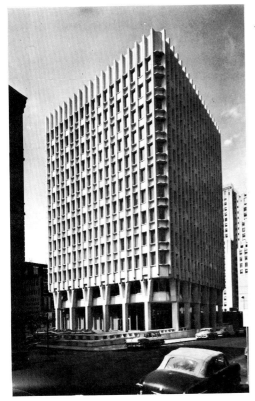

437. Boston, Massachusetts. Blue Cross Building. 1960. Paul Rudolph.

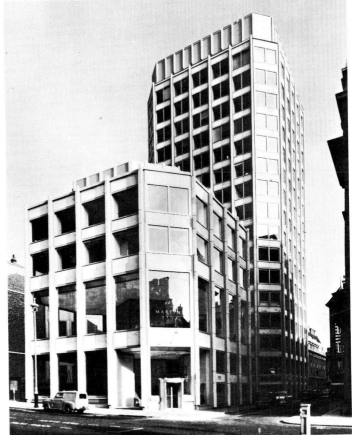

438. London. The Economist Group. 1964. Alison and Peter Smithson.

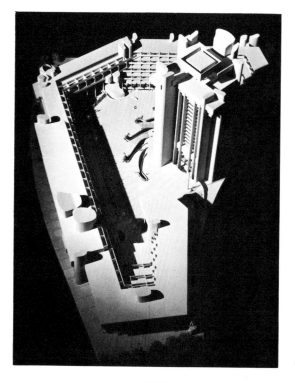

439. Project for Government Services Building, Government Center. Boston, Massachusetts. 1964. Paul Rudolph. Perspective view of tower.

440. Boston, Massachusetts. City Hall. 1963. Kallmann, McKinnell and Knowles. Perspective view of site.

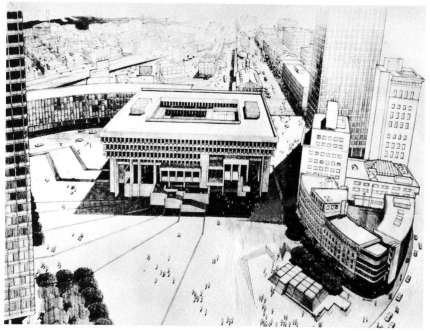

work his way out of aggressive assertions, now turning hollow, toward a more relaxed and sustaining kind of design. But on the other hand, Rudolph's great gifts in plastic organization may be finding their true means and programs in the megastructures he now projects. His studies of trailers lifted as living units into towered frames date back to the 1950's. Now, inspired by Habitat at Expo '67 *(Figs. 473, 474)*, he goes beyond that building in terms of functional and structural rationalism, discretion, and flexibility, and proposes hoisting the products of Magnolia Mobile Homes, of Vicksburg, Mississippi, into concrete frames rising out of the Hudson near the tip of Manhattan *(Figs. 298, 299)*. The stepped organization enhances the old pyramid of skyscrapers, and it shows how the scale could have been exploded without destroying them visually, as Yamasaki's towers will probably do. The legal, structural, and functional problems of Rudolph's project have already been solved; it could well be realized. Whatever the case, it represents the closest any architect has yet come to the physical realization of that industrialized plug-in city which the English Archigrammists like Peter Cook have so delightfully presented in graphic form. When transportation is included in it, as it will be in Rudolph's forthcoming

study of the Manhattan Expressway, all the elements of megastructural urbanism will finally be present, perhaps rather closer to realization in key areas than might have seemed possible even a year or so ago. Behind it all, surely, stands not only the dynamism of Russian Constructivism but also the giant figure of Le Corbusier.

The Boston City Hall is another example of Le Corbusier's influence *(Figs. 432, 440, 441)*. La Tourette ultimately inspired it, but here an English building, Caius College, Cambridge, by Martin and Wilson, was the link between the two. A good deal of history repeats itself in this: a European original, sculptural and humanistically generous, gives rise to a smaller and tighter English derivation, which suggests an American variation with a totally different function, and which here jumps about rather more nervously than the other two. The whole competition for the City Hall is of considerable interest, like that for the Chicago Tribune Tower. Here, though, most of the designs were even more, even indescribably, inept: swollen glass boxes or Yamasaki-like temples. The winner's only strong rival was Romaldo Giurgola's entry, closely derived from the work of Louis I. Kahn, whose influence now rivals Le Corbusier's in any event.

441. Second prize competition award for City Hall. 1963. Romaldo Giurgola.

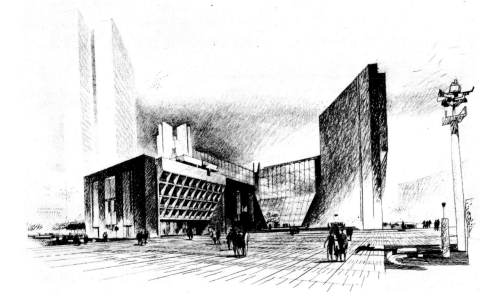

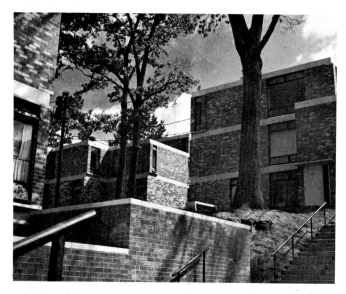

Yet the originating theory and practice of Le Corbusier is everywhere felt in Europe and America alike. The concrete lintels and brick walls of his Maisons Jaoul, for example, inspiring Stirling and Gowan's Ham Common in England and hundreds of buildings in America, created what appears to be the fundamental vernacular architecture of the 1960's. Americans could even make it superficial and picturesque *(Fig. 442)*. But its beginnings were included in what Reyner Banham perhaps rather overinclusively called the "New Brutalism," and some of its examples are indeed consciously rough and active in their *brut*

442. New Haven, Connecticut. Yale University. Married Graduate Student Housing. 1962. Paul Rudolph.

443. Cambridge, Massachusetts. Massachusetts Institute of Technology. Baker House Dormitory. 1947–48. Alvar Aalto.

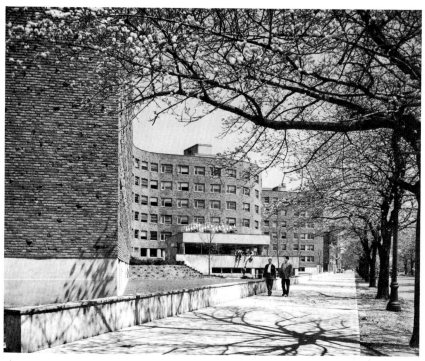

concrete and strongly massed and articulated forms. Alvar Aalto's dormitory at MIT, of 1947–48 *(Figs. 443, 444)*, reinforced that movement toward strong, rough shapes articulated according to their special functional characters much more than the International Style, with all its polemic about function, had usually cared to do. One is reminded, despite differences of shape, and perhaps less by Aalto than by others, of mid-nineteenth-century "masculine," Gothic Revival building. Banham's criteria, as well, are, in the end, the traditionally ethical ones of the Gothic Revival. On the whole, developed Brutalism

444. Baker House Dormitory. Exterior showing stairways.

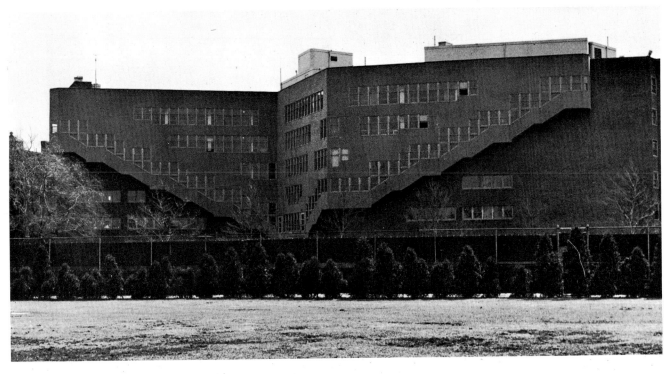

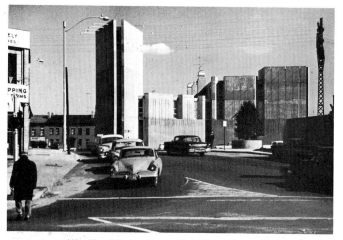

is indeed a straightforward and rather traditional way of making architecture. The way in which Peter Millard was able to incorporate its elements, first to shape an active concrete castle of a building *(Fig. 445)*, rising above railroad tracks, and next in order to respect the scale of a traditional residential street of clapboarded wooden houses *(Fig. 446)*, is a telling example of that, as is John Johansen's firm relationship of his strongly massed if rather classicizing theater to some good old Beaux-Arts buildings in Baltimore *(Fig. 447)*. One therefore tends to feel that Brutalism, though now disavowed by Banham as ethically impure, did in fact begin to break through the old abstract, International Style model toward something much more naturally applicable to existing conditions and programs. Its concrete and brick are still the least expensive of permanent materials,

445. New Haven, Connecticut. Central Fire Station. 1959–62. Earl P. Carlin, Architect; Paul E. Pozzi, Peter Millard, Associates.

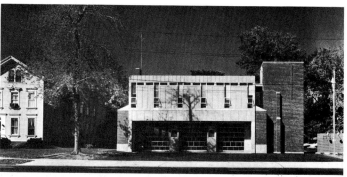

446. New Haven, Connecticut. Whitney Avenue Fire Station. 1964. Earl P. Carlin, Architect; Paul E. Pozzi, Peter Millard, Associates.

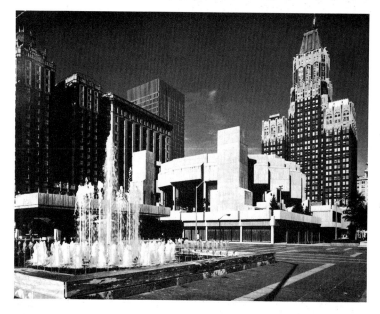

447. Baltimore, Maryland. Morris Mechanic Theatre. 1965–67. John Johansen.

and so can properly be superseded in a vernacular architecture only by fully industrialized, mass-produced, clip-on systems as of plastics and alloys, when and if such come into being. Yet, aside from Buckminster Fuller's geodesic dome—which I take, for all its airy and spidery splendor as seen at Montreal *(Figs. 448, 449)*, to be only one component of an articulated industrial architecture, since it can do only one thing and make only one shape—only Rudolph seems to have an archigram-scaled industrialized image anywhere near production *(Figs. 298, 299)*. Many architects, however, are giving it some thought, and Moshe Safdie, the designer of Habitat, has related projects under way.

Yet one cannot bring oneself to dismiss Fuller quite so parenthetically as the paragraph above does. His unique intellectual resources are all directed

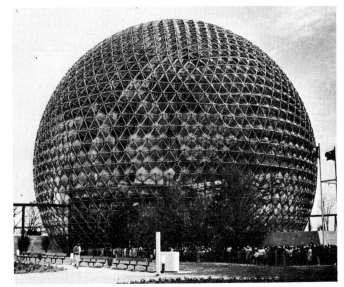

448. Montreal, Canada. Expo '67. American Pavilion. 1967. Geodesic dome by R. Buckminster Fuller.

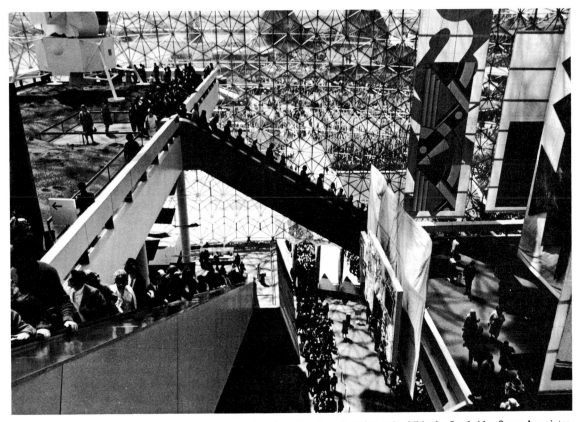

449. American Pavilion. Interior and exhibits by Cambridge Seven Associates.

toward compelling the individual to recognize the wild splendor of the physical universe and its metaphysical unity in the mind of man. So in architecture he concentrates upon imagining perfectly structured models of the cosmos: his geodesic domes and now his World Game, which will be a sphere. That is why the act of building one of these mechanisms is more than a mechanical experience for Fuller and his followers; it is a mystical rite, to be repeated with little variation over and over again, eternally wonderful, always complete.*

Slightly different is the American attempt to computerize design, which is best associated with the researches of Christopher Alexander and his teaching at Berkeley. Like Fuller's dome, it is indeed very American, seeking a method technologically sophisticated, very clear, promising mechanical answers. Its deterministic purism is sympathetic to much American thought, but it hardly satisfies all American objectives. One might better argue that Kahn is the architect whose work, at this time, most fully embodies American conditions and aspirations. The geometric compulsion, with its strong classicizing strain, the determined search for probity and integration, the struggle necessary to make contact with reality and with the place, the tendency toward technological determinism, too, all of these have been consistent American characteristics, and all have been turned to creative use by Kahn. With them he was finally able, after long years, to include that ingredient most generally lacking in America: the capacity to embrace and to be sustained by the nature of things as they are, most especially by the light of everyday. In his latest works it is, in fact, light which he most celebrates and which he can now combine with his geometric and structural imagination to make new forms. Related to acceptance of the world is Kahn's slow growth to a perception of the shapes which functions may suggest and to an instinct for the way in which what he calls "human institutions" may give rise to physical shapes. That capacity to invent shapes out of programmatic perceptions has been rarest of all in America, despite the persistent American myth to the contrary. Only Sullivan and Wright seem really to have had it, and they now long ago. In Kahn, it once more breaks through the colonialistic tendency, so often noted in these pages, to adapt European forms picturesquely for programs with which they originally had nothing to do. Kahn somehow fought his way through that pervasive cultural block and so through and out of the superficially packaging pseudoclassicism of the decadent International Style of the 1950's. Yet Kahn's ability to collect and employ sociological data is limited by his temperament and training, and in the American way, classicism's preconceived shapes are powerfully operative upon him, too, so that the grueling three-way contest which goes on in his process of work is between those shapes, the institution to be served, and the structure which will make a physical reality of the whole. Kahn has recognized the existence of that struggle and has learned how to use it in the sequence which he calls that of "Form" and "Design."

The Forms are Kahn's first conception of the shape in terms of its requirements; and since forms normally pre-exist (how difficult to imagine new ones), those first shapes are usually based not a little upon those of pre-existing monuments: Hadrian's Villa has figured often for Kahn, Viollet-le-Duc's Carcassonne has appeared, and Piranesi's Rome. Then, however, the Forms are bombarded by the empirical realities of the particular program, as Kahn tries his best to bring all its aspects of functional and structural possibility to bear, so that the original Form is deformed by Design. Slowly, if it was generally based on the proper conception to begin with, the process will give rise to a constructed shape which is a new form, and one peculiarly appropriate to the institution at hand. If not, then the preconceived Form is presumably thrown out and the process starts over. The whole represents a realistic appraisal by Kahn of himself—and perhaps of the way all human "creation" actually works: first the general conception, really a kind of preconception hammered out largely below the surface of consciousness from what one knows and remembers; this shapes the symbolic configuration which enables the mind to ask new questions in a pragmatic sense, which may lead finally, if rarely, toward something with its own proper character, unique, perhaps new.

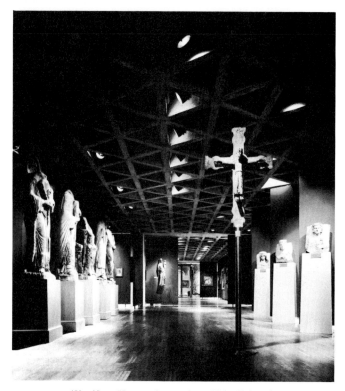

450. New Haven, Connecticut. Yale University. New Art Gallery. 1951–53. Louis I. Kahn. Interior.

Kahn came to all this most slowly, which is not in the normal American pattern at all. But his career has otherwise been an American archetype: Jewish immigrant child in the slums of Philadelphia at the beginning of the century; scholarship at the University of Pennsylvania and a Beaux-Arts education there; first trip to Europe in the 1920's; Depression, teaching, and war. Finally, as America began to unfold during the 1950's into its affluent postwar phase, Kahn's first real chance came. This was the new Art Gallery at Yale, with which he was entrusted through the efforts of George Howe, who had once been his partner (*Figs. 434, 435, 450*). We cannot review Kahn's career here, but his way of growth should be clear. The new Art Gallery is imperfect, but its struggle for probity is felt by everyone who sees it; the building has an authentic force, a Gothic Revival "reality," and it played a good part in the formation of the Brutalist aesthetic. The little Bath House at Trenton goes further. The structure made major spaces and service spaces, each one Roman and discrete, and yet there was a cross-axis, recalling Jefferson's and Wright's. The climax came with the Richards Medical Research Laboratories at the Uni-

451. Philadelphia, Pennsylvania. University of Pennsylvania. Alfred Newton Richards Medical Research Laboratories. 1957–61. Louis I. Kahn.

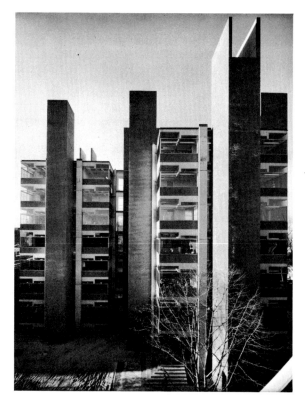

versity of Pennsylvania *(Figs. 451, 452)*. Impossible to look at them without thinking of the Larkin Building and its service towers, vertical piers, and interwoven spandrels *(Fig. 229)*. Impossible not to recall Alvar Aalto at MIT *(Figs. 443, 444)*, and much early semi-Brutalist architecture, including that of Le Corbusier. Impossible not to think of San Gimignano, as Saarinen was to do in a wholly picturesque, but functionally no less than scenographically rather successful way, in his Stiles and Morse colleges at Yale. But the Richards Laboratories, despite their medieval towers, are fundamentally not picturesque; they are grimly fashioned out of an obsessive structural determinism and a kind of tragic perception of what actually goes on inside. They are a castle of pain and a town of colleagues, but in a material sense they function not perfectly at all. The spaces are cramped by the structural conception; there is no sun protection, only the tightly stretched surface without apology. Again, illogically, a kind of awesome probity is felt, an archaic determination. Such is weaker in the Biology Laboratories, but there Kahn's experiments with the window and with light had begun *(Fig. 453)*. These cul-

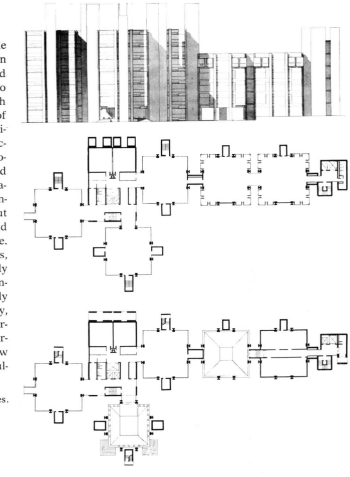

452. Alfred Newton Richards Medical Research Laboratories. Plan and elevation.

453. Alfred Newton Richards Medical Research Laboratories. View from the south.

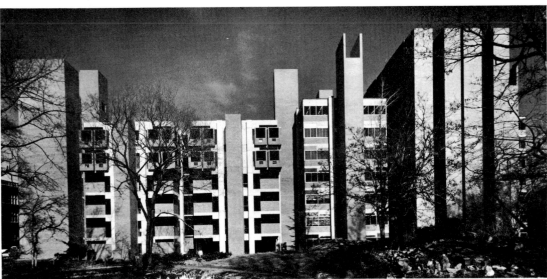

minated in the Unitarian Church at Rochester, where the whole massing and profiling of the exterior and the marvelous plasticity of its walls derive from the lighting of the interior and its protection from glare *(Figs. 454–56).* The grand structure of the noble, cinder-blocked meeting room, as well as the touchingly scaled window seats in the small rooms around it, are alike involved in that articulation of the light. Despite the vast amount of church and synagogue

454. Rochester, New York. First Unitarian Church. 1963–64. Louis I. Kahn.

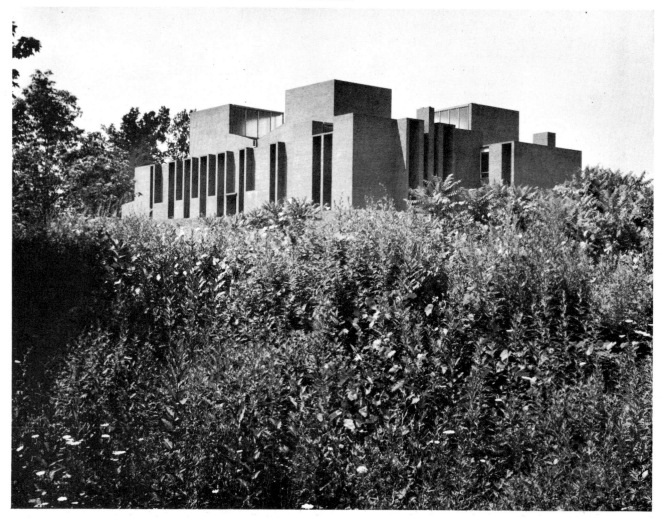

building which goes on in America, the Unitarian Church is one of the few examples which is neither domestic nor theatrical. Most are embarrassing displays of financial affluence and spiritual poverty. Contrasted with the piercing spires of colonial Boston or with the proud, high, silvered roofs that dominate every village in French Canada, their shapes have the nervous smirks of barely tolerated performers.

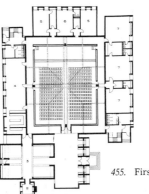

455. First Unitarian Church. Plan.

456. First Unitarian Church. Main meeting room.

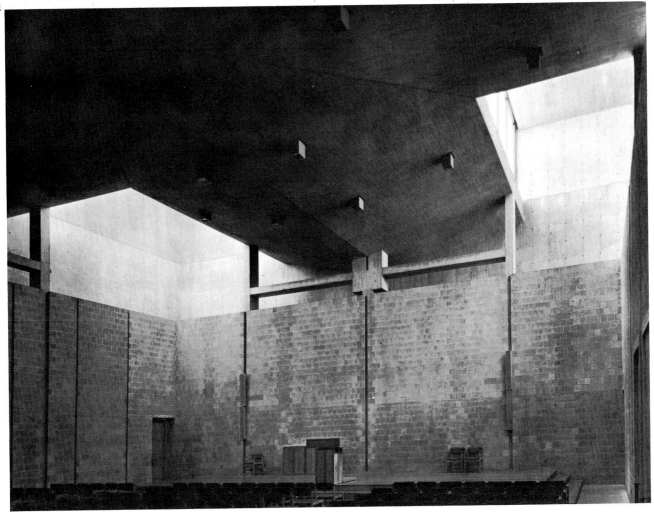

Kahn's church has the strength of something thought through in reverence for the facts of things: here, for light. The process of Form and Design as a whole is especially clear in it, as in its gentler sister, the dormitory at Bryn Mawr where, inside and out, everything works. Inside: staircase settings for human beings scaled as by Giotto *(Figs. 457, 458)*, top-lighted dining and living rooms, window-seated bays. Outside: these shapes faced over the block with delicately cut slate panels and precast concrete bindings *(Figs. 459, 460)*. The building reads as a low garden wall down the hill slope, when it is approached from the main campus above, and as a high palisade when it is seen from below. Never at any time is the strict geometry of the three squares in plan physically perceived. The whole is limpid with the sweetness of its program, and it flows with the land, beautifully sited there, as the Unitarian Church is not. One should contrast, in terms of the institution, Saarinen's packaging conception for a girls' dormitory at the University of Pennsylvania: Château d'If outside, Blanche DuBois within.

457. Bryn Mawr, Pennsylvania. Bryn Mawr College. Residence Hall. 1964–65. Louis I. Kahn. Stair hall.

458. Bryn Mawr College. Residence Hall. View of stair hall from landing.

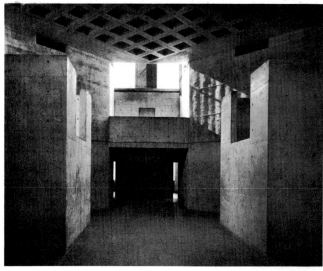

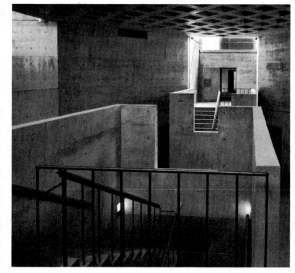

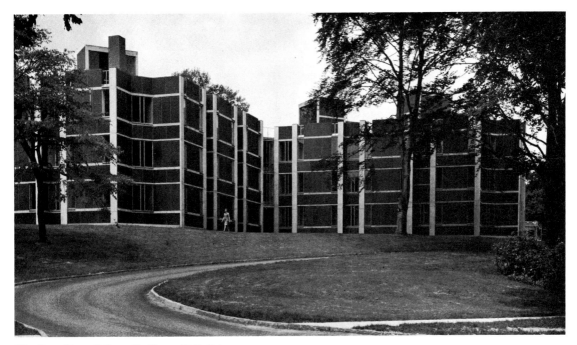

459. Bryn Mawr College. Residence Hall. Exterior.

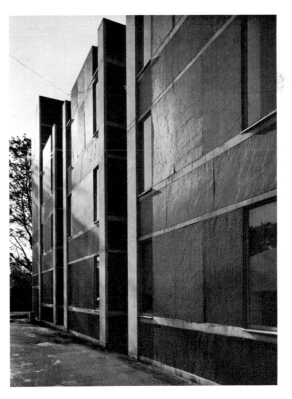

460. Bryn Mawr College. Residence Hall. Exterior wall detail.

219

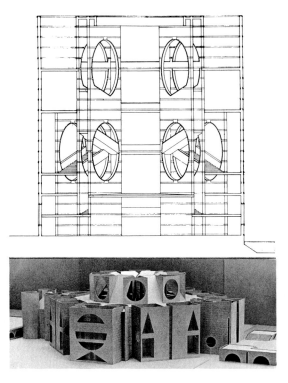

461. Project for Second Capital at Dacca, East Pakistan. 1966. Louis I. Kahn. Meeting hall.

462. Second Capital of Pakistan. Dacca, East Pakistan. Arches under Presidential Square.

463. Second Capital of Pakistan. Detail of arches.

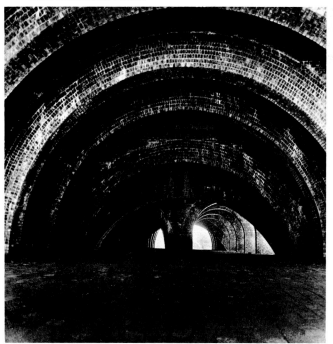

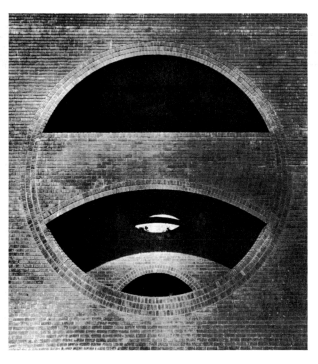

Kahn is now generally regarded by professionals in Europe and America as America's outstanding architect. His buildings in India and Pakistan have joined those of Le Corbusier and Lutyens as the finest examples of modern architecture on the subcontinent. And in the Indian architect and teacher, Doshi, his influence upon architectural education in Asia merges, as it were, with that of Le Corbusier. His Asian forms have exploited light and structure to the utmost, creating a brick and concrete structural and spatial order and proliferating with a kind of opulent visual excess appropriate to the traditions of the area *(Figs. 461–66)*. The Salk Center in

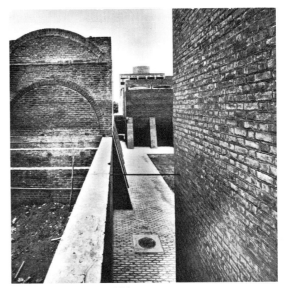

466. Indian Institute of Management.

464. Ahmedabad, India. Indian Institute of Management. 1964–66. Louis I. Kahn.

465. Indian Institute of Management. Detail of arches.

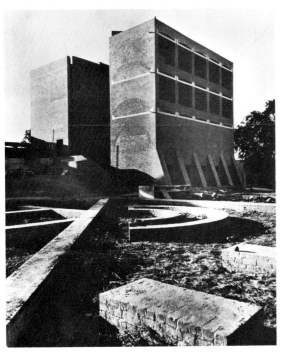

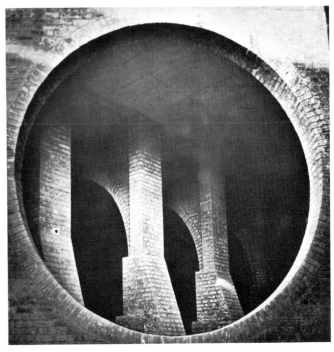

San Diego vastly improved the functional concepts of laboratory and study proposed in the buildings at Pennsylvania, and it did so with some of the most beautifully made structure to be found in America: a concrete poured with marvelous joints as smooth as silk, contrasted with sawn wooden boards set as panels within the concrete frames *(Figs. 467, 468)*. All the first shapes for the Salk project, closely based as they were upon Hadrian's Villa at Tivoli, took on their own unique forms as their functions and the structure appropriate to them were further studied. Kahn's most recent projects all seem to have even more of that greater freedom from precedent, perhaps the Philadelphia College of Art most of all, though it embodies a force reminiscent at once of Furness and Hugh Ferriss *(Figs. 170, 306, 307, 469)*. In these ways Kahn has been able to make use of his whole past, Beaux-Arts training and all, in order to break out of the rather frozen formalistic pattern of the 1950's.

467. La Jolla, California. Jonas B. Salk Center for Biological Research. 1962–66. Louis I. Kahn.

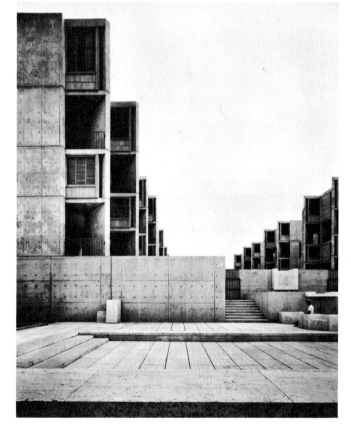

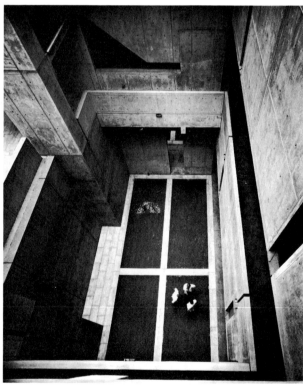

468. Jonas B. Salk Center. Courtyard.

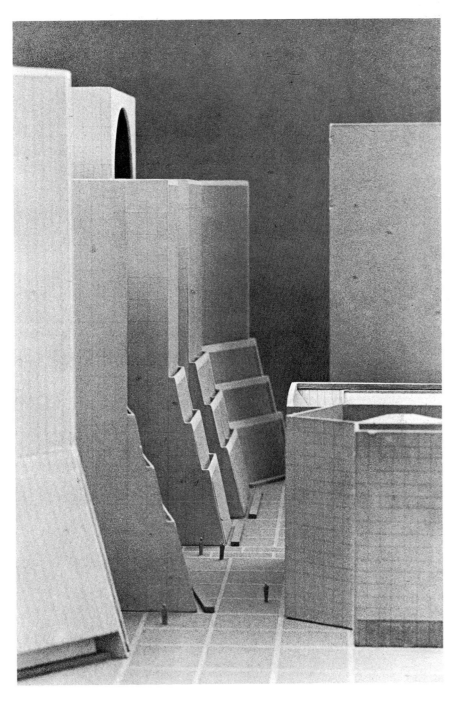

469. Project for Phila-
delphia College of
Art, Philadelphia,
Pennsylvania. 1966.
Louis I. Kahn.

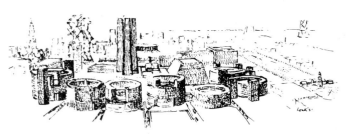

470. Project for the center of the city, with parking towers, Philadelphia, Pennsylvania. 1956. Louis I. Kahn. Perspective view.

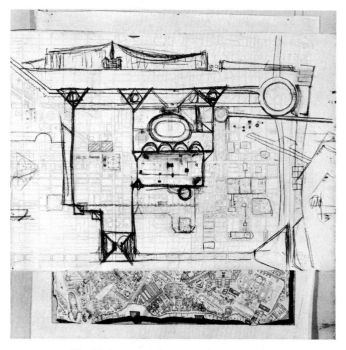

471. Viaduct architecture for Philadelphia, Pennsylvania. 1962. Louis I. Kahn. Plan drawn over Piranesi's plan of the Campus Martius.

Yet Kahn's aspirations, like those of the best of the 1950's, are heroic, too. In this he resembles Le Corbusier *(Figs. 377, 432)*. The Philadelphia College of Art shows it, as do his urbanistic projects for Philadelphia. They are grandiose and cataclysmic, like Le Corbusier's schemes *(Figs. 470, 471)*. Yet they have another aspect as well, in that they do in fact try to accommodate themselves to existing realities rather than to bomb the whole city and start over, as Le Corbusier would ideally have done. In Philadelphia, for example, the existing traffic pattern was to be respected and manipulated. The throughways and connectors which are blowing the hearts out of American cities everywhere were to be trapped into becoming a viaduct (that concept, Le Corbusier's), but here acting as a wall which would surround the center of the city precisely to protect it from disintegration by the automobile *(Fig. 471)*. That wall of cars, with its shops and so on in it, was, like Le Corbusier's, a megastructure itself. Yet the

472. Proposal for the center of the city, Fort Worth, Texas. 1956. Victor Gruen Associates. View of model.

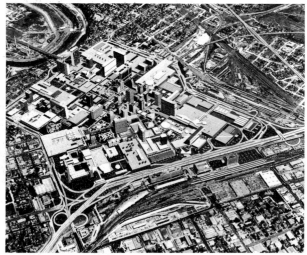

cars were not to be kept entirely out of the center, as Victor Gruen had proposed at Fort Worth *(Fig. 472)*, but were to be filtered in, baffled where necessary, invited where practicable. At one stage, garage towers were conceived of as ringing the center with new, integrally monumental forms growing out of the automobile's requirements *(Fig. 470)*. It is, in the end, a kind of compromise with, or—in terms of Kahn's own method of Form (here Roman) and Design—a rationalization of Le Corbusier in the light of existing conditions.

One fruitful result of that kind of combination of Le Corbusier and Kahn is Habitat *(Figs. 473, 474)* at Expo '67 in Montreal. That Canadian fair as a whole, despite its lack of general order, painfully showed up the crass disaster at New York of 1964–65. Expo's splendid demonstration of various types of public transportation, now almost everywhere atrophying in the United States, was especially welcome. So was Habitat. The setback of its

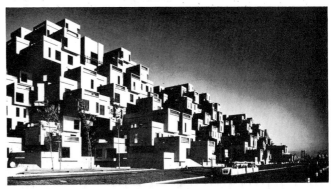

473. Montreal, Canada. Expo '67. Habitat. 1967. Moshe Safdie. General view.

474. Habitat. Detail.

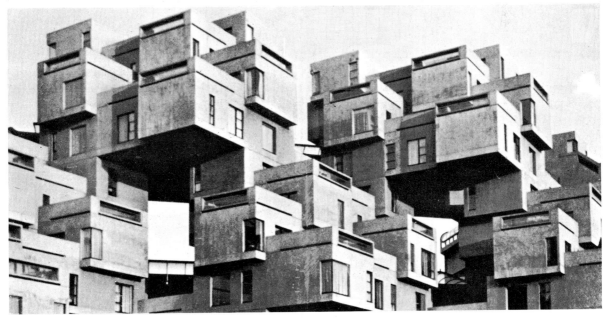

apartment units recalls Le Corbusier's projects for terraced apartments in North Africa, of the early 1930's. The desire to use the major spatial unit of the apartments as a structural beam is a device for the integration of institution with physical structure which is typical of Kahn. And Safdie, the brilliant young architect of Habitat, was for a time a pupil of Kahn's and worked in his office. But the units do not really work that way in Habitat; they all look alike, but those lower down are taking tremendous compressive forces, and the vertical expansion joints show us that the actual structure is of huge vertical piers more or less leaning against each other. But, visually, the building, with terraces on the roofs and fine views to be had by its occupants through it and under it, as well as across it, recalls the Pueblo architecture with which this book began *(Fig. 28)*. The comparison is so obvious that it has come to be derided, but it involves more than a matter of superficial resemblance in massing, because pueblos are the expression of a people living closely together in peace, loving the place, nonaggressive, finding their satisfaction in the rituals of productive life. It is not a bad image for the city of the future. And it will be a more effective one when it is carried out in true mass production with lighter materials, more consistent dry structure, and so on. As James Rouse noted and Paul Rudolph has shown, it should be built of trailers in a frame, demountable and mobile, functionally integral but structurally separable *(Figs. 298, 299)*. It now points up, in any event, the challenge of the future, which will be to create an environment industrially produced but infinitely varied, offering some satisfaction to everyone in a crowded world.[10]

The capacity of architects to create something of the sort for the urban environment as a whole will come more than anywhere else from their view of themselves. At present, the principles of the American Institute of Architects have something in common with those of the American Medical Association. In both cases, the status of the members of the profession as competing if mutually congratulatory individuals is supported and protected. All this is well and good, but the architect is now being employed more and more by redevelopment agencies, which bring a new collective force to bear upon him. That force is wielded mostly by certain kinds of lawyers and civil administrators, full of lies and dodges, with hearts like small stones. These men implement planning and redevelopment tactics, under the strategic direction of their patron politician, while the architects and planners employed by the agencies make many fundamental decisions about design and order their nonagency colleagues about. Unhappily, it is no secret that too many of them, especially in smaller cities, drifted more or less by accident into redevelopment and planning during the past decade. With some strikingly idealistic exceptions, they tended to be something less than the best qualified in the profession, since the talented man had more than the usual inducements during that period to go out in the traditional way and make a great name on his own. Now, however, still alone, he is meeting his bureaucratic contemporary on the other side of the table, and the power of final decision lies over there, often exercised by relatively unqualified people. It is a situation common in revolutions, and America is involved in an urban revolution today. In order to survive in that context the architect needs power. Perhaps spiritual power would be enough, because he has not shown up too well in the confrontation so far. The larger firms have milked the situation for profit, and all have been too easily diverted from larger considerations by the timely gift of a commission or two. This would be all right if the architect were simply a servant. Perhaps he is. But during the past generations he has given himself airs as a social engineer, a man of high ideals and touchy honor. If so, it is probably time for him to draw the stub of whatever remains to him now. Perhaps he will get on the other side of the table himself, as Barnett, Stern, Robertson, and others have done in New York and elsewhere, since the most challenging and rewarding projects of the future, such as proper mass housing and so on, will be handled there, and real professional competence must be available lest all be lost. To save his soul he may take up Advocacy Planning of the kind organized through the Architects' Renewal Committee in Harlem (ARCH) by Richard Hatch, since succeeded by Max Bond, as the black community moves toward the control of its own neighborhoods. Perhaps the architect will organize in other ways outside the agencies, reshaping the American Institute of Architects to act as a true

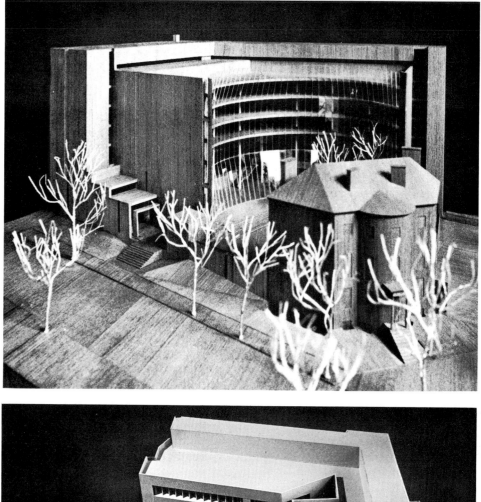

475. Project for headquarters for the American Institute of Architects. Washington, D.C. 1966. Romaldo Giurgola. View of model.

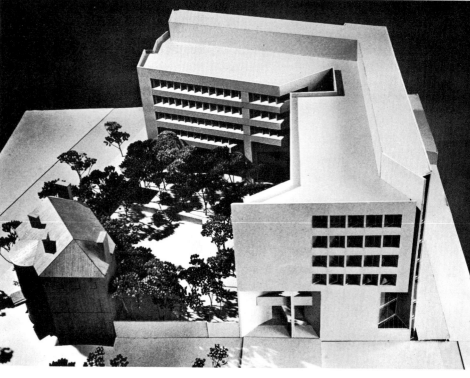

476. Project for AIA Headquarters. Washington, D.C. 1968. Romaldo Giurgola. Final scheme.

477. (*Opposite*) Project for Transportation Square Office Building. Washington, D.C. 1968. Caudill Rowlett & Scott, Venturi and Rauch, architects. Perspective view.

urban force as he himself slowly grows into an understanding of what such forces are. In that connection, it will be interesting to see if the A.I.A. will attempt to defend the commendable design by Romaldo Giurgola for its own projected building in Washington *(Fig. 475)*, to which it gave a prize in an honest competition, and to which Washington's Fine Arts Commission has since denied a building permit. "You will thank us someday, Mr. Giurgola," one of the more unlikely members of that commission was heard to say. (As this book went to press, in late 1968, Giurgola had been forced to return some half-dozen times with changes required by the Commission's undeniably offensive and certainly narrow-minded dominant architectural member. Finally, after having injured his light and buoyant design considerably in order to conform to the Commission's ponderously classicizing taste *(Fig. 476)*, Giurgola was forced by his own professional integrity to resign the commission. The A.I.A. backed him not at all. Again, Robert Venturi's design for the Transportation Square Office Building, also a competition winner and already approved by the Washington Redevelopment Authority, was denied a permit in a hearing that was conducted at such a low level of personal and professional abuse that the Commission refused to release its transcript. Since Venturi's drawings make it clear enough that the building would have considerably enhanced its site *(Fig. 477)*, firmly defining the street intersection and finely complementing the older buildings round about, it is again difficult to agree with the Commission's puristic and vulgarly genteel criteria. These call the whole problem of review boards into question, since they seem about to impose upon the nation's capital

a pompous aridity and a jealous authoritarianism which may be appropriate enough for Lyndon Johnson's Washington but hardly for that of its founders.)

Clearly enough, there are two counterprinciples at work and in conflict in American life and in American architecture and urbanism at the moment: the aggressively pretentious and the reasonably accommodating. In a sense, Habitat or Rudolph's trailers combine both, and surely no one is prepared to deny the need for large schemes and general conceptions. Yet many now agree with Robert Venturi that the principle of "accommodation" is the more significant, or the more necessary to respect, at the present time. The word so employed is Venturi's own, and was used by him in his book, *Complexity and Contradiction in Architecture*, published in 1967. The principles of compromise and multiplicity suggested there have never been popular in America, despite the pluralism of the American condition. It is undoubtedly because of that very heterogeneity that Americans have so often preferred "unifying," homogenized solutions. The self-righteousness of American puritanism, which must see alternatives in terms of black or white, also continues to play a part. Irony, especially, tends to be venomously resented; and "accommodation" requires and is sweetened by irony, which is aware that nothing is final and perfect and that human beings must give and take a little all the time. One cannot really live in a city (or in the modern world, for that matter) without it, as the Greeks, for all their heroic aggression, understood perfectly well. Le Corbusier, for example, invariably balanced his heroic actions with urbanely ironic qualifications and so made them consistently believable in modern terms. Most of

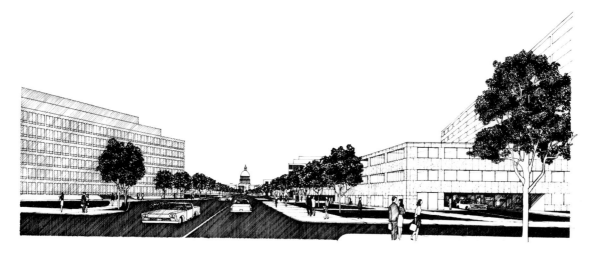

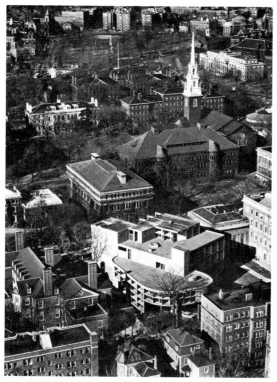

478. Cambridge, Massachusetts. Harvard University. Carpenter Center for the Visual Arts. 1963. Le Corbusier. Air view.

479. Carpenter Center for the Visual Arts. Approach from Quincy Street.

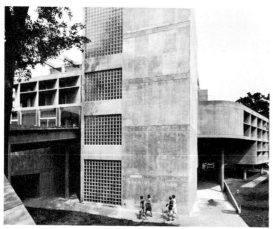

all, it was exactly that kind of building which he designed for Cambridge, Massachusetts. While his followers there had been producing some quite fine housing, as well as some rather overstated *béton brut* in the master's late manner, he himself was preparing a building with slender columns of smooth, plywood-molded concrete, soft as a cloud, sharp-edged as a cigar box, for America. His Carpenter Center for the Visual Arts at Harvard is pure volume, or volumes, each space articulated from the other and enclosed as a discrete shape in a cool shell of flat or curving walls *(Figs. 478, 479)*. The ramp leads the undergraduate seeking a short cut through the block into the building's cumulous folds, shows him the studios blooming with light, and induces him, presumably, to take part at some future date in the various programs for making things that the Center so proudly affords. Space-positive, mass-negative, ballooning, tautened, and column-stretched as the building is, it enhances the hard, dry closed cubes of the others near it and gently echoes the swell of its only true comrade, Richardson's Sever Hall, diagonally across the way *(Fig. 179)*. It is respectful urbanism, and excellent for the street, despite the fact that it is not set parallel to it. But it is ironic, too: complex, contradictory, and full of easy accommodations and Pop asides, a master's sketch, in fact (how appropriate to the Fogg Museum next door), but in all ways more understood, apparently, by Venturi than by any other architect in America.

Few architects anywhere have been able to accommodate contradiction and to suggest irony through their forms. Perhaps Furness could a little, or Maybeck; Wright, not at all, nor Saarinen, nor Rudolph, nor Johnson, who probably understands the principle but cannot embody it. Not Kahn. But with Venturi it is fundamental and is without doubt the major reason why he has so far enjoyed little popular success and incurred surprising professional resentment. (After one of the usual rebuffs, his indispensable partner, John Rauch, said, "Don't take it so hard. You're only a failure. I'm an assistant failure.") On the one hand, Venturi's lovely house for the distinguished historian of the *trecento*, Millard Meiss, a wise and gentle comment upon the nature of Italy and of art history alike, was never built *(Figs. 480–82)*. On the other, his early Pop

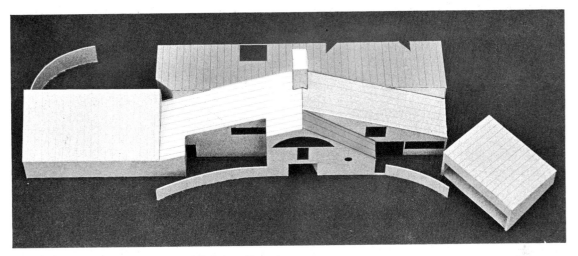

480. Project, house for Millard Meiss. 1962. Robert Venturi.

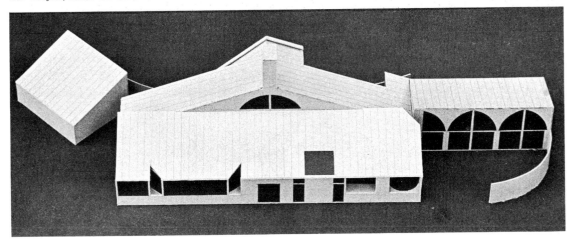

481. House for Millard Meiss. View of model.

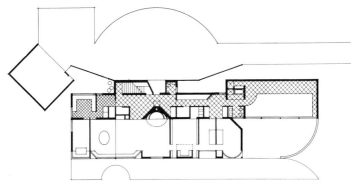

482. House for Millard Meiss. Plan.

231

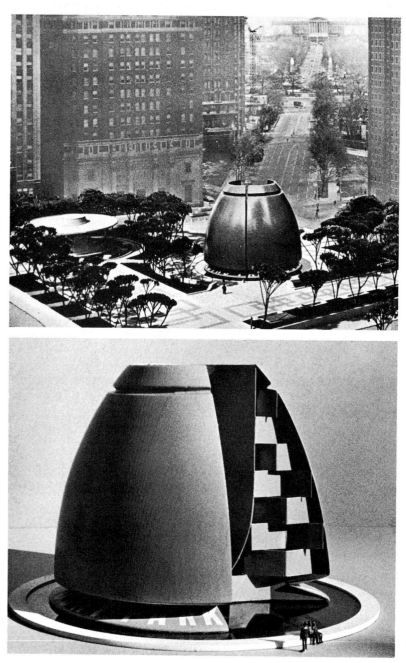

483. Competition entry for fountain, Philadelphia, Pennsylvania. 1964. Venturi and Rauch; Denise Scott Brown. Photomontage.

484. Competition entry for fountain. Model.

restaurant was destroyed by the gentility of the owner, while the entrepreneur, if that is the correct term in this connection, of the Princeton Memorial Park cemetery decided to make it "colonial" *(Fig. 485)*. Needless to say, none of Venturi's earlier entries in competitions gained a prize, neither his Roosevelt Memorial, where sculpture became wholly environmental, nor his fountain for Philadelphia, where it became an ominous object, focusing its water jet, scaleless, immanent as the casing of a shell *(Figs. 483, 484)*.

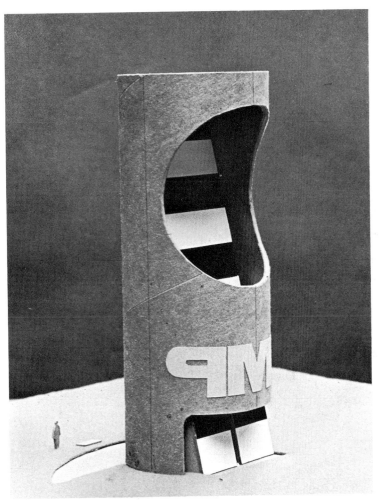

485. Project for a monument for Princeton Memorial Park. Hightstown, New Jersey. 1966. Venturi and Rauch.

Venturi's own house of 1962 is like Wright's of 1889 *(Fig. 221)*, an *ur* dwelling as a child would draw it *(Figs. 486, 487)*. But Venturi dumps the thing on the ground, splits the protective gable into a baroque apotheosis, nodding ironically to Blenheim *(Fig. 65)*, and in general comments lightly about that fearsome institution which real-estate operators have a distressing tendency to refer to as a Home. Inside, as out, there are recollections of the Shingle Style *(Figs. 212, 215, 216)*, before Wright forced all plans into puristic geometries, and the spatial areas expand and contract according to their functional requirements rather than to a preconceived concept of abstract order. Already, the difference from Kahn, Venturi's most important mentor, is striking. There is no real struggle with structural or geometric considerations; these "accommodate" easily to the spaces conceived as human beings will use them. One is reminded of Alvar Aalto, to whom Venturi also owes a great deal, and in whose timely dormitory at M.I.T., of 1949, Kahn was apparently to perceive the corner towers; Venturi, like many other young architects, the function-accommodating housing of the stairs.

But again, it is perhaps the ironic comment upon America's middle-class suburban dream, *le rêve à deux millions*, which has, consciously or unconsciously, formed the reaction of most observers to Venturi's work. In Charles Moore's design *(Fig. 488)*, in some measure derived from Venturi's, as Moore would ironically agree, the comment sometimes becomes strident, the laughter so picturesquely maniacal that it upsets nobody. (Though Moore has since come rather nobly and spaciously into his own, as his Faculty Club for the University of California, at Santa Barbara [*Fig. 489*], now shows.) But Venturi is a deeply systematic and fundamentally monumental architect, whose themes cannot help but turn serious and tragic in his hands. The absurdity of the mass-produced dream world is inescapably suggested by his buildings *(Figs. 485, 486)*.

486. Chestnut Hill, Pennsylvania. Venturi House. 1962. Venturi and Rauch.

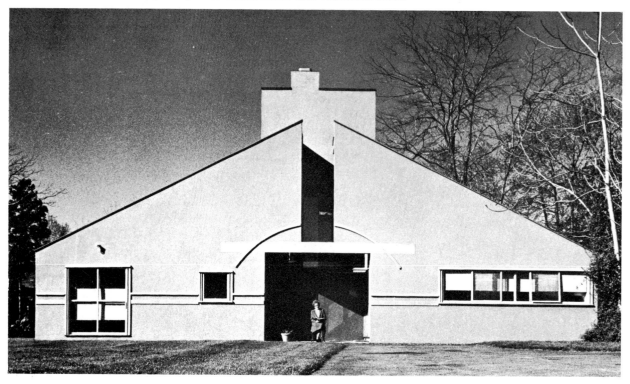

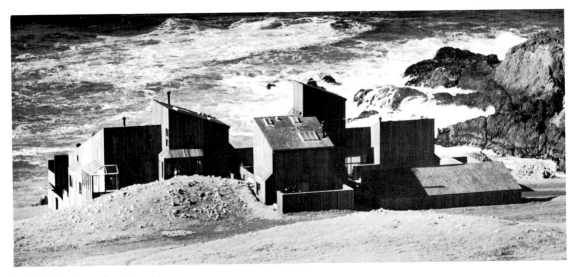

488. Sea Ranch, California. 1966. Moore, Lyndon, Turnbull, and Whitaker.

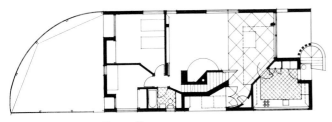

487. Venturi House. Plan.

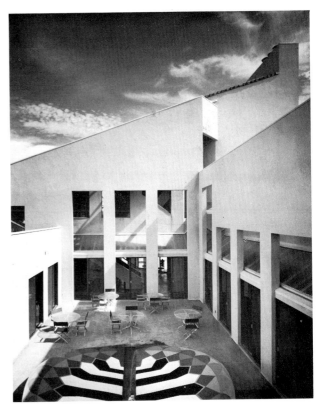

489. Santa Barbara, California. University of California. Faculty Club. 1966. Moore, Lyndon, Turnbull, and Whitaker.

His Guild Housing for the Aged surely does so *(Figs. 490, 491, 494)*. Most of the profession dislikes it. Contrast with Oskar Stonorov's prize-winning building in the same city for the same program is instructive. The latter is what we have been taught to expect: windows ceiling to floor, carpeting at least spiritually wall to wall, Miami Beach for everyone. Venturi's is a brick building with windows in it on a street in Philadelphia, in scale with the older and pretty good housing behind it and with the street, which it respects. Like Sullivan, as we have already noted *(Fig. 242)*, Venturi creates several scales. The various sorts of room have the several sizes of window appropriate to their use, cut into the brick skin over the concrete frame. Hence the design, while not inexpressive of the structural facts, is functionally rather than technologically directed. Contrast should be drawn with Skidmore, Owings and Merrill's office tower on their mechanistic campus for the University of Illinois, in Chicago *(Fig. 492)*. There, a largely arbitrary diagrammatic representation of the compressive forces in the frame is used to design the façade. This is pseudo-technological domination, not functional expression; the spaces used by men inside are not employed to design the surface. Le Corbusier, in his Secretariat at Chandigarh, both shows us the frame and varies the expression of the major offices, so causing the building to breathe with human action *(Fig. 493)*. Venturi covers the frame but shows the wall as thin and brings it to generous life with variants and hierarchies of spatial use. In the simplest sense, Venturi's design is humanistic, in contrast to that of too many contemporary architects, especially in America, who take refuge from human complexity in technological diagrams—not in true technology, which enhances the choices for human behavior. Therefore, the demands of the exterior must also be considered, no less humanistic those, and also to have an effect on the wall. So the whole mass steps up to the street, defines it with a flat and "decorated" façade, identifies itself with lettering brasher than Roman, expansively Pop, and blooms generously upward to the large, arched opening of a common living room with a television aerial rising above it *(Figs. 490, 494)*. This last feature obsessively infuriates Kahn. Again, his is the heroic reaction: Those old people had better shape up and do a little reading. Venturi would shrug: So they look at TV, don't they? With whatever pre-existed on the street, Venturi's building gets along; with what will follow it, since it gives itself no special airs, it will always be in keeping. It avoids aggressive gestures but has its own monumentality, ironically proletarian and antigenteel. Rather an aristocratic position, in fact. This again may well be why it annoys almost everyone.

490. Philadelphia, Pennsylvania. Guild House. 1960–63. Venturi and Rauch; Cope and Lippincott. Friends' housing for the elderly.

491. Guild House. Plan.

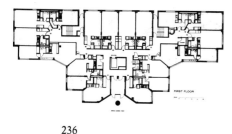

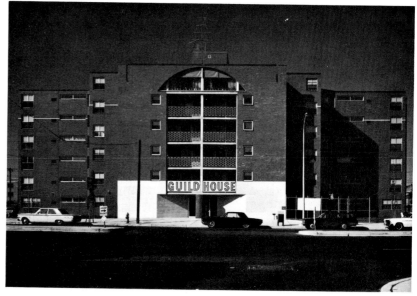

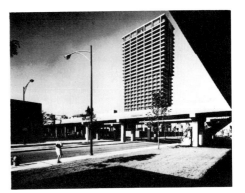

492. Chicago, Illinois. University of Illinois, Chicago Circle Campus. Administration Tower. 1964. Skidmore, Owings and Merrill.

493. Chandigarh, India. Secretariat. 1951–57. Le Corbusier.

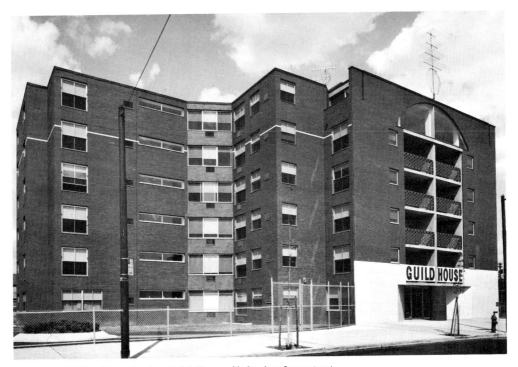

494. Philadelphia, Pennsylvania. Guild House. Angle view from street.

Venturi's project, with Clark and Rapuano, for the redevelopment of the center of the town of North Canton, Ohio, showed what he could do in working along the lines that the American small-town Main Street suggested *(Figs. 495–98)*. The second project, when the position of the city hall had to be changed, perhaps most forcefully shows his power of relationship and of what he calls "inflection." The principles upon which the buildings were based are in one sense the familiar Sullivanian ones, but there is an individual assimilation of suggestions deriving from sources as far apart as classical antiquity and the work of Lutyens. The project died with the death of its major sponsor; some reflection of it can be seen in the fire station for Columbus, Indiana, which, despite or because of its super-graphics and its irony, is somehow just like the cardboard house for the little red fire truck everybody had as a child *(Fig. 499)*. Whatever America had of a functionalist folk tradition is thus welcomed and employed,

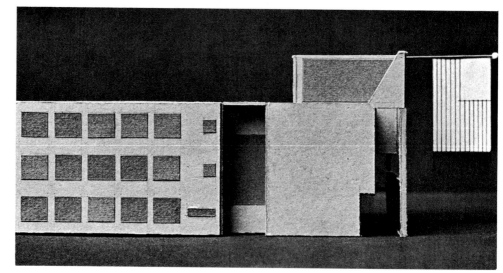

495. Project for town center, North Canton, Ohio. 1965. Venturi and Rauch; Clarke and Rapuano. View of model.

496. Project for a city hall, North Canton, Ohio. 1965. Venturi and Rauch; Clarke and Rapuano. View of model.

238

497. Project for a city hall, North Canton, Ohio. View of model.

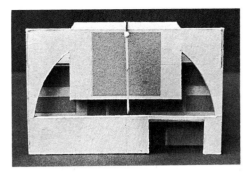

498. Project for a YMCA. North Canton, Ohio. Venturi and Rauch. Perspective view. Sketch by Robert Venturi.

499. Columbus, Indiana. Fire Station #4. 1965–67. Venturi and Rauch.

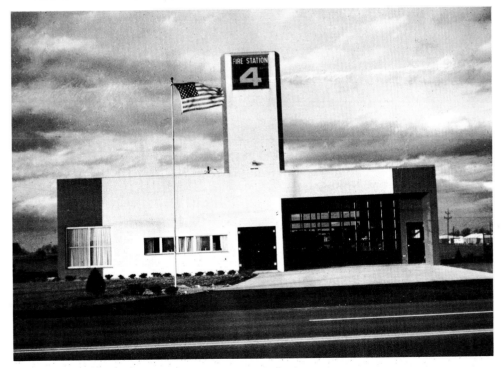

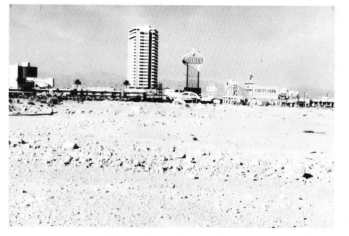

though not without comment, in Venturi's work, just as his and Kahn's together revive the more consciously artistic but no less functionally based architectural tradition which Sullivan and Wright had climaxed long before.

"Main Street is almost all right," wrote Venturi, here maddening those who had put their urbanistic marbles on a Clean-Up-America campaign. So Venturi's interest in the ecology of the Strip, the motel, the gas station, and so on *(Figs. 500–502)*, supported and in part suggested here by the motorized researches of John B. Jackson, the brilliant editor of *Landscape*, constitutes a willingness on his part to try to understand and, indeed, to enjoy the American scene as it is, in order to learn how to use its elements to make it function better as a general

500. Las Vegas, Nevada. The Strip from the desert.

501. Las Vegas, Nevada. The Strip.

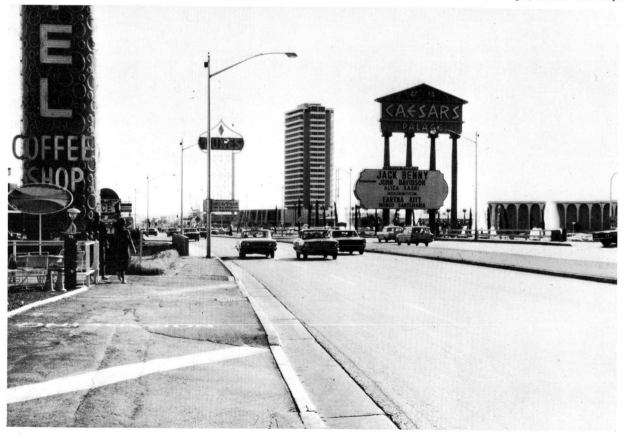

environment. How did the motel, for example, whose floating world Vladimir Nabokov made us see, grow from its separate splintery cabins of the 1930's (touching, threadbare old America), to its glittering horizontal continuities of the 1950's (Lolita at the Coke machine down the way), to its multistories of the 1960's, invading the towns, every room bugged and magic-fingered? Or, what is good about a parking lot? What can be gained from automobiles at rest as in motion? How do lights and signs function? How did they achieve their great size? How can the unilinear development of a road make volumes of space beside it? What are the positive qualities of visual shock and confusion, of the automobile oasis, the proletarianized cowboy's dreams? Here, again, the influence of the Pop painters and sculptors, felt throughout Venturi's later work, should be especially recognized *(Figs. 485, 503)*. They have indeed made many Americans begin to see the challenge of the billboards, just at the moment when other Americans have been getting around to tearing them down or, like those who would "beautify" Las Vegas, planting them out with trees. In any event, the fact of the matter is that the electric signs now tower like the dying elms.

There is a more menacing scale to these problems, of which Venturi, Jackson, and all those who now look about them cannot be unaware *(Fig. 504)*. There can be a horrid viciousness in the Strip. Some of the growth is cancerous, perhaps deadly. Frontier hedonism has always teetered on the edge of murder. Yet it is at the vaster scale of throughway

502. Las Vegas. Motel and gas station.

503. Roy Lichtenstein: *Hot Dog.* 1962.

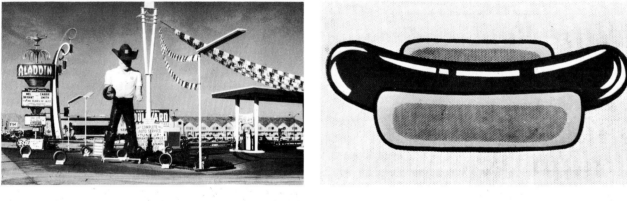

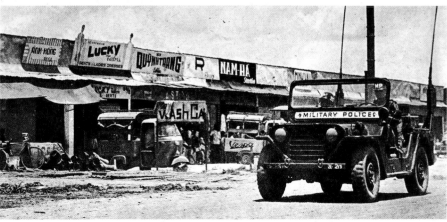

504. Tananhoi, South Vietnam. Frontier Strip, export model. 1967.

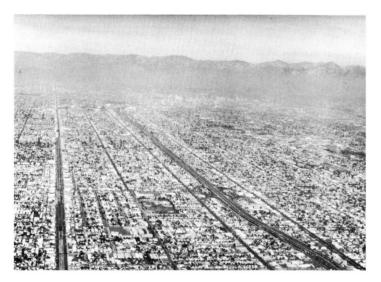

505. Los Angeles, California. Freeway.

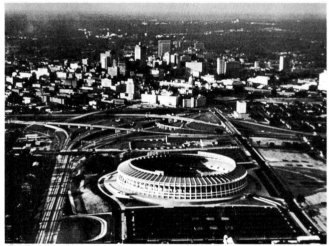

506. Atlanta, Georgia. Air view.

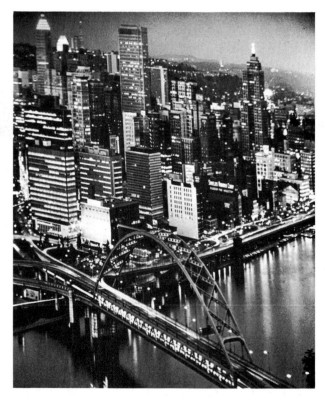

507. Pittsburgh, Pennsylvania. The Golden Triangle.

and connector that the most devastating achievements of modern industrial life now grandly and savagely unfold *(Figs. 505–8)*. The rush of the movement itself, only partly under control and wild with danger, is the right and appropriate way to perceive the new urban scene, with its promise of smashed bodies, its mechanical roar, and its rubbery scream, just as the laggard footpace accompanied by the sound of human voices was the proper way to ascend the Spanish Stairs. That norm was peace; ours is apparently mechanized war. One now dives rattling past the towers of the city, lighted in rising tiers, and flashes through its heart, high above the little houses, released from confinement as through one reckless act of destruction and escape. It is the jailbreak of the urban masses, one-handed with a beery tattoo on the roof at seventy miles an hour in two tons of old iron. Baseball-bat-basher, beer-belly,

breaker of cities, comes into his own in ours—"a savage servility / slides by on grease," wrote Lowell.

This urban scene is truly of America's making. It is the really new thing. European observers can afford to romanticize it, but Americans are forced to take note of the violent and ungenerous social attitudes which seem to accompany it in those areas, like Los Angeles, where its automobilized aspect is most fully developed. In consequence, we can hardly help but question its value, but in perceiving works of art there comes a moment when we must pass beyond preconceptions to an empirical recognition of what exists. Otherwise we can never learn anything. And all this is here; some of our greatest painters have seen it *(Fig. 509)*. It is our most complete work of art, multiple and tremendous. Its uniqueness, its inconceivable brutality, even only its visual magnificence, can never be denied.

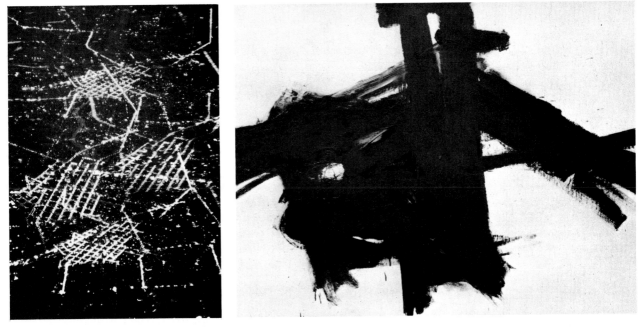

508. Minneapolis–St. Paul, Minnesota. Air view at night.

509. Franz Kline: *Crosstown.* 1955.

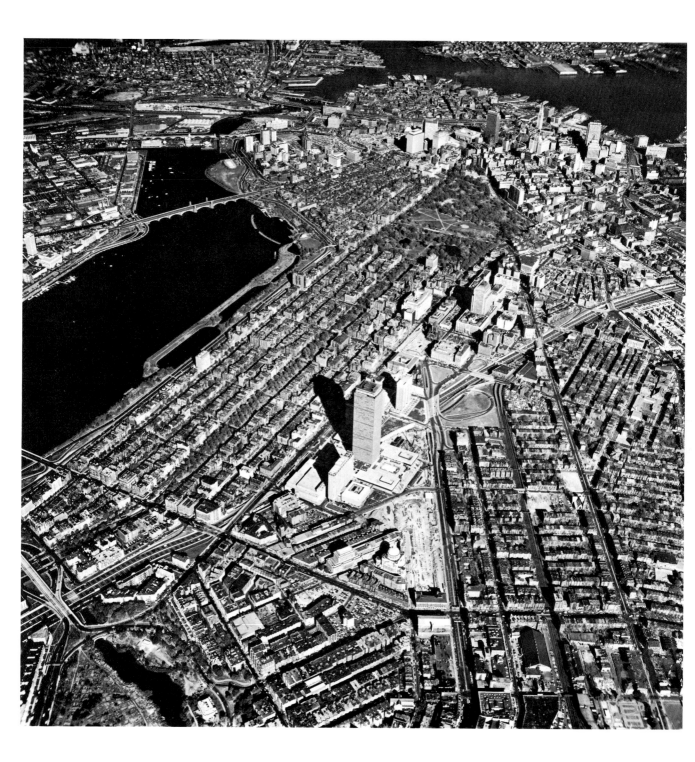

The memory of Sullivan, though perhaps unexpected in this connection, should again be invoked, since the more particular local traditions which Sullivan represented at both small scale and large fell, as we have seen, before an international style, the Beaux-Arts, which worked from a model of reality which was most of all preconceived, and also genteel, generalized, and abstract. Even more abstract, and puristic, was the architectural and urbanistic model employed by the International Style as America understood it, whose development owed something important to the early work of Sullivan himself in its search for what Sullivan had called "the demonstration so broad as to allow of no exception." The result may be said to be Boston's Prudential Building, standing in a wasteland of its own making (Fig. 510). Therefore, during the 1960's it became perfectly obvious that exceptions had become mandatory, and that the preconceived formal model of the International Style, already a generation old, needed to be revised and humanized in terms of the actual complexity of human life and urban building. Philosophically, the shift was from the existentialist heroic-idealism of the 1950's toward a more empirical position, from what Lévi-Strauss termed the "dialectic" of Sartre to the "analysis" which he himself proposed; from a confrontational stance to a more ecological one. Yet it is the older attitude which is now bearing rather frightening fruit

at all levels, domestic and international, of American life. It is the outmoded model, applied after its utility is gone by those who do not understand it and under circumstances which make it highly destructive as well. One of the outstanding challenges at this moment involves breaking the grip of that "form" upon the minds of architects and planners (politicians and policy makers) before it wholly blinds us to reality and humanity alike and, in combination with related social factors, tears our cities, and with them probably our society and the world, totally apart.

Cataclysmic, automotive, and suburban: these have been the pervasive characteristics of Urban Redevelopment in America. They were all present in the conception of the Prudential and its related throughway. They derive, as we have already noted, from the same kind of combination of Le Corbusier's Ville Radieuse with Howard's Garden City which marked Wright's Broadacre City. As such, they are exactly in accord with the most persistent American myths and desires: the city is *bad;* tear it down, get on the road, be a pioneer, live in Greenwich like a white man. So redevelopment became a way to appear to plan but not really to plan. It encouraged all kinds of forces that existed: real-estate men, automobiles, and so on, and it came to function as such forces suggested or required.

510. Boston, Massachusetts. Prudential Life Insurance Company. Air view.

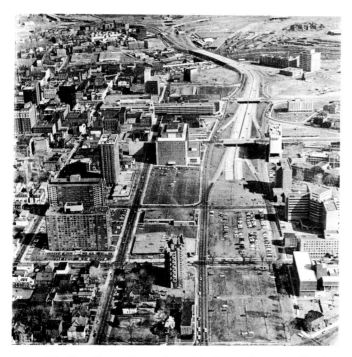

511. New Haven, Connecticut. Oak Street Connector. Air view.

512. Oak Street Connector, facing west in direction of expansion. Middle distance: Crawford Manor by Paul Rudolph.

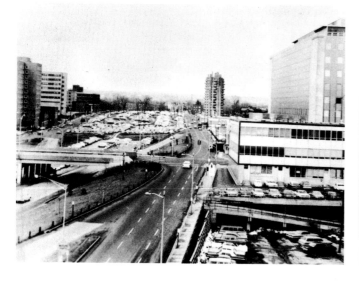

The redevelopment of New Haven, Connecticut, may appropriately be considered a fair example. The process has probably advanced as far there as anywhere else in America because of the energy of Edward Logue, archetypal redeveloper (who then went on to Boston and is now in New York), and of Mayor Richard C. Lee, who has ground considerable political mileage out of it. Though a Democrat, Lee was able to engage the support of most of the conservative Republican businessmen of the city (most of whom lived in the suburbs) for a program which appealed not only to their pocketbooks but also to their sincerely self-righteous view of what society should be and how people ought to live: cutting their grass on the outskirts, apparently. Well and good; but it has not worked out quite that way. Redevelopment has demolished about 5,000 living units of the poor in New Haven during the past twelve years or so but has built only about 1,507, of which about 793 have been luxury housing and 445 middle-income, with only 12 low-income public-housing units, and 257 for the elderly, constructed during that period. All the rest of New Haven's public housing, and not too much of it at that, was built before Redevelopment under earlier administrations. Just about 200 rent subsidies for proper housing elsewhere have also come along late in the period.

513. *Across the Continent.* 1868. Currier and Ives colored lithograph; drawing by F. F. Palmer.

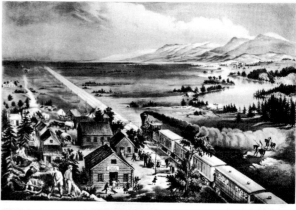

Redevelopment's Oak Street Connector shows the
system at work: a slum was cleared to provide a
huge connector, that good old American Open Road,
designed as if for the prairie, which was intended
to bring suburbanites into the center of the city,
which would then compete with suburban shopping
centers and, in the process, began to look rather
like a suburban shopping center itself *(Figs. 511–14)*.
Public transportation decayed; the automobile proliferated, so requiring more connectors, which would
eventually cut the city up into fragments in the Garden City manner *(Fig. 515)*, bursting through parks,
devouring neighborhoods. The Oak Street Connector
is now to be continued through a low-income neighborhood as Route 34, literally twice as wide as it
needs to be, in order to clear out as large an area
as possible *(Figs. 512, 515)*. (Now, in late 1968, after
years of pressure, 100 feet or so have been sub-
tracted from the gargantuan right of way, but the
neighborhood has already been largely destroyed
before it.) In these ways, the suburb is brought into
the city, which is in turn scattered into the suburbs,
while the dense old slum is replaced by vast open
spaces defined by commercial buildings and luxury
apartments *(Fig. 514)*. The slum is now high rise,
and, like Robert Moses' Lincoln Towers and Washington Square Village, it is upper-middle income as
well. Who gains? Not the poor. Rudolph's old peo-

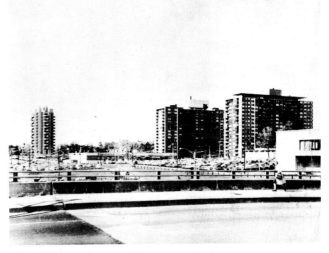

514. Oak Street Connector. Luxury apartments.

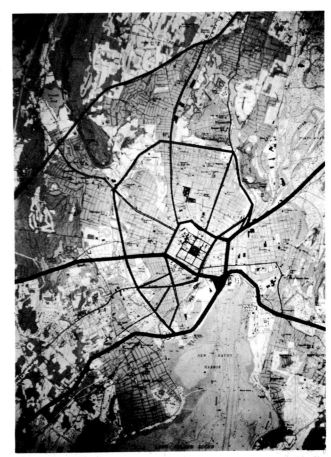

515. New Haven, Connecticut. Plan: projection of proposed
throughways, connectors, and enlarged streets.

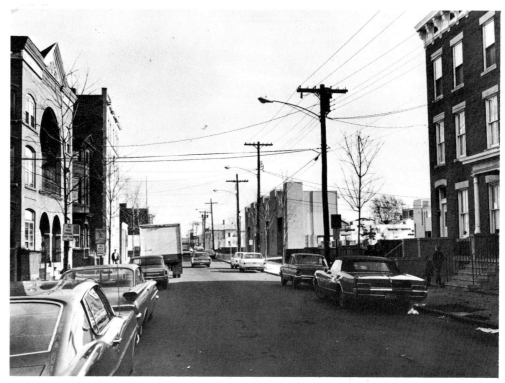

516. New Haven, Connecticut. Columbus Mall houses. 1963.
Earl P. Carlin, Architect; Paul E. Pozzi, Peter Millard,
Associates. View on street.

517. Columbus Mall Houses.

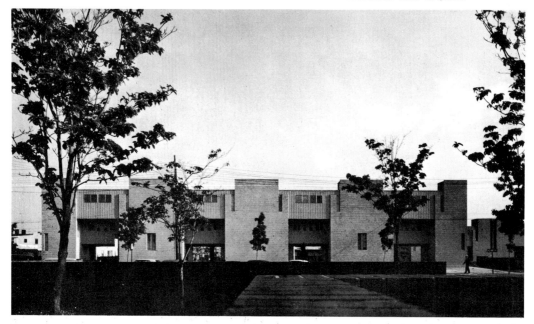

ple's tower, called Crawford Manor, is the only public housing envisaged in the area of the Oak Street Connector. Roche's Knights of Columbus Building will rise in it, too, a jackbooted sentinel of corporate power *(Figs. 426, 427, 512)*. In a superficial sense it is all exactly in Le Corbusier's image, the monumental slabs standing huge and free in space *(Figs. 337, 346)*. But here it is not the anguished grouping of low-income housing towers which New York and Chicago most earnestly raised *(Fig. 345)*. It is, instead, another gross, pictorial distortion of a European program. Because the poor were scattered, and their neighborhood was destroyed for profit sanctified by puritan conviction, since—as Herbert J. Gans showed in his book *The Urban Villagers*, about the similar destruction of a neighborhood in Boston—their way of life did not fit the middle-class dream. Where did the poor go? ("To Bridgeport," is the waggish reply in New Haven.) Some, especially the Blacks, of whom more than 40 percent of those living in the city have been affected, and to whom most of even the rattiest suburbs are closed, went to the area known as the "Hill." More than a few had been forced to move out in front of redevelopment several times before.

The middle-income housing that was built in various redeveloped areas was mostly shockingly deficient in any sense of place, public space, or neighborhood grouping. The best of it, though in-jured by the Redevelopment Agency's palsied landscaping, was surely Carlin and Millard's Columbus Mall Housing off Wooster Square *(Figs. 516, 517)*, where the archaic massing and tense surface of the American tradition produced forms grand, even noble, on their street. They were not inappropriate *palazzi* for their predominantly Italian neighborhood, which was, on the whole, able to exert enough political power and picturesque appeal to be handled with some care, while Interstate 91 was pushed eastward away from it, eventually separating it from the largest black enclave in the area. No low-income public-rental housing whatever was built, except for the aged, until Carlin, Pozzi, and Associates' twelve units, designed by Bart Kaltenbach and completed in 1967 *(Fig. 518)*. This housing reversed the puristic pattern. Its citation in 1967 by the Connecticut chapter of the A.I.A. read as follows:

A good example of anti-cataclysmic redevelopment, appropriate to the pre-existing street and to the fabric of life which it houses. The jury welcomes New Haven's first foray into low income public housing under redevelopment, and is pleased that it clearly respects the neighborhood and its people. Indeed it is largely for that reason that the result shows infinitely more architectural quality than the high-cost, middle-class apartments which have so often been encouraged in the past.

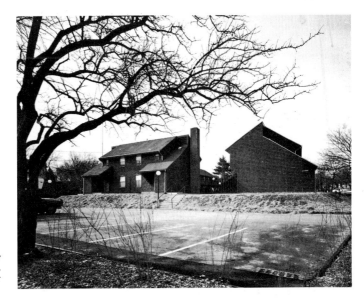

518. New Haven, Connecticut. Riverview Houses. 1967. Carlin, Pozzi & Associates, Architect; Peter Millard, Bart Kaltenbach, Associates.

But the Redevelopment Agency had long before announced its intention of redeveloping the "Hill." The disintegration of the district had accelerated at once, and over the long interval of waiting which ensued, because the future was now uncertain for it. Such is an element of redevelopment strategy in New Haven, as everywhere else, and during that period, one is told, the incidence of recorded emotional disturbances increased threefold in the "Hill." The Agency's plan *(Fig. 519)*, when published, superficially resembled that of the first village center at Reston, with its tower, and so on *(Fig. 520)*. Again, the model is everywhere. In Reston, however, the suburb was to be tightened up and made somewhat more urban; but in the "Hill," the lower-income urban neighborhood, already existing, was to be cleaned out and suburbanized. The process

519. New Haven, Connecticut. Project for redevelopment of the "Hill" neighborhood. 1966. New Haven Redevelopment Agency. Perspective view.

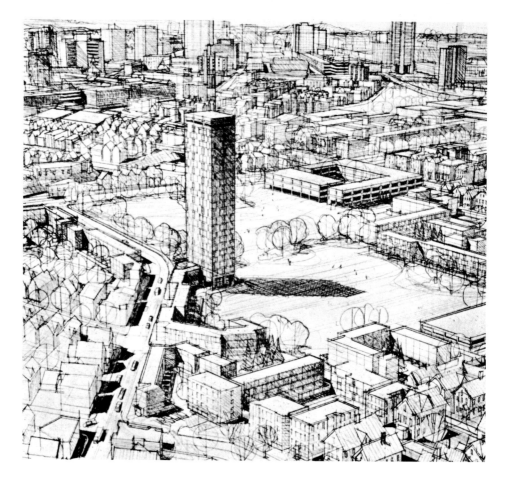

might be described as escalation on the home front. The proposal was to bulldoze the center of the area, to stick up a tower full of old folks rescued from their obliterated village, and to leave a vast empty space defined by garden apartments intended to harbor only a fraction of those whose houses were to be destroyed *(Fig. 519)*. There were going to be fewer people there afterward than there were before, and probably different people, so making the whole thing cleaner and neater and more like God's own suburb. Two schools ("everything for the kids, Granny") were to share the central desert as a playground. Purism and a distaste for life's messy multiplicity could go no further here.

We can hardly be surprised that New Haven's own special riot during the summer of 1967 exploded in the "Hill," with this threat hanging over

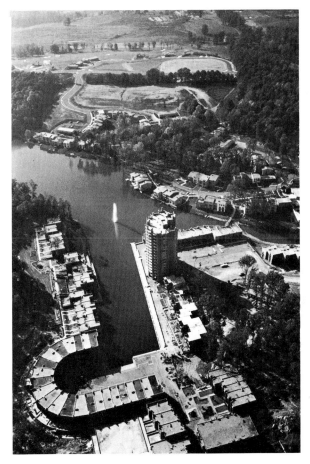

520. Reston, Virginia. 1961. Robert E. Simon, Jr., developer. View of Village Center, by Conklin and Whittlesey.

251

it. Though comparatively minor by current standards, the disturbance set up tremors that were felt as far as Washington, because New Haven had been heavily propagandized as a model city. The mayor of New Haven denied this title, and unlike the mayor of Newark, who blamed "outside agitators" for his troubles, Lee stated that it was merely "Urban America, 1967," which was at fault.

For this avoidance of a demagogic opportunity something can be forgiven him. But the problem remains before him so long as the model of redevelopment adhered to continues to be a sociologically hypocritical and an architecturally outdated one. For example, the Agency had already responded to various pressures by hiring Kahn to take over the Hill project and to redesign it with "a free hand." By the summer of 1967, Kahn had made preliminary proposals to the Agency which retained a great number of the houses the Agency wanted to tear down. His engineers vouched for the structural solidity of every one so saved. The families who lost their houses would in many cases never be able to own a house of their own again. Hence Kahn threw out the tower and broke up the open space around it into better-scaled areas utilizing existing houses. The Agency resisted all these proposals and still wanted the area emptied and the eye of the beholder knocked out. Gee, that tower and those, wow, schools. The latter they insisted upon placing at the busiest intersection, apparently for purposes of touristic visibility. One is reminded of Nasser's "free, public heart clinic for orphans," prominently labeled and crowded up to the cacophonic tourist-camel approach to the pyramids.

(By the end of 1968 the Agency had continued to demolish houses, while Kahn had failed to keep himself properly informed of the situation, and a three-way deadlock had therefore developed between the Agency, Kahn, and an outraged, increasingly resentful community, both black and white. The installation of a unit of the Federal Housing and Urban Development organization [HUD], and the acquisition of funds under the Model Cities Program show few results so far. All progress is at a standstill; something is wrong with the entire program, which clearly has to be reconsidered in terms of who does what for whom and who controls it. The whole is an arresting symbol of a national impasse.)

Therefore, like other Americans in positions of even more frightening power in 1967, the mayor of New Haven and his advisors were really operating under an old model of reality now about fifteen years out of date, a model at its worst simplistic and arrogant, at its best demanding uncompromising confrontation rather than civilized accommodation, a model which needed to be everywhere revised in terms of common humanity if catastrophe was to be avoided. That the model had nothing intrinsic to do with reality can be seen by comparing the Redevelopment Agency's proposal for a new Federal Complex east of the New Haven Green with its proposal for the Hill *Figs. (519, 521, 523)*. The schemes were exactly the same in form despite the polarity of their functions. A free-standing tower beat its breast in a vast open space defined by a horizontal stage set of buildings. It was the old classicism of the 1950's, coming into popularized use fifteen years or so after its time. Considering the agonized reappraisal of urbanistic questions which has taken place since, this was a serious cultural lag. Cataclysmic as could be, the project was intended to tear down almost every building in the block, including the really fine Post Office by James Gamble Rogers, in order to provide continuous basement parking for the bank, as the architect was once moved to say. The Post Office could go because advanced taste, at the Agency's level, as formed, say, by Giedion (through a kind of criticism in which the present writer was by no means guiltless), had not yet come around to valuing any building designed by the Beaux-Arts. A fragment of the City Hall could be left, though cowering under the tax-subsidized, speculative office tower owned by the bank *(Fig. 523)*, because advanced taste, at least in New Haven, had just about gotten around to the Gothic Revival. (Not that of the President of Yale, however, who characterized two fine buildings by J. C. Cady as "monsters" and had them torn down during the summer of 1967 to make way for a huge radio cabinet. In 1968, the mayor took a leaf from the president's book and removed the tower of City Hall during the summer season. He pledges its restoration but points ominously to the cost, while Rudolph hovers in the background waiting to build a new City Hall.)

The definition of the Green, developed over the centuries, would have been destroyed by the redundantly open plaza of the project *(Fig. 522)*, and its scale would have been ground down by the tower, which was in truth intending to use it as a doormat. The project was blocked by citizen action, for which we give thanks, since its sterile pretension would have easily rivaled that of Mussolini's E.U.R.[11]

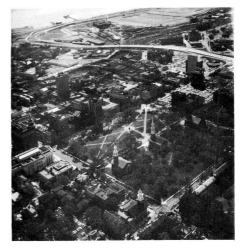

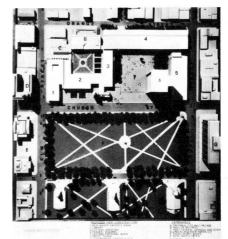

521. New Haven, Connecticut. The Green. Air view. Early nineteenth-century churches. Gothic Revival City Hall; 1859; Henry Austin. Beaux-Arts Post Office; 1910–17; James Gamble Rogers. Redevelopments and connectors beyond.

522. Proposed City Government project and speculative office tower, with the Green. New Haven, Connecticut. 1966. View of model from above.

523. Proposed City Government project and speculative office tower, and New Haven Green. View from ground level.

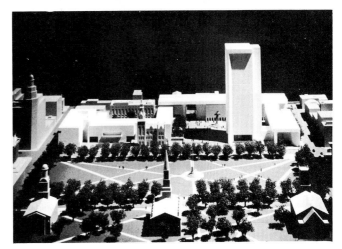

It seems obvious, therefore, that the packaged solutions of the last generation are no longer of much use in the social and architectural problems of the late 1960's. They must all be thought through again, in terms of the lives of all of us. We can hardly flee our neighbors along the ringing highroad forever. Crazy the image, and dear to us; and if we are fortunate, we shall make more and more of it in the future, farther out and wilder. But it cannot be all *(Figs. 524, 525)*. Its pursuit is of emptiness, and we must stand up now to urban life with our fellows, in our feared and hated cities, though the smell of the morning break the heart on the high plains.

Yet, happy the moment when professional questions are finally perceived in relation to everything else, as they demand to be these days. They help us

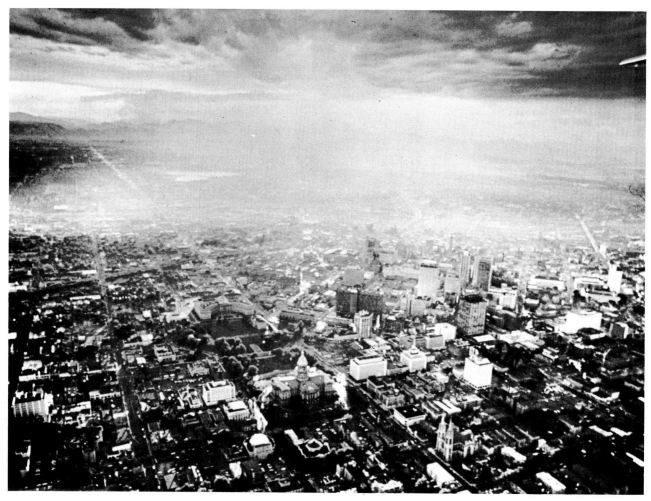

524. Denver, Colorado. View in 1966.

to see that the brutal forcing of present reality into old models is always Procrustean folly. It is, of course, the way in which most states and individuals have encompassed their own collapse before now. The brain hates to think things through afresh; sometimes it chooses death instead. It resists most of all the abandonment of childish dreams and illusions, worn-out myths, and violent evasions. Life is calling the United States to face its realities now.

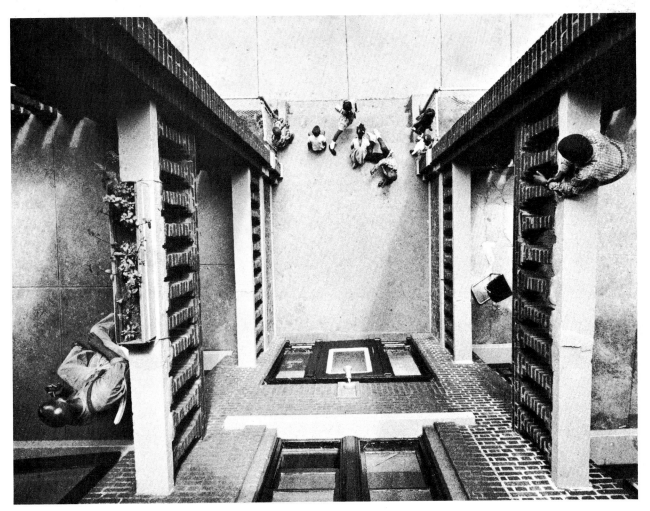

525. Cleveland, Ohio. "Garden Towers."

1988

An architectural revolution—some might call it a counterrevolution—has taken place since the previous page was written. It began with the publication of Venturi's *Complexity and Contradiction in Architecture,* of 1966, which let the air out of the late manifestations of the International Style and paved the way for a revival of what Leon Krier has since called "The Classical and Vernacular Traditions." That movement was later dubbed "Post-Modernism" by Charles Jencks, but the name implies that the International Style had been the only modern architecture, which was far from the case. It might be more accurate to say that the new movement in fact released Modernism as a whole from the entirely unnecessary reductionism, iconoclasm, and aesthetic hermeticism of the International Style—and that liberation can still be seen best in Venturi's own work.

Venturi's Trubek and Wislocki houses of 1971–72 *(Figs. 526, 527)* went beyond his family's house of ten

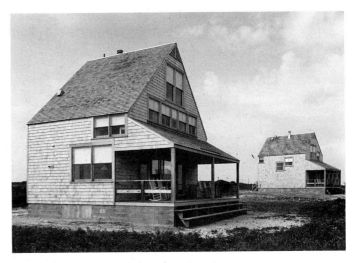

527.   Trubek and Wislocki houses. View from the sea.

526.   Nantucket Island, Massachusetts. Trubek (right) and Wislocki houses. 1970–71. Venturi and Rauch. View from the land side.

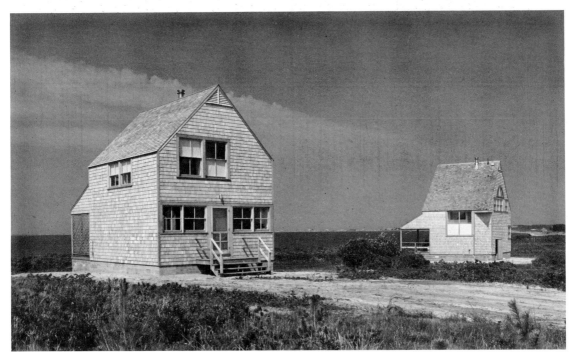

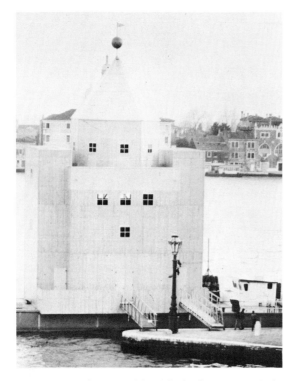

528. Venice, Italy. Teatro del Mondo, for the Venice Biennale. 1980. Aldo Rossi.

529. Block Island, Rhode Island. Coxe-Hayden Studio Houses. 1979–82. Venturi and Rauch. From the land side.

years before *(Fig. 486)* to embrace the Shingle Style tradition more fully. References to Frank Lloyd Wright's early work again play a part, but the general effect is of a wholly traditional architecture, indigenous to Nantucket, which has been snapped into contemporary expression by powerful gestures within the vernacular context. The double-hung window of the Trubek House, for example, has been made enormous in scale. The two square, cross-mullioned windows of the Wislocki House are like eyes, and its massing is as vertical as an arrow, while that of the Trubek House is broad on that side but compressed on the other. The porches which face the splendid view across the upper reaches of Nantucket Harbor are as sharply drawn as the beaks of birds, and the two houses together stand alertly on their bluff, turning slightly toward each other like, on the one hand, Greek temples, or, on the other, seabirds themselves. All this produces a modern architecture which is liberated from abstraction by its link to vernacular traditions and to simple, ageless building types. The work of Aldo Rossi in Italy turned out by the early eighties to be much the same, involving a few clear types and the revival of vernacular and classical traditions. In Rossi's case these were, of course, primarily Italian ones, but they produced forms which were in the end much like Venturi's, suggesting some special sweetness and innocence, and similarly alive

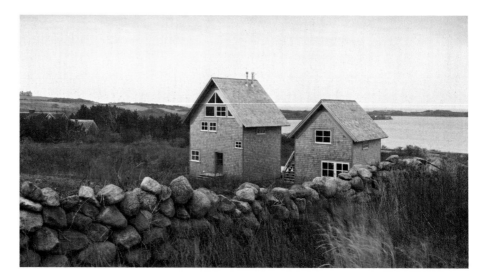

with square, cross-mullioned windows like eyes *(Fig. 528)*.

Venturi's wonderfully tall, lonely, sharp-edged cottages on Block Island *(Fig. 529)* might almost have been designed by Rossi, but his Flynt House in Delaware *(Figs. 530, 531, 532)* has other characteristics more peculiarly his own: among them its decoration. The firm of Venturi, Rauch, and Scott Brown has been foremost in attempting to open up that traditional resource to architects once more. The International Style had consigned ornament to the uttermost pits of hell—we remember that Adolf Loos' splendid and truly mad essay of 1905 had equated it with crime—but in the Flynt House it plays a central role. As an arched screen it masks the large upper windows of the entrance side and so at once unifies that façade and builds up its scale, while from the inside it moves like a great ghost outside the music room of the second floor, which is itself decorated in ways that suggest at once the joy and the notation of music. On the other side of the house vast modern comments on the most primitive of Doric columns, originally round in Venturi's first sketches, loom outside the windows. They are much broader in elevation than they could have been if rounded but are thinned out in section to the thickness of the other walls and so enhance the building's volumetric unity of the in-walled enclosure.

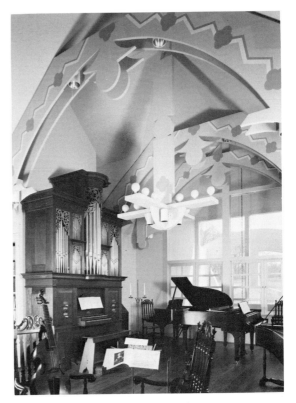

531. Flynt House. Music room.

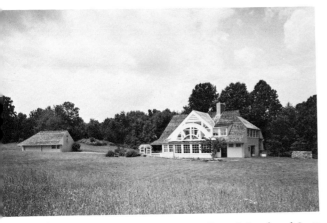

530. Delaware. Flynt House. 1984. Venturi, Rauch and Scott Brown. Entrance side.

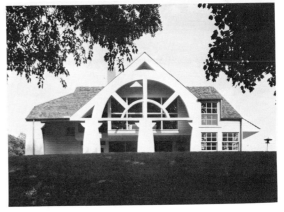

532. Flynt House. Columned façade.

259

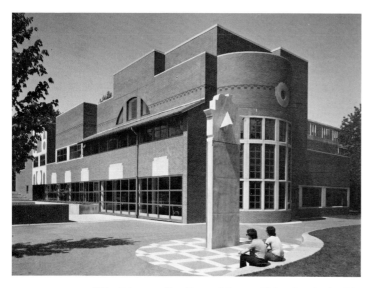

533. Princeton, New Jersey. Princeton University, Gordon Wu Hall. 1980. Venturi, Rauch and Scott Brown. Entrance side.

Venturi is unique in his capacity to cite many kinds of architecture and to tap the strength of traditional ways of building while at the same time endowing the whole with a curiously vital tension and wit that can be nothing but contemporary. His Tudor-evoking Wu Hall at Princeton, wholly contextual with its pre-existing neighbors, does exactly this, inside and out, stretching its surface, throwing up a signboard over the entrance, and cascading the great staircase of the interior down from an enormous Tudor window bay to double as the seats of an impromptu theater *(Figs. 533, 534, 535).* No other contemporary American architect can quite bring off that syncretism of past and present, even though architecture's most intrinsic quality over the ages has always been exactly that, or can seem so to transcend abstract formal manipulation as to deal only with meaning itself.

That quality has now been recognized in England, where Venturi has been selected over a number of distinguished British architects to design the addition to the National Gallery in London. Earlier International Style proposals for that vexed and difficult

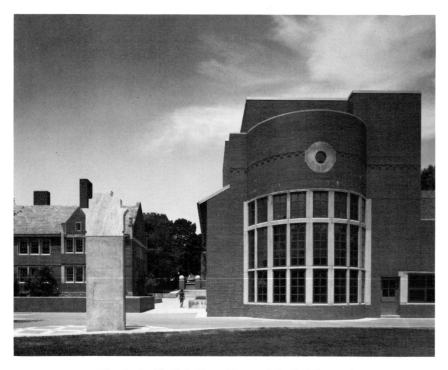

534. Gordon Wu Hall. View with pre-existing buildings to the left.

535. Gordon Wu Hall. Stairs.

project, situated at the very heart of empire on Trafalgar Square, aroused the ire of the Prince of Wales among others, and the choice of Venturi to put things right—a generous and courageous act in itself—represents the first significant public recognition of his special gifts. It is touching that it should have come in England rather than the United States. Though a number of American architects have built in England over the past century and are building there right now, this is by far the most important public commission ever awarded an American (indeed, intensive research might well show it to be the only one). This book has noted the historical flow of influence from England to America. The British themselves have generously reversed that trend in this instance. Venturi has surely repaid them in part by the sensitive adjustment to the site shown in his first drawings for the project and by his enhancement of the qualities of rhythm and scale he has perceived in the existing building—which has up till now been nobody's favorite *(Figs. 536, 537, 538)*. His "cadenzas" of pilaster celebrate its colossal colonnades, no less than Nel-

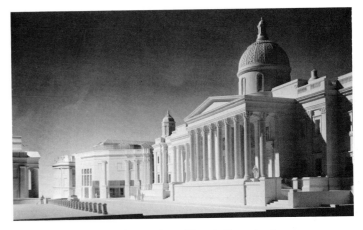

536. London, England. The Sainsbury Wing: An Extension to the National Gallery. 1986–. Venturi, Rauch and Scott Brown. (*Right to left*) original building by Wilkins and entrance façade of Sainsbury Wing.

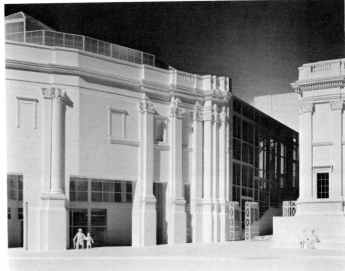

537. The Sainsbury Wing. Entrance façade, detail.

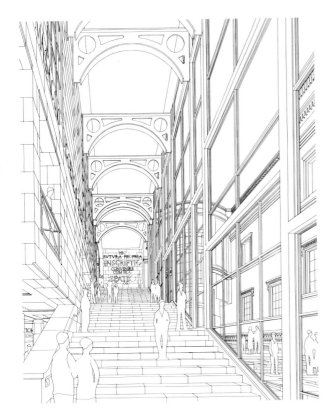

261

538. The Sainsbury Wing. Main stairway.

son's lone column out in the square, while the wall of glass behind them offers one great view of the old building with the square beyond it. The whole is bold and gentle, at once generous and respectful, specifically designed not to parade its own virtues but to make the square a little better than it was before.

Many other architects have taken part in this general movement of liberation and healing. Charles Moore, as we have noted, was very early on the scene, moving from the eloquent vernacular of his Sea Ranch *(Fig. 488)*, shaped by the sea wind, and which has since inspired thousands of condominiums, none so eloquent as itself, to his Faculty Club at Santa Barbara *(Fig. 489)*, where Louis I. Kahn's doctrine of deformation—through which Kahn himself intended to suggest the need for new formal beginnings—was developed as a positive agent to give the building as

a whole a vital stretch. At Santa Cruz, Moore creates a campus-street suggesting a street-theater *(Fig. 539)*, and his major contribution to contemporary sensibility is surely his lively and playful urbanism, as seen in the Piazza d'Italia in New Orleans *(Fig. 540)*, and in that city's World's Fair of 1984.

The classical details of the Piazza d'Italia are made mostly of plastic and are in general of a witty and rather ironic character, but a number of architects have been trying very hard over the past decade to work themselves back into the vernacular and classical traditions from a more literal point of view. Robert Stern, who began his career while still in architecture school as one of the first young architects to appreciate Venturi's work, has continued to improve as a designer the closer he has approached to straight vernacular forms. In his case they are fun-

539. Santa Cruz, California. Kresge College, University of California at Santa Cruz. 1974. Charles Moore.

540. New Orleans, Louisiana. Piazza d'Italia. 1977–78. Charles Moore.

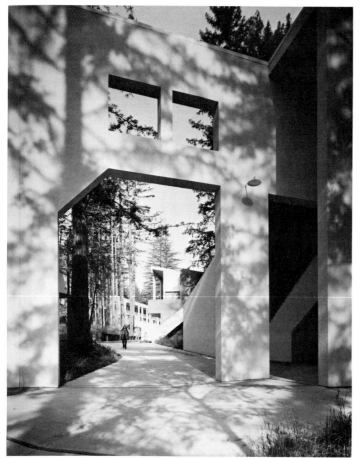

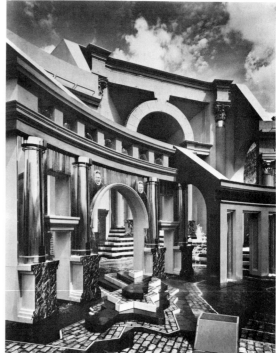

damentally those of the Shingle Style, but his work also tends to have a strong English cast, suggestive of his admiration for Lutyens, to whom, again, he was largely introduced by Venturi's example. Stern's powerful shingled cottage on Martha's Vineyard can stand for a mode of which he has by now produced scores of examples *(Figs. 541, 542)*. It is beautifully built, with the kind of vernacular details which have never entirely disappeared in American popular practise but which the International Style despised. The interior, as in all Stern's houses, is studied with profound attention to those details and to such larger Shingle Style elements as the open staircase, while the exterior greets the visitor with the Shingle Style's archetypal frontal gable.

Stern has also built one of the best of the new condominiums, most of which also seem based on the Shingle Style. His group at St. Andrews shows what can be done with traditional structure, shingles, and good solid window frames with real mullions rather than the clip-on variety that stock windows are nowadays provided with *(Fig. 543)*. There are thousands of similar housing groups throughout the United States, many of at least comparable quality. It is a renewed way of traditional building in the uniquely contemporary program of the condominium. It would require only a small diversion of funds from "Star Wars" and other inflationary projects to build much of the low-cost public housing American society so desperately needs right now in exactly this traditional and humane way.

In that connection, Seaside, a traditionally planned and designed community on the Florida coast, by the young husband-and-wife team of Elizabeth Plater-

541. Martha's Vineyard, Massachusetts. House at Chilmark. 1983. Robert A. M. Stern. Entrance façade.

542. House at Chilmark. Interior with stairs.

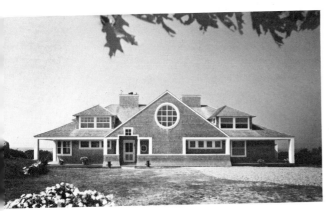

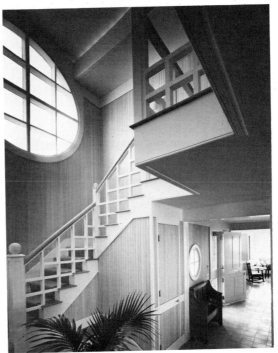

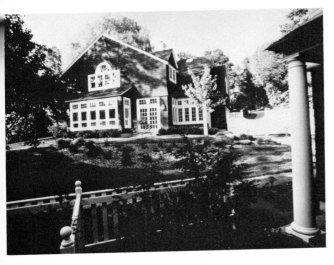

543. Hastings-on-Hudson, New York. St. Andrews: A Jack Nicklaus Golf Community. 1982–. Robert A. M. Stern.

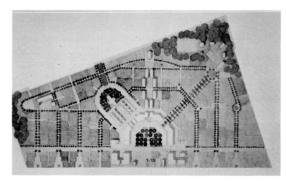

544. Seaside, Florida. Housing Community at Seaside. 1980–. Andres Duany and Elizabeth Plater-Zyberg. Plan.

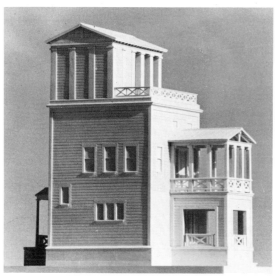

547. Seaside, Florida. House. 1985. Leon Krier. Model.

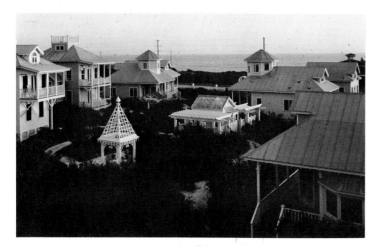

545. Seaside, Florida. Overview of Rosewalk Cottages, gardens, and garden architecture. 1981. Orr & Taylor, Architecture and Gardens.

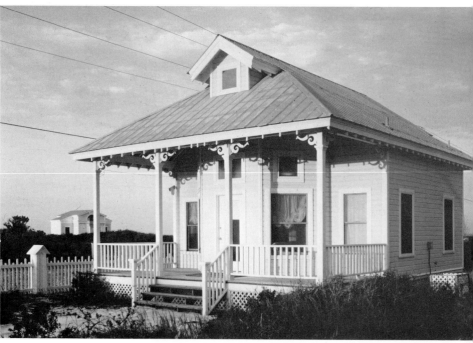

546. Seaside, Florida. Rosewalk Bungalow.

Zyberg and Andres Duany, has been criticized for its very virtues by some students *(Fig. 544)*. That is to say, it is like a town, invoking traditional town values of coherent layout and mixed population, but it is not a town, precisely because the economics of development will not permit it to be one. It is a luxury group, as all such developments are. But the point, I think, it not that Plater-Zyberg and Duany were unable to change the economic structure of the moment but that they have in fact shaped a model that could stand for more democratic housing programs. A number of excellent architects have been engaged to build individual buildings there, including Stern and Alex Gorlin. Robert Orr and Melanie Taylor have built a whole sympathetically scaled, Southern Stick Style neighborhood *(Figs. 545, 546)*. Even Leon Krier has consented to participate and has designed his first projects for America—which may turn out to be his first built anywhere: a Greek Revival house for himself and a tall tower as a marker for the town. The house *(Fig. 547)*, a bit like Claude Lorrain's painting of Delphi, supports a couple of temples on a blocky mass in a somewhat surreal way.

Aldo Rossi has also begun to practise in the United States with his project for the Architectural School at the University of Miami, now in the final stages of design *(Fig. 548)*. Its colorful, geometric, Mediterra-nean forms should go well with the more or less Spanish, limestone and stucco vernacular of the region and under its incomparable skies. Rossi's Teatro del Mondo for the Venice Biennale of 1980 *(Fig. 528)* was to have been resurrected as a library standing in the lake, which is inhabited, so it is said, by one alligator, but that building may not in fact be built.

In all these developments the question of the place and future of classical architecture is never far away. The vast project planned by the Catalan architect Ricardo Bofill for the banks of the Hudson River opposite lower Manhattan will, if built, be the most conspicuous of all the new classical buildings *(Fig. 549)*. In a series of public housing projects around Paris, Bofill has moved since the late seventies step by step toward a severe, correct, rather eighteenth-century type of classicism employing rustication, pediments, balustrades, pilasters, and so on. These are shaped out of a rigorously disciplined system of cast concrete, but the ensemble closely resembles Beaux-Arts classical buildings of the early twentieth century in Barcelona, as do Bofill's hemicyclical plans. These too are traditionally classic, and their hemi-cycles, axes, formal gardens, and so on bring a welcome sense of order into the degraded chaos of the French "New Towns," where the destructive effect of International Style urbanism can be seen at its worst.

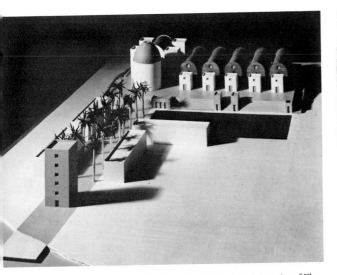

549. New Jersey. Drawing for Hudson River Development. 1986–. Ricardo Bofill. View from the river.

265

548. Miami, Florida. Architectural School at University of Florida. 1986–. Aldo Rossi. Model.

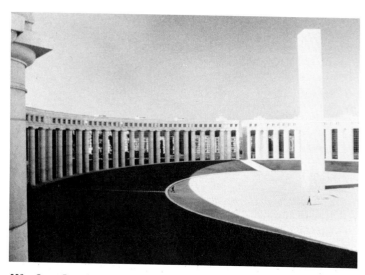

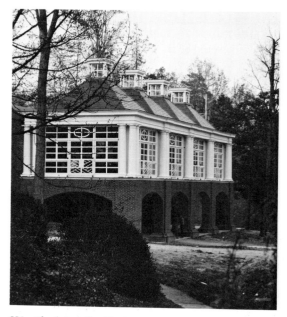

550. Cergy-Pontoise, France. Housing group. 1984–86. Ricardo Bofill.

551. Charlottesville, Virginia. University of Virginia, Observatory Hill Dining Hall. 1982–84. Robert A. M. Stern.

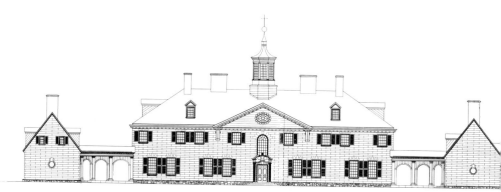

552. Connecticut. Farmhouse. 1979–83. Allan Greenberg. Entrance elevation.

266

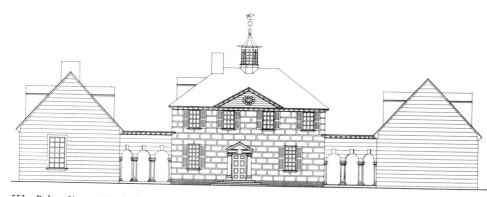

553. Robert Venturi. Study for a house after Mount Vernon. Front elevation.

The housing group at Cergy-Pontoise *(Fig. 550)* is the most developed, and wholly classic, of all Bofill's designs, but it would be far surpassed in size and visual effect by the colossal colonnade projected for the Hudson. Typically, however, the program has changed from that of low-cost public housing in France to luxury apartments in America. It may indeed be that Bofill's classicism is so much more rationalized and worked out than that of any American architect at present precisely because the great social programs which classicism can handle so well are available to it only in Europe. The Americans are working with what they have, sometimes, perforce, in more superficial ways. Stern's white-painted classical columns are conspicuous in most of his houses, for example, succeeding his Mannerist enlargements and rustications of an earlier day, and he has tried to develop more wholly classical systems in other projects, most appropriately at the University of Virginia *(Fig. 551)*. Allan Greenberg is one among numerous architects, perhaps the most determined and conspicuous among them, who are now trying to do the whole thing absolutely straight. His big, earnest essay on Mount Vernon, built in Greenwich for the Brants, should be contrasted in this regard with Venturi's perhaps slightly malicious comment on the same project, where Mount Vernon's disarming irregularities and indecisions are the starting point for further highly articulate distortions and surprises *(Figs. 552, 553)*. Greenberg, on the other hand, straightens everything out, makes it all symmetrical and bigger in scale, and creates a highly impressive if rather solemn mansion which might have been better if the clients had

not required him to remove its cupola, thin down its columns, and regularize its terrace-plinth with a wall. Inside, every molding has been studied in terms of traditional classical elements, and some powerful frames and pediments have resulted, again recalling those of Lutyens but with which, it might be said, the rather second-rate Pop Art paintings of the owner's collection go very badly. Their irony looks shoddy in relation to their surroundings. Or is it that their surroundings look humorless compared to them?

In his great arch to commemorate the Holocaust, projected for construction on the Battery in New York, Greenberg's architecture shakes free of such domestic considerations and mounts, I think, to a profoundly moving, tragic eloquence of its own *(Fig. 554)*. Out of the mighty rustication of the arch a squat chimney rises; massive compressive weight is metamorphosed above the keystone into an upward movement suggestive of the fire. Only the great elements of classical architecture, here in very simple form, could create such effects, and we are again reminded of Lutyens, especially of his incomparably moving memorial to the dead of the Somme at Thiepval.

Greenberg has received Federal sponsorship as well and has designed several major conference rooms for the State Department in Washington. The political significance of such rooms cannot be overestimated, in view of the fact that in them the United States puts forth the image of itself with which it wishes to impress foreign diplomats. In this case that face is of a rather lush classicism, somewhat shaky in scale but tirelessly optimistic in detail *(Fig. 555)*. There is a curiously Augustan passion for abundance

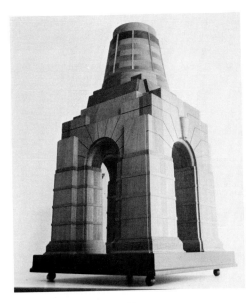

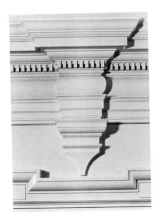

555. Washington, D.C. Entablature with over-door capital and pendant from the George C. Marshall Reception Room in the State Department Building. 1986. Allan Greenberg.

554. Allan Greenberg. Proposed arch to commemorate the Holocaust. 1984. Model.

in it, especially in its great Corinthian capitals with their seal. Greenberg can hardly be blamed for trying to pack everything in, given such a chance to do so. The resultant interior is not threatening in any event but is redolent of too much money, powerfully applied.

Thomas Gordon Smith is a very different kind of classical architect. He has built some rather touching and extremely personal houses employing the classical language. He brings to them not only the talents of scholar and archaeologist but those of painter and poet as well. They are at once haunted and alive, in some ways recalling Jefferson's work with their big details, grandly out of scale on little buildings. As with Jefferson, they are regarded by Smith as part of an intellectual system, an educational process, and, in the grand tradition, he has written a systematic treatise on how classical architecture is to be done, illustrated with some spectacular drawings of his own. There, as in some of his buildings, he goes back to what are really pre-classic forms, as in the early Ar-

chaic Temple of Apollo at Thermon, so that the special vitality, the touching awkwardness, of new beginnings (so beloved by Kahn) is embodied in his work *(Figs. 556, 557)*.

Despite all this, a question still remains about how far toward a fully classical architecture modern architecture may now go. There are no real reasons, not even technical ones, why it could not supplement other kinds of architecture and so go the whole way in programs appropriate to it. Critics who claim that such cannot properly be done today are voicing an opinion, not a fact: It is the old *zeitgeist* obsession all over again. There seems, however, to be no question whatever about the continuing revival of the vernacular as such, especially since, by definition, it varies from region to region and material to material. For a while, especially during the oil shortages of the seventies, it seemed to some people, if not to others, that the possibilities of passive and active solar design might well help create new vernacular forms. That enthusiasm seemed to have waned by the later

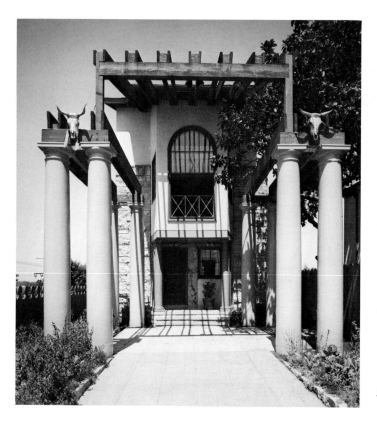

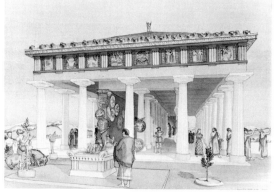

557. Thomas Gordon Smith. Reconstruction perspective of Temple of Apollo at Thermon. 1985.

556. Richmond, California. Richmond Hill House. 1983. Thomas Gordon Smith. Front elevation.

eighties, by which time a good many of the features of solar design had indeed merged more or less imperceptibly into the general vernacular—in which they seem, nevertheless, to occupy only a minor place. So out on the prairies where Wright once invoked primitive beginnings and, incidentally, created an ideal solar system by burying a house partly underground and opening it to the whole arc of the southern horizon *(Figs. 356–357)*, Tom Beeby now erects his tall, thin-skinned farmhouse, which might be a setting for one of Willa Cather's novels *(Fig. 558)*. Wright's reference was to the primitive sod huts of the region. He, like the more purely International Style architects, was willing enough to refer to the primordial or the exotic, while Beeby's reference is more generally to nineteenth- and twentieth-century Middle Western culture, invoking as it does the long-standing wooden vernacular of the place. Elsewhere, as in his Hansen House, Beeby invokes other, somewhat more Italianate aspects of the rural and suburban villa tradition *(Fig. 559)*.

558. Wisconsin. Beasley House. 1979. Thomas Beeby. Gable view.

559.   Wilmette, Illinois. Hansen House. 1986-87. Thomas Beeby.

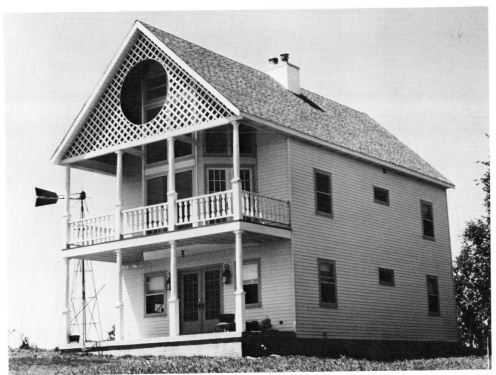

269

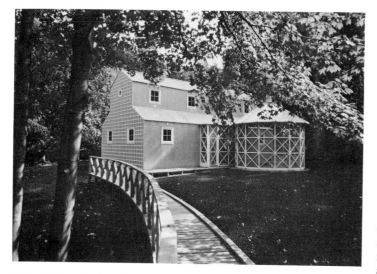

560. Michigan. Weekend House. 1983. Stanley Tigerman and Margaret McCurry.

Stanley Tigerman, though always full of cultural references as well as endlessly fertile in invention, is perhaps closer to the Modernist position. His own rather endearing little house, designed with his wife, Margaret McCurry, is a simple gabled structure, but it specifically refers to barns rather than to traditional houses and employs corrugated metal siding and a porch adapted from prefabricated silos *(Fig. 560)*. Frank Gehry, well laid back in California, goes further with what might be called an animated subversion of the vernacular. His own house, one of the first of his mature works, seems always in course of construction, with the frame exposed in part and loose boards hanging around *(Figs. 561, 562, 563)*. It, too, is endearing, a hymn to vernacular process, loving even the chain-link fence of redneck boundaries and shuffling about to protect itself from, all the while revealing itself to, the suburban street. Whether it is an affront to the neighborhood rather than an enhancement of it is, however, a debatable point. Gehry

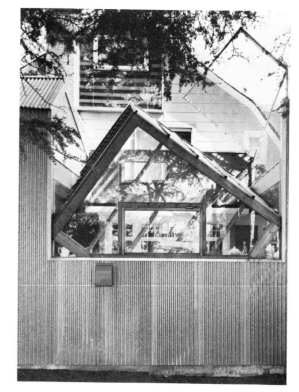

561. Santa Monica, California. Gehry House. 1977-78. North side at kitchen. Frank Gehry.

562. Wayzata, Minnesota. Winton Guest House. 1983-87. Exterior showing stone-clad bedroom, metal-clad living room, and brick fireplace alcove. Frank Gehry.

may in fact be the most anarchically original of all neo-Modernists. His later work suggests just that: so varied that it is always more or less contextual but supremely contemptuous of traditional urbanistic norms, owing a good deal to Graves and Rossi but irrepressibly lighthearted, childlike, released, as if in fact there were no other world than its own. Gehry is a transcendent sculptor who somehow knows how to keep the rain out.

Other architects, like Charles Gwathmey, remain unreconstructedly International Style, and there is clearly room for any kind of fantasy in domestic design in rural and suburban areas where no question of urban contextuality need arise. But the reason the suburban single family house in America is in better shape at present than it has been in several genera-

tions is precisely that its architects have on the whole been led by Venturi to value its traditional sources once more. If so, what is the status in that regard of the perennial complement to the suburban house in American life, the center-city office building? Here we find that a similar revitalization of traditional points of view has taken place. The Municipal Services Building in Portland, Oregon, by Michael Graves, is an early example of that revival *(Fig. 564)*. Portland's downtown is shaped by a grid plan marked by small, square blocks; it is set down on the more or less level ground which lies between the Willamette River and the chunky bluffs behind it. The International Style skyscrapers which had been built on the site had trashed the grid with their captious placement and their open plazas and had ignored the

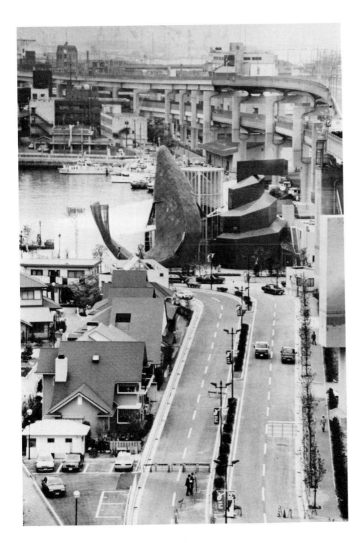

271

563. Kobe, Japan. "Fishdance" Restaurant. 1986-87. Frank Gehry.

scale of the bluffs with their height. Graves, however, related the solid block of his building to both conditions: respecting the grid, echoing the bluffs. Though restrained by budget from articulating the surface of the building by anything other than truly superficial devices, such as changes of material or only of paint, Graves still managed to decorate his block with considerable monumental effect. It has some sculptural presence and achieves an appropriately governmental scale. Like Sullivan's Guaranty Building *(Fig. 197),* it is most of all a solid building unit out of which a coherent downtown can be put together.

Such, however, was the unbridled hostility toward Graves' design shown by the so-called modern ("academic" would be a more correct adjective in this case) architects of Portland that Graves was forced to win the competition twice and was later prevented from building the little village which was intended to populate his building's top *(Fig. 565).* This was too bad, because the bluffs beyond are crowned with houses in much the same way, and the contextual references would thereby have been completed. The fundamental intolerance of International Style aesthetics could hardly have been demonstrated more abjectly, or the paranoia which its apologists of a past generation, such as Sigfried Giedion, ascribed to the Beaux-Arts, been more clearly revealed as its own.

The generous upward gesture of the Municipal Building's main façade, like a flat curtain lifting, will, however, furnish a splendid backdrop for the action of the monumental, classical figure of Portlandia, which will eventually be installed above the entrance. That relationship will physically demonstrate the fundamental character of architecture as creating an environment, a setting, and of sculpture as embodying action in relation to, and sometimes against, that setting. Here, as Mies van der Rohe understood so well, it is figural sculpture that works best, since it literally embodies human action seen

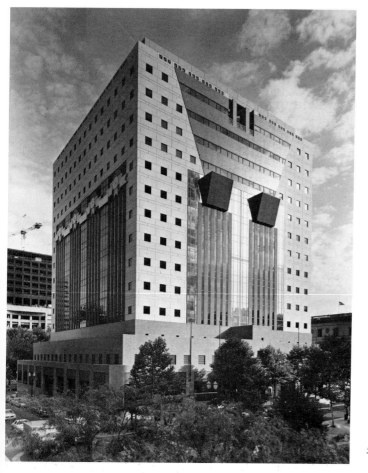

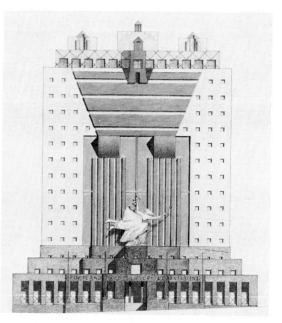

565. Municipal Services Building. Drawing with village on roof.

564. Portland, Oregon. Municipal Services Building. 1980. Michael Graves. View from Fifth Avenue.

in relation to the natural and the man-made worlds. All the great ages of architecture have related figural sculpture to buildings in many varied and culturally characteristic ways. Sculpture which does not employ the human body is clearly at a disadvantage in that relationship, but if it can be made to look active or even strikingly out of scale in relation to its setting it may approximate the effect, as does Picasso's admittedly rather feeble effort at the Civic Center in Chicago *(Fig. 393)*. But if the object also has an identity which is, for example, incongruously changed in size, perhaps blown up in scale, like Oldenburg's delightful colossi, the effect can be much more intense, because a powerful associational element is bound up with it. What one does not want are dead masses resembling elephant droppings or the remains of a cannibal feast, like the objects scattered about in front of the City Hall in Dallas, whose mindless inertia should be contrasted with Oldenburg's alert, lively, intrusive *Lipstick* as it invaded Beinecke Plaza at Yale *(Figs. 566, 567)*. The herd of mustangs, if that is the correct term, which runs through the fountain in the otherwise horrendously sterile urban center of the Las Colimas development near Dallas, though deprecated as representational by Dallas' artistic avant-garde, is also infinitely preferable *(Fig. 568)*. Sculpture is life, acting in a space, a place. If it is too spatial itself, like Richard Serra's long wall which divided the barren Federal Plaza in New York *(Fig. 569)*, it may well, and perhaps rightly, be in trouble. Serra's wall, however, may have been unjustly condemned. Its interruption of a smug plaza brought a new kind of vitality to the place, introducing a kind of threat,

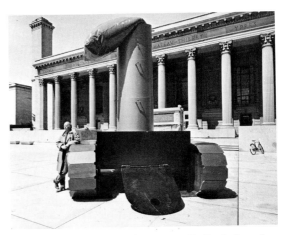

567. Claes Oldenburg: *Lipstick on Caterpillar Tracks Ascending*, Yale University. New Haven, Connecticut. 1969. Sculpture with artist in Beinecke Plaza.

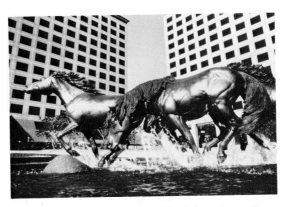

568. Robert Glen: *The Mustangs of Las Colimas*, Irving, Texas. 1977–84.

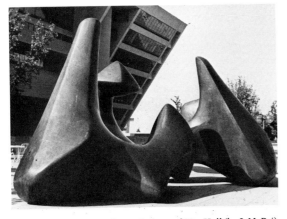

566. Henry Moore: Sculpture in front of City Hall (by I. M. Pei), Dallas, Texas.

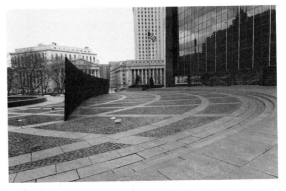

569. Richard Serra: *Tilted Arc*, Federal Plaza, New York, New York. 1981.

a spatial mugging. Clearly enough, as part of the present revival of respect for architectural traditions, the relation of sculpture to building is becoming better understood with every passing day, and it does not necessarily deal with harmony or security. The streets of our inner cities call up the junkies of Duane Hanson and our breakfast tables his women in house dresses, while the grates from which heat rises between the White House and the Mall in Washington are in fact covered by the sleeping figures of homeless persons, shapeless piles of old clothes like Hanson's Bowery bums with their naked feet and poor backsides exposed. The more sculpture becomes "real," as it is in Hanson's hands, the more it calls up the true symbolic population of the world we have made.

Graves himself is extremely sensitive to sculptural issues, and he is therefore also able to endow his buildings with whatever sculptural energy may be proper to a building, as a form which is primarily the shaper of an environment rather than a figural actor in it. His Municipal Services Building was not beyond criticism in that regard, perhaps only because of the enforced thinness of its detailing, but those criticisms were soon answered by Graves in his Humana Building for Louisville (Fig. 570). Here again, his design was a well-deserved competition winner, out of which came a building respecting the street with its pre-existing storefronts and rising out of them in considerable grandeur. Once again, as in the projected village on the roof at Portland, the influence of Leon Krier can be felt, here in the truss structure of the balcony high above, and perhaps that of Aldo Rossi in the profile of the building as a whole, but the intricate and correct adjustments to the site all belong to Graves. Unlike the inert slab next door, the design is once again wholly contextual, like that of the Municipal Services Building, and in similarly appropriate ways. At the lower levels it is contextual with the immediate street setting, as we have seen, and up above, where fantasy should clearly be encouraged, with Louisville's old iron bridges and, at the very top, with the dams of the T.V.A. not so far away. There is also, as there had so strongly been in the Art Deco skyscrapers of the twenties and thirties, a strong suggestion of the upward-leaping temple bases of Mayan Tikal as well.

Graves' first project for an extensive addition to Marcel Breuer's Whitney Museum in New York civilized that architect's iconoclastic intrusion on the street by swathing it in what amounted to a traditional classic palazzo, upon whose roof a high-stepped mass with a low, long, arched window in it supported something very close to an antique temple (Figs. 571, 572). The combination closely recalled Gilley's project for a monument to Frederick the Great, considerably modified to work appropriately in this place. Moreover, every one of Graves' new elements deferred to Breuer's original building, whose forward lunge now seemed to support the great mass above it and so to be much more solid and powerful itself than it had ever looked before. This was all a considerable achievement, and it showed that Graves' design, rather than approaching a dead end, as some perhaps rather jealous critics had wished to believe, was in fact growing in power and in its capacity to relate both to older buildings and to the urban structure as a whole. Most of Graves' city buildings do in fact suggest a revival of Art Deco or of what was called in its period "Modern Classic" precedent. This makes sense, because Art Deco and Modern Classic alike respected the traditional urban conditions the International Style came to flout.

Once again, however, Graves aroused the Modernists' ire, and a strong wave of opposition to his project for the Whitney swept through the architects of New York. That movement was eventually successful enough to force Graves to redesign his proposal in ways that, on the one hand, may be regarded as having weakened it considerably or, on the other, as having released Breuer's building from a considerable load (Fig. 573). In early 1988 its future was still in doubt. It is instructive to note that there was no such popular movement among architects to protest Gwathmey's proposal for an addition to Wright's Guggenheim Museum—on the face of it a much more destructive addition to a much better, a much gentler, building. It is true that there was eventually a good deal of opposition to Gwathmey's scheme, and it is now being redesigned, but it never aroused the bitterness, indeed the viciousness, with which Graves' proposal was greeted (Fig. 574). The point was surely that the architects were out to save Breuer's Whitney as a symbol of the International Style, and their movement has grown since that time until it has become a considerable, though probably temporary, force among architectural students. It is precisely Breuer's contempt for the urban setting they most admire. The fact that the Whitney is a harsh, hard-edged, scaleless object intended to outrage the pre-existing civil architecture of Madison Avenue is all to the good so far as these young architects are concerned. They are tired of hearing the older generation talk about contextuality and are sick of the whole revival of the vernacular and classical tradition in

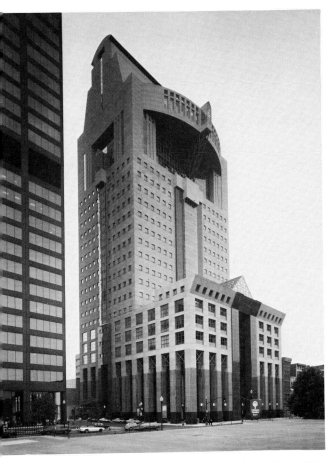

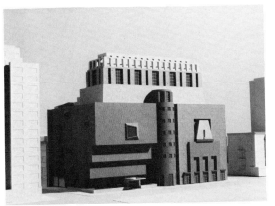

572. Addition to Whitney Museum of American Art. March 1985. Michael Graves. Model of Madison Avenue façade.

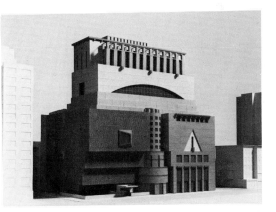

570. Louisville, Kentucky. The Humana Building. 1982. Michael Graves. Façade from Main Street.

573. Addition to Whitney Museum of American Art. Revised version. May 1987. Michael Graves.

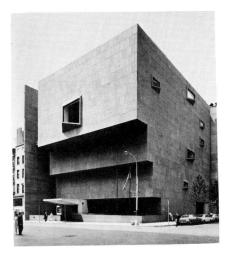

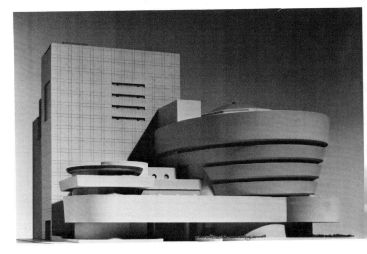

571. New York, New York. Whitney Museum of American Art. 1963. Marcel Breuer.

574. Proposed addition to Guggenheim Museum. New York, New York. 1987. Gwathmey Siegel & Associates Architects. West façade.

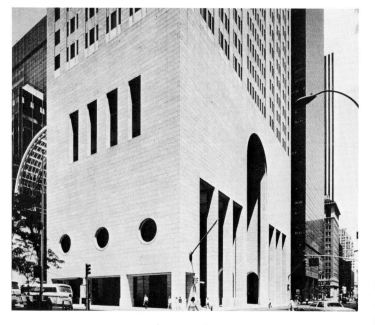

575. New York, New York. AT&T World Headquarters. 1984. Philip Johnson/John Burgee Architects. View looking up Madison Avenue.

which the Venturi generation has been involved. There are some cogent reasons for this from their point of view. Contextuality is difficult to achieve. An architect needs a good deal of cultivation—he needs to know a lot and to be able to draw very well—in order to design traditional architecture. On the other hand, the International Style is easy to do, all lines and planes devoid of difficult details, and demanding nothing much to learn so far as an architectural language is concerned. Even more to the point, contextuality demands a good deal of humility from the architect: he must respect what has gone before and subordinate the more egregious aspects of his own personality to it. How much more satisfying the Rambo role offered him by the International Style: the past is junk, the architect is epic hero, reinventing the wheel every time. To this attitude was coupled, by 1987, the kind of political outrage felt by many of the young. Eight years and more of enshrined greed and social cruelty had surely sickened some of them, but those conditions also furnished a pretext for them to turn on their elders and against the kind of architecture they had produced during that period. Not wishing to recognize the fact that the International Style had itself become the essential architecture of

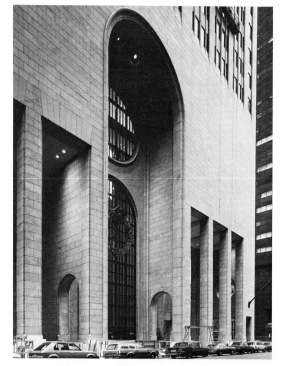

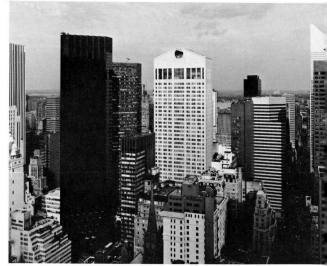

577. AT&T Headquarters on the skyline.

576. AT&T Headquarters. Detail of Madison Avenue façade.

the corporate program, they opted, as Marxist critics had done before them, for its reductionism, its nihilism, its obvious contempt for the past. It suited their mood in 1987—a state of mind which, however transitory, was right in line with the kind of architecture easiest to learn, and to teach, in architectural schools. Whatever the case, not only the rebellious young, the "slashers," as Graves called them, but also their elders found plenty to criticize in some of the best buildings in the eighties.

Johnson's AT&T Building on Madison Avenue is a case in point *(Figs. 575, 576, 577)*. It at once acknowledges the rush of the street and rounds it out into an event. It shapes a place, suggesting the volumetric stability of an urban plaza dominating the traffic flow. It stands on legs—though on the side streets they are rather droopy-drawered ones—and its entrance arch rises high, embellished with a rich classical surround. The whole building is symmetrical. Indeed, it behaves like an integral body, standing firmly on its feet and rising up continuously to the open gesture of its broken pediment. It is in fact much like the Seagram Building with its firm inflection to the street *(Fig. 389)*, so contrary to the destructive turning of Lever Brothers' slab *(Fig. 390)*, that is now enhanced

by the entrance arch and the crowning pediment. AT&T's stance has the effect of making the other new buildings around it look obsolete. Why do they have flat tops, we ask? Why is the corner of one of them cut away and the lower floors of another slanted outward? In a way, they don't look like buildings at all, and in an urbanistic sense they are not. They are objects, scaleless, which happen to be large and are set down in a city but have nothing to do with the concept of city. Johnson, on the other hand, has clearly looked at older urbanistic models, at Rockefeller Center, for example. But it is here, in fact, that his design gives pause, insofar as it is thinner, less generous, more brittle than that of his models. Is this a matter of economics, as Cesar Pelli claims it to be? Is it a residue of the original International Style aesthetic, with its linear intersections and planar surfaces? Or is it expressive of something more pervasively contemporary, having to do with the state of architectural patronage or even with the character of society as a whole? Here a project by Pelli himself might help us approach the question. It is his mammoth group of buildings at Battery Park City *(Fig. 578)* for the developer Olympia and York, where the magnificent master plan was by Alexander Cooper and Stan-

578. New York, New York. World Financial Center, Olympia and York Developers. Design 1981–85. Construction 1982–87. Cesar Pelli & Associates. Planners: Alexander Cooper & Stanton Eckstutt.

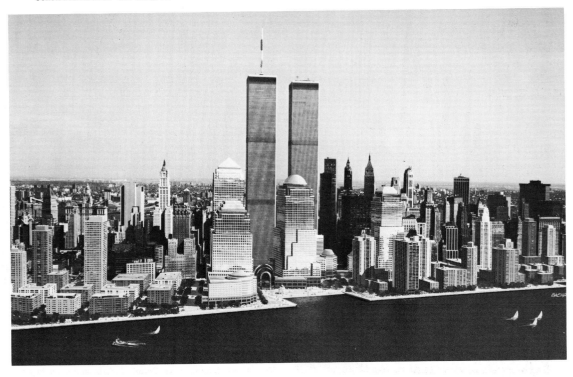

ton Eckstutt. Even more directly than Johnson, Pelli was inspired here by the RCA Building and the pointed tops of other Art Deco skyscrapers. But his buildings are much thicker, more bulbous, than their prototypes. They are certainly robust, but they are also rather swollen, not at all the elegant, faceted towers or slabs which their predecessors, the Empire State, the Chrysler, and the RCA, had been. Is this so because their developer was not willing to give up the rentable space which earlier clients were perfectly ready to cede in their buildings in order to endow them with an elegant profile? Or is it only that Pelli is responding to the special conditions of his site, as the earlier architects were to theirs? Moreover, the thin curtain wall, which Pelli insists is the only viable cladding under present economic circumstances, creates an insubstantial and transparent effect consorting strangely with the mountainous massing of the buildings as a whole and very different from the densely articulated surfaces of the earlier skyscrapers. But it works very well in this place. The buildings do seem to stretch and loom, creating a great landing place off the Hudson, ringed by vast, magical beings, mediators with the World Trade towers behind them. The massing of the whole group is grand and firm, standing up to the river no less than to Manhattan's higher towers, as each great block divests itself of its lower floors and rises up shining in the sun. It is one

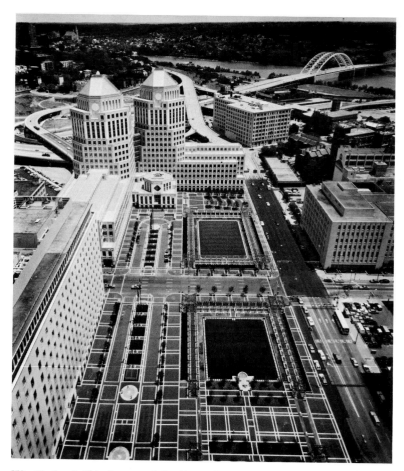

579. Cincinnati, Ohio. Procter and Gamble Headquarters. 1985. Kohn Pedersen Fox with Perkins and Will.

278

of the major urban groupings of the past two generations, in that sense surely the worthiest descendant of Rockefeller Center yet created in New York. The Procter and Gamble buildings in Cincinnati, by the firm of Kohn Pedersen Fox, also build up to solidly urban shapes, well in the best tradition of the twenties and thirties *(Fig. 579)*

Few other architects can do so well at present. Though the greatest days of the American skyscraper are being invoked once more, the results are, with the exceptions already noted, decidedly disappointing. We ask ourselves why this should be so and are led to consider the present state of architecture as a whole—that is, of the man-made environment entire—somewhat more broadly than we have yet attempted to do in this postscript. And there, according at least to the questions raised earlier in this text, the overall view tends to be a spectacularly depressing one. It is not too much to say that every major battle this book identified in 1969 as essential for architecture and society to win has been lost. Or almost all; others, such as those relative to preservation and rehabilitation, have taken some odd turns, which deserve to be explored later. But Black Americans, whose plight seemed to constitute a central urban problem sixteen years ago, are in many ways worse off than ever. Subject as they have been to the neglect, sometimes even the harassment, of Washington, their economic position has progressively worsened in a comparative sense; their ghettoes are more devoid of hope and thus more terrifying. We have noted the important new developments toward the liberation and enrichment of domestic architecture that have taken place in the past sixteen years and have seen that none of them have been used to help the poor or to replace the ghetto. Almost the sole exception, and that only a project, was Robert A. M. Stern's proposal for what he called a "Subway Suburb," to be built in the South Bronx *(Fig. 580)*. Whether the people whom the Reagan administration so unctuously referred to as the "truly needy" could have afforded those houses is an open question. The few which have been built in that area, as if in response to Stern's broader suggestion, can certainly not be afforded by the general run of its inhabitants.

The large-scale Federal program of jobs and housing needed to remedy that situation, and which the present state of architectural knowledge might well make much more livable and symbolically sympathetic than the old "projects" were, will not be forthcoming in any foreseeable future. In the meanwhile

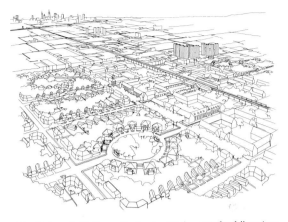

580. Robert A. M. Stern. Design for "Subway Suburb" project in the South Bronx, New York. 1976.

the poor are paying for the Federal government's arms buildup with their lives. We have already noted what the two major programs of building are right now: suburban houses and center-city corporate office buildings and, of course, the fresh armies of condominiums, all blindingly expensive. But there is a third program, the museum, which, considering its specialization, has also been spectacularly on the rise. The present pattern of house and office building seems to be rounded out by it. It is the ritual center, the new church, as art seems in many ways to be the major religion now. Where can we see this pattern at its clearest? The answer surely is, in the Sun Belt, and especially out there in the old Southwest where this book began.

Dallas is a good place to see it all, because there the towers and their attendant museum are set in the most expressive relation to each other, wherein we can hardly fail to see who is calling the tune. The first urbanistic factor of all, though, is the automobile, which connects downtown with the suburban developments way out in space. So the center of Dallas is ringed by freeways, as are all American cities today. The old cities of the Northeast, as we have noted, were laid waste by the automobile, but in the Sun Belt there was so much less of the old city to destroy and economic resources were so great that a wild and quite new urban pattern has emerged. The freeways flash around the city center, a choir of gleaming towers. Each of these has been designed as an architectural one-liner, intended to knock our eyes out for a fleeting instant as we glimpse it from behind the wheel. Philip Johnson has shown himself to be especially skilled at this kind of thing, particularly in Houston, and he has gained a popular reputation as the foremost living American architect through precisely that talent, which is in accord at once with his quickness of perception, his impatience, and his ruthlessly empirical historical sense. The two towers of his Pennzoil Place Building in Houston *(Fig. 582)*

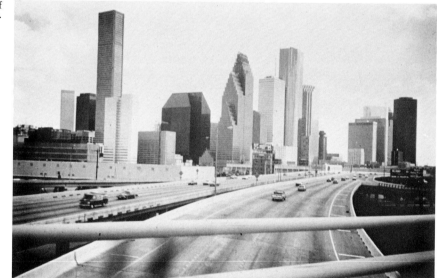

581. Houston, Texas. View of skyscrapers from freeway.

may even be said to have initiated the mode, though it surely had some precursors in the work of Roche and Portman. Other buildings picked it up: anything for a memorable shape to be seen at great speed from afar—and really only from there. Are such buildings "signs" in the semiotic sense explored by Venturi, signs which communicate some special meaning to us? Hard to say, because there does not seem to be any special meaning to these shapes, not even anything specifically relevant to the character of the corporations they serve—unless it is the rather empty PR of advertising in which they all engage, each claiming in this way a wholly spurious uniqueness. Yet, in order to produce such shapes Johnson, for example, has clearly invoked the old mountain image of Hugh Ferriss and based his Republic Bank Building in Houston on one of the Finnish entries in the Chicago Tribune Competition of 1922, which had a distinctly mountainous profile. Here, though, it is only the distant image that counts. When we dare to leave

our cars and get down in among the towers we find that we are at the heart of a void. There is nothing there—nothing that can be called a city as we ever knew a city to be, because the skyscrapers have no scale or function in relation to the street. Indeed, they do not encourage pedestrian traffic among them. The streets are not enjoyed and packed with people as they had been, and still are, in the beloved canyons of New York. Consequently, when the buildings are seen close up no details emerge. They become blanker and more inarticulate the closer they are. The old skyscrapers looked loved, so lovingly and intricately detailed they were, right down to the street. The new ones look despised, and so cannot sustain a conversation, having nothing to say after they utter their one loud cry from afar.

So much for the corporate towers. What about the museums? They have had a spectacular development over the past twenty years. The most dignified new examples were built by Louis I. Kahn before his death

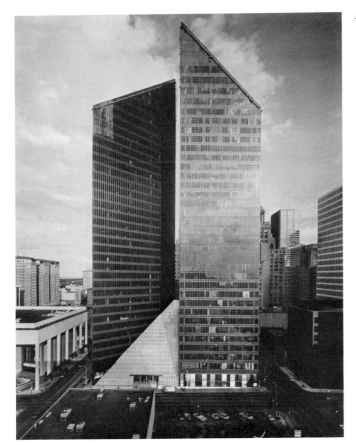

582. Houston, Texas. Pennzoil Place. 1974. Philip Johnson/John Burgee Architects.

281

in 1974. His Kimbell Museum in Fort Worth *(Figs. 583, 584, 585)* lies at the bottom of a gently sloping park below Johnson's Amon Carter Museum on the crest. If the Kimbell Museum were entered from the park, as it was originally intended to be, the experience would be an intense and moving one. Dwarf trees are planted so as to march with us as we enter the entrance court, beyond which the strong and gently vaulted gallery space spreads out symmetrically on either side. Everything in the building has gone into that vault. It is the source of light, sets the scale, creates the atmosphere, and shapes the exterior, which thereby offers no way to get into it integrally except through the happy device of the trees. Unhappily, the only entrance now normally open is the automobile loading dock on the other side. This must originally have been conceived of as a subsidiary, almost a service, entrance, but it is now the main one and badly needs decoration of some kind. That is an idea which Kahn would have found unspeakably repellent, but it is called for here. The point is that the building is severely hurt because it was not designed to accommodate the dominance of the automobile or to tame it.

Kahn's other greatest museum, the British Art Center for Yale, does not have that problem *(Figs. 586, 587, 588)*. It strictly conforms to the existing street almost directly across from Kahn's first mature work, the Yale Art Gallery of 1951–53. In part because Kahn had come to believe that the open loft

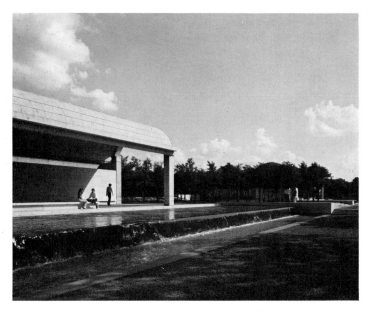

583. Fort Worth, Texas. Kimbell Art Museum. 1966–72. Louis I. Kahn. Park side with trees, northwest corner.

584. Kimbell Art Museum. Interior with stairs, gallery, and vaults.

585. Kimbell Art Museum. Auto entrance and south façade.

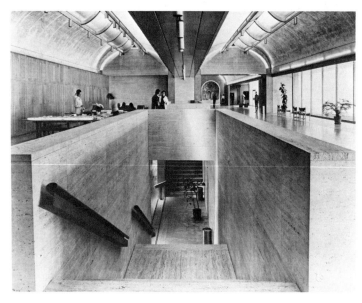

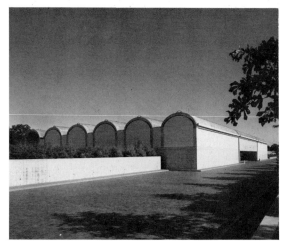

spaces of his Art Gallery had been ruined later because they were so easy to remodel, he constructed the British Center on a clear and quite small bay system. Its columns and bays divide the interior and articulate the exterior wall, where stainless steel panels and sheets of glass are set within the concrete frame. The effect is rather Miesian, and suggests a kind of dignified, if reductive, classicism a good deal like that of Mies; but the reflections in the glass are miraculous, contrasting as they do with the utterly matte surface of the steel panels and picking up flashes of the fine old Beaux-Arts Art Gallery across the way. Finally, though, we are impressed most of all by the solemn dignity of Kahn's building technique. The materials are assembled reverently at beautifully detailed joints, so that the whole does in fact give that effect of "Silence" Kahn so desired. This is especially true of the interior, with its grand Tudorish hall and oak paneling, and most of all of the calm gallery spaces, defined by their structural bays but opening to hall or court as well and, on the top floor, lighted from above as lovingly as at the Kimbell. In such a building it is hard not to feel that Kahn is still incomparable among the architects of the past thirty years, if only for one fundamental reason: that he learned so thoroughly how to build well. Because of that his buildings embody some deep, mute, physical presence, some total stasis, which more gestural, perhaps even more sophisticated, kinds of design do not seem able to equal.

586.   New Haven, Connecticut. Yale Center for British Art. 1974–77. Louis I. Kahn. View along Chapel Street.

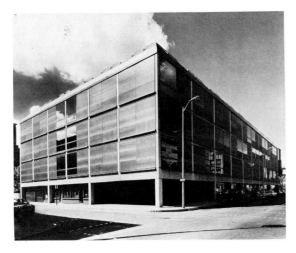

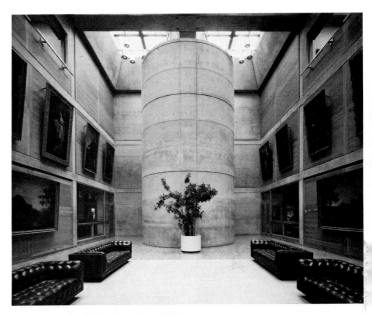

587.   Center for British Art. Great Hall.

588.   Center for British Art. Interior gallery space.

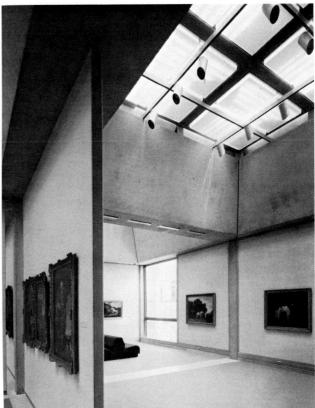

Kahn has not built the only new museums or even the most typical ones. Venturi designed a subtly contextual addition to a fine old building by Cass Gilbert at Oberlin *(Fig. 589)*. But Richard Meier's late International Style virtuosity, wholly abstract and even anti-contextual as it is, seems to have struck the most popular chord. Museums like Meier's High Museum in Atlanta are, perhaps appropriately, wholly removed from everything else and from most associations other than those of a dreamlike, high-tech fantasy *(Figs. 590, 591)*. Works of art can best float in them, as works of art now mostly seem to do, untrammeled by any connection with anything but ourselves. They are *our* individual fetishes; they must belong to no one else. Meier is surely more successful at this even than I. M. Pei, whose addition to the National Gallery of Art comes off not too strongly in terms of dream worlds when compared with John Russell Pope's colossally columned rotunda in the original *(Figs. 592, 593)*. In Los Angeles, the Museum of Contemporary

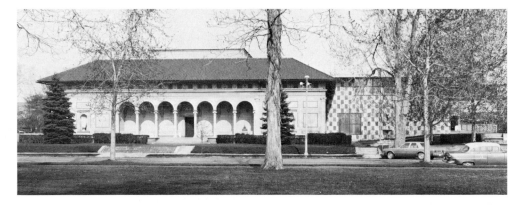

589. Oberlin, Ohio. Expansion of Allen Art Museum at Oberlin College. 1973. Robert Venturi.

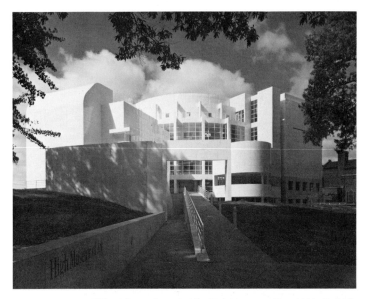

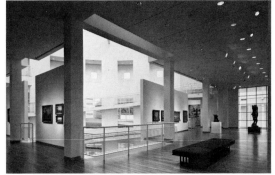

591. The High Museum of Art. Interior.

590. Atlanta, Georgia. The High Museum of Art. 1980–83. Richard Meier.

Art by Arata Isozaki is perhaps more powerful, though considerably more surreal: abstract, disorienting, but with an eerie sense of body, of cult, that only the Japanese seem able to suggest *(Fig. 594)*. And once again, in museums as in houses, Frank Gehry seems to have developed a way of design special to himself. These larger buildings combine that special sense of common process, of life going on, which we noted in his own house of some years earlier, with the powerfully anarchic geometry that shapes his more recent work and with his special talent as a maker of figural images. Gehry is still willing to go further than any other architect today toward the creation of dream states, charged with unexpected displacements of conventional reality. A blend of Gaudí, Maybeck, and Bruce Goff, he differs from those and other expressionist architects in the mordant modernity of his irony and his wit. He understands the city as it is, but fits his buildings only eccentrically into it, while, at the same time, they celebrate the richness and autonomy of a secret, eccentric life inside: in museums, the life of objects, the aura of art.

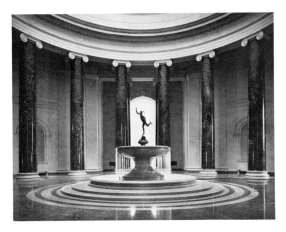

593. National Gallery of Art. John Russell Pope. Rotunda.

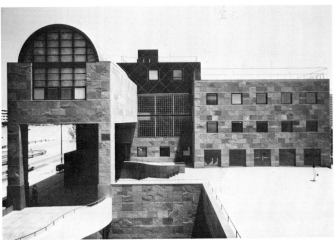

594. Los Angeles, California. Museum of Contemporary Art. 1981–83. Arata Isozaki.

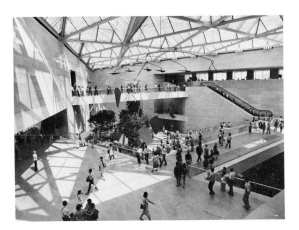

592. Washington, D.C. East Wing of National Gallery of Art. 1978. I. M. Pei.

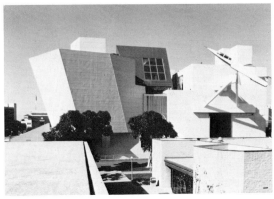

595. Los Angeles, California. Aerospace Museum. 1982-84. Frank Gehry.

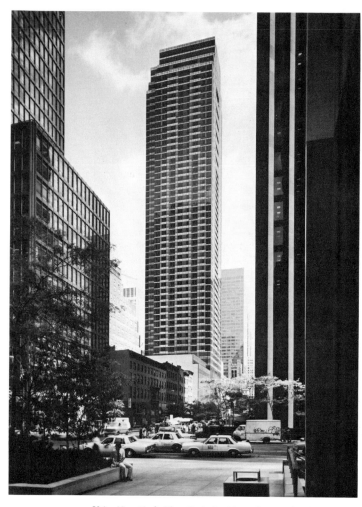

596. New York, New York. Residential tower for the Museum of Modern Art. 1984. Cesar Pelli & Associates.

Yet the Museum of Modern Art in New York is in every fundamental way the mother of all the new museums. It is of course less than two generations old itself, but it was the first museum which consciously set out to incorporate modern art into American life and, in a sense, to domesticate it through what the museum called "Good Design." Russell Lynes, in his bright biography of MOMA, ascribes to its history a continual and revealing struggle between art and business. Its founders and principal backers were enormously wealthy people with collections of their own, and their views about what the museum ought to be and what the museum ought to house have sometimes been at odds with those of the director. If so, we may legitimately surmise that business has won the most recent round in the contest, because it is now the museum's new rentable apartment tower that dominates the complex of buildings as a whole. It is a tower elegantly detailed as to profile and surface, but its placement leaves much to be desired. That it rises directly from the street is an excellent thing, but the flapping piece of flashing with which it is tenuously connected to the roof of the older building can hardly be credited. More seri-

597. Museum of Modern Art. Escalator housing and tower from sculpture garden.

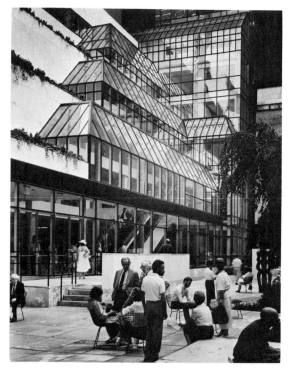

ously, its bulk severely compromises the privacy and scale of the sculpture court behind it—a garden which the late Alfred Barr, the museum's immortal director, used to characterize, conservatively, as the most beautiful space in New York *(Figs. 596, 597)*. The definition of the garden as an enclosed volume of space (a *paradeisos*) is further disturbed by the greenhouse which now flops down into it and houses the escalator in the museum's new circulation space. That necessary area of, it is true, a scale formerly lacking in the museum, has now, however, come to resemble that of a shopping mall, loud and confusing, while the galleries behind it have turned into labyrinths through which it is difficult, not to say meaningless, to find one's way and in which the paintings, now bereft of their frames, get mixed up with the air-conditioning ducts. One feels that for the first time in its history something has gone really wrong with the Modern, something of which the tower, now dominant over the garden like business over art, must be the symbol.

So we return at last to Dallas, and there a similar pattern is clear to see. The brilliantly designed new museum by Edward Larrabee Barnes lies literally supine, horizontal on the slope below the towers *(Fig. 598)*. We approach it from the freeway through its parking lot at the foot of the slope. The skyscrapers rise above it. A wide ramp leads up through the body of the building toward them until, at the top of the ramp, they fill the void and dominate our view. A weak secondary axis crosses the ramp halfway up. This is part of a contemplated pedestrian way intended to serve the rest of an arts complex along the slope. It is as arty to walk as to jog these days, and it threatens neither the automobiles nor the towers to do so. The feeling is that all this cultural activity is being *permitted*, as the sanctioning towers are permitting all the boisterous hell the big paintings are raising in the white galleries below them. Modern art has indeed been incorporated, as the Modern first showed that it could be. Its personal whoop-de-do, however irreverent, serves the corporation too. It is all consumer goods after all, and it is obsessive consumption, directed by corporate enterprise, that the newest museums unquestionably celebrate and encourage.

All that, of course, leads us to the single most significant architectural movement of the past twenty

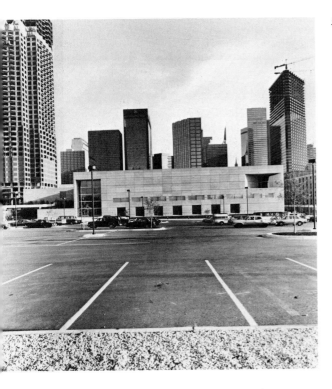

598. Dallas, Texas. Dallas Museum of Art. 1983–84. Edward Larrabee Barnes. View from parking lot.

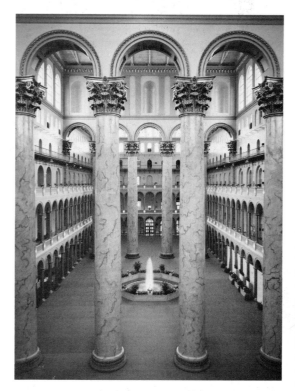

599. Washington, D.C. Great Hall of the National Building Museum (formerly Pension Building). 1881–87. Montgomery C. Meigs.

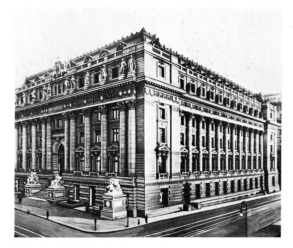

600. New York, New York. Customs House. 1910. Cass Gilbert.

601. Washington, D.C. Office building at 1001 Pennsylvania Avenue. 1985. Hartman-Cox Architects.

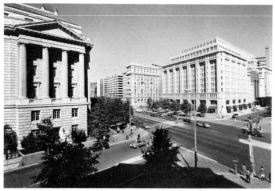

years, that for Preservation, which has risen up, with vast popular support, to combat the destruction occasioned by the automobile and the all-consuming office towers. Has it done so effectively? To some extent certainly. Buildings such as Mullet's grand State, War, and Navy Building, the old Pension Building with its continuous figural frieze and colossal columns, which has become a museum of American architecture (Fig. 599), the Patent Office, now a national portrait gallery, the Federal Post Office—all these in Washington—and in New York Cass Gilbert's Customs House (Fig. 600), Potter's Jefferson Market Court House, the Astor Library, and innumerable others throughout the country are still with us because of the efforts of dedicated preservationists everywhere. More than that, the best new buildings are not only so designed as to fit into the existing urban context but are also protecting old buildings, sometimes enshrining them. An excellent example of that double action is the big office and retail block, a grand palazzo, by Hartman-Cox at 1001 Pennsylvania Avenue in Washington, which gives a much-needed lesson in manners to the brutal, Late Modern, FBI Building across the avenue (Fig. 601). It is directly adjacent to the Post Office and honors it in its own forms while at the same time literally enfolding and protecting five delightful earlier buildings on the site. A generation or so ago such buildings would have disappeared without trace. One reason, without question, why many of them are still around is because of a pervasive feeling on the part of the informed public that "modern" architecture has failed. That public has begun to harbor the suspicion that anything new will be worse than whatever is there already, and it has to be admitted that most of the productions of the late International Style made that lamentable suspicion a reasonable one.

New Haven, alas—whose redevelopment was treated earlier in this book—finally lost most of its City Hall to one of Redevelopment's last and most arrogant acts of demolition. The present city government, along with everyone else, would be glad to have it back. However, the new building which is proposed to replace it is no longer of the late International Style, as the previous project of the sixties was. Instead, an attempt has been made, if with only moderate success so far, to design it in context with the remains of the original building *(Fig. 602)*. This is surely a step forward, not back, because it now transcends recent and destructive concepts of "style" and "modernity" in favor of the more enduring and traditional urbanistic principles of suitability, type, and contextuality. But again, an office building, in every likelihood of much less satisfactory design, will dominate the whole complex. We are almost back to the original proposal of 1966, are we not *(Fig. 523)*? It is the developer who must pay for, thus "permit," the government building. Now, though, the open space of the Green will be respected and defined, so that a few urban lessons at least have been learned in the intervening years. But the office building still dominates. City Hall, like the museum, lies in the shadow of the corporate towers—while, across the Green, the elegantly contextual library by Cass Gilbert, of 1908–9, though now saved, has been periodically threatened by developers' schemes for luxury condominiums, probably the least appropriate program imaginable for such a public place, charged as it is with the symbols of the community as a whole.

Preservation itself, admirable though it is, and symptomatic of some of the most important changes in architectural thinking that have taken place during the past sixteen years, also tends to be dominated by a debilitating, bowdlerizing, commercial spirit. Faneuil Hall and the Quincy Market area in Boston and South Street Seaport in New York, despite their many admirable qualities, show what comes of that *(Figs. 603, 604)*. The old existing buildings are cleaned, scraped, and cutesied up. New buildings seeking to emulate them have a distinctly homogenized char-

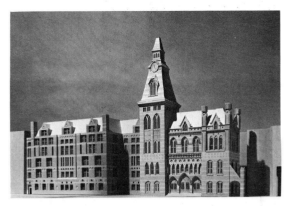

602. New Haven, Connecticut. City Hall Renovation. Model of project. 1986–89. Herbert S. Newman Associates.

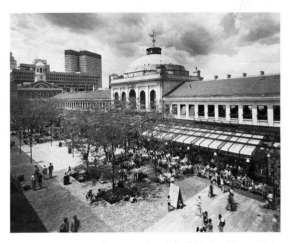

603. Boston, Massachusetts. Faneuil Hall Market Place. 1976–78. Benjamin Thompson & Associates.

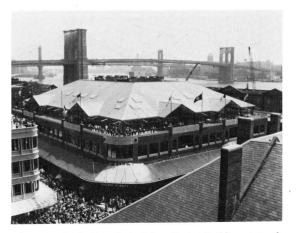

604. New York, New York. Fulton Market Building at South Street Seaport. 1983–84. Rouse Company. Opening-day festivities.

acter. They are feebler than their models, somehow diminished. One suspects that this is so in part because all the variety of action originally embodied in the areas in question—involving loading and unloading, outfitting, bulk storage, retail trading, hard drinking, and fighting—has been reduced to the simple consumption of luxury goods, exemplified by what might be called "cute eating," upon which the Rouse Company apparently places all its bets. Ethnic foods of every kind are the draw at South Street, as they are in Rouse's renovation of the Chapel Square Mall in New Haven *(Fig. 605)*. That lugubrious non-street, one of the first monuments to Redevelopment, has been brought up to a much more cheerful state of life by Rouse's architect, Herbert Newman. It is a welcome change to see a bad building of the sixties livened up rather than a strong nineteenth-century street reduced. And it is true that one does not wish to cavil over something, whatever its limitations, which is clearly better than its predecessors. Seattle, for example, has done all this with more vigor along its vast waterfront, where the activities are more varied and from which a great flight of stairs mounts to an authentically tough old market on the bluff, around which cluster new buildings that are at least attempting to shape a densely urban environment. In the end, though, it seems to be the developer who calls most of the shots and whose characteristic product, the office tower, defines and limits the basic character of our world.

There is a deep problem here, because office buildings are intrinsically less interesting and lively than almost any other kind of building, than houses, farms, or factories, for example, and much less complicated and dense in meaning than temples or cathedrals or even city halls. Never before in human history have cities been dominated by forms growing out of a program so fundamentally inane—a program saved once in its infancy by Sullivan's obsessively caring ornamentalism and again by the dear competitive fancy of New York. That fancy was very special, and some few architects, like Philip Johnson, have seemed to understand it today. So we are particularly struck when Johnson proposes an office building for Third Avenue which is pure Houston *(Fig. 606)*. In the recent past we have seen Houstonization almost completely destroy the fine old downtowns of cities like Denver, where the process was courageously opposed by a citizens' group called Historic Denver and by many public officials. We have noted how Graves began to turn the process around in Portland and Louisville, while Johnson's AT&T Building was good

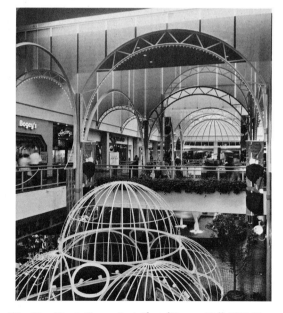

605. New Haven, Connecticut. Chapel Square Mall. 1984. Herbert S. Newman Associates.

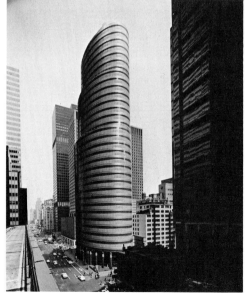

606. New York, New York. Office building for Gerald Hines on Third Avenue. 1984–86. John Burgee Architects with Philip Johnson. View from Third Avenue.

old New York in every important way. We realize, however, that Third Avenue is not Madison. It is wide and raw, with every kind of change of scale. It is a frontier street, upon which Johnson's glossy wraparound, designed for his Houston developer, Gerald Hines, takes up a weirdly appropriate stance. However unsympathetic to it our original reactions are, it may do well in that place.

There is surely a lesson in this. It is true that the architectural situation as a whole may appear to be a bit discouraging, but the present can never be easily summed up or too firmly categorized. New things, thank heaven, are incessantly growing up about us, and we do not always see them right away. Our models of reality are inevitably a little behind the times. Westway was a good example of that. By the time that proposal was ready, public opinion had begun to turn against the destruction of the urban fabric by throughways—and, as we have seen, rightly so. The only trouble was that Westway was something else: the throughway put to the service of a grander urban scheme involving much needed housing and, perhaps most of all, a great public park, a waterfront of classical grandeur designed by Venturi and one of his finest works. It would have created one of the noblest and most civilized spaces in New York, a grand esplanade with strong sculptural details, running along the Hudson *(Figs. 607, 608, 609)*. But the image of it that dominated the public and probably even the official mind was of an overblown Connector, and so in the end it was defeated on ecological pretexts of dubious relevance. Irony upon irony for the historian: having railed against the automobile

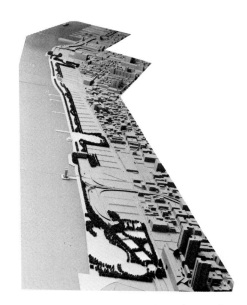

607. New York, New York. Westway, design for river-front park along Hudson River. Preliminary design. 1985. Venturi, Rauch and Scott Brown. Model of ninety-seven-acre project.

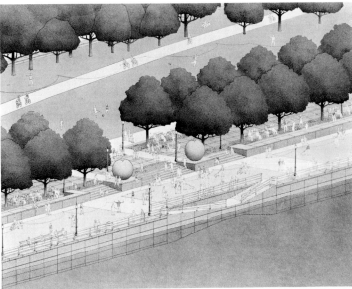

608. Westway. Detail drawing with *Big Apple* sculptures.

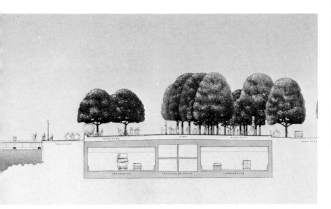

609. Westway. Elevation from river, showing underground highway for cars.

291

for a generation, he is witness to the frustration of a magnificent urban prospect because of its connection with the automobile.

We are always a little slow to learn; our models contain us. Yet in the end it is art more than anything else that helps us to break those models and to grow. After all, the work of architecture that has most excited the imagination and attracted, indeed, released the love of the American people during the past decade has been neither an office building, a museum, nor a condominium, but a gentle memorial to the dead of a hateful war. It was designed by none of the architects we have mentioned but by a young girl of Chinese descent who won a massive competition for it when she was still an undergraduate in Yale College. I refer, of course, to the Vietnam Memorial on the Mall in Washington by Maya Lin *(Figs. 610, 611, 612)*. This dark but shining wall of names leads us chronologically with the dead down into the depths of the war and then rises slowly up again to direct our attention far out across space to the Washington Monument on one side and the Lincoln Memorial on the other. Sunk down into the earth, set over to one side, and screened by trees, the Memorial still completes the great vistas of the Mall and unites them into one achingly contemporary emotional experience as no more obtrusive monument would have been able to do. It is a memorial not to victory but to grief—and to the mortality that underlies all human hopes. But it invokes immortality too, because that state of being resides in the human capacity to remember and to name. So the crowds reach out to touch the wall, descending into the depths it defines, while it leaps out arrowlike beyond them, pointing to Lincoln's temple with its image and Washington's obelisk rising toward the sun.

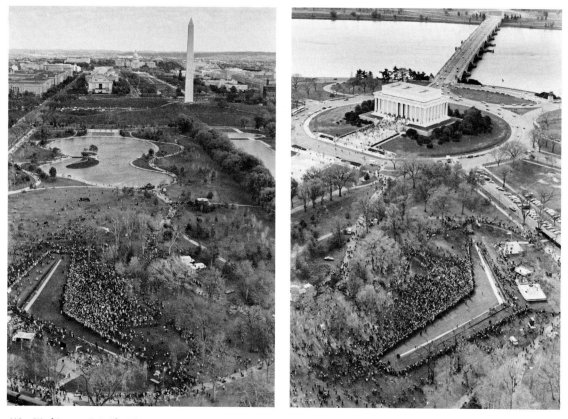

610. Washington, D.C. The Vietnam Veterans Memorial. 1982. Maya Lin. Aerial photograph taken during dedication ceremonies.

611. The Vietnam Veterans Memorial with Lincoln Memorial.

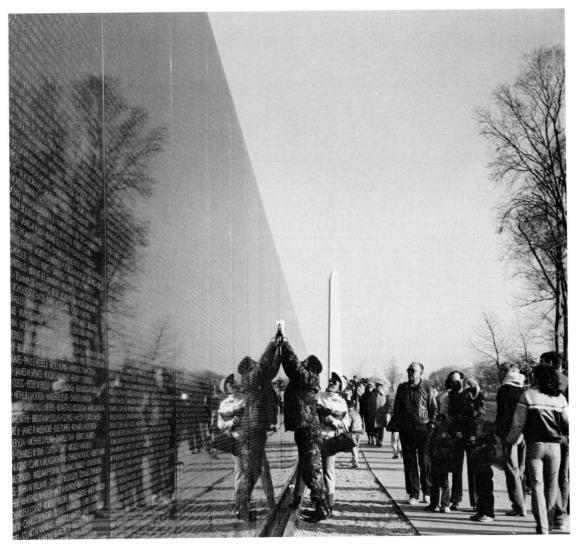

612. The Vietnam Veterans Memorial. Soldier in uniform making a rubbing of a name on the wall.

Notes

1. The sequence above about automobiles and the frontier seems questionable now. It is still, I think, a fair description of the way things appeared to be in 1969, but by 1988 the automobile had dwindled. It is true that there are more of them than ever and that the pattern of the new cities, such as Houston, Dallas, and so on, has been wholly set by them, but they themselves have become smaller, less symbolic in design, and enormously expensive. So many of them are also of foreign, especially Japanese, manufacture, or imitate the foreign types, that they can no longer be described as peculiarly American in form or symbol. Their physical presence as a whole is no longer mythic and fantastic, and their emotional appeal is much less. Paradoxically, though they have come to control the shape of the city, their day as shapers of myth has apparently passed away. It is possible that some of the special American bafflement apparent in 1988 derives in part from that fact. New automobiles, like new houses, have become too expensive for most people to buy. The very industries upon which the prosperity of the modern United States has been founded are foundering, and along with them the unique way of mass life they made possible. Hence basic symbols are changing.

   Mobile homes have also changed. They are still being made in great numbers and are to be found seeded throughout the more poverty-stricken districts of rural America, but they are no longer the special economic bargain they once seemed to be. Nor do the possibilities they appeared to offer for industrially produced housing fascinate architects any longer. Paul Rudolph's intricately conceived group for New Haven, Connecticut *(Fig. 5)*, has become a horrendous example of what might happen to mobile-home units and a cautionary tale against their use. The whole group has literally fallen apart, simply disintegrated under weather and habitation. It was also progressively torn to pieces by its infuriated inhabitants and, step by step, abandoned, until only a few families crouched in the ruins, surrounded by acres of rotting plywood packing-cases. Soon they too were gone. The scene was definitive. The epic time of the mobile home, like that of the automobile, had gone by.

2. The Wainwright certainly needed the buildings around it, as the well-intentioned but disastrous isolation of it that was decided upon in 1974 has so sadly shown. It is indeed a traditional palazzo block, solidly defining its street. It is a type, like the other office buildings of its time which surrounded it and with which it worked to shape the solid fabric of its downtown. It differed from those other buildings only in what might be called its surface decoration, which was, as a matter of fact, a good deal like that of Palladio's Palazzo Valmarana in Vicenza. Indeed, from Vicenza to Chicago ran an urban tradition in which city buildings were treated as simple blocks, each one resembling and enhancing the other, to shape the city as a whole. So the great façades of the Wainwright Building needed to be complete only on the street elevations; at its other extremities it is only a couple of bays deep, and the rear elevations are totally undesigned. When the buildings around it were torn down—an act which derived in the end from sensibilities shaped by the anti-urbanism of

294

International Style buildings like Lever Brothers—it became apparent that Sullivan had counted on those buildings and the general urban concept of the solid street façade.

3. There was a good deal that is problematic in that development, however, and much that turned out to be architecturally reductive and urbanistically destructive. The Guaranty, like the Wainwright, had only two designed façades, and was therefore still conceived by Sullivan in a traditional urbanistic context—one which the later generation was to destroy to the detriment of the urban fabric as a whole.

4. But there is something deeper going on. The evocation of colonial architecture refers here to its earlier, more medieval phases, surely seen, with an eye like that of Hawthorne, as something incredibly ancient, much older than it actually was, soaked in myth and legend—and moldering back into the landscape itself so that it, too, began to seem a natural landscape form. Here, for a curious wonder, the ancient Amerindian doctrine of imitation seems to surface again. Richardson, as O'Gorman has shown, seems to have employed it, and so, as Levine's forthcoming book demonstrates, did Frank Lloyd Wright, especially in his later work.

5. The two preceding paragraphs should now be read with all polemical, and especially pejorative, adjectives eliminated from them. I leave them here as a reminder of what not to do in future. The development to stripped form had nothing intrinsically evil in it. It was simply part of the general trend toward simplification, and its productions were generally called "Modern Classic" at the time. The kind of mass envelope it created served as an appropriate method to shape and surface some very good buildings, notably the Art Deco skyscrapers of New York. These, and the government buildings such as post offices that were built in great numbers at the same time, look much better to us today than most of their more "modern" contemporaries and successors. They are solid and permanent, built with considerable care and excellent materials. Only an extremely hermetic aesthetic could prefer the generally shoddy, undignified, loveless buildings of the present to them. As to their relation to totalitarianism and so on: associational meanings drain in and out of buildings though their forms remain the same. They will therefore always be experienced according to the cultural stance of the observer, which will invariably change over time. "Fascist" and "Nazi" build-

ings will seem much less so to observers as time goes on and those absurd and abominable regimes recede ever further into the past. Their buildings, which in fact belong to a large international group, will then take on other associations. Is the Folger Library any more or less intrinsically "totalitarian" than the stripped classical buildings constructed by Mussolini and Hitler which derive in part from it? The recent work of Aldo Rossi in Italy and the projects of Leon Krier have opened our eyes to heavy, simplified classical forms once again, leaving one a little embarrassed by one's own conditioned reflexes to them in the past. Forms are "heavy" or "light" or whatever; these are empathetic reactions. They are "democratic" or "totalitarian"; these are associational responses. Can they be "good" or "evil"? Applied to buildings rather than to good works or crimes, such terms seem to be simple projections. Our experience of any work of art will in any event be a complicated one, in which every kind of response and conditioning is involved and inextricably interwoven. Historians should be aware of the process.

6. But the grand axis of French academic urbanism is much more than that, just as the great plan it completed in Washington was much more than simply a strong frame for future building. It was the ultimate urban declaration of humanity's confidence in its own political destiny—in its capacity to control the world through human will and reason. Following Le Nôtre's Versailles, Washington and modern Paris together culminated the whole development of the classic plan that had run from Delphi through Olympia and Athens to Kos, Praeneste, and Baroque Rome. The great avenues "radiate." They are "stars," cosmic in scale, leaping out across space. Perhaps the Washington Monument was finally built as a simple obelisk in the 1880's, to balance the Capitol's dome, because it was an obelisk in the Place de la Concorde which called attention to the dome of the Invalides as it is seen on that bearing rising behind the Chambre des Députés. But the completion of the Mall endowed the United States with the most purely classical government complex in the world. As such, it has shown the durability of classicism to embody permanent ideals which can outlive generations and lend the resonant dimension of time to present reality. Classicism has a history which is political as well as religious, and it endows contemporary events with those associational references. In this dimen-

sion Lincoln does become the martyred god in his tomb, witnessing the Kennedy funerals, which in this setting become those of the Gracchi, Tribunes of the people, slaughtered, after which more conservative forces progressively take command.

7. This favorable assessment must be modified negatively in 1988. Rudolph's project would have cast a fearful shadow over a good bit of the west side, not to mention the fact that, in view of the fate of his trailers in New Haven described in Note 1, the permanence of the scheme might well have been in doubt. Comparison should now be made with Pelli's great group a little farther downtown *(Fig. 578)*, where the existing towers of the city are complemented by traditional building types rather than by megastructural fantasies, and where the World Trade Center in particular is pulled into some kind of contextual unity, especially as seen from the Hudson.

8. The PSFS was a fine building, but it was already beginning to lose the special magic with which New York's more Art Deco skyscrapers had been endowed. The postcards of them reproduced by Rem Koolhaas in his delightful book, *Delirious New York*, of 1978, capture the feeling: The Empire State is seen as leaping to the sky gods, scraping the clouds, like the temples of Tikal. So is its contemporary, the Chrysler Building, covered with automobile imagery and thinning itself down to the narrowest towers in order to pierce the heavens with its shining needle. But the Chrysler Building seems to play the female role when Koolhaas puts it and the Empire State Building in bed together. Empathetic personification can hardly go further. So by 1978 the Beaux-Arts "Modern Classic" skyscrapers of New York, once despised by modernist critics, had become everyone's darlings. And rightly so.

9. The word "unsuccessful" in the preceding paragraph should simply be deleted. A word more should be said about Mies' buildings. They came closer than the buildings of any other architect of the International Style toward creating a coherent architectural language. Their parts were articulated like parts of speech, fixed parts of speech, so that they spoke the same comprehensible idiom always. The major problem was that theirs was a reductive language when compared, for example, to that of classicism itself; it had many fewer words and systems of construction. This was inevitable, since it was the cre-

ation of one man. Still, it was a dignified dialect, and it came much closer than the more idiosyncratic assertions of Le Corbusier toward founding a set of more or less permanent architectural types. In this it was of course an urban architecture, and in some ways a traditionally classic one, but here again it was reductive. Though Mies' instinct for traditional urban relationships was surer than that of other International Style architects, he failed, like them, to value the street and its life. Insisting on the slab standing on its legs, he could not use the splendid device Sullivan had imagined and New York had put into practise of keeping the street solidly defined with palazzo blocks (full of shops at sidewalk level) and allowing fancy free rein up above. His buildings, too, therefore tended toward the destruction of the urban fabric, though rarely to the degree achieved by most other late International Style structures.

10. Now, in 1988, I totally disagree with everything I wrote in the paragraphs immediately above. The whole megastructural concept should, I think, be seen as a desperate attempt by late International Style architects (and apparently by myself as a critic at that time) to escape from the obvious fact that traditional urbanism means fundamentally good architecture and has to be respected in new buildings. There is no need either to try to stand on one finger in order to be different from everything else or to invent new types of cities. Every one of those attempts, from Rudolph's Mobile Homes in New Haven to Cumbernauld in Scotland, has turned out in practise to be an unmitigated disaster—simply because everything about such schemes, Habitat most of all, is tormented, artificial, and unrealistic. In that connection, too, Habitat's strained and arbitrary structural system has nothing whatever to do with the solemn probity of Kahn's design, with its sense of system and rightness and its strict avoidance of gesture—out of which Kahn's special silence and peace arise.

11. I now think the E.U.R. was much better than the New Haven project and not all that sterile. It created an environment haunted by Italian memory, and it has emphatically outlived the regime that created it. It is now much desired as a place to live and has played a part in inspiring some of the most eloquent of contemporary Italian architecture, that of Aldo Rossi in particular.

A Note on Method and Bibliography

A word about what needs to be written in the future, in a purely art-historical sense, may not be out of place at the start. One point is now clear, and the historian must make it without blushing. It is that history is essential for architecture, because the architect, who must now deal with everything urban, will therefore always be dealing with historical problems—with the past and, a function of the past, with the future. So the architect should be regarded as a kind of physical historian, because he constructs relationships across time: civilization in fact. And since civilization is based largely upon the capacity of human beings to remember, the architect builds visible history. For this reason, art history ought to be able to help him if he will let it do so, because it will cause him to focus on new things, to value more things, and, most of all, to sense and to love their relationships to each other and to the multilevel life of humanity.

Odd that such should need saying, but there is still a good deal of iconoclasm in America, which produces some individuals, architects among them, who resent the past bitterly and so are apparently incapable of affecting civilization in other than destructive ways. There can be no doubt, as Lawrence sensed (D. H. Lawrence, *Studies in Classic American Literature, London,* 1922), that the American genius has been a highly destructive one, of old patterns of behavior and of old things. To discard and to move on always westward or upward; there is force in the movement, but it has been and can be crushing too, especially of anything or anyone that gets in its way. Hence, we should no longer romanticize our frontier, as even Frederick Jackson Turner's great study surely tended to do (*The Frontier in American History,* New York, 1920), but should see its effects objectively. One of them is provincialism, with its concomitant social timidity. Another is violence. Baffled by differences of race or opinion, the frontier rages; checked, it turns suicidal, fearful of nothingness if the momentum goes. That phase of hysterical mobility is at its ultimate crisis now, in external as well as internal affairs, in foreign policy no less than in redevelopment. And it should be obvious that history—which always looks for the complexity of the truth beyond the spurious simplicity of the myth, and seeks out the complex relationships beneath the polemic stance—can serve the cause of humanity critically in both areas. It can multiply the choices, soothe the destructive fury of either-or and, beyond sterile hysterics, rediscover over and over again the common simple fact of life which is the point of it all.

Art history must therefore be conservative, experimental, and ethical. It loves old and new things, and it demands value. The line between history and criticism should therefore be difficult to draw in any field; in the modern field, it must be almost nonexistent. What needs to be written, then, is more history, and in art especially, broader history, embracing more things. At this moment, it is the special task of the architectural historian to broaden his field. He must now bring into it all the elements of urbanism and social organization which he can grow to apprehend. Here the anthropologist and the sociologist, of whom some have already shown themselves sympathetic to art-historical collaboration, can help him enormously and be helped in turn. The art historian's contribution to his common problem can best be made in two ways: through his perception of the formal (some would now say "structural") relationships between things and through his unwearying insistence upon the depths of human meaning which all man-made things embody in varying degrees. His approach must therefore always be intuitive and emotional as well as intellectual—as if the distinctions made any sense any more, which of course they do not. Consequently, he must be more interested in experience than in criteria. For this he must never apologize, because it is precisely here that the task is hardest for all men: how to experience and to implement in physical form what the mind well knows but for which it can never easily find emotional equivalents or physical embodiments. Art history must work in that unique area, or it need not exist. Beyond the sum of its knowledge and experience, in a way yet unknown, lies some absolute connection with the existential loneliness of perception and choice, and the sudden stumble of action, when a new thing is born.

This book owes something to the work of other people and to earlier publications of my own, from which some, though I hope minimal, repetitions could hardly be avoided. It seems best to refer here largely, though not exclusively, to more available published sources and to books rather than articles where possible: first, though not so available as it ought to be, to The American Guide, E. G. Alsberg, editor (New York, 1949), which grew out of the WPA State Guides of the 1930's, some of which can still be found. Most cities have their own architectural guidebooks or special studies of one kind or another, usually available through local museums or historical and preservation societies. Among many fine examples, A Guide to the Architecture of Washington, D.C., done under the auspices of the American Institute of Architects, Hugh Newell Jacobsen, editor, and with an introduction by Francis Donald Lethbridge (New York, 1965), comes to mind as an excellent type—or, for pictorial histories, works such as John A. Kouwenhoven, The Columbia Historical Portrait of New York (New York, 1953); or R. H. Howland and E. P. Spencer, The Architecture of Baltimore (Baltimore, 1953). Everyone should probably own the guide for his own city and, if one is not available, might take steps to have one made in order to fight effectively for his town in the years to come—as he will have to do if he wants to keep it. He will also find many new paperback editions of the titles mentioned below and of others, some useful, some not.

The first general histories of American architecture (Talbot Hamlin, The American Spirit in Architecture, New Haven, 1926; Thomas E. Tallmadge, The Story of Architecture in America, New York, 1927; Fiske Kimball, American Architecture, New York, 1928) all appeared, it will be noted, during the opulent 1920's and are of most interest today as reflections of Beaux-Arts attitudes; they should be used to redress the balance tipped toward the Bauhaus or the Bay Region by books of the immediately

postwar era (Sigfried Giedion, Space, Time and Architecture, Cambridge, Mass., 1941; James Marston Fitch, American Building, the Forces That Shape It, New York, 1948, new edition, American Building, the Historical Forces That Shaped It, New York, 1966; John A. Kouwenhoven, Made in America: The Arts in Modern Civilization, Newton Centre, Mass., 1948; and, in its own way, Bruno Zevi, Towards an Organic Architecture, London, 1950; New York, 1966). These works surely owed something to the writings of Lewis Mumford, whose beautiful Sticks and Stones (New York, 1924; Dover paperback, 1966) and Brown Decades: A Study of the Arts in America, 1865–1895 (New York, 1931; Dover paperback, 1966)—along with many essays culminating later in those published in The Highway and the City (New York, 1953; Mentor paperback 1964)—had begun to look at the history of American architecture afresh through the eyes of a Garden City humanitarian; and of Henry-Russell Hitchcock, whose more strictly art-historical method had, along with more specialized studies, both identified modern architecture (Henry-Russell Hitchcock, Jr., Modern Architecture, Romanticism and Reintegration, New York, 1929) and named the International Style (Henry-Russell Hitchcock and Philip Johnson, The International Style: Architecture Since 1922, New York, 1932; new edition, New York, 1966), and had begun to re-evaluate nineteenth-century American architecture (Rhode Island Architecture, Providence, 1939).

Since historians normally have something to prove, most later general books have some easily identifiable bias. Wayne Andrews, Architecture, Ambition and Americans: A History of American Architecture (New York, 1955; new edition, Architecture, Ambition and Americans: A Social History of American Architecture, Chicago, 1964), might be more precisely described as a socialite history, while Christopher Tunnard and Henry Hope Reed, The American Skyline (Boston, 1955; Mentor paperback, 1956), is invaluable for its command of planning and of the environment as a whole but flighty in its architectural judgments, wherein the balance back toward the Beaux-Arts is perhaps overly redressed—as it also is in the rather bureaucratically conceived John Burchard and Albert Bush-Brown, The Architecture of America: A Social and Cultural History (Boston, 1961; paperback, 1966). There is now a study of American planning which stops much earlier than one would like (about 1910), is perhaps overly topographical, but is most welcome nonetheless: John W. Reps, The Making of Urban America: A History of City Planning in the United States (Princeton, N.J., 1965); and, for an anthology of texts related to city planning, David R. Weimer, editor, *City and Country in America* (New York, 1962). Also, for all traditional, pre-Ville Radieuse urban preoccupations, Camillo Sitte, *City Planning According to Artistic Principles* (original edition, Vienna, 1889; now with elaborate commentary by George R. Collins and Christiane Crasemann Collins, 2 vols., New York, 1965). Useful as a handy source of illustrations and basic data, with short critical essays, is *Arts of the United States: A Pictorial Survey*, edited by William H. Pierson, Jr. and Martha Davidson (New York, 1960), in which the section on colonial architecture was compiled and written by Hugh Sinclair Morrison, that on the nineteenth century by William H. Jordy, and that on the twentieth century by myself.

In general, one turns with relief to more restricted studies. For pueblo architecture, though its history as an art has hardly been written, there are the authoritative archaeological accounts, with good bibliographies, of Alfred Vincent Kidder, *An Introduction to the Study of Southwestern Archaeology* (New Haven, 1924; new revised edition with an introduction by Irving Rouse, New Haven, 1963), and H. H. Wormington, *Prehistoric Indians of the Southwest* (Denver, 1947; six printings to 1964). Don Watson, *Cliff Dwellings of the Mesa Verde* (Mesa Verde National Park, Colo., n.d.) has excellent photographs. And now there is a good archaeological handbook for all the pre-Columbian art of this continent: Gordon R. Willey, *An Introduction to American Archaeology; Vol. I: North and Middle America* (Englewood Cliffs, N.J., 1966). For the Spanish colonies: Rexford Newcomb, *Spanish Colonial Architecture in the United States* (New York, 1937), and George A. Kubler, *The Religious Architecture of New Mexico in the Colonial Period and Since the Colonial Occupation* (Colorado Springs, 1940). And for the necessary hemispherical and European background: George A. Kubler, *The Art and Architecture of Ancient America* (Harmondsworth and Baltimore, 1962; revised edition in press), and George A. Kubler and Martin Soria, *Art and Architecture in Spain and Portugal and Their American Dominions, 1500–1800* (Harmondsworth and Baltimore, 1959).

For colonial architecture in general, including that of the Eastern Seaboard, and with bibliography: Hugh Morrison, *Early American Architecture* (New York, 1952), which, though remarkably complete, can be supplemented by Anthony Garvan, *Architecture and Town Planning in Colonial Connecticut* (New Haven, 1951); and by Thomas Tileston Waterman, *The Dwellings of Colonial America* (Chapel Hill, 1950); and Frederick D.

Nichols, *The Early Architecture of Georgia* (Chapel Hill, 1957); and Henry Chandlee Forman, *Old Buildings, Gardens, and Furniture of Tidewater Maryland* (Cambridge, Md., 1967); and by Louis B. Wright *et al*, *The Arts in America: The Colonial Period* (New York, 1966); also, for general aesthetic considerations, John W. McCoubrey, *American Tradition in Painting* (New York, 1963); and my "The Precisionist Strain in American Architecture," *Art in America*, 3 (1960), 46–53. For Jefferson there is Fiske Kimball, *Thomas Jefferson, Architect* (Boston, 1916; new edition, New York, 1968); I. T. Frary, *Thomas Jefferson, Architect and Builder* (Richmond, 1931); and Clay Lancaster, "Jefferson's Architectural Indebtedness to Robert Morris," *Journal of the Society of Architectural Historians*, 10 (March, 1951), 3–10. European, especially English, relationships were overly ignored in earlier American studies; so: Nikolaus Pevsner, *An Outline of European Architecture* (6th, Jubilee edition, Baltimore, 1960; or 7th edition, Penguin paperback, 1963 *et seq.*); and Kerry Downes, *English Baroque Architecture* (London, 1966); and John Summerson, *Georgian London* (London, 1945; revised edition, Penguin paperback, 1962), and his *Architecture in Britain, 1530–1830* (4th edition, Baltimore, 1963); also Emil Kaufmann, *Architecture in the Age of Reason* (Cambridge, Mass., 1955).

Talbot Hamlin, *Greek Revival Architecture in America* (New York, 1944; Dover paperback, 1964), is so broad in coverage (though see also Rexford Newcomb, *Architecture of the Old Northwest Territory*, Chicago, 1950) that it should properly be entitled "Romantic-Classic Architecture in America," but its conclusions need to be revised and extended through a consideration of European materials and of the general architectural development of the time, as by Henry-Russell Hitchcock, *Architecture: Nineteenth and Twentieth Centuries* (Harmondsworth and Baltimore, 1958; new edition, 1963), which should indeed be consulted for the proper relationship between European and American events and stylistic developments to, at least, 1939, and whose bibliography, like those of most of the other titles cited here, can also be consulted with profit. For my view of the period, my *Modern Architecture: The Architecture of Democracy, c. 1789–1960* (New York, 1961).

For the nineteenth century, Carroll L. V. Meeks, "Picturesque Eclecticism," *Art Bulletin*, 32 (1950), 226–35, proposed a key concept. Note should also be taken of Hitchcock's *Early Victorian Architecture in Britain* (New Haven, 1954), and of his *American Architectural Books: A List of Books, Portfolios, and Pamphlets on*

Architecture and Related Subjects Published in America Before 1895 (3d edition, Minneapolis, 1946). An anthology of texts for this period and later is Lewis Mumford's Roots of Contemporary American Architecture (New York, 1952). Among these, Horatio Greenough (Form and Function: Remarks on Art, Berkeley, 1949), whose "functional" view is, I feel, fundamentally Greek Revival in character, should be especially noted, as well as the picturesque and balloon-frame pattern books which I discussed in my articles noted below. My treatment of the Stick and Shingle Styles in this book is based upon my doctoral dissertation of 1949 and my chapters of the same names in Antoinette F. Downing and Vincent J. Scully, Jr., The Architectural Heritage of Newport, Rhode Island, 1640–1915 (Cambridge, Mass., 1952; 2d edition revised with new introductions, New York, 1967); and upon my "Romantic Rationalism and the Expression of Structure in Wood: Downing, Wheeler, Gardner and the 'Stick Style,' 1840–1876," Art Bulletin, 35 (1953), 121–42; and my "American Villas," Architectural Review (March, 1954), 168–79; and The Shingle Style (New Haven, 1955). James Early, Romanticism and American Architecture (New York, 1965), is a fairly sound review of most of the literature of the period. For Furness and the neo-grec, I am indebted to the unpublished master's thesis by Neil Levine, submitted at Yale in 1967, in relation to which we should not forget the remarks by Leopold Eidlitz on "empathy," in his The Nature and Function of Art, More Especially of Architecture (London, 1881); and, for some basic ideas about American pictorialism, to my colleague George Hersey, "Replication Replicated, or, Notes on American Bastardy," Perspecta, 9–10 (1965), 211–48. For another anthology, rather overtitled but with some Eidlitz and Furness included: The Literature of Architecture: The Evolution of Architectural Theory and Practice in Nineteenth-Century America, edited by Don Gifford (New York, 1966).

For Richardson one must not only turn back if one can to Mrs. Schuyler Van Rensselaer, Henry Hobson Richardson and His Works (Boston and New York, 1888), but to Henry-Russell Hitchcock, The Architecture of H. H. Richardson and His Times (New York, 1936; new edition, Hamden, Conn., 1961; and M.I.T. paperback, 1965). For Sullivan we are indebted to another pathfinding work: Hugh Morrison, Louis Sullivan, Prophet of Modern Architecture (New York, 1935; new edition, 1952; Norton paperback, 1962), to which, for my thoughts on Sullivan's ornament and the importance of his late work, I diffidently add my own "Louis Sullivan's Architectural Ornament: A Brief Note Concerning

Humanist Design in the Age of Force," Perspecta, 5 (1959), 73–80. Also, Winston Weisman, "Philadelphia Functionalism and Sullivan," Journal of the Society of Architectural Historians, 20 (1961), 3–19. Good photographs are in Albert Bush-Brown, Louis Sullivan (New York, 1960). But for Sullivan we are fortunate in possessing extensive writings of his own, especially Kindergarten Chats and Other Writings (New York, 1947) and The Autobiography of an Idea (New York, 1934, 1949, 1956). Sherman Paul, Louis Sullivan: An Architect in American Thought (Englewood Cliffs, N.J., 1962), treats Sullivan as a progressive sociologist. During the Richardson-Sullivan era there was a distinguished contemporary critic, Montgomery Schuyler, whose criteria, if they can be said to have had a systematic framework, were generally based upon the structural determinism of the ubiquitous Viollet-le-Duc, whose Discourses on Architecture were published in America in 1875–81. See Montgomery Schuyler, American Architecture (New York, 1892), especially the edition edited by William H. Jordy and Ralph Coe (2 vols., New York, 1961). Schuyler is especially good on the early skyscrapers. For Chicago: Thomas E. Tallmadge, Architecture in Old Chicago (Chicago, 1941); and Carl W. Condit, The Rise of the Skyscraper (Chicago, 1952) and The Chicago School of Architecture (Chicago, 1964).

Frank Lloyd Wright also wrote prolifically, sometimes in Sullivan's Whitmanesque prose, sometimes more tersely. His writings are most readily available in Frank Lloyd Wright: Writings and Buildings, selected by Edgar Kaufmann and Ben Raeburn (Cleveland and New York, 1960). For Wright's buildings to 1941: Henry-Russell Hitchcock, In the Nature of Materials, 1887–1941: The Buildings of Frank Lloyd Wright (New York, 1942); and for the early period, Grant Manson, Frank Lloyd Wright to 1910: The First Golden Age (New York, 1958). One should remember the splendid publications of Wright's work in Berlin, of 1910 and 1911, by Ernst Wasmuth (Ausgeführte bauten und entwürfe von Frank Lloyd Wright, Berlin, 1910; and Frank Lloyd Wright: Ausgeführte bauten, Berlin, 1911; the first recently reprinted as Frank Lloyd Wright: Buildings, Plans, and Designs, New York, 1963). These were the major vehicles for Wright's critical influence in Europe during the teens. For the stylistic analysis upon which my text here is largely based, see my Frank Lloyd Wright (New York, 1960); and "Frank Lloyd Wright and Twentieth-Century Style," in Studies in Western Art: Acts of the Twentieth International Congress of the History of Art, IV, Problems of the Nineteenth and Twentieth Century (Princeton, 1963),

7–21; shorter version, "Wright, International Style and Kahn," in *Arts Magazine*, March, 1962. The work of the other architects of the Prairie School is discussed by H. Allen Brooks, "The Prairie School, the Midwest Contemporaries of Frank Lloyd Wright," in the same volume of the *Acts of the Twentieth International Congress of the History of Art* cited above, 22–33; and by M. L. Peisch, *The Chicago School of Architecture: Early Followers of Sullivan and Wright* (New York, 1965); and David Gebhard, "Louis Sullivan and George Grant Elmslie," *Journal of the Society of Architectural Historians*, 19 (May, 1960), 62–68; and his *A Guide to the Existing Buildings of Purcell and Elmslie, 1910–1920* (Roswell, N.M., 1960). For that period in California, with Greene and Greene, Maybeck, Gill: Stephen W. Jacobs, "California Contemporaries of Wright," *Acts of the Twentieth International Congress of the History of Art*, 34–63; and for them and Schindler, the labor of love by Esther McCoy, *Five California Architects* (New York, 1960); by her also, *Richard Neutra* (New York, 1960).

The Beaux-Arts eclectics are treated in the general books mentioned at the beginning of this note, as well as in monographs such as *A Monograph of the Work of McKim, Mead and White, 1879–1915* (4 vols., New York, 1914–15); and Charles Moore, *The Life and Times of Charles Follen McKim* (Boston, 1929), and his *Daniel H. Burnham* (2 vols., Boston and New York, 1921); and Charles C. Baldwin, *Stanford White* (New York, 1931). Also, a beautiful book with many illustrations, excellent for the New York skyscrapers and for general considerations of planning and group design in city and suburb alike: Werner Hegemann (with Elbert Peets), *Amerikanische Architektur und Stadtbaukunst* (2d printing, Berlin, 1927), also in English as *Civic Art: The American Vitruvius*. For the Garden City and its derivatives, see David R. Weimer, noted earlier, and also his *City as A Metaphor* (New York, 1966); and especially Ebenezer Howard, *Garden Cities of To-Morrow* (London, 1898; new edition, Cambridge, Mass., 1965); and Clarence S. Stein, *Toward New Towns for America* (New York, 1957; M.I.T. paperback, 1966); and Henry S. Churchill, *The City is the People* (New York, 1945; new edition, Norton paperback, 1962).

For the most characteristic attitudes of modern architecture in Europe, besides Giedion: Walter Gropius, *The New Architecture and the Bauhaus* (London, 1935; reprinted 1956, M.I.T. paperback, 1965); Nikolaus Pevsner, *Pioneers of Modern Design from William Morris to Walter Gropius* (New York, 1949; revised edition, Penguin paperback, 1960); and Reyner Banham, *Theory and Design in the First Machine Age* (New York, 1960), and his *The New Brutalism, Ethic or Aesthetic?* (New York, 1966). For American architecture of the 1930's and the postwar period, one might again refer to Hitchcock and to my *Modern Architecture;* also to Elizabeth Mock, *Built in U.S.A., 1932–1944* (New York, 1944), and to Henry-Russell Hitchcock and Arthur Drexler, *Built in U.S.A.: Post-War Architecture* (New York, 1952). Also to my "Doldrums in the Suburbs," *Journal of the Society of Architectural Historians*, 24 (March, 1965), 36–47, and *Perspecta*, 9–10 (1965), 281–90. For the 1950's in their freshness: Ian McCallum, *Architecture U.S.A.* (New York, 1959); and for individual architects: Arthur Drexler, *Ludwig Mies van der Rohe* (New York, 1960); John Jacobus, *Philip Johnson* (New York, 1962); Allan Temko, *Eero Saarinen* (New York, 1962); and *Eero Saarinen on His Work*, edited by Aline B. Saarinen (New Haven, 1962); and John McHale, *R. Buckminster Fuller* (New York, 1962), and for the incomparably technocratic Bucky himself: R. Buckminster Fuller, *Nine Chains to the Moon*, (Philadelphia, 1938; new paperback edition, Carbondale, Ill., 1963); and for high-keyed individual buildings: John Jacobus, *Twentieth-Century Architecture: The Middle Years, 1940–65* (New York, 1965); and for architects discussing their work, mostly making small sense: Paul Heyer, *Architects on Architecture: New Directions in America* (New York, 1966); and for low-keyed urbanism: Kevin Lynch, *The Image of the City* (Cambridge, Mass., 1960); and Martin Meyerson *et al, Face of the Metropolis* (New York, 1963); and for the design of freeways, subdivisions, and so on: Christopher Tunnard and Boris Pushkarev, *Man-Made America: Chaos or Control* (New Haven, 1963); and messy America: Peter Blake, *God's Own Junkyard* (New York, 1964); and the glories of redevelopment and new towns, Julian Eugene Kulski, *Land of Urban Promise* (Notre Dame, Ind., 1966) and for wrong-headedness so consistent as to present an incomparable image of the cataclysmic Ville Radieuse–Garden City model: Percy Johnson-Marshall, *Rebuilding Cities* (Chicago, 1966); and for Las Vegas, signs, hot rods, and customs, upon which all kinds of work still needs to be done: Tom Wolfe, *The Kandy-Kolored, Tangerine-Flake, Streamline Baby* (New York, 1965).

Since 1961, I have learned a good deal, I hope, from my colleagues and students, cited in various places above, such as Robert A. M. Stern, whose book on George Howe should appear shortly and to whom I am indebted for advice about housing. Also, for the Philadelphia Savings Fund Society Building, see the articles by Stern and Jordy in *Journal of the Society of Archi-*

tectural Historians, 21 (May, 1962), 47–102. Since 1961: I suppose that the continued rise of Kahn, as America's first great innovator since Wright, has been a major event (for which see my *Louis I. Kahn*, New York, 1962, and my articles in *Architectural Forum*, *121*, August–September, 1964, 162–70, and *Zodiac*, *17*, 1967, where the impressive exhibition of Kahn's work, organized by Arthur Drexler at the Museum of Modern Art in 1966, is published in part), while the development of Venturi's theory and work has been, in my opinion, the most important new phenomenon (Robert Venturi, *Complexity and Contradiction in Architecture*, New York, 1967; as well as, for Venturi and other contemporary events, *Perspecta*, *9–10*, 1965, and *11*, 1967, and the aforesaid *Zodiac*, 1967).

For me the major change since 1961 has been one away from what might charitably be called a religiophilosophical position toward a more socio-functional one, from which, however, I trust that neither philosophy nor religion is wholly absent. History and architecture always go together, as I noted in the text in relation to my work on the Stick Style and American domestic architecture of the late 1940's; my concentration during the later 1950's upon architecture's heroic aspects in Greek temples (*The Earth, the Temple, and the Gods: Greek Sacred Architecture*, New Haven, 1962; revised edition, New York, 1969) paralleled similar concerns in American architects (as shown in my own *Modern Architecture* of 1961), and it reflected, like their work, strong influences from Le Corbusier—to whose great books some reference must here be made: especially to *Vers une Architecture* (Paris, 1923; translated as *Towards a New Architecture*, London, 1927); and *Manière de Penser l'Urbanisme* (Paris, 1946); and *La Ville Radieuse* (Paris, 1935; now translated as *The Radiant City*, New York, 1967; as to all seven volumes of his *Oeuvre Complète*, *1910–1965*, gathered together in *Le Corbusier, 1910–1965*, edited by W. Boesiger and H. Girseberger (New York, 1967). Yet these heroic pretensions now seem, alas, to be in a bureaucratized and highly dangerous phase in all walks of our life. One seeks a newly empirical, less doctrinaire approach to the world, and is thereby led toward a gentler and more embracing urbanism (as to the pueblos) and to a perception of the way in which preconceived social and architectural images have deformed it at present. Here note should be taken once more and the value acknowledged of Jane Jacobs, *The Death and Life of Great American Cities* (New York, 1961). My own very preliminary views can be found in "The Death of the Street," *Perspecta*, 8 (1963), 91–102, and "America's Architectural Nightmare," *Holiday* (March,

1966), reprinted in *Zodiac*, *17* (1967), and in my introduction to Venturi's book listed above, also reprinted in the same issue of *Zodiac*. These fundamentally aesthetic reactions led me more or less unwillingly to sociological conclusions regarding planning and redevelopment, and their connection with national policies as a whole, outlined in the abstract of a talk, "The Threat and the Promise of Urban Redevelopment in New Haven," given in New Haven in October, 1966, and also published in *Zodiac* (1967) and, rather more developed, in this book. In all this I was immeasurably moved by Herbert J. Gans, *The Urban Villagers* (New York, 1962). For varying points of view: James Q. Wilson, editor, *Urban Renewal: The Record and the Controversy* (Cambridge, Mass., 1966).

1988

Since 1969 the rate of research in American architecture has enormously accelerated. Reference should be made to the *Papers of the American Association of Architectural Bibliographers* (Charlottesville: University of Virginia Press); to the *Bibliographic Guide to Art and Architecture* (Boston: G. K. Hall, 1981); and to Charles B. Wood's essay on architecture, which is volume I of Bernard Karpel's *Arts in America: A Bibliography*, 4 volumes (Washington, D.C.: Smithsonian Institution Press, 1979). Leland M. Roth's *A Concise History of American Architecture* (New York, 1979) is an unexceptionable survey of the field with an excellent working bibliography. Its companion volume, Roth's *America Builds: Source Documents in American Architecture and Planning* (New York, 1983), is a useful anthology of otherwise widely scattered materials. The field of study which has grown most significantly since 1969 is that concerned with vernacular architecture, apparently triggered by Fred Kniffen, "Folk Housing: Key to Diffusion," *Annals of the Association of American Geographers*, 55 (1965), 549–77, encouraged by Henry Glassie, *Pattern in the Material Folk Culture of the Eastern United States* (Philadelphia, 1969), and best described by Dell Upton, "Ordinary Buildings: A Bibliographical Essay on American Vernacular Architecture," *American Studies International*, 19 (1981), 57–75. The writings of J. B. Jackson, especially his early articles from his magazine *Landscape*, collected in *Selected Writings of J. B. Jackson*, edited by Ervin R. Zube (Amherst,

1970), and his *The Necessity for Ruins and Other Essays* (Amherst, 1980), have also exerted a considerable influence on other scholars.

Guidebooks of all kinds have also enjoyed a welcome boom in recent years, as it was hoped they would do in this Note. Among them the most general is G. E. Kidder Smith, *The Architecture of the United States: An Illustrated Guide to Notable Buildings Open to the Public* (New York, 1981). Those put together by David Gebhard and his collaborators in California are excellent regional examples: David Gebhard and Harriette Von Breton, *Architecture in California, 1869–1968* (Santa Barbara, 1968); and David Gebhard, Roger Montgomery, Robert Winter, Sally and John Woodbridge, *A Guide to Architecture in San Francisco and Northern California* (Santa Barbara and Salt Lake City, 1973). The ongoing publications of the admirable and active Historic American Buildings Survey, arranged by state, city, building type, and special subjects, should also be consulted, noting especially Alicia Stamm, *Historic America: Buildings, Structures, and Sites Recorded by HABS and HAER* (Washington, D.C., 1983–85), and also in that connection, Adolf K. Placzek, editor, *Macmillan Encyclopedia of Architects* (New York, 1982).

More specialized studies which might be mentioned are, taken in chronological order, my *Pueblo: Mountain, Village, Dance* (New York, 1975), which attempts to discuss the relation of Pueblo architecture to landscape and ritual, and William Pierson, *American Buildings and Their Architects: The Colonial and Neo-Classical Styles* (Garden City, N.Y., 1976), which, as the title indicates, discusses the period in familiar stylistic terms. A more archaeological approach is found in Abbott Lowell Cummings, *The Framed Houses of Massachusetts Bay, 1625–1725*, (Cambridge, Mass., 1979), and, more startling in its results, Gary Carson et al., "Impermanent Architecture in the Southern American Colonies," *Winterthur Portfolio, 16* (1981), 135–96, wherein that most permanent of archaeological records, the empty hole, is used to reconstruct the houses of post-hole construction in wood which once constituted the great bulk of Colonial building in the South—constructions which, unlike the wooden houses on stone foundations of the North, have since disappeared without other trace.

For furniture, so central to the Colonial experience: Charles F. Montgomery and Patricia Kane, *American Art, 1750–1800: Towards Independence* (New Haven, 1976), and, among many, Oscar P. Fitzgerald, *Three Centuries of American Furniture* (Englewood Cliffs, N.J., 1982), and, especially for its bibliography, Jonathan L. Fairbanks and Elizabeth Bates, *American Furniture, 1620 to the Present* (New York, 1981), and for a consideration of furniture in relation to the other arts, the two television films I wrote and narrated for WNET and the Metropolitan Museum of Art, produced by Lorna Pegram, now in publication as *Household Gods and Sacred Places: American Art and the Metropolitan Museum* (New York Graphic Society, 1988).

For the nineteenth century there is Edgar Kaufmann Jr., editor, *The Rise of an American Architecture* (New York, 1970), to which Albert Fein contributed a much-needed study of America's greatest landscape architect, Frederick Law Olmsted, and I an article on houses. Nineteenth-century domestic architecture has recently been the subject of a good deal of sociological interest, not unconnected with vernacular questions and the new women's history, as embodied in David Handlin, *The American Home, 1815–1915* (Boston, 1979); Gwendolyn Wright, *Moralism and the Model Home: Domestic Architecture and Cultural Conflict in Chicago, 1873–1913* (Chicago, 1980); and Dolores Hayden, *The Grand Domestic Revolution: A History of Feminist Designs for American Homes, Neighborhoods, and Cities* (Cambridge, 1981). To these should be added Robert A. M. Stern, with John Montague Massengale, *The Anglo-American Suburb* (London, 1981), though its focus is more on architectural form.

There have been many more traditional studies, such as H. Allen Brooks, *The Prairie School* (New York, 1972); William H. Jordy, *American Buildings and Their Architects*, vol. 3: *Progressive and Academic Ideals at the Turn of the Twentieth Century* (Garden City, N.Y., 1972), and, vol. 4: *The Impact of European Modernism in the Mid-Twentieth Century* (Garden City, N.Y., 1972), and numerous monographs on or special studies of individual architects, some of them dealing with Beaux-Arts and traditional architects whom modernist historians had previously ignored. One thinks, more or less chronologically, of Donald Hoffman, *The Architecture of John Wellborn Root* (Baltimore, 1973); James O'Gorman, *The Architecture of Frank Furness* (Philadelphia, 1973), and his *H. H. Richardson and His Office: Selected Drawings* (Cambridge, 1974); Theo B. White, *Paul Philippe Cret, Architect and Teacher* (Philadelphia, 1973); Janann Strand, *A Greene and Greene Guide* (Pasadena, 1974); William R. and Karen Current, *Greene and Greene, Architects in the Residential Style* (Fort Worth, 1974); Thomas S. Hines, *Burnham of Chicago: Architect and Planner* (New York, 1974); and his *Richard Neutra and the Search for a Modern Architecture* (New York, 1982); Robert A. M. Stern, *George*

Howe: *Toward a Modern American Architecture* (New Haven, 1975); Douglas S. Tucci, *Ralph Adams Cram, American Medievalist* (Boston, 1975); Sarah Bradford Landau, *Edward T. and William A. Potter, American Victorian Architects* (New York, 1979); and her *P. B. Wright: Architect, Contractor and Critic, 1838–1925* (Chicago, 1981); Paul R. Baker, *Richard Morris Hunt* (Cambridge, Mass., 1980); Richard Oliver, *Bertram Grosvenor Goodhue* (New York and Cambridge, 1983); Leland M. Roth, *McKim, Mead and White, Architects* (New York, 1983, though written as a dissertation much earlier); William Morgan, *The Almighty Wall: The Architecture of Henry Vaughan* (New York and Cambridge, 1983).

The rise of interest in decorative design, furniture, and ornament and their role in architecture has been signaled by David Hanks, *The Decorative Design of Frank Lloyd Wright* (New York, 1979); Catherine Lynn, *Wallpaper in America from the Seventeenth Century to World War I* (New York, 1980); Damie Stillman, *Architecture and Ornament in Late Nineteenth-Century America* (Newark, Del., 1981); and Robert Judson Clark, David De Long et al., *Design in America: The Cranbrook Vision, 1925–50* (New York, 1984). A renewed appreciation for the work of the great English architect of the early twentieth century, Sir Edwin Lutyens, as championed anew by Venturi and Greenberg and by Robert Grant Irving, *Indian Summer: Lutyens, Baker and Imperial Delhi* (New Haven and London, 1981), has also had considerable effect on American revisionist criticism. More general studies opening up the Beaux-Arts tradition to sympathetic consideration were initiated with the exhibition of drawings at the Museum of Modern Art in 1975, resulting in Arthur Drexler, *The Architecture of the Ecole des Beaux-Arts*, with essays by Richard Chaffee, Arthur Drexler, David Van Zanten, and Neil Levine (New York, 1977), followed by Richard N. Murray, Dianne H. Pilgrim, and Richard Guy Wilson, *The American Renaissance, 1876–1917* (New York, 1979); and, most important in terms of method, by Robert A. M. Stern's contextual study (with Gregory Gilmartin and John Montague Massengale) of the city as a whole, *New York 1900: Metropolitan Architecture and Urbanism, 1890–1915* (New York, 1983).

For reasons which are obvious enough in the text, Stern's books seem to me to demonstrate one important way—perhaps the most important—in which architectural history ought to be written right now: synchronically and in terms of the whole urban fabric and its types. The American college campus has also received welcome attention as a special American environment and a type itself, as by Paul Venable Turner, *Campus: An American Planning Tradition* (New York and Cambridge, 1984); and Helen Lefkowitz Horowitz, *Alma Mater: Design and Experience in the Women's Colleges from their Nineteenth-Century Beginnings to the 1930s* (New York, 1984). Several studies of New York skyscrapers, following the sympathetic treatment of them in this text, have also appeared; among them Cervin Robinson and Rosemarie Bletter, *Skyscraper Style: Art Deco New York* (New York, 1975); the incomparably perceptive and zany Rem Koolhaas, *Delirious New York, A Retroactive Manifesto for Manhattan* (New York, 1978); and Paul Goldberger, *The Skyscraper* (New York, 1981). It should also be said that the standard of criticism which Paul Goldberger has sustained in the *New York Times*, if sometimes rather Olympian in tone, has clearly served the cause of architecture and urbanism exceedingly well in recent years and seems to be growing in courage all the time. Critical considerations prompted any number of articles during the seventies to take on semiotic slants of greater or lesser degrees of relevance and comprehensibility; my own interest turned toward the early writings of Freud and their analysis of the dream work, as in "Frank Lloyd Wright and the Stuff of Dreams," *Perspecta, 16* (Cambridge, Mass., 1980), 3–31; followed by my introductions to the new facsimile edition of Wasmuth's *Ausgeführte Bauten und Entwürfe von Frank Lloyd Wright* (Berlin, 1910), (Tübingen, 1986), and to the symposium on the Robie House published by the University of Chicago Press in 1988, and my keynote address to the symposium on Falling Water held at Columbia University in 1986 and in process of publication.

Robert Venturi's *Complexity and Contradiction in Architecture*, of 1966, as indicated in the text, turned out in fact to constitute a watershed in architectural theory and criticism and in the practise of architecture itself. It was followed by important studies in architectural symbolism which also had vernacular and pop art connections: Robert Venturi, Denise Scott Brown, and Steven Izenour, *Learning from Las Vegas* (New York, 1972). The Venturis' perhaps even more useful study of symbolism in suburban housing, "Learning from Levittown," has never had the kind of publication it deserves but has exerted an enormous influence nevertheless. Historians such as myself have since written about the movement initiated by Venturi, as in my *The Shingle Style Today, or the Historian's Revenge* (New York, 1974); and in Charles Jencks' influential books, almost entirely semiotic in method, which attempted to apply the term *Post-Modern* to the movement as a whole, as in his *The*

Language of Post-Modern Architecture (New York, 1977). Various architects and critics have produced a number of studies of the issues involved: for example, Robert A. M. Stern, whose *New Directions in American Architecture* (revised edition, New York, 1977) was followed by his "The Doubles of Post-Modernism," *The Harvard Architectural Review, 1* (1980), 75–87. Stern also had what amounted to the last word in the controversy, producing a few of the usual low blows, which took place between the so-called Whites and Grays in the early seventies and was occasioned by Peter Eisenman et al., *Five Architects* (New York, 1972), and more or less came to a close in Peter Eisenman and Robert A. M. Stern, editors, "White and Gray," *Architecture and Urbanism, 52* (1975), 3–180.

The theory and practise of several contemporary European architects, such as Aldo Rossi, *A Scientific Autobiography* (Cambridge, Mass., 1981), for which I wrote a postscript; and his *The Architecture of the City* (Cambridge, Mass., 1982); and for Rossi's work, the extra edition of *Architecture and Urbanism*, November, 1982, and Aldo Rossi, *Buildings and Projects 1959–1983*, edited by Peter Arnell and Ted Bickford (New York, 1983), for which Rafael Moneo and I wrote essays; and Leon Krier, *Drawings, 1967–1980* (Brussels, 1980), have also had a considerable effect upon American thought, surely upon my own. American "Post-Modernism" is treated in its international context in Paolo Portoghesi, *After Modern Architecture* (English translation, New York, 1981), for which I wrote a foreword.

The definitive biographical and critical study which Louis I. Kahn deserves has not yet been written. There is a book with fine photographs: Romaldo Giurgola and Jaimini Mehta, *Louis I. Kahn* (Boulder, Colorado, 1975). Articles such as Christian Norbert-Schulz, "Kahn, Heidegger and the Language of Architecture," *Oppositions, 18* (Fall 1979), 29–47, are describing tangential, not consequential, phenomena, while Kieffer's interesting exploration into the relation of Kahn's theory and design to Jewish mysticism still awaits publication. The dis-

covery of Kahn's early watercolors and many previously unknown pastels was a happy event: Vincent Scully, *The Travel Sketches of Louis I. Kahn*: introduction to an exhibition at the Pennsylvania Academy of Fine Arts, Philadelphia, 1978. See also *Notebooks and Drawings of Louis I. Kahn*, edited and designed by Richard Saul Wurman and Eugene Feldman (New York, 1962, 2d edition, Cambridge, Mass., 1973). Venturi, Rauch, and Scott Brown's work has found publication in their own writings, as noted above, and in many articles, such as mine in *Architectural Digest*, March, 1985, and there is now a useful traveling exhibition, *Venturi, Rauch, and Scott Brown: A Generation of Architecture*, with an introduction by Rosemarie Bletter, sponsored by the University of Illinois at Urbana-Champaign. The papers from a symposium on Venturi held in Albuquerque in 1985, edited by Christopher Last, are now in press. Philip Johnson's work is continually published, but his own writings remain more interesting than those written about him, as in *Philip Johnson, Writings*, with a commentary by Robert A. M. Stern, an introduction by Peter Eisenman, and a foreword by myself (New York, 1979). For Richard Meier: the monograph compiled by himself with an introduction by Joseph Rykwert (New York, 1984). Michael Graves has had a number of monographical studies, as, David Dunster, editor, *Michael Graves* (London, 1979); and *Michael Graves, Buildings and Projects 1966–1981*, edited by Karen Vogel Wheeler, Peter Arnell, and Ted Bickford (New York, 1981), for which I wrote an essay; and also my postscript to *A Tower for Louisville: The Humana Competition*, edited by Peter Arnell and Ted Bickford (New York, 1982). Robert A. M. Stern has been similarly published, as in Peter Arnell and Ted Bickford, editors, *Robert A. M. Stern, Buildings and Projects 1965–1980: Towards a Modern Architecture After Modernism* (New York, 1981), and David Dunster, editor, *Robert Stern* (London, 1981), for which I wrote the introduction. Beyond all this, attention is directed in general to the architectural magazines, where a spate of publication such as the world has never seen flows on.

Picture Credits

1. Peabody Museum of Natural History. Yale University, New Haven, Conn. 2. Courtesy Chrysler Historical Collection. Chrysler Corporation, Detroit. 3. Smithsonian Institution, Washington, D.C. In W. T. Hagan, *American Indians*, Chicago, 1961. 4. Courtesy R. Buckminster Fuller, Carbondale, Ill. 5. Courtesy Paul Rudolph, New York. 6. Collection Vincent Scully, New Haven, Conn. 7. Photo: William Alex, New York. 8. Collection Vincent Scully, New Haven, Conn. 9. Smithsonian Institution, Washington, D.C. In W. T. Hagan, *American Indians*, Chicago, 1961. 10. Photo: Denise Scott Brown, Philadelphia. 11. The Ohio State Archaeological and Historical Society, Columbus, Ohio. In E. O. Randall, *The Serpent Mound*, Columbus, 1905. 12. Smithsonian Institution, Washington, D.C. In W. T. Hagan, *American Indians*, Chicago, 1961. 13. Photo: Vincent Scully, New Haven, Conn. 14. Photograph Collection, Yale University Art Library, New Haven, Conn. 15. Smithsonian Institution, Washington, D.C. In H. H. Wormington, *Prehistoric Indians of the Southwest*, Denver, 1947. 16. Redrawn from Roberts, 1929. In G. R. Willey, *An Introduction to American Archaeology*, Englewood Cliffs, N.J., 1966. 17. Collection Vincent Scully, New Haven, Conn. 18. After Jackson. In A. V. Kidder, *An Introduction to the Study of Southwestern Archaeology*, New Haven, 1924. 19. After Judd. National Geographic Society. In A. V. Kidder, *An Introduction to the Study of Southwestern Archaeology*, New Haven, 1924. 20. National Park Service. In H. H. Wormington, *Prehistoric Indians of the Southwest*, Denver, 1947. 21. Photo: William R. Current, Carmel, Calif. 22. Collection Vincent Scully, New Haven, Conn. 23. National Park Service. Collection Vincent Scully, New Haven, Conn. 24. Photo: Vincent Scully, New Haven, Conn. 25, 26, 27. Courtesy Mesa Verde Museum Association, Inc., Mesa Verde National Park, Colo. 28. Collection Vincent Scully, New Haven, Conn. 29, 30. Photos: Wayne Andrews, Grosse Pointe, Mich. 31. In G. A. Kubler, *The Religious Architecture of New Mexico*, Colorado Springs, Colo., 1940. 32. Photograph Collection, Yale University Art Library, New Haven, Conn. 33. Museum of New Mexico, Santa Fe, N.M. 34. Photo: Vincent Scully, New Haven, Conn. 35. The I. N. Phelps Stokes Collection of American Historical Prints. New York Public Library, New York. 36, 37. In D. Lyman, *Atlas of Old New Haven*, New Haven, Conn., 1929. 38, 39. Photograph Collection, Yale University Art Library, New Haven, Conn. 40. Historic Urban Plans, Ithaca, N.Y. 41. Photograph Collection, Yale University Art Library, New Haven, Conn. 42, 43, 44. In W. Hegemann and E. Peets, *Amerikanische Architektur und Stadtbaukunst*, Berlin, 1927. 45. Tyler Papers, Earl Gregg Swem Library, The College of William and Mary in Virginia. 46. Library of Congress, Washington, D.C. 47. The New-York Historical Society, New York. 48. Photograph Collection, Yale University Art Library, New Haven, Conn. 49. Photo: Wayne Andrews, Grosse Pointe, Mich. 50. Philip White, after Millar. In H. Morrison, *Early American Architecture*, New York, 1952. 51. The Walpole Society, Boston. In H. Morrison, *Early American Architecture*, New York, 1952. 52, 53. Photos: Samuel Chamberlain, Marblehead, Mass. 54. Courtesy Harvard Law School, Cambridge, Mass. (Oil 56 3/16 in. x 77 3/4 in.) 55. Photograph Collection, Yale University Art Library, New Haven, Conn. After H. Morrison, *Early American Architecture*, New York, 1952. 56. The Metropolitan Museum of Art, New York. 57. Harold Fowler, Whittlesey House/McGraw-Hill, New York. 58. Courtesy Wadsworth Atheneum, Hartford, Conn. 59. Photo: Frank Cousins. Photograph Collection, Yale University Art Library, New Haven, Conn. Reproduced with the permission of Warner House Association, Portsmouth, N.H. 60. Photo: Hedrich-Blessing, Chicago. 61. Colonial Williamsburg, Williamsburg, Va. 62. Photo: Sandak, New York. Reproduced with the permission of the owner, Bruce Crane Fisher, Charles County, Va. 63, 64. Photos: Wayne Andrews, Grosse Pointe, Mich. 65. Photo: A. F. Kersting, London. 66. The Preservation Society of Newport County, Newport, R.I. 67. In W. Hegemann and E. Peets, *Amerikanische Architektur und Stadtbaukunst*, Berlin, 1927. 68. Photo: Wayne Andrews, Grosse Pointe, Mich. 69. Photo: Sandak, New York. Reproduced courtesy of the congregation of First Parish Unitarian Church, Hingham, Mass. 70. Photo: Sandak, New York. 71. The I. N. Phelps Stokes Collection of American Historical Prints. New York Public Library, New York. 72, 73. The Preservation Society of Newport County, Newport, R.I. 74. Photo: Wayne Andrews, Grosse Pointe, Mich. 75. National Buildings Record, London. 76. Photograph Collection, Yale University Art Library, New Haven, Conn. 77. Courtesy Yale University Art Library, New Haven, Conn. 78. Photograph Collection, Yale University Art Library, New Haven, Conn. 79. Photo: Sandak, New York. 80. Art Work of Boston. In T. Hamlin, *Greek Revival Architecture in America*, New York, 1944. 81, 82. From Robert Morris' *Select Architecture*. In T. T. Waterman, *Mansions of Virginia*, Chapel Hill, N.C., 1945. 83. Coolidge Collection, Massachusetts Historical Society. In F. Kimball, *Thomas Jefferson, Architect*, Boston, 1916. 84. In F. Burger, *Die Villen des Andrea Palladio*, Leipzig, 1910. 85, 86, 87, 88, 89. In I. T. Frary, *Thomas Jefferson, Architect and Builder*, Va., 1931. 90. Collection Vincent Scully, New Haven, Conn. 91. Courtesy the University of Virginia Information Service, Charlottesville, Va. 92. Photo: Ralph Thompson. Courtesy the University of Virginia Information Service, Charlottesville, Va. 93. Courtesy the University of Virginia Information Service, Charlottesville, Va. 94, 95, 96. In I. T. Frary, *Thomas Jefferson, Architect and Builder*, Richmond, Va., 1931. 97.

Photo: Sandak, New York. *98.* Photograph Collection, Yale University Art Library, New Haven, Conn. *99.* In I. T. Frary, *Thomas Jefferson, Architect and Builder*, Richmond, Va., 1931. *100, 101.* Photos: Sandak, New York. *102.* In *Magazine of Art*, February, 1948. *103.* In N. P. Willis, *American Scenes*, London, 1840. *104.* Photo: Sandak, New York. *105.* In T. Hamlin, *Greek Revival Architecture in America*, New York, 1944. *106.* Photo: George Heard Hamilton. Photograph Collection, Yale University Art Library, New Haven, Conn. *107.* Photo: R. Kraeling. Photograph Collection, Yale University Art Library, New Haven, Conn. *108.* Photo: Milton Pearce, Tiverton, R.I. *109, 110.* Photos: Sandak, New York. *111, 112.* Photograph Collection, Yale University Art Library, New Haven, Conn. *113.* The New-York Historical Society, New York. *114.* From Ross's illustrated letter in Loudon's *The Architecture Magazine*, Vol. II, December, 1835. In T. Hamlin, *Greek Revival Architecture in America*, New York, 1944. *115.* The Bostonian Society, Old State House, Boston. In J. M. Howells, *Lost Examples of Colonial Architecture*, New York, 1931. *116.* Picture Collection, New York Public Library, New York. *117.* Photo: Wiles-Hood. In T. Hamlin, *Greek Revival Architecture in America*, New York, 1944. *118.* Photo: Sandak, New York. Reproduced with the permission of the owner, Mrs. Andrew Stewart, Vacherie, La. *119.* Photo: Wayne Andrews, Grosse Pointe, Mich. *120.* Photo: Sandak, New York. Reproduced with the permission of Belmont College, Nashville, Tenn. *121, 122.* Library of Congress, Washington, D.C. *123.* Picture Collection, New York Public Library, New York. *124.* In N. P. Willis, *American Scenes*, London, 1840. *125, 126.* Library of Congress, Washington, D.C. *127, 128, 129.* Fine Arts Commission, Washington, D.C. *130.* *The Architectural Record*, June, 1923. *131.* Litton Industries, Aero Service Division, New York. *132.* Photo: Joseph Klima, Jr. Courtesy Burton Historical Collection, Detroit Public Library, Detroit. *133.* Library of Congress Map Division, Washington, D.C. *134.* The New-York Historical Society, New York. *135.* The I. N. Phelps Stokes Collection of American Historical Prints. New York Public Library, New York. *136.* Photo: Rudolph Burckhardt. Leo Castelli Gallery, New York. (Lithograph. 33¾ in. x 26¼ in.) *137.* Library of Congress Map Division, Washington, D.C. *138.* Photograph Collection, Yale University Art Library, New Haven, Conn. *139.* Photo: Vincent Scully, New Haven, Conn. *140.* Courtesy Standard Oil Company (New Jersey), New York. *141.* Historic American Building Survey, Library of Congress, Washington, D.C. *142.* Photo: Louis Eiford, Baltimore, Md. *143.* Photo: Alexis L. Pierson, Baltimore, Md. *144.* In W. Hegemann and E. Peets, *Amerikanische Architektur und Stadtbaukunst*, Berlin, 1927. *145.* Photo: Vincent Scully, New Haven, Conn. *146.* Collection Vincent Scully, New Haven, Conn. *147.* Photo: Sandak, New York. *148.* Photo: Lou Marinoff. New York City Housing Authority, New York. *149.* The I. N. Phelps Stokes Collection of American Historical Prints. New York Public Library, New York. *150.* The New-York Historical Society, New York. *151, 152.* New York Public Library, New York. *153.* The Preservation Society of Newport County, Newport, R.I. *154.* From Andrew Jackson Downing, *The Architecture of Country Houses*, New York, 1850. *155, 156.* Jinny and Wendy Neefus, Hudson, N.Y. *157.* In W. E. Bell, *Carpentry Made Easy*, Philadelphia, 1858. *158.* The Preservation Society of Newport County, Newport, R.I. *159.* Photo: Wayne Andrews, Grosse Pointe, Mich. *160.* The Preservation Society of Newport County, Newport, R.I. *161.* In A. Downing and V. Scully, *The Architectural Heritage of Newport Rhode Island 1640–1915*, Cambridge, Mass., 1952. *162, 163.* Photograph Collection, Yale University Art Library, New Haven, Conn. *164.* Photo: George M. Cushing. Courtesy of the Boston Athenaeum, Boston. *165.* Photo: Sandak, New York. *166.* Photo: William Alex, New York. *167.* Photo: Sandak, New York. *168, 169.* Photograph Collection, Yale University Art Library, New Haven, Conn. *170.* *The Architec-tural Review,* London. *171.* Photograph Collection, Yale University Art Library, New Haven, Conn. *172.* Photo: Sandak, New York. *173, 174, 175, 176, 177.* Photograph Collection, Yale University Art Library, New Haven, Conn. *178, 179.* Yale University Art and Architecture Library, New Haven, Conn. *180.* In Mrs. S. Van Rensselaer, *Henry Hobson Richardson and His Works*, Boston, 1888. *181.* Photo: Wayne Andrews, Grosse Pointe, Mich. *182.* In Mrs. S. Van Rensselaer, *Henry Hobson Richardson and His Works*, Boston, 1888. *183.* Photograph Collection, Yale University Art Library, New Haven, Conn. *184.* Photo: Chicago Architectural Photographing Company, Chicago. *185.* In H-R. Hitchcock, *The Architecture of H. H. Richardson and His Times*, New York, 1936. *186.* Photo: Victor Turl, Bristol, England. Smith College Department of Art, Northampton, Mass. *187.* Photo: Berenice Abbott, New York. *188, 189.* The Museum of Modern Art, New York. *190.* Photograph Collection, Yale University Art Library, New Haven, Conn. *191.* In A. T. Andreas, *History of Chicago*, Chicago, 1884–86. *192.* In F. A. Randall, *History of the Development of Building Construction in Chicago*, Urbana, Ill., 1949. *193.* Photograph Collection, Yale University Art Library, New Haven, Conn. *194.* In *Industrial Chicago*, Chicago, 1891. *195.* Photo: Chicago Architectural Photographing Company, Chicago. *196.* Photo: Hedrich-Blessing, Chicago. *197.* Photo: Chicago Architectural Photographing Company, Chicago. *198.* Photo: Richard Wurts, Litchfield, Conn. *199, 200.* Photos: Chicago Architectural Photographing Company, Chicago. *201.* The Museum of Modern Art, New York. *202.* The Preservation Society of Newport County, Newport, R.I. *203.* From *New York Sketch Book*, #2, 1875. In V. Scully, *The Shingle Style*, New Haven, Conn., 1955. *204.* From *Building News*, May 8, 1874. In V. Scully, *The Shingle Style*, New Haven, Conn., 1955. *205.* Photograph Collection, Yale University Art Library, New Haven, Conn. *206.* In H-R. Hitchcock, *The Architecture of H. H. Richardson and His Times*, New York, 1936. *207.* In V. Scully, *The Shingle Style*, New Haven, Conn., 1955. *208, 209.* Stanhope Collection, Newport, R.I. In A. Downing and V. Scully, *The Architectural Heritage of Newport, Rhode Island 1640–1915*, Cambridge, Mass., 1952. *210.* Photo: Wayne Andrews, Grosse Pointe, Mich. *211.* In G. W. Sheldon, *Artistic Country Seats*, Vol. I, New York, 1886–87. *212.* Plan in *American Architect and Building News*, #17, 1885. Sketches by Eldon Deane, in *American Architect and Building News*, #17, 1885. *213.* From the *American Architect*, #10, 1881. In V. Scully, *The Shingle Style*, New Haven, Conn., 1955. *214, 215.* In G. W. Sheldon, *Artistic Country Seats*, Vol. I, New York, 1886–87. *216.* Photo: Wayne Andrews, Grosse Pointe, Mich. *217, 218, 219, 220.* In G. W. Sheldon, *Artistic Country Seats*, Vol. II, New York, 1886–87. *221.* Collection Professor Henry-Russell Hitchcock, Northampton, Mass. *222.* Reproduced with the permission of Verlag Ernst Wasmuth, Tübingen, Germany. In H-R. Hitchcock, *In the Nature of Materials, 1887–1941: The Buildings of Frank Lloyd Wright*, New York, 1942. *223.* Photo: Chicago Architectural Photographing Company, Chicago. *224.* Reproduced with the permission of Verlag Ernst Wasmuth, Tübingen, Germany. In C. R. Ashbee, *Frank Lloyd Wright: Ausgeführte Bauten*, Berlin, 1911. *225.* From *Ladies' Home Journal*, February, 1901. In H-R. Hitchcock, *In the Nature of Materials, 1887–1941: The Buildings of Frank Lloyd Wright*, New York, 1942. *226.* Collection Professor Henry-Russell Hitchcock, Northampton, Mass. *227.* In H-R. Hitchcock, *In the Nature of Materials, 1887–1941: The Buildings of Frank Lloyd Wright*, New York, 1942. *228.* Reproduced with the permission of Verlag Ernst Wasmuth, Tübingen, Germany. *229.* Photograph Collection, Yale University Art Library, New Haven, Conn. *230.* Reproduced with the permission of Verlag Ernst Wasmuth, Tübingen, Germany. In C. R. Ashbee, *Ausgeführte Bauten und Entwurfe von Frank Lloyd Wright*, Berlin, 1910. *231.* The Museum of Modern Art, New York. *232.* In Le Corbusier, *Vers Une Architecture*, Paris, 1923. *233, 234, 235.* Reproduced with the permission of Verlag Ernst Wasmuth, Tübingen, Germany. In C. R. Ashbee, *Frank Lloyd Wright: Ausgeführte Bauten*, Berlin, 1911. *236.* Reproduced with the permission of Verlag Ernst Wasmuth, Tübingen, Germany. In C. R. Ashbee, *Ausgeführte Bauten und Entwurfe von Frank Lloyd Wright*, Berlin, 1910. *237.* The Museum of Modern Art, New York. *238, 239.* Photos: Wayne Andrews, Grosse Pointe, Mich. *240.* Reproduced with the permission of Verlag Ernst Wasmuth, Tübingen, Germany. In C. R. Ashbee, *Ausgeführte Bauten und Entwurfe von Frank Lloyd Wright*, Berlin, 1910. *241.* Collection Vincent Scully, New Haven, Conn. *242.* Photo: Infinity Inc., Minneapolis, Minn. *243.* Photo: Richard Nickel, Park Ridge, Ill. *244.* Courtesy George Braziller, Inc., New York. *245.* Photo from *Western Architect*, 1911. In H-R. Hitchcock, *In the Nature of Materials, 1887–1941: The Buildings of Frank Lloyd Wright*, New York, 1942. *246.* Photo: Vincent Scully, New Haven, Conn. *247.* Photograph Collection, Yale University Art Library, New Haven, Conn. *248.* Photo: Vincent Scully, New Haven, Conn. *249.* Photo: Marvin Rand, Los Angeles. *250.* In Jacobs, *Studies in Western Art: Acts of the Twentieth-International Congress of the History of Art, IV*, Princeton, N.J., 1963. *251.* Photo: Marvin Rand, Los Angeles. *252.* In E. McCoy, *Five California Architects*, New York, 1960. *253.* Photo: Marvin Rand, Los Angeles. *254.* Collection Esther McCoy, Santa Monica, Calif. Print courtesy the University of California Art Gallery, Santa Barbara, Calif. *255.* In E. McCoy, *Five California Architects*, New York, 1960. *256.* Photo: H. Pascal Webb. In R. Newcomb, *Spanish Colonial Architecture in the United States*, New York, 1937. *257.* Photo: Irving Gill. Collection Esther McCoy, Santa Monica, Calif. *258.* Photo: Marvin Rand, Los Angeles. *259.* Reproduced with the permission of Anton Schroll & Company, Vienna. In L. Munz and G. Kunstler, *Adolf Loos: Pioneer of Modern Architecture*, New York, 1966. *260.* Collection Esther McCoy, Santa Monica, Calif. *261.* Photo: Julius Shulman, Los Angeles. *262.* Photo: Roy Flamm, San Francisco. *263.* Albright-Knox Art Gallery, Buffalo, N.Y. (Oil on wood. 17¾ in. x 16 in.) *264.* Photo: Roy Flamm, San Francisco. *265, 266.* Photos: Wayne Andrews, Grosse Pointe, Mich. *268.* Courtesy Philip Johnson, New York. *268.* In H. H. Bancroft, *The Book of the Fair*, Vol. I, Chicago, 1893. *269.* Photo: Sandak, New York. Reproduced with the permission of the Hon. Kevin White, Mayor of Boston. *270.* In H. H. Bancroft, *The Book of the Fair*, Vol. I, Chicago, 1893. *271.* Photograph Collection, Yale University Art Library, New Haven, Conn. *272.* Photo: Sandak, New York. *273, 274.* In D. H. Burnham and E. H. Bennett, *Plan of Chicago*, Chicago, 1909. *275.* Bancroft Collection, University of California Library, Berkeley, Calif. *276, 277.* In D. H. Burnham, *Report on a plan for San Francisco*, San Francisco, 1905. *278.* Courtesy Penn Central Railroad, New York. *279.* In *A Monograph of the Work of McKim, Mead and White, 1879–1915*, New York, 1914–15. *280.* Thomas Airviews. Courtesy Madison Square Garden Center, New York. *281, 282.* Courtesy Penn Central Railroad, New York. *283.* In *Look at America, New York City*, Boston, 1948. *284.* Photograph Collection, Yale University Art Library, New Haven, Conn. *285.* Litton Industries, Aero Service Division, New York. *286.* Courtesy the Empire State Building, New York. *287.* Photo: Elwood P. Johns. Courtesy Chase Manhattan Bank, New York. *288.* From *Scribner's Magazine*, September, 1909. In M. Schuyler, *American Architecture*, New York, 1892. *289.* Photo: Sandak, New York. *290.* From *Scribner's Magazine*, September, 1909. In M. Schuyler, *American Architecture*, New York, 1892. *291.* Courtesy Woolworth Building, New York. *292, 293.* In W. Hegemann and E. Peets, *Amerikanische Architektur und Stadtbaukunst*, Berlin, 1927. *294.* Courtesy Trinity Church Corporation, New York. *295.* In *King's Views of New York*, New York, 1908. *296.* Photograph Collection, Yale University Art Library, New Haven, Conn. *297.* Collection Vincent Scully, New Haven, Conn. *298, 299.* Photos: Ezra Stoller, Mamaroneck, N.Y. Courtesy Paul Rudolph, New York. *300.* Photo: Chicago Architectural Photographing Company, Chicago. *301, 302, 303, 304, 305.* In *The International Competition for a New Administration Building for the Chicago Tribune*, Chicago, 1923. *306, 307.* In H. Ferriss, *The Metropolis of Tomorrow*, New York, 1929. *308.* Courtesy New York Telephone Company, New York. *309, 310.* Photograph Collection, Yale University Art Library, New Haven, Conn. *311.* Photo: Thomas Airviews, Bayside, N.Y. Courtesy Rockefeller Center, Inc., New York. *312, 313.* Photos: Sandak, New York. *314.* Courtesy William Lescaze and Associates, New York. *315.* Photo: Wayne Andrews, Grosse Pointe, Mich. *316.* Photograph Collection, Yale University Art Library, New Haven, Conn. *317.* From G. W. Sheldon, *Artistic Country Seats*, Vol. II. New York, 1886–87. *318.* In H-R. Hitchcock, *In the Nature of Materials, 1887–1941: The Buildings of Frank Lloyd Wright*, New York, 1942. *319.* Photo: Wayne Andrews, Grosse Pointe, Mich. *320.* Reproduced with the permission of Artemis Verlag, Zurich. In Le Corbusier, *Oeuvre Complète, 1910–65*, Zurich, 1967. *321.* University of California Art Galleries, Santa Barbara, Calif. *322.* Photo: Luckhaus Studio, Los Angeles. Courtesy Richard J. Neutra, Los Angeles. *323.* Photo: Hedrich-Blessing, Chicago. *324, 325.* In *Architectural Forum*, January, 1938. *326.* In E. Howard, *Garden Cities of To-Morrow*, London, 1898. *327, 328, 329.* In W. Hegemann and E. Peets, *Amerikanische Architektur und Stadtbaukunst*, Berlin, 1927. *330.* In C. S. Stein, *Toward New Towns for America*, New York, 1957. *331.* Photo: Gottscho-Schleisner, Jamaica, N.Y. *332.* Photo: Charles F. Doherty, New York. Courtesy Clarence S. Stein, New York. *333.* Library of Congress photo by Fairchild Aerial Surveys, New York. In C. S. Stein, *Toward New Towns for America*, New York, 1957. *334.* Courtesy Clarence S. Stein, New York. *335.* Photo: Fairchild Aerial Surveys, New York. In C. S. Stein, *Toward New Towns for America*, New York, 1957. *336.* Courtesy Levitt and Sons, Lake Success, N.Y. *337, 338.* Reproduced with the permission of Artemis Verlag, Zurich. In Le Corbusier, *Oeuvre Complète, 1910–65*, Zurich, 1967. *339.* Courtesy Greater London Council, Inner London Education Authority, London. *340.* Reproduced with the permission of Artemis Verlag, Zurich. In Le Corbusier, *Oeuvre Complète, 1910–65*, Zurich, 1967. *341.* The Museum of Modern Art, New York. *342, 343.* Courtesy New York City Housing Authority. *344.* Courtesy Metropolitan Life Insurance Company, New York. *345.* *The New York Times*, New York. *346.* Reproduced with the permission of Artemis Verlag, Zurich. In Le Corbusier, *Oeuvre Complète, 1910–65*, Zurich, 1967. *347.* Reproduced with the permission of Artemis Verlag, Zurich. In Le Corbusier, *Manière de Penser l'Urbanisme*, Paris, 1946. *348.* Photo: Robert Perron, New Haven, Conn. *349.* Photograph Collection, Yale University Art Library, New Haven, Conn. *350.* Reproduced with the permission of Artemis Verlag, Zurich. In *La Ville Radieuse*, Paris, 1964. *351.* Photograph Collection, Yale University Art Library, New Haven, Conn. *352.* In H-R. Hitchcock, *In the Nature of Materials, 1887–1941: The Buildings of Frank Lloyd Wright*, New York, 1942. *353.* Photo: Hedrich-Blessing, Chicago. *354, 355.* In *Architectural Forum*, January, 1938. *356, 357.* Photos: Ezra Stoller, Mamaroneck, N.Y. *358.* In *Architectural Forum*, January, 1948. *359.* Photo: Pedro E. Guerrero, New York. *360.* Collection Professor Henry-Russell Hitchcock, Northampton, Mass. *361.* Photograph Collection, Yale University Art Library, New Haven, Conn. *362.* Photo: Vincent Scully, New Haven, Conn. *363.* Photograph Collection, Yale University Art Library, New Haven, Conn. *364.* Photo: Reimar A. Frank, Milwaukee, Wis. *365.* Courtesy George Braziller, Inc., New York. *366.* Photo: Robert E. Mates, New York. *367.* In A. Meigs, *An American Country House*, New York, 1925. *368.* Photograph Collection, Yale University Art Library, New Haven, Conn. *369.* Photo: Richard T. Dooner. In *Architectural Forum*, March, 1935. *370.* Photo: Ben Schnall, New York. *371.* The Museum of Modern Art, New York. *372.*

Photo: Robert Damora, Bedford, N.Y. *373.* Yale University Art Gallery, Collection of the Société Anonyme, bequest of Katherine S. Dreier. (Oil on galalith [?]. 16 in. x 20⅜ in.) *374.* Photograph Collection, Yale University Art Library, New Haven, Conn. *375.* Photo: Pedro E. Guerrero, New York. Courtesy Marcel Breuer & Associates, New York. *376.* Photo: Lee Hanley. Courtesy Marcel Breuer & Associates, New York. *377.* Photograph Collection, Yale University Art Library, New Haven, Conn. *378.* In E. B. Mock, *If You Want to Build a House,* New York, 1946. *379.* Photo: Wayne Andrews, Grosse Pointe, Mich. *380.* Photo: Roger Burke. Photograph Collection, Yale University Art Library, New Haven, Conn. *381.* Photo: Robert Damora, Bedford, N.Y. *382.* The Museum of Modern Art, New York. *383, 384.* Photos: Hedrich-Blessing, Chicago. *385.* In *Werk,* November, 1964. *386* Photo: Robert A. M. Stern. Photograph Collection, Yale University Art Library, New Haven, Conn. *387.* Photo: William Alex, New York. *388.* Photo: Hedrich-Blessing, Chicago. *389.* Photo: Alexandre Georges, Pomona, N.Y. *390.* Photo: Ezra Stoller, Mamaroneck, N.Y. *391.* Courtesy the United Nations, New York. *392.* Photo: Bill Engdahl, Hedrich-Blessing, Chicago. *393.* Photo: Ezra Stoller, Mamaroneck, N.Y. Courtesy Public Building Commission of Chicago. © 1967, All Rights Reserved. *394.* Photo: Hedrich-Blessing, Chicago. *395.* Photograph Collection, Yale University Art Library, New Haven, Conn. *396, 397.* Photos: Hedrich-Blessing, Chicago. *398.* Photo: Bill Hedrich, Hedrich-Blessing, Chicago. *399.* Photo: Stewarts, Colorado Springs, Colo. Courtesy Skidmore, Owings and Merrill, Chicago. *400.* Photo: Hedrich-Blessing, Chicago. *401.* Photo: Balthazar Korab, Birmingham, Mich. *402.* Photo: Rondal Partridge, Berkeley, Calif. Courtesy Edward Durell Stone, New York. *403.* Courtesy Edward Durell Stone, New York. *404, 405.* In *Arkhitektura SSR,* January, 1960. *406.* Photograph Collection, Yale University Art Library, New Haven, Conn. *407.* Collection Vincent Scully, New Haven, Conn. *408.* Photo: Ezra Stoller, Mamaroneck, N.Y. *409.* Photo: Joseph W. Molitor, Ossining, N.Y. *410, 411.* Photos: Ezra Stoller, Mamaroneck, N.Y. *412.* Courtesy Philip Johnson, New York. *413.* Photo: Bruce Cunningham-Werdnigg, Guilford, Conn. *414.* Photo: Hedrich-Blessing, Chicago. *415.* Photo: Ezra Stoller, Mamaroneck, N.Y. Courtesy General Motors Corporation, Detroit. *416.* Photo: Balthazar Korab, Birmingham, Mich. *417, 418.* Photos: Vincent Scully, New Haven, Conn. *419.* Photo: Geoffrey Clements, New York. Collection Carroll Janis. Courtesy Sidney Janis Gallery, New York. (Wash, crayon. 23½ in. x 17½ in.) *420.* Photo: Ezra Stoller, Mamaroneck, N.Y. *421.* Photo: Ezra Stoller, Mamaroneck, N.Y. Courtesy Trans World Airlines, New York. *422.* Photo: Robert A. M. Stern, New York. *423.* Photo: Ezra Stoller, Mamaroneck, N. Y. Courtesy Deere & Company, Moline, Ill. *424.* Photo: Ezra Stoller, Mamaroneck, N.Y. *425.* Courtesy CBS, New York. *426, 427.* Courtesy Kevin Roche, John Dinkeloo, and Associates, Hamden, Conn. *428.* Photo: Ezra Stoller, Mamaroneck, N.Y. *429.* Courtesy Kevin Roche, John Dinkeloo, and Associates, Hamden, Conn. *430.* Photo: Ezra Stoller, Mamaroneck, N.Y. Courtesy Ford Foundation, New York. *431.* Photo: Yuji Noga, New Haven, Conn. *432.* Collection Professor Henry-Russell Hitchcock, Northampton, Mass. *433.* Courtesy Paul Rudolph, New York. *434.* Photo: Yuji Noga, New Haven, Conn. *435.* Photo: Yuji Noga, New Haven, Conn. Photograph Collection, Yale University Art Library, New Haven, Conn. *436.* Photo: Bruce Cunningham-Werdnigg, Guilford, Conn. *437.* Photo: Joseph W. Molitor, Ossining, N.Y. *438.* Photo: William J. Toomey. Courtesy *The Architects' Journal,* London. *439.* Photo: Ezra Stoller, Mamaroneck, N.Y. *440.* Photograph Collection, Yale University Art Library, New Haven, Conn. *441.* Courtesy Mitchell/Giurgola Associates, Philadelphia. *442.* Courtesy Yale University News Bureau, New Haven, Conn. *443, 444.* Courtesy Massachusetts Institute of Technology, Cambridge, Mass. *445.* Photo: Bruce Cunningham-Werdnigg, Guilford, Conn. *446.* Photo: David Hirsch, New York. Courtesy Carlin, Pozzi & Associates, New Haven, Conn. *447.* Courtesy John Johansen, New York. *448, 449.* Photos: Ernest Barbee. Courtesy Cambridge Seven Associates, Inc., Cambridge, Mass. *450.* Photo: Lionel Freedman, New York. *451.* Photo: Malcolm Smith, New York. *452.* Courtesy Louis I. Kahn, Philadelphia. *453, 454.* Photos: John Ebstel, New York. In *Progressive Architecture,* April, 1961. *456, 457, 458, 459, 460.* Photos: John Ebstel, New York. *461.* Photo: George Pohl, Philadelphia. *462, 463, 464, 465, 466.* Photos: Neil Thompson. Courtesy Louis I. Kahn, Philadelphia. *467, 468.* Photos: Marvin Rand, Los Angeles. *469.* Photo: George Pohl, Philadelphia. *470.* Courtesy Louis I. Kahn, Philadelphia. *471.* Photo: Marshall D. Meyers, Philadelphia. Courtesy Louis I. Kahn, Philadelphia. *472.* Photo: Gordon Sommers, Beverly Hills, Calif. Courtesy Victor Gruen Associates, New York. *473.* Photo: Jerry Spearman, New York. *474.* Courtesy Moshe Safdie, Montreal. *475.* Photo: Rollin R. La France. Courtesy Mitchell/Giurgola Associates, Philadelphia. *476.* Photo: William Watkins, Philadelphia. Courtesy Mitchell/Giurgola Associates, Philadelphia. *477.* Courtesy Venturi and Rauch, Philadelphia. *478.* Photo: Laurence Lowry, Beverly, Mass. *479.* Photo: Bruce Cunningham-Werdnigg, Guilford, Conn. *480, 481.* Photos: George Pohl, Philadelphia. Courtesy Venturi and Rauch, Philadelphia. *482.* Courtesy Venturi and Rauch, Philadelphia. *483, 484.* Photos: Rollin R. La France, Philadelphia. Courtesy Venturi and Rauch, Philadelphia. *485.* Photo: George Pohl, Philadelphia. Courtesy Venturi and Rauch, Philadelphia. *486.* Photo: Rollin R. La France, Philadelphia. Courtesy Venturi and Rauch, Philadelphia. *487.* Courtesy Venturi and Rauch, Philadelphia. *488, 489.* Photos: Morley Baer, Berkeley, Calif. *490.* Photo: Skomark Associates, Philadelphia. Courtesy Venturi and Rauch, Philadelphia. *491.* Courtesy Venturi and Rauch, Philadelphia. *492.* Photograph Collection, Yale University Art Library, New Haven, Conn. *493.* Reproduced with the permission of Artemis Verlag, Zurich. In W. Boesiger, ed., *Le Corbusier 1910–65,* New York, 1967. *494.* Photo: William Watkins. Courtesy Venturi and Rauch, Philadelphia. *495.* Photo: Robert Talbous, Clarke & Rapuano, Inc. Courtesy Venturi and Rauch, Philadelphia. *496, 497.* Photos: George Pohl, Philadelphia. Courtesy Venturi and Rauch, Philadelphia. *498.* Sketch by Robert Venturi. Courtesy Venturi and Rauch, Philadelphia. *499.* Photo: Robert A. M. Stern, New York. Courtesy Venturi and Rauch, Philadelphia. *500, 501, 502.* Photos: Denise Scott Brown, Philadelphia. *503.* Private Collection, Paris. Courtesy Ileana Sonnabend Gallery, Paris. (24 in. x 36 in.) *504.* In *The New York Times,* New York, October 29, 1967. *505.* Photo: Denise Scott Brown, Philadelphia. *506, 507, 508.* Photos: Howard J. Sochurek, New York. *509.* Photo: Olivor Baker Associates, New York. Collection Dr. and Mrs. Frank Stanton, New York. Courtesy Sidney Janis Gallery, New York. (48 in. x 63 in.) *510.* Courtesy Prudential Life Insurance Company of America, Boston. *511.* Photo: Yuji Noga, New Haven, Conn. *512.* Photo: Vincent Scully, New Haven, Conn. *513.* The Harry T. Peters Collection. Museum of the City of New York. *514, 515.* Photograph Collection, Yale University Art Library, New Haven, Conn. *516.* Photo: Charles R. Schulze, New Haven, Conn. Courtesy Carlin, Pozzi & Associates, New Haven, Conn. *517.* Photo: Bruce Cunningham-Werdnigg, Guilford, Conn. *518.* Photo: Charles R. Schulze, New Haven, Conn. Courtesy Carlin, Pozzi & Associates, New Haven, Conn. *519.* Photograph Collection, Yale University Art Library, New Haven, Conn. *520.* Photo: Stan Wayman, *Life* Magazine © Time Inc., New York. *521.* Courtesy New Haven Redevelopment Agency, New Haven, Conn. *522.* Photograph Collection, Yale University Art Library, New Haven, Conn. *523.* Photograph Collection, Yale University Art Library, New Haven, Conn. *524.* Photo: Howard J. Sochurek, New York. *525.* Photo: Burk Uzzle, © 1968 Magnum Photos, New York. *526, 527.* Courtesy Venturi and Rauch,

Philadelphia. *528.* Photo: Charles Jencks. *529.* Photo: Tom Bernard. Courtesy Venturi and Rauch, Philadelphia. *530.* Photo: Matt Wargo. Courtesy Venturi, Rauch and Scott Brown. *531.* Photo: Matt Wargo. *532.* Photo: Matt Wargo. *533.* Photo: Tom Bernard. Courtesy Venturi, Rauch and Scott Brown. *534.* Photo: Tom Bernard. *535.* Photo: Tom Bernard. *536, 537, 538.* Courtesy Venturi, Rauch and Scott Brown. *539.* Photo: Morley Baer. Courtesy Centerbrook Architects and Planners. *540.* Photo: Norman McGrath. Courtesy Centerbrook Architects and Planners. *541.* Photo: Peter Aaron/Esto. Courtesy Robert A. M. Stern. *542.* Photo: Peter Aaron/Esto. *543.* Photo: Ed Stoecklein. Courtesy Robert A. M. Stern. *544.* Courtesy Andres Duany and Elizabeth PlaterZyberg. *545.* Photo: Mick Hales. Courtesy Orr & Taylor, Architecture and Gardens. *546.* Photo: Mick Hales. Courtesy Orr & Taylor, Architecture and Gardens. *547.* Photo: A. W. El Wakil. Courtesy Leon Krier. *548.* Photo: Ned Matura. Courtesy Aldo Rossi. *549.* Courtesy Ricardo Bofill. *550.* Courtesy Ricardo Bofill. *551.* Photo: Timothy Hursley. Courtesy Robert A. M. Stern. *552.* Courtesy Allan Greenberg. *553.* Courtesy Robert Venturi. *554.* Courtesy Allan Greenberg. *555.* Photo: Richard Cheek. Courtesy Allan Greenberg. *556.* Photo: Henry Bowles. Courtesy Thomas Gordon Smith. *557.* Courtesy Thomas Gordon Smith. Watercolor on Fabriano paper, for *Classical Architecture: Rule and Invention* (1987). *558.* Courtesy Thomas Beeby. *559.* Thomas Beeby. *560.* Photo: Jim Hedrich/Hedrich-Blessing. Courtesy Stanley Tigerman and Margaret McCurry. *561.* Courtesy Frank Gehry. *562.* Courtesy Frank Gehry. *563.* Courtesy Frank Gehry. *564, 565.* Photos: Paschall/Taylor. Courtesy Michael Graves. *566.* Courtesy Henry Moore. *567.* Photo: Claes Oldenburg. Courtesy *ARTnews. 568.* Courtesy Robert Glen. *569.* Photo: Michael Abramson. Courtesy Richard Serra. *570.* Photo: Paschall/Taylor. Courtesy Michael Graves. *571.* Courtesy Marcel Breuer. *572, 573.*

Photo: Paschall/Taylor. Courtesy Michael Graves. *574.* Photo: Dan Cornish/Esto. Courtesy Gwathmey Siegel & Associates Architects. *575.* Courtesy Philip Johnson/John Burgee Architects. *576.* Photo: Wolfgang Hoyt/Esto. Courtesy Johnson/Burgee Architects. *577.* Photo: Richard Payne, AIA. Courtesy Johnson/Burgee Architects. *578.* Photo: Kenneth Champlin Photos. Courtesy Cesar Pelli & Associates. *579.* Courtesy Kohn Pedersen Fox with Perkins and Will. *580.* Courtesy Robert A. M. Stern. *581.* Photo: Blair Kamin. *582.* Richard Payne, AIA. Courtesy Philip Johnson/John Burgee Architects. *583, 584, 585.* Photo: Bob Wharton. Courtesy Louis I. Kahn. *586.* Photo: Tom Brown. Courtesy Louis I. Kahn. *587.* Photo: Joseph Szaszfai. Courtesy Yale Center for British Art. *588.* Photo: Courtesy Yale Center for British Art. *589.* Photo: Tom Bernard. Courtesy Robert Venturi. *590.* Photo: Ezra Stoller/Esto. Courtesy Richard Meir. *591.* Photo: Ezra Stoller/Esto. Courtesy Richard Meir & Partners. *592.* Courtesy National Gallery of Art. *593.* Courtesy Yale Slide and Photograph Collection. *594.* Photo: Tim Street-Porter. Courtesy Arata Isozaki. *595.* Courtesy Frank Gehry. *596, 597.* Photo: Cervin Robinson. Courtesy Cesar Pelli & Associates. *598.* Photo: Roberto Schezen. Courtesy Edward Larrabee Barnes. *599.* Photo: Harlan Hambright & Associates. Courtesy Harlan Hambright & Associates. *601.* Photo: Gregory Murphy. Courtesy Hartman-Cox Architects. *602.* Photo: Nathaniel Lieberman. Courtesy Herbert S. Newman Associates. *603.* Photo: Steve Rosenthal. Courtesy Benjamin Thompson & Associates. *604.* Photo: The Rouse Company. *605.* Photo: Norman McGrath. Courtesy Herbert S. Newman Associates. *606.* Courtesy John Burgee Architects with Philip Johnson. *607.* Courtesy Venturi, Rauch and Scott Brown. *608.* Courtesy Venturi, Rauch and Scott Brown. *609.* Courtesy Venturi, Rauch and Scott Brown. *610, 611.* Photo: Charles Pereira, U.S. Park Police. *612.* Photo: Peter Aaron/Esto.

Index

Numerals in *italics* are page numbers of illustrations.

312

Library, University of Pennsylvania, Philadelphia, 97–98; *98, 99*
Lichtenstein, Roy, *241*
Lima, Ohio, *13, 41*
Lin, Maya, 292; *292*
Lincoln, Mass., 180; *180, 181*
Lincoln, Nebr., 139; *139*
Lincoln Memorial, Washington, D.C., 74, 140; *74, 75*
Lincoln Towers, New York, 247, 253
Litchfield, Conn., 32; *32*
Lloyd Lewis House, Libertyville, Ill., 173; *172*
Logue, Edward, 246
Lönberg, Knut, 151, 154; *151*
London, 34, 48, 167, 260–62; *34, 48, 167, 261*
Long Island, N.Y., *162, 163, 198*
Long Wharf, New Haven, Conn., 170
Loos, Adolf, 132, 151; *133, 150*
Lorillard House, Tuxedo Park, N.Y., 157; *157*
Los Angeles, 159, 284–85; *131, 159, 165, 183, 242, 285*
Louisville, Ky., 274, 290; *275*
Lovell Beach House (Schindler), Newport Beach, Calif., 158; *158*
Lovell House (Neutra), Los Angeles, 159; *159*

MacArthur, John, *93*
McCoy, Esther, 131
McCurry, Margaret, 270; *270*
McGraw-Hill Building, New York, 154; *155*
McGregor Memorial Conference Center, Wayne State University, Detroit, *191*
McIntire, Samuel, 50
McKim, Mead and White, 115, 117, 118, 137, 144, 148, 195; *57, 114, 117, 118, 136, 139, 142*
Macpheadris-Warner House, Portsmouth, N.H., *13, 41*
Madison, Wis., *174*
Madison Square Garden Center, New York, *142*
Magnolia Mobile Homes, Vicksburg, Miss., 207; *15*
Mahoney, Marion, 126
Maison Carrée, Nîmes, France, 60
Maisons Jaoul, 208
Manchester-by-the-Sea, Mass., *116*
Marina City, Chicago, *188*
Married Graduate Student Housing, Yale University, New Haven, Conn., *208*
Marshall Field Warehouse, Chicago, 104, 108, 117; *104*
Martha's Vineyard, Mass., 263; *263*
Martin and Wilson, 207
Martin House, Buffalo, N.Y., *122*
Mason City, Iowa, *128*
Masonic Temple, Woodbury, Conn., 65
Maybeck, Bernard, 133–35, 139, 230; *134, 135*
Mayhew, Clarence, *183*
Meier, Richard, 284; *284*
Meigs, Montgomery C., 288; *288*
Mellor, Meigs and Howe, *179*
Memorial Hall, Harvard University, Cambridge, Mass., 92; *93*

Memorial to Robert Gould Shaw, Boston, 139; *138*
Merchants' National Bank, Grinnell, Iowa, *128*
Merchants' National Bank, Winona, Minn., 126, 127; *126*
Merrick, Long Island, N.Y., *16*
Mesa Verde, Colo., 19, 23; *18, 19, 22, 23*
Metapontum, Italy, 30
Mexico City, 26; *26*
Meyer, Adolf, 151; *151*
Miami, Fla., 265; *265*
Middletown, R.I., *91*
Mies van der Rohe, Ludwig, 108, 159–60, 184–85, 188–91, 272; *184, 185, 186, 187, 189, 190*
Millard, Peter, 210, 249; *210, 248*
Millard House, Pasadena, Calif., 158; *158*
Millard Meiss House (proposed), Philadelphia, 230; *231*
Miller, J. Marshall, *132*
Mills, Robert, 63; *63*
Mills and Casey, 74
Minneapolis, Minn., *243*
Modified Basketmaker pit house, Mesa Verde, Colo., *18*
Moffatt, Captain John, 40
Moffatt-Ladd House, Portsmouth, N.H., 40
Moholy-Nagy, Laszlo, 180; *181*
Moline, Ill., 198; *199*
Momo, Giuseppe, 176
Monadnock Building, Chicago, 107; *107*
Monastery of La Tourette, Eveux, France, 202–3, 207; *202*
Montauk Building, Chicago, *106, 107*
Monticello, Charlottesville, Va., 51–54; *52, 53, 54, 55*
Montreal, Canada, 207, 211, 225; *211, 225*
Monument Valley, Ariz., *16*
Moore, Charles, 130, 234; *235*
Moore, Henry, *273*
Moore, Lyndon, Turnbull, and Whitaker, *235*
Morris, Robert, 52
Morris Mechanic Theatre, Baltimore, 210; *210*
Morse College, Yale University, New Haven, Conn., 215
Moscow, 148, 193; *148, 192, 193*
Mossdor, Heinrich, *151*
Mt. Desert Island, Maine, 178; *179*
Mount Vernon, Va., 267
Mt. Vernon Place, Baltimore, *82*
Mulberry Castle, Berkeley County, S.C., 42; *43*
Mumford, Lewis, 171
Munday, Richard, 44; *44*
Municipal Building, New York, 148
Municipal Services Building, Portland, Ore., 271, 274; *272*
Museum of Contemporary Art, Los Angeles, 284–85; *285*
Museum of Fine Arts, Houston, 191; *190*
Museum of Modern Art, New York, 286; *286*

Nakoma Country Club (proposed), Madison, Wis., 157; *157*